Learning ASP.NET C

Build modern web apps with ASP.NET Core 2.0, MVC, and EF Core 2

Jason De Oliveira
Michel Bruchet

BIRMINGHAM - MUMBAI

Learning ASP.NET Core 2.0

First published: December 2017

Production reference: 1111217

Published by Packt Publishing Ltd.
Livery Place
35 Livery Street
Birmingham
B3 2PB, UK.

ISBN 978-1-78847-663-8

www.packtpub.com

Credits

Authors
Jason De Oliveira
Michel Bruchet

Reviewer
Alvin Ashcraft

Commissioning Editor
Merint Matthew

Acquisition Editor
Chaitanya Nair

Content Development Editor
Akshada Iyer

Technical Editor
Abhishek Sharma

Copy Editor
Safis Editing

Project Coordinator
Prajakta Naik

Proofreader
Safis Editing

Indexer
Aishwarya Gangawane

Graphics
Jason Monteiro

Production Coordinator
Deepika Naik

Foreword

If I find the right solution, you have to offer me a coffee!—An informal discussion between a software development veteran and a newbie around the coffee machine.

Working as a professional in software development for over 20 years, I have been lucky to be an actor and user of .NET technologies since the early beginnings. While working on many software development projects as tech-lead and application architect, I was also one of the first MSDN seminar and DevDays speakers in France and Switzerland, teaching and explaining the amazing new features of C# Beta 1 a long time ago.

I still remember the first French edition of the Professional Developer Conference (PDC) in 2001, where Microsoft's evangelists showed the first public demo of .NET, C#, and ASP.NET (it was Web Forms era). Every attendee, who were mostly developers, writing rich VB6 client applications or web applications using ASP, VBScript, or Visual InterDev, had discovered how easy it was to write .NET applications using the already well-known paradigms from VB6. However, they also learned how professional tooling offered by .NET and Visual Studio together with modern languages such as C, C++, or Java could lead to more productivity and efficiency. It was a big success.

As a result, I spent a lot of time learning and acquiring deep knowledge of .NET, the CLR, and other CLR languages (C#, VB.Net, and C++/CLI) either through professional projects, personal applications, blog posts, or by speaking about various subjects during technical events and conferences.

At that time, high-quality technical information was concentrated on some reference websites (with special tributes to the fabulous Dotnet Guru, TechHeadBrother).

Since then, the internet and its major application—the web—became essential to the world economy. Then, cloud computing appeared. It allowed exceptional growth, faster than ever, which not only transformed software hosting and development practices, but also business models. Time-To-Market became very important, which meant that the development of applications and services had to be done in an extremely short and fast time scale to have an advantage over the competition.

Regardless of the size of the project, it became inevitable to envision continuous delivery, continuous integration, test automation, and build pipelines. Topics such as Scale-out, microservices and clouds patterns, operating system agnostic technologies, IaaS/PaaS/SaaS, API cultures, and other trendy subjects had to be considered and integrated in application architecture and design decisions.

Today, choosing a development technology is not guided by the hosting operating system anymore, but instead by the matching of application requirements and the richness of the technical ecosystem around that technology (developer community, additional software packages, compatibility and interoperability with other technologies and so on).

.NET succeeded in its evolution (or maybe even its revolution?) mainly because it was adapted to match these new requirements and development processes. It transformed from an open and standardized platform (since 2002: ECMA-334 and ECMA-335, with the shared source CLI 'Rotor' implementation, then ISO-23270 since 2003) into a new multi-platform technology. With .NET Core and ASP.NET Core, it reached even farther by fully embracing the collaborative open source development concepts and methodologies. This allows .NET to remain on the top list of 'first-class citizen' technologies, seamlessly adapted to cloud providers (Microsoft Azure, Amazon AWS and so on).

The fast-changing characteristics of development technologies entails to quickly identify trustable information sources and reliable learning channels for newbies and even for more experienced developers. This continuous knowledge quest is one of the most interesting and inspiring tasks of our job.

The internet contains such a vast quantity of information with more or less documented code samples (from few lines to thousand lines of code) and varying quality, that finding the right information to a problem is a challenge by itself.

As the saying goes: *too much information, kills the information*. If you need a guided journey for a technology, ranging from the starting point to the target line, the choices can be very limited or lost in a crowd of information.

Being able to trust professionals who make their professional experiences accessible through a didactic book is an awesome gain of time and productivity, which will also increase the quality of your future code.

During these past few years, I had the opportunity to collaborate with Jason and Michel at multiple times. Whether it be in the Microsoft Most Valuable Professional (MVP) and Regional Director (RD) worldwide community, or through joint professional projects.

I feel perfectly safe letting you start a fabulous journey with ASP.NET Core 2.0 and this book.

Good reading ... and you will no longer have to thank veterans with caffeinated drinks anymore ... you will become a veteran yourself!

Nicolas Clerc
Cloud Architect, Microsoft France

About the Authors

Jason De Oliveira works as a CTO for MEGA International (http://www.mega.com), a software company in Paris (France), providing modeling tools for business transformation, enterprise architecture, and enterprise governance, risk, and compliance management. He is an experienced manager and senior solutions architect, with high skills in software architecture and enterprise architecture.

He loves sharing his knowledge and experience via his blog, speaking at conferences, writing technical books, writing articles in the technical press, giving software courses as MCT, and coaching co-workers in his company. He frequently collaborates with Microsoft and can often be found at the Microsoft Technology Center (MTC) in Paris.

Microsoft has awarded him for more than 6 years with the Microsoft® Most Valuable Professional (MVP C#/.NET) award for his numerous contributions to the Microsoft community. Microsoft seeks to recognize the best and brightest from technology communities around the world with the MVP Award. These exceptional and highly respected individuals come from more than 90 countries, serving their local online and offline communities and having an impact worldwide.

Feel free to contact him via his blog if you need any technical assistance or want to talk about technical subjects (http://www.jasondeoliveira.com).

Jason has worked on the following books:

- *.NET 4.5 Expert Programming Cookbook* (English)
- *WCF 4.5 Multi-tier Services Development with LINQ to Entities* (English)
- *.NET 4.5 Parallel Extensions Cookbook* (English)
- *WCF Multi-layer Services Development with Entity Framework* (English)
- *Visual Studio 2013: Concevoir, développer et gérer des projets Web, les gérer avec TFS 2013* (French)

I would like to thank my lovely wife, Orianne, and my beautiful daughters, Julia and Léonie, for supporting me in my work and for accepting long days and short nights during the week, and, sometimes, even during the weekend. My life would not be the same without them!

Michel Bruchet works as an application architect for MEGA International (http://www.mega.com), a software company in Paris (France), providing modeling tools for business transformation, enterprise architecture, and enterprise governance, risk, and compliance management. He has more than 20 years of experience as a senior architect, working on complex projects in IT and development departments.

Michel has published several publications on the internet (SlideShare, LinkedIn, and more). He has worked for big companies in France, such as Sanofi, Pierre et Vacances – Center Parcs, Banque de France, BPCE, and BNP.

He is also the main driving force and mastermind behind the Ingenius Solution, which provides efficient e-business solutions to customers around the world.

I would like to thank my family for accepting that I had to work hard and, sometimes, until late into the night in my free time to write this book!

About the Reviewer

Alvin Ashcraft is a software developer living near Philadelphia, PA. He has dedicated his 22-year career to building software with C#, Visual Studio, WPF, ASP.NET, HTML/JavaScript, UWP, and Xamarin apps and SQL Server. He has been awarded as a Microsoft MVP nine times; once for Software Architecture, seven times for C# and Visual Studio & Tools, and for Windows Dev in 2018-2019. You can read his daily links for .NET developers on his blog at `alvinashcraft.com` and UWP App Tips blog at `www.uwpapp.tips`.

He currently works as a Principal Software Engineer for Allscripts, developing clinical healthcare software. He has previously been employed with several large software companies, including Oracle, Genzeon, and Corporation Service Company. There, he helped create software solutions for financial, business, and healthcare organizations using Microsoft platforms and solutions.

He was a technical reviewer for *NuGet 2 Essentials* and *Mastering ASP.NET Core 2.0* by Packt.

I would like to thank my wonderful wife, Stelene, and our three amazing daughters for their support. They were very understanding while I read and reviewed these chapters on evenings and weekends to help deliver a useful, high-quality book for the ASP.NET Core developers.

www.PacktPub.com

For support files and downloads related to your book, please visit www.PacktPub.com.

Did you know that Packt offers eBook versions of every book published, with PDF and ePub files available? You can upgrade to the eBook version at www.PacktPub.com and as a print book customer, you are entitled to a discount on the eBook copy. Get in touch with us at service@packtpub.com for more details.

At www.PacktPub.com, you can also read a collection of free technical articles, sign up for a range of free newsletters and receive exclusive discounts and offers on Packt books and eBooks.

www.packtpub.com/mapt

Get the most in-demand software skills with Mapt. Mapt gives you full access to all Packt books and video courses, as well as industry-leading tools to help you plan your personal development and advance your career.

Why subscribe?

- Fully searchable across every book published by Packt
- Copy and paste, print, and bookmark content
- On demand and accessible via a web browser

Customer Feedback

Thanks for purchasing this Packt book. At Packt, quality is at the heart of our editorial process. To help us improve, please leave us an honest review on this book's Amazon page at `https://www.amazon.com/dp/1788476638`.

If you'd like to join our team of regular reviewers, you can e-mail us at `customerreviews@packtpub.com`. We award our regular reviewers with free eBooks and videos in exchange for their valuable feedback. Help us be relentless in improving our products!

Table of Contents

Preface

Everyday, software developers, application architects, and IT project managers work on building applications as quickly as possible to be a leader in their respective markets: time to market is of utmost importance. Unfortunately, the quality and performance of those applications are often not as expected, since they have not been fully tested, optimized, and secured.

During the past few years, ASP.NET has evolved into becoming one of the most consistent, stable, and feature-rich frameworks available in the market for web application development. It provides all expected characteristics you can think of concerning performance, stability, and security out of the box.

For some time now, the IT market has been changing. Compliance with different standards is now required and customers expect industrialized, high-performing, and scalable applications, while developers ask for frameworks that allow higher productivity and extensibility to adapt to specific business needs. This has lead Microsoft to completely rethink their web technologies accordingly.

As a result, Microsoft has built ASP.NET Core, which gives developers the capacity to do the following:

- Creating applications and compile them in a specific environment, but then run them in any environment (such as Linux, Windows, or macOS)
- Using third-party libraries with additional functionalities
- Working with various tools, frameworks, and libraries
- Adopting the most up-to-date best practices for frontend development
- Developing flexible, responsive web applications

ASP.NET Core 2.0, together with Microsoft Visual Studio 2017, includes several features to make your life as a web developer easier and more productive. For example, Visual Studio offers project templates, which you can use to develop your web applications. Visual Studio also supports several developments modes, including using Microsoft Internet Information Services (IIS) directly to test your web applications during development time and using a built-in web server and developing your web applications over FTP.

With the debugger in Visual Studio, you can run through your application and step through the critical areas of your code to find problems. With the Visual Studio Editor, you can effectively develop user interfaces.

And when you are ready to deploy your application, Visual Studio makes it easy to create a deployment package for deployment on Azure, Amazon Web Services, and Docker, or any other platform including Linux and macOS. These are but a few of the features built into the ASP.NET Core framework when paired with Visual Studio.

This book provides the latest best practices and ASP.NET Core guidance to get you up to speed quickly. Each section of this book presents specific ASP.NET Core 2.0 features in an easily readable format with detailed examples. The step-by-step instructions yield immediate working results. Most of the key features of ASP.NET Core are illustrated using succinct, easily understandable, and reusable examples. The examples are rich to illustrate features without being overbearing.

In addition to showing ASP.NET Core features by example, this book contains practical applications of each feature so that you can apply these techniques in the real world. After reading this book and applying the exercises, you will have a great head start into building efficient web applications that include modern features, such as MVC, Web APIs, custom view components, and tag helpers.

We hope this book will help you in your daily job as a developer and reading it will give you as much joy as writing it has given us.

Once upon a time, NGWS and the .NET Framework

The following is a little bit of history to explain how the .NET Framework has evolved over the years and why you have to consider the .NET Core Framework today:

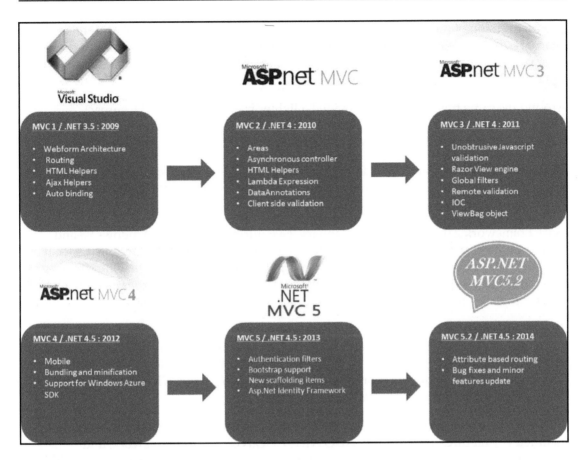

Microsoft has started working on what we know now as the .NET Framework in the late 1990s and has released a first beta version of .NET Framework 1.0 in late 2001.

Originally, the framework was named NGWS for Next Generation Windows Services (internal codename Lightning/Project 42). In the beginning, developers could only use VB.NET as a programming language. More than 10 Framework versions later, a lot has been achieved. Today, you can choose between a large number of languages, frameworks, and technologies.

In the beginning, InterDev was the primary development environment to develop ASP Pages, and you had to use a command-line VBC compiler tool to compile your code.

The first version of our beloved Visual Studio development environment was published in February 2002, bringing with it a common runtime environment for the Windows client and Windows server family (NT 4, Windows 98, Windows ME, Windows XP, and then Windows 2000).

Around the same time, Microsoft provided a lighter framework, named Compact Framework, to execute Windows CE on Windows Mobile. The last version was published in January 2008 as Version 3.5 RTM before it was replaced by newer mobile technologies.

The first .NET SDK was published in April 2003 as .NET Framework 1.1 and was included in Visual Studio 2003. It was the first version to be included in the Windows Server OS and shipped together with Windows 2003.

.NET Framework 2.0 was released in January 2006 during the time of Windows 98 and Windows Me. It provided a major upgrade to the Common Language Runtime (CLR). It was the first version to fully support 64-bit computing and fully integrate with Microsoft SQL Server. It also introduced a new Web Pages Framework, providing features such as skins, templates, master pages, and style sheets.

.NET Framework 3.0 (WinFX) was released in November 2006. It included a new set of managed code APIs. This version added several new technologies to build new types of applications, such as Windows Presentation Foundation (WPF), Windows Communication Foundation (WCF), Windows Workflow Foundation (WWF), and Windows CardSpace (later integrated into Windows Identity Foundation).

.NET Framework 3.5 extended the WinFX features one year later in 2007. This version included key features such as Linq, ADO.NET, ADO.NET Entity Framework, and ADO.NET Data Services. Furthermore, it shipped with two new assemblies that would later be the foundation of the MVC framework: System.Web.Abstraction and System.Web.Routing.

.NET Framework 4.0 was published in May 2009; it provided some major upgrades to the Common Language Runtime (CLR) and added Parallel extension to improve support parallel computing, dynamic dispatch, named parameters, and optional parameters, as well as code contracts and the BigIntegerComplex numeric format.

After the release of .NET Framework 4.0, Microsoft released a set of improvements to build microservices in the form of the Windows Server AppFabric framework. Essentially, it provided an InMemory distributed cache and an application server farm.

.NET Framework 4.5 was released in August 2012; it added a so-called Metro style application (which later evolved into Universal Windows Platform applications), the Core features, and the Microsoft Extension Framework (MEF).

Concerning ASP.NET, this version was more compatible with HTML5, jQuery, and provided bundling and minification for improved web page performance. It was also the first to support WebSockets and asynchronous HTTP requests and responses.

.NET Framework 4.6.1 was released in November 2015; it required Windows 7 SP1 or later, and was an important version. Some of the new features and APIs included were support for SQL Connectivity for AlwaysOn, Always Encrypted, and improved connection resiliency when using Azure SQL Databases. It also added Azure SQL Database support for distributed transactions using the updated System.Transactions APIs and provided many other performance, stability, and reliability related fixes in RyuJIT, GC, and WPF.

.NET Framework 4.6.2 was released in March 2016; it added support for paths longer than 260 characters, FIPS 186-3 DSA in X.509 certificates, and localization of data annotations, and the resources files were moved to the App_LocalResources folder. Additionally, the ASP.NET session provider and local cache manager were made compatible with the asynchronous framework.

.NET Framework 4.7 was released in April 2017; it was included in the Windows 10 Creators update. Some of the new features included enhanced cryptography with elliptic curve cryptography and improved Transport Layer Security (TLS) support, especially for version 1.2. It also introduced the object cache store, which enabled developers to provide custom providers easily by implementing the ICacheStoreProvider interface.

There was also a better integration between the application and the memory monitor and the famous memory limits reactions, which enables developers to observe the CLR when it truncates objects cached in memory and overrides the default behavior.

Then, Microsoft developed a completely new .NET Framework with open source multi-platform in mind from the beginning. It was introduced as ASP.NET 5 and later renamed ASP.NET Core Framework.

The first release, 1.0, was announced by Richard Lander (MSFT) in June 2016; the ASP.NET MVC and Web API frameworks were merged into a single framework package that you could easily add to your projects via NuGet.

The second release, .NET Core Framework 1.1, was published in November 2017; it ran on more Linux distributions, its performance was improved, it was released with Kestrel, the deployment on Azure was simplified, and the productivity was improved. Entity Framework Core started to support SQL Server 2016.

Note that .NET Core Framework 1.0 and 1.1 will be supported by Microsoft until June 2019.

The latest release of the .NET Core Framework is 2.0. A first preview version was released in May 2017. A second preview version—published in June 2017 and the final version, on which this book is based—was released in August 2017.

Microsoft has vastly improved the .NET Core Framework. The improvements and extensions are the result of the vision for .NET Core 2.0; it enables you to use more of your code in more places.

The following improvements are included in .NET Core 2.0:

- Massive API increase (>100%) relative to .NET Core 1.x
- Support for .NET Standard 2.0
- Support to reference .NET Framework libraries and NuGet packages
- Support for Visual Basic

Furthermore, the .NET Standard 2.0 brings these new features:

- Bigger API surface—it's extended to cover the intersection between .NET Framework and Xamarin. This also makes .NET Core 2.0 much bigger as it implements .NET Standard 2.0. The total number of APIs added to .NET Standard is ~20,000.
- It can reference existing .NET Framework libraries. The best thing is—no recompile required, so this includes existing NuGet packages.
- .NET Core supports more Linux distribution. Samsung is working to provide support for the mobile OS Tizen.
- And, most importantly, .NET Core is the fastest application runtime available in the .NET world.

Also, note that most of the regular libraries are available on GitHub. They can be forked and rebuilt by anyone who wants to extend or change any standard behaviors.

What this book covers

This book is organized into multiple chapters that explain ASP.NET Core 2.0 features in an easy and understandable format with practical examples. Most of the key features of ASP.NET Core 2.0 are illustrated using succinct, efficient examples and step-by-step instructions yield immediate working results.

You don't have to read the chapters in any order to find the book useful. Each chapter stands on its own, except for the first chapter, which details the fundamentals of ASP.NET Core—you might want to read it first if you've never ventured beyond desktop application development.

The following topics will be covered throughout the book:

Chapter 1, *What is ASP.NET Core 2.0?*, describes the features and functionalities of ASP.NET Core 2.0, but also the technical restrictions, which should allow you to understand in which cases it could be a good fit for your own needs and what to expect.

Chapter 2, *Setting Up the Environment*, gives a detailed explanation of how to set up your development environment and how to create your first ASP.NET Core 2.0 application. You will learn how to either use Visual Studio 2017 or Visual Studio Code, how to install the runtime, and how to use Nuget to retrieve all necessary ASP.NET Core 2.0 dependencies.

Chapter 3, *Creating a Continuous Integration Pipeline in VSTS*, shows how to set up a complete Visual Studio Team Services (VSTS) Continuous Integration Pipeline. You will learn how to fully automate building, testing, and deploying your applications using VSTS in the cloud.

Chapter 4, *Basic Concepts of ASP.NET Core 2.0 – Part 1*, explains the basic structure and concepts of ASP.NET Core 2.0 applications. It shows how everything works internally and what classes and methods can be used to override basic behavior. It also provides the theoretical background for all the other chapters.

Chapter 5, *Basic Concepts of ASP.NET Core 2.0 – Part 2*, following up on the concepts covered in Chapter 4, *Basic Concepts of ASP.NET Core 2.0 – Part 1*, this chapter delves deeper into essential ASP.NET Core 2.0 concepts. You will learn about components and features offered by ASP.NET Core to build responsive web applications.

Chapter 6, *Creating MVC Applications*, provides all the concepts and everything necessary to create your first ASP.NET Core 2.0 MVC application. You will learn the specifics of MVC applications and how to implement them efficiently. Additionally, you will see how unit tests and integration tests will help you build better applications with fewer bugs, resulting in lower maintenance costs.

Chapter 7, *Creating Web API Applications*, covers the Web API Framework and provides everything essential to create your first ASP.NET Core 2.0 Web API. You will see different Web API styles, such as RPC, REST, and HATEOAS, and learn when to use them and how to implement them in an effective way.

Chapter 8, *Accessing Data Using Entity Framework Core 2*, shows how to access databases using Entity Framework Core 2, while using all the advanced features (Code First, Fluent API, Data Migrations, InMemory Databases, and more) it offers.

Chapter 9, *Securing ASP.NET Core 2.0 Applications*, explains how to use the built-in ASP.NET Core 2.0 features for user authentication and how to extend them by adding external providers. If you need to secure your applications, then this chapter is where you want to go.

Chapter 10, *Hosting and Deploying ASP.NET Core 2.0 Applications*, is about the various options you have when it comes to hosting and deploying your ASP.NET Core 2.0 web applications on premises and in the cloud. You will learn how to choose the appropriate solutions for a given use case, which will allow you to make better decisions for your own applications.

Chapter 11, *Managing and Supervising ASP.NET Core 2.0 Applications*, is finally going to be a chapter on how to manage and supervise your production-ready applications after deployment. It will greatly aid you in diagnosing problems for your ASP.NET Core 2.0 web applications during runtime and reduce the time to understand and fix bugs.

What you need for this book

You will either need Visual Studio 2017 Community Edition or Visual Studio Code, which are both free of charge for testing and learning purposes, to be able to follow the code examples found within this book. You could also use any other text editor of your choice and then use the dotnet command-line tool, but it would be advised to use one of the development environments mentioned earlier for better productivity.

Later in the book, we will work with databases, so you will also need a version of SQL Server (any version in any edition will work). We advise using SQL Server 2016 Express Edition, which is also free of charge for testing purposes.

There might be other tools or frameworks that will be introduced during the following chapters. We will explain how to retrieve them when they are used.

If you need to develop for Linux, then Visual Studio Code and SQL Server 2016 are your primary choices, since they are the only ones running on Linux.

Additionally, you will need an Azure Subscription and Amazon Web Services Subscription for some of the examples shown within the book. There are multiple chapters dedicated to show you how to take advantage of the cloud.

Who this book is for

This book is for developers who would like to build modern web applications with ASP.NET Core 2.0. No prior knowledge of ASP.NET or .NET Core is required. However, basic programming knowledge is assumed. Additionally, previous Visual Studio experience will be helpful but is not required, since detailed instructions will guide you through the samples of the book. This book can also help people who work in infrastructure engineering and operations to monitor and diagnose problems during the runtime of ASP.NET Core 2.0 web applications.

Conventions

In this book, you will find a number of text styles that distinguish between different kinds of information. Here are some examples of these styles and an explanation of their meaning.

Code words in text, database table names, folder names, filenames, file extensions, pathnames, dummy URLs, user input, and Twitter handles are shown as follows: "Start Visual Studio 2017, open the *Tic-Tac-Toe* ASP.NET Core 2.0 project you have created, create three new folders called Controllers, Services, and Views, and create a subfolder called Shared in the Views folder."

A block of code is set as follows:

```
[HttpGet]
public IActionResult EmailConfirmation (string email)
{
  ViewBag.Email = email;
  return View();
}
```

Any command-line input or output is written as follows. The input command might be broken into several lines to aid readability, but needs to be entered as one continuous line in the prompt:

```
sudo apt-get install code
```

New terms and **important words** are shown in bold. Words that you see on the screen, for example, in menus or dialog boxes, appear in the text like this: "Open Visual Studio 2017, go to the **Team Explorer** tab, and click on the **Branches** button".

Warnings or important notes appear like this.

Tips and tricks appear like this.

Reader feedback

Feedback from our readers is always welcome. Let us know what you think about this book—what you liked or disliked. Reader feedback is important for us as it helps us develop titles that you will really get the most out of.

To send us general feedback, simply email `feedback@packtpub.com`, and mention the book's title in the subject of your message.

If there is a topic that you have expertise in and you are interested in either writing or contributing to a book, see our author guide at `www.packtpub.com/authors`.

Customer support

Now that you are the proud owner of a Packt book, we have a number of things to help you to get the most from your purchase.

Downloading the example code

You can download the example code files for this book from your account at `http://www.packtpub.com`. If you purchased this book elsewhere, you can visit `http://www.packtpub.com/support` and register to have the files emailed directly to you.

You can download the code files by following these steps:

1. Log in or register to our website using your email address and password.
2. Hover the mouse pointer on the **SUPPORT** tab at the top.
3. Click on **Code Downloads & Errata**.
4. Enter the name of the book in the **Search** box.
5. Select the book for which you're looking to download the code files.
6. Choose from the drop-down menu where you purchased this book from.
7. Click on **Code Download**.

Once the file is downloaded, please make sure that you unzip or extract the folder using the latest version of:

- WinRAR / 7-Zip for Windows
- Zipeg / iZip / UnRarX for macOS
- 7-Zip / PeaZip for Linux

The code bundle for the book is also hosted on GitHub at the following repositories:

- `https://github.com/JasonDeOliveira/Learning-ASP.NET-Core-2.0/commits/master`
- `https://github.com/PacktPublishing/Learning-ASP.NET-Core-2.0`

We also have other code bundles from our rich catalog of books and videos available at `https://github.com/PacktPublishing/`. Check them out!

Errata

Although we have taken every care to ensure the accuracy of our content, mistakes do happen. If you find a mistake in one of our books—maybe a mistake in the text or the code—we would be grateful if you could report this to us. By doing so, you can save other readers from frustration and help us improve subsequent versions of this book. If you find any errata, please report them by visiting `http://www.packtpub.com/submit-errata`, selecting your book, clicking on the **Errata Submission Form** link, and entering the details of your errata. Once your errata are verified, your submission will be accepted and the errata will be uploaded to our website or added to any list of existing errata under the Errata section of that title.

To view the previously submitted errata, go
to `https://www.packtpub.com/books/content/support` and enter the name of the book in
the search field. The required information will appear under the **Errata** section.

Piracy

Piracy of copyrighted material on the internet is an ongoing problem across all media. At
Packt, we take the protection of our copyright and licenses very seriously. If you come
across any illegal copies of our works in any form on the internet, please provide us with
the location address or website name immediately so that we can pursue a remedy.

Please contact us at `copyright@packtpub.com` with a link to the suspected pirated
material.

We appreciate your help in protecting our authors and our ability to bring you valuable
content.

Questions

If you have a problem with any aspect of this book, you can contact us
at `questions@packtpub.com`, and we will do our best to address the problem.

1
What is ASP.NET Core 2.0?

The first preview release of ASP.NET came out almost 15 years ago as part of the .NET Framework. Since then millions of software developers have used it to build and run all types of great web applications. Over the years Microsoft has added and evolved many of its features until coming up with a complete redesign of the ASP.NET Framework called **ASP.NET Core** in June 2016. After ASP.NET Core 1.0 and 1.1, version 2.0 is the third and latest installment of ASP.NET Core. Let's see what it offers and when it makes sense to use it in your projects.

ASP.NET Core 2.0 is a new open-source and cross-platform framework for building modern cloud-based applications, such as web applications, **Internet of Things** (**IoT**) applications and even mobile backend.

ASP.NET Core 2.0 applications run on the .NET Core Framework as well as on the full .NET Framework. The ASP.NET Core Framework was architected to provide an optimized development framework for applications, which have to be deployed either within the cloud or on-premises. It consists of modular components with minimal overhead, so you retain a high degree of flexibility when conceiving and implementing your software solutions. You can develop and run your ASP.NET Core 2.0 applications on Windows, Linux, and macOS.

In the following diagram you can see how the different .NET Framework versions and components work together:

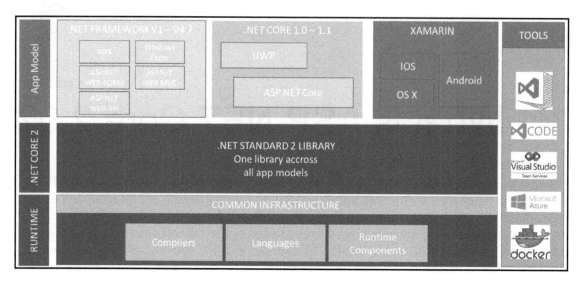

ASP.NET Core 2.0 includes several architectural changes that result in a much leaner and more modular framework when compared to the framework that came before it. It is no longer based on `System.Web.dll`, instead, it uses a set of granular and well factored NuGet packages. This allows optimizing of applications to include just the NuGet packages that are really needed.

The benefits of a smaller application surface area include:

- Better security
- Reduced dependencies between components
- Improved performance
- Decreased optimized financial costs in a pay-for-what-you-use cloud consumer world

As a developer, when building applications based on the classic .NET Framework, you must choose between six application models (WPF, Windows Forms, Web Forms, Web MVC, Web API, and Xamarin), which can be confusing and not very productive.

With the release of the ASP.NET Core 1.0 and 1.1, this was optimized and reduced to three different application models, with the drawback that you cannot share code between them.

With ASP.NET Core 2.0, the number of application models was further reduced to two and code is now sharable, meaning that you can now reuse more than 90% of your code. For you as a developer, this makes you more productive and allows for switching between application models quickly and easily.

In this chapter, we will cover the following topics:

- ASP.NET 2.0 features
- Cross-platform support
- Microservice architecture
- Working with Docker and containers
- Performance and scalability
- Side-by-side deployments
- Technology restrictions
- When to choose ASP.NET Core 2.0

ASP.NET Core 2.0 features

The new `Microsoft.AspNet.Core.All` package contains all ASP.NET Core 2.0 features in a single library. It includes authentication, MVC, Razor, monitoring, Kestrel support and many others. They are explained in more detail later in the book.

> Note that if you want to selectively add packages one by one, you can still reference them manually instead of using the single packages that contain it all but then you will miss several advantages as you will see here.

The **runtime store** is an important new component shipped with ASP.NET Core 2.0. It contains compiled packages, which were compiled using the native machine language and it is key for improved performance. All applications using the `Microsoft.AspNet.Core.All` package benefit from it, because they do not need to be deployed with all the dependent packages anymore. Everything is already there, so their deployment size will be reduced and their execution time will be optimized.

ASP.NET Core 2.0 allows you to create well-factored and testable web applications that follow the **Model-View-Controller** (**MVC**) pattern. We have dedicated a full chapter to this topic later in the book.

Furthermore, you can build HTTP services with full support for content negotiation using custom and built-in formatters such as JSON or XML as well as RESTful services.

ASP.NET Core 2.0 fully supports Razor which contains an efficient language for creating your views and Tag Helpers enable server-side code to participate in creating and rendering HTML elements in Razor files.

Model binding automatically maps data from HTTP requests to action method parameters and model validation automatically performs client and server side validation.

In terms of client-side development, ASP.NET Core 2.0 is designed to integrate seamlessly with a variety of client-side frameworks including AngularJS, KnockoutJS, and Bootstrap.

Additionally, it provides the following fundamental improvements:

- ASP.NET MVC and Web API have been combined into a single framework
- Modern client-side frameworks and development workflows
- Environment-based configuration system ready for cloud hosting
- Built-in dependency injection functionalities
- New light-weight and modular HTTP request pipeline
- Host the same application in IIS, self-host, Docker, Cloud and even in your own processes
- Hosts multiple versions of an application or a component side-by-side
- Ships entirely as NuGet packages
- New tooling that simplifies modern web development
- Simplified `csproj` file, making it easier to work with development environments other than Visual Studio (on Linux and macOS, for example)
- The `Program.cs` class has been extended to fully automate the integration of Kestrel, the setting of the `ContentRootPath`, loading the configuration files, initializing the logging middleware, and other steps by only calling a single method
- The `Startup.cs` has been simplified by moving logging and configuration into the WebHost builder initialization

Cross-platform support

As explained before, the ASP.NET Core 2.0 framework has been built, from the beginning, with cross-platform support in mind. It supports a wide variety of operating systems and technologies such as Windows, Linux, macOS, Docker, Azure, and others.

ASP.NET Core 2.0 currently supports the following Linux distributions:

- Ubuntu 14, 16
- Linux Mint 17, 18
- Debian 8
- Fedora
- CentOS 7.1 and Oracle 7.1
- SUSE Enterprise Server 64 bits
- OpenSuse 64 bits

Concerning macOS, it currently only supports (other versions might be added later):

- macOS 10.11
- macOS 10.12

For application development, you may develop on Windows using Visual Studio or Visual Studio Code and then deploy your ASP.NET Core 2.0 application to your target system.

 Note that the target system can use a completely different underlying operating system. For instance, you can develop and test on Windows and then deploy your applications to a Linux server for performance, stability or cost reduction reasons.

If you choose so, you can of course directly develop on Linux and macOS using several system-specific source code editors. On Linux, you could use Visual Studio Code, VIM/VI, Sublime, or Emacs for example. On macOS, you could use Visual Studio for Mac, Visual Studio Code or any other Mac-specific text editor.

The Visual Studio 2017 or Visual Studio Code developer environments would be the preferred choice though, since they provide everything necessary to be highly productive and to be able to debug and understand your code as well as navigate within it easily. That is why we are going to use those IDEs throughout the rest of the book.

After building your application, you can use several web servers to run it. Here are some examples:

- Apache
- IIS
- Kestrel self-host
- Nginx

Microservice architecture

Microservices also known as the microservice architecture, is an architectural layout that structures an application as a collection of loosely coupled services, which implement business capabilities. It can be used to build e-commerce system, business application, and IOT.

ASP.NET Core 2.0 is the best candidate when you want to embrace this system architecture. The ASP.NET Core 2.0 framework is lightweight and its API surface can be minimized to the scope of a specific microservice. A microservice architecture also allows you to mix technologies across service boundaries, enabling for a gradual transition to ASP.NET Core.

Notice that microservices built with ASP.NET Core 2.0 can work together with services using other technologies such as the full classic .NET Framework, Java, Ruby, and even other more legacy technologies. This is a big advantage when you need to progressively transform monolithic applications into more (micro)service-oriented applications.

You are not bound to a specific underlying infrastructure, instead, you have a wide choice since ASP.NET Core 2.0 supports nearly all the technologies that you can think of today. Additionally, you can modify the infrastructure when needed so there is no technological lock-in for applications that have been developed based on it.

Your primary choice for orchestrating and managing microservices written in C# efficiently and at high scale, on-premises, and in the cloud, should be Microsoft Service Fabric. It was conceived exactly for that and is used by Microsoft for various Azure services (SQL Database, and more) for many years already.

A microservices Docker container approach might also fit your needs, we are going to explain its use cases in the next paragraphs. To sum it up, ASP.NET Core 2.0 is the ideal choice for implementing and hosting your microservices in any kind of technical environment.

Working with Docker and containers

Docker and containers are everywhere at the moment. Everybody is speaking about them and there are so many use cases where they seem to be a great fit. They provide an efficient, lightweight and self-contained approach for packaging applications with their dependencies while re-using the underlying operating system files and resources.

They are a perfect fit for microservice architectures, but can also be used for any other application archetypes. They work exceptionally well together with ASP.NET Core 2.0 applications since both have been conceived with modularity, performance, scalability, lightweight nature, and efficiency in mind.

 Note that Docker container images including ASP.NET Core 2.0 applications are much smaller than images with classic ASP.NET applications, meaning that they are faster to deploy and to start-up.

Both, Docker containers and the ASP.NET Core 2.0 framework, provide full cross-platform support (Windows, Linux, and macOS). Furthermore, you can host your containers on-premises and in the cloud. You can use Azure for example, either via **IAAS** deployments or via Azure Container Services, which additionally allows for mixing and matching different operating systems and technologies.

Performance and scalability

If you need the best possible performance and support high scalability scenarios then you need to absolutely use ASP.NET Core 2.0 and the underlying .NET Core Framework. ASP.NET Core 2.0 has been built from the ground up for high performance and high scalability scenarios. It really shines in these areas and it can be considered as the best choice.

It is ten times faster than classic ASP.NET, you can even think of it to be the fastest web application runtime in the .NET world currently available!

Furthermore, it provides the best solution for microservices architectures, where performance and scalability are extremely important. No other technology is as efficient while consuming such low system resources, which also leads to reduced infrastructure and cloud hosting costs.

Side-by-side deployments

If you want to be able to install applications with dependencies on different versions of the .NET Framework, then you should consider using the ASP.NET Core 2.0 framework, since it provides 100% side-by-side deployment capabilities.

Side-by-side deployments of different .NET Core and ASP.NET Core versions allow for having multiple services and applications on the same server. Each of them can be using their own dedicated versions of the respective frameworks, thus eliminating risks and saving money when doing application upgrades and common IT operations.

Technology restrictions

Please look carefully at the technologies shown in this section. If you use a technology or framework within your current application, which is listed here and which is not (yet) supported, then you might find it difficult or even impossible to migrate to ASP.NET Core 2.0.

Not all current .NET Framework technologies are available in ASP.NET Core 2.0 and some might never be ported over, since they do not comply with the new .NET Core specific paradigms and patterns.

The following list shows the most common technologies not directly found in ASP.NET Core and .NET Core, knowing that some can be used via the multi-targeting features:

- **ASP.NET Web Forms applications**: The legacy Web Forms technology is only available using the full classic .NET Framework, you cannot use ASP.NET Core and .NET Core for these types of applications.
- **ASP.NET Web Pages applications**: They are not included in ASP.NET Core 2.0 as such, but it is possible to use the Razor web pages engine to provide the same functionalities.
- **ASP.NET SignalR applications**: Currently, ASP.NET SignalR is not available for ASP.NET Core. However, you can find a first preview version in the corresponding server-side and client library GitHub repositories, so they should be included in one of the next releases.
- **WCF Services**: ASP.NET Core 2.0 contains a WCF client for accessing WCF services, but creating WCF services is not supported. This feature might be added in future releases though.

- **Workflow Services**: Windows Workflow Foundation, Workflow Services, and WCF Data Services are not supported and there are no plans for adding them to ASP.NET Core in the future.
- **WPF and Windows Forms applications**: Windows Presentation Foundation and Windows Forms cannot be built with ASP.NET Core, it would go against the cross-platform paradigm. You could, however, replace your WPF applications by UWP applications provided by the XAML2 Universal standard.

Not all .NET languages are currently supported by ASP.NET Core 2.0. For example, F# does not have any tooling support. Visual Basic support has been added in the latest version of Visual Studio 2017. There will be more and more languages that will be supported.

In addition to the official ASP.NET Core roadmap, there are other frameworks and technologies, that are planned to be ported over to .NET Core in the next months. To get further information on what will be ported over and what will not, go to the GitHub repository of the .NET Core Libraries (`https://github.com/dotnet/corefx`).

For those that are planned, there is no assurance that they will really get ported over, though. But you will find a good indication of what you can expect in the next versions of ASP.NET Core. Note that you can, in some cases, use the multi-targeting features of ASP.NET Core 2.0 for being able to call frameworks that are currently not directly supported by ASP.NET Core 2.0.

If you care about a specific framework or component that you need within your projects, consider participating in the discussions on GitHub. Maybe others will have the same requirements and Microsoft decides to prioritize their .NET Core migration accordingly.

Some Microsoft services, and even some third-party platforms, do not support ASP.NET Core. For example, some Azure services such as Service Fabric Stateful Reliable Services and Service Fabric Reliable Actors require the full classic .NET Framework.

Also, sometimes ASP.NET Core SDKs are not provided or not yet available. In the meantime, you can always use the equivalent REST APIs instead of the client SDKs and then replace them later. Be assured, all Azure services are going to support ASP.NET Core in the future as can be seen on the respective product roadmap.

When to choose ASP.NET Core 2.0

After having seen the various features and functionalities provided by ASP.NET Core 2.0, you could ask yourself if it will replace the full classic .NET Framework in the future. It is true that ASP.NET Core 2.0 and the underlying .NET Core Framework provide some major enhancement and performance improvements, but there are still some specific scenarios, where those new application patterns do not apply and where the full .NET Framework will be the best and sometimes even the only choice.

Migrating your whole existing applications to ASP.NET Core right from the start might be difficult or even impossible to do. You should think about how to transform your applications progressively to lower the risk of failure or over-complexification and give yourself time to really understand the new patterns and paradigms.

You could start for instance by only using ASP.NET Core 2.0 for all new developments, then see how to migrate your legacy code later and sometimes even leave it be since there will be no real benefits for migrating it over. If you are really interested in the migration topic, please consider the appendix, since we have a full chapter dedicated to this important topic.

ASP.NET Core and the .NET Core Framework get more and more framework and client library support each day. Microsoft, tool and framework vendors, and the different developer communities work hard to provide a large set of functionalities for allowing feature-rich and high performing web applications. Everybody wants to work on this promising technology that could shape the future in a sustainable way.

The possibility to use .NET Core and .NET Framework libraries together at the same time when using .NET Standard 2.0 extends the possibilities even more and gives developers a temporary solution until every important feature and every major framework will be available in .NET Core.

To recap what has been discussed in this chapter, you should use ASP.NET Core 2.0 for your server applications when:

- You have cross-platform needs
- You are specifically targeting microservices
- You want to use Docker containers
- You need high performance and highly scalable applications
- You need to put multiple applications with different .NET versions side by side
- The presented technical restrictions do not apply to your application requirements

Summary

In this chapter, you have learned about the ASP.NET Core 2.0 framework and its features. You have seen that it includes everything necessary to work efficiently in a cross-platform environment while using microservices architectures and container technologies such as Docker.

Furthermore, you have learned that it provides very good performances and exceptional scalability for your web applications and that even side-by-side deployments are supported.

At the end, we have talked about technical restrictions and when it is advisable to use the ASP.NET Core 2.0 framework.

In the next chapter, we will talk about how to set up your development environment including either Visual Studio 2017 or Visual Studio Code as an integrated development environment.

2
Setting Up the Environment

You have decided to learn about ASP.NET Core 2.0, the most advanced and efficient cross-platform web application framework on the market today. A very good choice! You are surely eager to start programming right away, but before we can begin, we must set up the required technical prerequisites and tools.

In this chapter, we are going to introduce Visual Studio 2017 Community Edition and Visual Studio Code, and then install either one of them as a development environment. Then, we are going to build a simple sample application based on the ASP.NET Core 2.0 Framework.

In this chapter, we will cover the following topics:

- Visual Studio 2017 as a development environment
- How to install Visual Studio 2017 Community Edition
- Creating your first ASP.NET Core 2.0 application in Visual Studio and via the command line
- Visual Studio Code as a development environment
- How to install Visual Studio Code on Linux
- Creating your first ASP.NET Core 2.0 application in Visual Studio Code
- Creating your first ASP.NET Core 2.0 application in Linux

Visual Studio 2017 as a development environment

As a developer, you need an environment for your daily development tasks, and Microsoft Visual Studio 2017 is just that. It provides a very efficient and productive **Integrated Development Environment** (**IDE**) for creating new software projects and developing, debugging, and testing them. It will help you to build high-quality applications in a very quick and intuitive way. Many of its features have been built around common development tasks and how to streamline and optimize them within a single tool.

You can create web applications, web services, desktop applications, mobile applications, and many other types of applications not covered within this book.

Additionally, you can use a wide range of programming languages such as C#, Visual Basic, F#, JavaScript, and even Java.

There are different editions of Visual Studio 2017, each with their own unique features and licenses. The Visual Studio 2017 Community Edition, for instance, is free of charge but cannot be used for applications running in production environments. The main goal of this version is private usage and learning purposes.

The Visual Studio 2017 Professional and Enterprise Editions contain everything, including the necessary licenses, to build and run applications in production environments.

The Visual Studio 2017 Professional Edition contains a subset of all features that are offered in the Enterprise Edition. It is usually sufficient to start with this edition and then upgrade to the Enterprise Edition if necessary.

The Visual Studio 2017 Enterprise Edition contains a lot of additional features to improve developer productivity even more, such as live dependency validation, testing, architecture diagrams, architecture validation, code cloning, and many others. If you need these features, then you need to use this edition.

 Note that multiple versions of Visual Studio (2013, 2015, 2017, 2017 Preview, and more) can be installed side by side on a developer machine, which has earlier versions of the Visual Studio IDE installed.

Traditionally, Visual Studio was released only for Windows, but a macOS version has existed since 2016 called Visual Studio for macOS. You can use it for developing your .NET applications on this operating system.

The Visual Studio 2017 Community Edition is exactly what we need for trying out and understanding the examples illustrated in this book, so that is why we are going to use this edition throughout the rest of the chapters.

How to install Visual Studio 2017 Community Edition

Visual Studio 2017 Community Edition is installed like any other Windows application.

 Note however that you need administrator rights during the installation. These rights will not be required when developing with Visual Studio later.

For the Visual Studio 2017 Community Edition installation, you can choose between the following three different Visual Studio 2017 installation modes:

- The **Express Installation** installs all of the components that are considered default components by Microsoft in an easy and quick way. If you need specific Visual Studio features not found in this list, then you need to use the Custom Installation.
- The **Custom Installation** gives you full choice over every Visual Studio 2017 feature you can install. You may, for instance, install complementary features such as Visual C++, F#, SQL Server Data Tools, the mobile platform, and several other SDKs, as well as specific language packs.
- When using the **Offline Installation**, you can install Visual Studio 2017 without any network connections. This is very handy when you cannot connect to the internet and nonetheless want to prepare a developer machine. In this case, you have to prepare an external support, such as a mobile hard disk or a USB key, and put the Visual Studio 2017 installer files on it beforehand.

One way to prepare such an external support is to download the necessary Visual Studio installer (Community, Professional, or Enterprise Edition) from the Visual Studio website, `https://www.visualstudio.com/downloads/`, and extract its contents into a folder. Then, you retrieve the various install packages by executing the command `<executable name> --layout` in a command-line window. After some time, everything is downloaded and you have an external support that can be used for offline installations.

Note that you can use the same procedure to download all of the installation files to a central network storage and then create a shared folder for being able to install Visual Studio 2017 from within your own network to optimize installation times and lower network bandwidth needs.

We will now see how to install Visual Studio 2017 Community Edition manually by using the downloaded setup program from the Microsoft Visual Studio website mentioned previously:

1. Start the Visual Studio 2017 Community Edition setup program and you will see a list of various installable workloads. By default, you will see Windows, web and cloud, mobile and gaming, and other toolsets:

2. Choose your desired components and they will get installed in the next steps. If that is all you need, then there is nothing else to be done. As explained before, this is the Express Installation.

3. If you need to customize the installed components, to either add or remove individual components, then you have to click on **Individual components**. Obviously, you will then be doing what is called a Custom Installation:

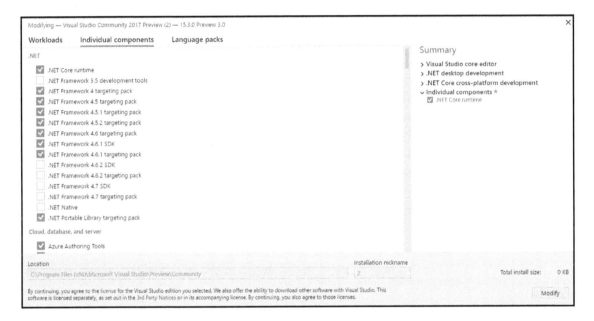

4. When you have finished selecting your desired workloads and components, the installation will start. The installation time is dependent on the number of workloads and components you have selected, as well as your internet connection speed, if you are not using the Offline Installation method described previously:

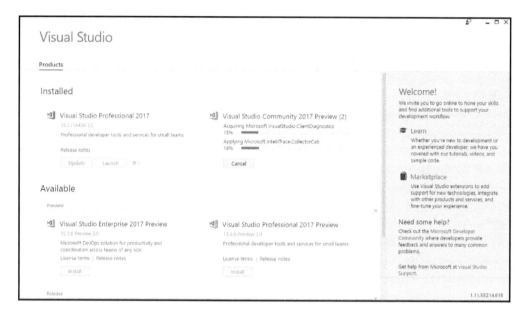

For more advanced scenarios, like automating and scripting the Visual Studio 2017 installation, you can start the setup program via the Command Prompt. There is a variety of command-line parameters, which help to define what needs to be installed where.

Following is a list of some of the command-line parameters with a brief description of what they do. Please go to `https://docs.microsoft.com/en-us/visualstudio/install/use-command-line-parameters-to-install-visual-studio` to get more information, as well as a full list of all existing command-line parameters:

Parameter	Description
`/AddRemoveFeatures`	This adds the features selected
`/AdminFile`	This specifies a file to install silently
`/CreateAdminFile`	This specifies to generate a silently response file after your installation
`/CustomInstallPath`	This specifies the target path
`/ForceRestart`	This forces your PC to restart
`/Full`	This installs all the features
`/noweb`	This disables internet searching features and downloading
`/ProductKey`	This specifies the key to be used

First steps with Visual Studio 2017

After installing Visual Studio 2017, you are now able to explore everything it has to offer for improving developer productivity. Following is a list of some of the features that are provided.

Start Visual Studio 2017 and the first thing you will see is the Visual Studio **Start Page**. It displays by default a **Get Started** section with a list of help topics, the history of projects you have recently worked on, a developer and community news feed, and some shortcuts to common developer tasks, such as creating or opening projects:

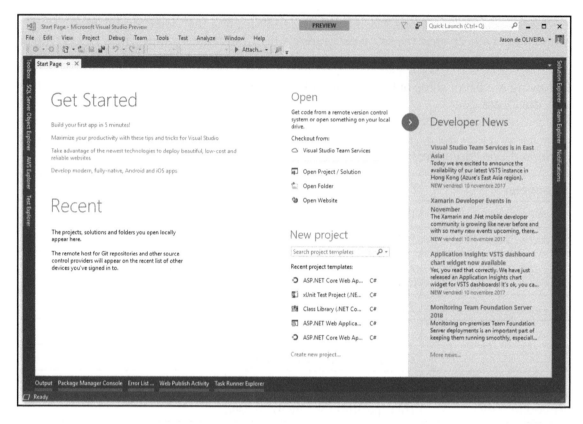

The **Start Page** is fully customizable, so if you do not want to see the news section, for example, containing developer news from Microsoft's official channels, then you just have to close the collapsed list or remove it completely. You can customize the Start Page much more, and you can look up the details in MSDN at
https://msdn.microsoft.com/en-us/library/ff425532.aspx, should you be interested in doing so.

One of the most important features of Visual Studio is IntelliSense. It helps developers to be much more productive by offering features like List Member, Parameter Info, Quick Info, and Complete Word. It has been improved in Visual Studio 2017 with some very interesting new features, since you can now filter by type (class, namespace, or keyword) and by CamelCase search.

It is also possible now to select the best matching results from the list of results, instead of just picking the top one:

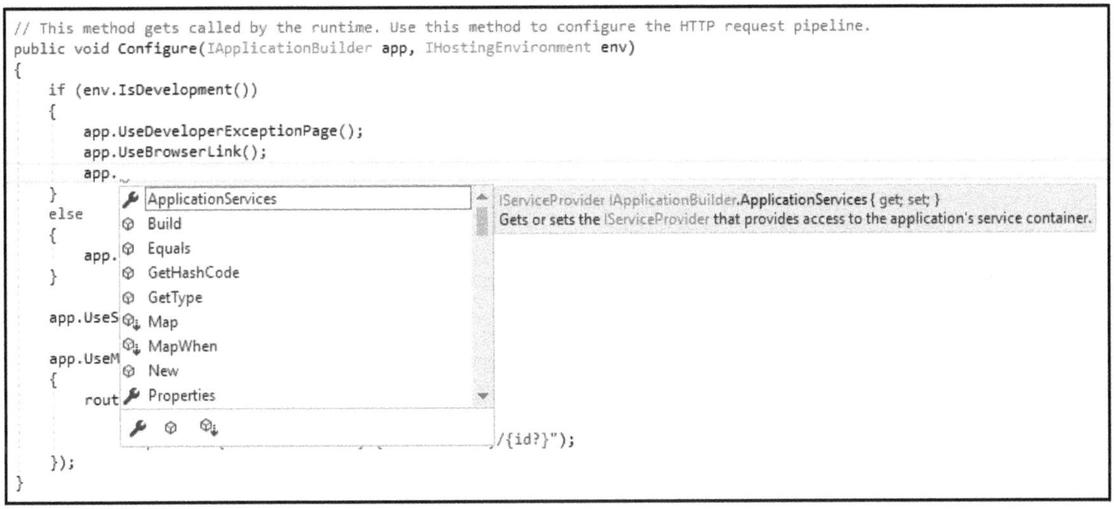

```
// This method gets called by the runtime. Use this method to configure the HTTP request pipeline.
public void Configure(IApplicationBuilder app, IHostingEnvironment env)
{
    if (env.IsDevelopment())
    {
        app.UseDeveloperExceptionPage();
        app.UseBrowserLink();
        app.
    }
    else
    {
        app.
    }
    app.UseS
    app.UseM
    {
        rout                                          /{id?}");
    });
}
```

ApplicationServices
Build
Equals
GetHashCode
GetType
Map
MapWhen
New
Properties

IServiceProvider IApplicationBuilder.ApplicationServices { get; set; }
Gets or sets the IServiceProvider that provides access to the application's service container.

The **Code Refactoring** and **Live Code Analysis** features of Visual Studio 2017 accelerate development and assure readable and maintainable code. For example, you can add missing namespaces or remove unnecessary namespaces automatically:

```
1   using System;
2   using System.Collections.Generic;
3   using System.Linq;
4   using System.Threading.Tasks;
5   using Microsoft.AspNetCore.Builder;
6   using Microsoft.AspNetCore.Hosting;
7   using Microsoft.AspNetCore.Mvc;
8   using Microsoft.Extensions.Configuration;
9   using Microsoft.Extensions.DependencyInjection;
10  using Microsoft.Extensions.Logging;
11
12      Remove Unnecessary Usings   ▶    using System;
13                                        using System.Collections.Generic;
14      public class Startup            using System.Linq;
15      {                               using System.Threading.Tasks;
16          public Startup(ICo          using Microsoft.AspNetCore.Builder;
17          {                           using Microsoft.AspNetCore.Hosting;
18              Configuration           using Microsoft.AspNetCore.Mvc;
19          }                           using Microsoft.Extensions.Configuration;
20                                      using Microsoft.Extensions.DependencyInjection;
21          public IConfigurat          using Microsoft.Extensions.Logging;
22
23          // This method get    Preview changes                the container
24          public void Configu   Fix all occurrences in: Document | Project | Solution
25          {
26              services.AddMvc();
27          }
```

Here is an example of a Code Refactoring suggestion:

```
23        // This method gets called by the runtime. Use this method to add services to the container.
24        public void ConfigureServices(IServiceCollection services)
25        {
26            services.AddMvc();
27    Use expression body for methods  ▶   ...
28                                              // This method gets called by the runtime. Use this method to add services to the container.
29        // This method g              public void ConfigureServices(IServiceCollection services)                    pipeline.
30        public void Conf              {
31        {                                 services.AddMvc();
32            if (env.IsDe              }
33            {                         public void ConfigureServices(IServiceCollection services) => services.AddMvc();
34                app.UseD   ...
35                app.UseB   Preview changes
36        }
```

As the name depicts, the **Find All References** feature allows a developer to easily and quickly find all references of a method or an object. Coloring, grouping, and a Peek Preview functionality aid visually to better navigate within your code and really help to understand it:

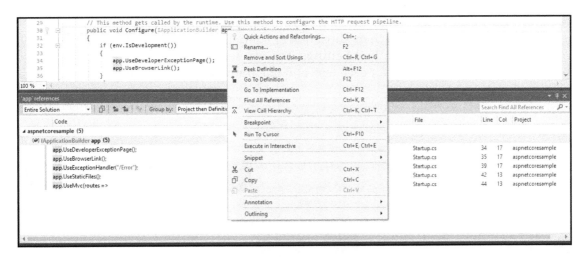

The **Peek Definition** and **Go to Definition** features serve to examine the definition of a method, interface, or class either within a popup window, without changing the current window, or by directly opening the file containing the source code with the requested definition. The **Go To Implementation** feature does the same, but navigates to the implementation instead:

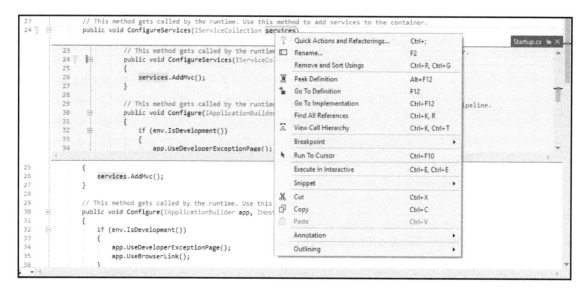

Another important feature, one of our favorite features, by the way, is **Live Unit Testing.** It requires Visual Studio 2017 Enterprise Edition and allows you to automatically run unit tests in the background after each modification or compilation of your code. It can be configured and activated in the **Test Settings**. You can set, for instance, the number of test processes, maximum duration for each test, and maximum memory consummation:

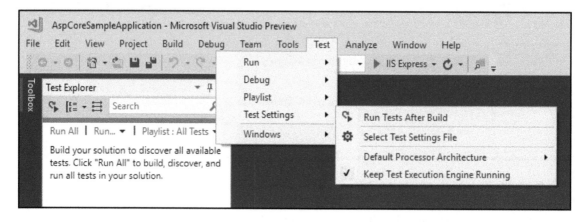

There are many more interesting and exciting features in Visual Studio 2017, and we invite you to visit the official Visual Studio web page at
`https://docs.microsoft.com/en-us/visualstudio/welcome-to-visual-studio` for more details. It is key for a developer to know his developer IDE as best as he can and to familiarize himself with a lot of its features which can then help him to do his job better and faster. So, do take some time to look at this before you start developing your applications.

Creating your first ASP.NET Core 2.0 application in Visual Studio 2017

You have patiently read the previous chapters, understood what you will be learning by reading this book, and prepared your developer machine. You are now ready to create your first sample application.

Let's look at the different options you have for creating your first ASP.NET Core 2.0 application in more detail.

When creating a new project in Visual Studio 2017, the first thing you see is the template explorer displaying a tree view for choosing between installed, language-specific, and online templates.

After having selected the template source in the tree view, the different templates are shown. For ASP.NET Core, you see **Console App**, **Class Library**, **Unit Test Project**, xUnit **Test Project**, and **ASP.NET Core Web Application (.NET Core)**, for example.

Since some of the templates integrate multiple application types, you sometimes have to make additional choices to specify what exact type of application you want to create. This is the case for ASP.NET Core web applications, since you have to choose between an empty, **Web API**, **Web Application**, or **Web Application (Razor Pages)** project template. Additionally, you can enable Docker support and change the authentication mode between no authentication, an individual user account, a work or school account, or Windows authentication.

The following are step-by-step instructions for creating your first ASP.NET Core 2.0 sample web application:

1. If the .NET Core 2.0 SDK is not yet installed, then download and install .NET Core Preview 2 from `https://www.microsoft.com/net/core/preview`.

 Note that this step might no longer be needed at the time of reading this book, since it should have been released officially by then.

2. Start Visual Studio 2017.

3. Create a new project by clicking on **File** | **New** | **Project**:

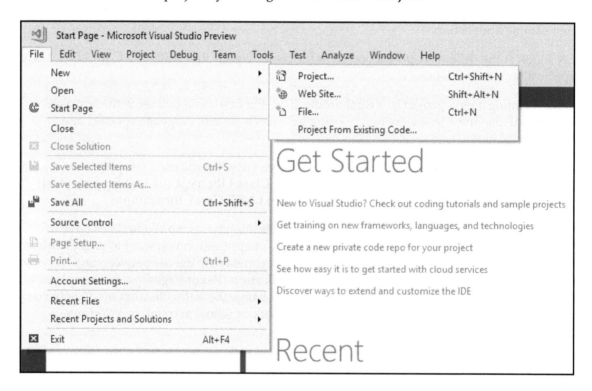

4. Select as project template **Visual C# | .NET Core | ASP.NET Core Web Application (.NET Core)**:

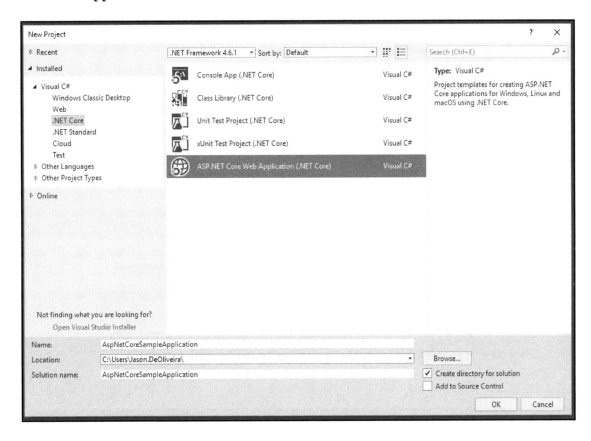

5. You are now able to select the specific web application type. Select **Web Application (Razor Pages)** and leave the Docker support (disabled) and authentication (**No Authentication**) options unchanged:

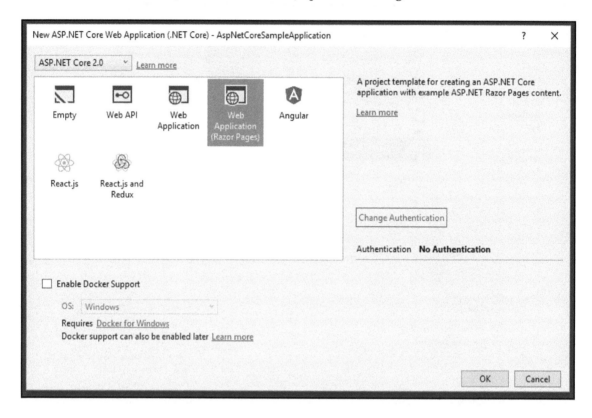

Note that at the time of the elaboration of this book, only Visual Studio 2017 Preview 15.3 had support for ASP.NET Core 2.0. It should be included in the standard version, though, and at the time of publication.

6. After the sample application project has been generated, a project start page is displayed. Here, you can configure additional options such as connected services (Application Insights, and more) and publishing targets (Microsoft Azure App Services, IIS, FTP, Folder, and more). Leave everything unchanged:

7. You can now start debugging your application by pressing *F5* or by clicking on **Debug | Start Debugging**:

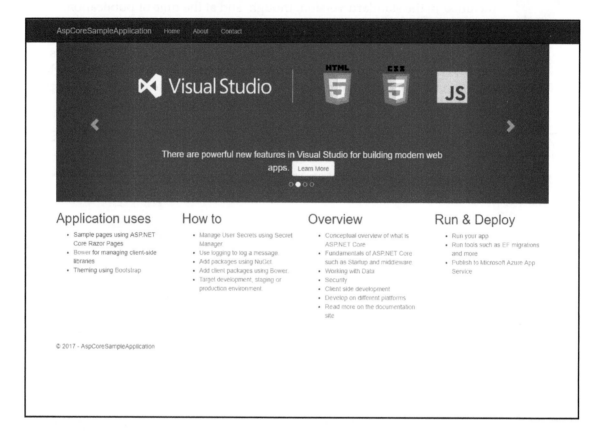

Creating your first ASP.NET Core 2.0 application via the command line

In the previous section, you saw how to create your first ASP.NET Core 2.0 sample application with Visual Studio 2017, and this should be the preferred method for most common developers.

However, if you prefer using the command line or Visual Studio Code, which we are going to introduce a little later in the book, then using Visual Studio 2017 is not really an option. Luckily, .NET Core and ASP.NET Core 2.0 provide full support for the command line. This might even be your only option on other operating systems such as Linux or macOS. The same command-line instructions work on all the different operating systems, so, once you get used to them, you can work on any environment.

Let's see now how creating your first sample application using the Windows command line works:

1. If the .NET Core 2.0 SDK is not yet installed, then download and install .NET Core Preview 2 from `https://www.microsoft.com/net/core/preview`.

 Note that this step might no longer be needed at the time of reading this book, since it should have been released officially by then.

2. Create a folder for your sample application, `mkdir aspnetcoresample`.
3. Move into the created folder, `cd aspnetcoresample`.
4. Create a new web application based on the empty ASP.NET Core 2.0 web application template, `dotnet new web`.

 Previous versions of .NET Core required an additional `-t` parameter for choosing the template (`dotnet new -t web`). If you get an error when executing `dotnet new web`, it is a good indication that you need to install .NET Core 2.0.

Note that you can verify your .NET version by entering `dotnet` (with no parameters) if you are not sure about your environment, since it will display the current .NET Core version.

5. Run the sample application by executing `dotnet run`:

```
Administrator: Command Prompt - dotnet  run                                          —    □    ×

C:\Users\Jason.DeOliveira>mkdir aspnetcoresample

C:\Users\Jason.DeOliveira>cd aspnetcoresample

C:\Users\Jason.DeOliveira\aspnetcoresample>dotnet new web
The template "ASP.NET Core Empty" was created successfully.
This template contains technologies from parties other than Microsoft, see https://aka.ms/template-3pn for details.

Processing post-creation actions...
Running 'dotnet restore' on C:\Users\Jason.DeOliveira\aspnetcoresample\aspnetcoresample.csproj...
  Restoring packages for C:\Users\Jason.DeOliveira\aspnetcoresample\aspnetcoresample.csproj...
  Generating MSBuild file C:\Users\Jason.DeOliveira\aspnetcoresample\obj\aspnetcoresample.csproj.nuget.g.props.
  Generating MSBuild file C:\Users\Jason.DeOliveira\aspnetcoresample\obj\aspnetcoresample.csproj.nuget.g.targets.
  Restore completed in 2,44 sec for C:\Users\Jason.DeOliveira\aspnetcoresample\aspnetcoresample.csproj.


Restore succeeded.

C:\Users\Jason.DeOliveira\aspnetcoresample>dotnet run
Hosting environment: Production
Content root path: C:\Users\Jason.DeOliveira\aspnetcoresample
Now listening on: http://localhost:5000
Application started. Press Ctrl+C to shut down.
info: Microsoft.AspNetCore.Hosting.Internal.WebHost[1]
      Request starting HTTP/1.1 GET http://localhost:5000/
info: Microsoft.AspNetCore.Hosting.Internal.WebHost[2]
      Request finished in 10.1007ms 200
info: Microsoft.AspNetCore.Hosting.Internal.WebHost[1]
```

6. Open a browser and go to `http://localhost:5000`. If everything worked correctly, you should see a **Hello World!** page:

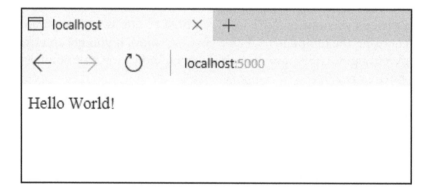

You have seen how to create your first sample application either by using Visual Studio 2017 or the command line. You will now see how to use Visual Studio Code and how it helps you when building an ASP.NET Core 2.0 application on Linux or macOS.

Visual Studio Code as a development environment

Visual Studio Code is a lightweight and powerful cross-platform development environment for Windows, Linux, and macOS.

You can use a wide range of programming languages such as JavaScript, TypeScript, and Node.js as well as C++, C#, Python, PHP, Go, and the .NET Core and Unity runtimes via language and runtime extensions.

It comes with a streamlined, clean, and very efficient user interface. There is a file and folder explorer on the left and a source code editor on the right, showing the contents of files you have opened and are currently working on:

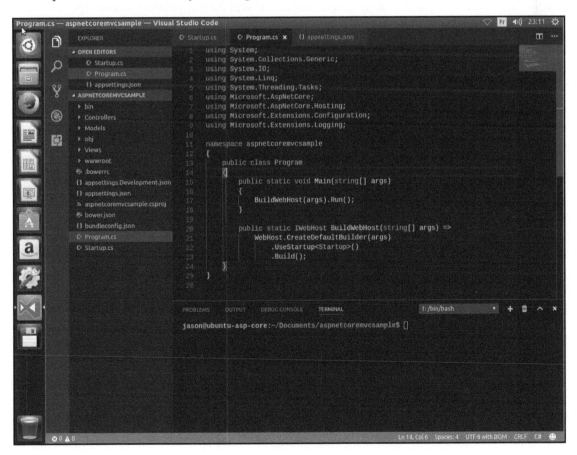

The user interface consists of the following areas:

- **Activity bar**: Provides several different views and additional context-specific indicators such as outgoing code changes when Git is enabled.
- **Sidebar**: Contains a file and folder explorer for working on your projects.
- **Editor groups**: This is the main area for working with your code and navigating within it. Up to three source code editor windows can be opened side by side at the same time.
- **Panels**: Serves to display panels with output or debug information, errors and warnings, or an integrated terminal.
- **Status bar**: Additional information concerning projects and files you have edited.

Please go to `https://code.visualstudio.com/docs` for additional information on Visual Studio Code and its capacities and functionalities. It will be our primary choice for illustrating how to build ASP.NET Core 2.0 applications on Linux.

How to install Visual Studio Code on Linux

We are now going to explain how easy and fast it is to install Visual Studio Code on Linux. One of the most popular Linux distributions, Ubuntu 16.04, will serve as an example.

If you do not have a physical or virtual installation of Linux Ubuntu available, you can easily install it in Azure for trying out Visual Studio Code and understanding the various ASP.NET Core 2.0 examples, and then connect via Microsoft Remote Desktop app to it.

In this case, select the Linux Ubuntu 16.04 LTS image from the Azure Marketplace and create a new Linux Ubuntu VM in Azure. Leave all of the default options, then configure it to allow remote desktop connections (install compatible desktop, install xrdp, open port 3389, and more):

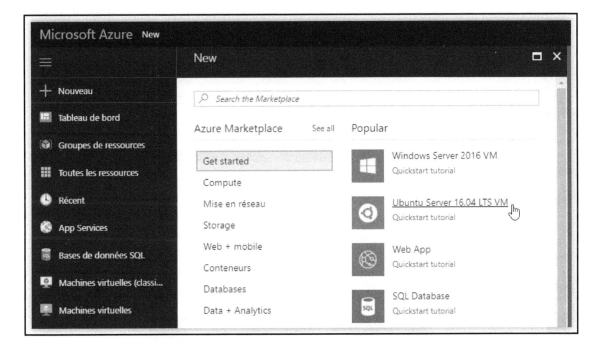

Let's see how to install Visual Studio Code on Linux Ubuntu:

1. First, download the Linux Ubuntu install `.deb` package (64-bit) from `https://go.microsoft.com/fwlink/?LinkID=760868`:

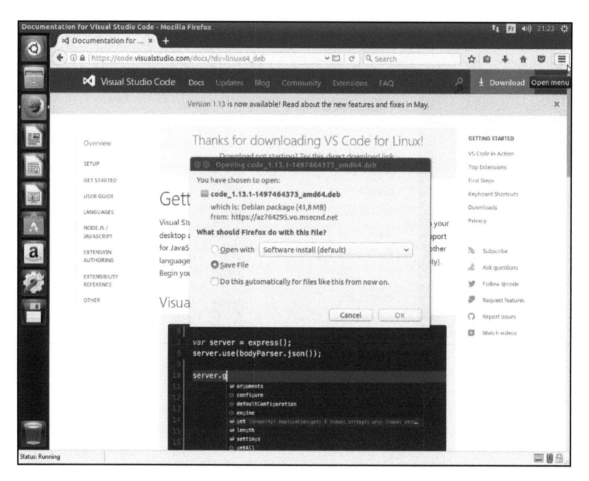

2. Open a new Terminal window in Ubuntu.
3. Install the downloaded package via `sudo dpkg -i <file>.deb`.
4. Then, enter `sudo apt-get install -f`.
5. Set Visual Studio Code as your default text file editor by typing the command `xdg-mime default code.desktop text/plain`.

The installation will begin and automatically install the APT repository and signing key for enabling automatic package updates, as well as Visual Studio Code:

```
jason@ubuntu-asp-core: ~/Downloads

jason@ubuntu-asp-core:~$ ls
Desktop    Downloads        Music      Public      Videos
Documents  examples.desktop Pictures   Templates
jason@ubuntu-asp-core:~$ cd Downloads/
jason@ubuntu-asp-core:~/Downloads$ sudo dpkg -i code_1.13.1-1497464373_amd64.deb

[sudo] password for jason:
Selecting previously unselected package code.
(Reading database ... 174260 files and directories currently installed.)
Preparing to unpack code_1.13.1-1497464373_amd64.deb ...
Unpacking code (1.13.1-1497464373) ...
Setting up code (1.13.1-1497464373) ...
Processing triggers for gnome-menus (3.13.3-6ubuntu3.1) ...
Processing triggers for desktop-file-utils (0.22-1ubuntu5) ...
Processing triggers for bamfdaemon (0.5.3~bzr0+16.04.20160824-0ubuntu1) ...
Rebuilding /usr/share/applications/bamf-2.index...
Processing triggers for mime-support (3.59ubuntu1) ...
jason@ubuntu-asp-core:~/Downloads$ sudo apt-get install -f
Reading package lists... Done
Building dependency tree
Reading state information... Done
0 upgraded, 0 newly installed, 0 to remove and 241 not upgraded.
jason@ubuntu-asp-core:~/Downloads$ xdg-mime default code.desktop test/plain
jason@ubuntu-asp-core:~/Downloads$
```

You can also manually install the repository and signing key, update the package cache, and then finally start the Visual Studio Code package installation, as follows:

1. Open a new Terminal window in Ubuntu:

   ```
   curl https://packages.microsoft.com/keys/microsoft.asc | gpg --
   dearmor>microsoft.gpg

   sudo mv microsoft.gpg /etc/apt/trusted.gpg.d/microsoft.gpg

   sudo sh -c 'echo "deb [arch=amd64]
   https://packages.microsoft.com/repos/vscode stable main" >
   /etc/apt/sources.list.d/vscode.list'

   sudo apt-get update

   sudo apt-get install code
   ```

2. Set Visual Studio Code as your default text file editor by typing the command `xdg-mime default code.desktop text/plain`.

For more information and details on how to install Visual Studio Code on other Linux distributions such as RHEL, Fedora, CentOS, openSUSE, SLE, or others, please go to `https://code.visualstudio.com/docs/setup/linux`.

Creating your first ASP.NET Core 2.0 application in Visual Studio Code

You will now see how to initialize your first ASP.NET Core 2.0 application using the built-in Visual Studio Code terminal window. Then, you are going to install all of the necessary extensions to be able to run and debug it at the end:

1. Start Visual Studio Code; no folder has been opened in the **Explorer** viewlet yet:

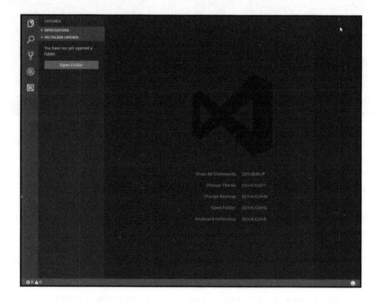

2. Click on **Open Folder**, and then click on **Create Folder**. Name the folder `aspnetcoremvcsample` and click on **OK**:

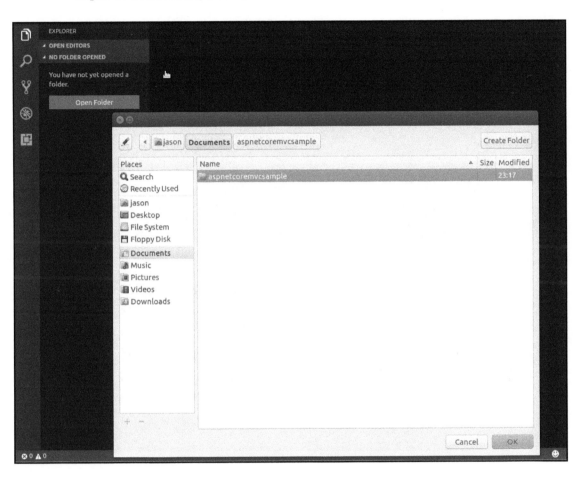

3. Display the integrated terminal window via **View** | **Integrated Terminal** and initialize a new ASP.NET Core 2.0 MVC project by entering `dotnet new mvc`:

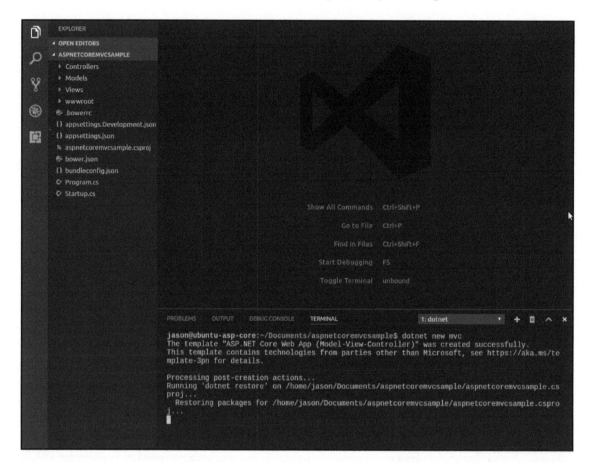

4. When opening any of the C# files, you are asked to install additional project dependencies and Visual Studio Code extensions. Do this to be able to build, run, and debug your application in the next steps:

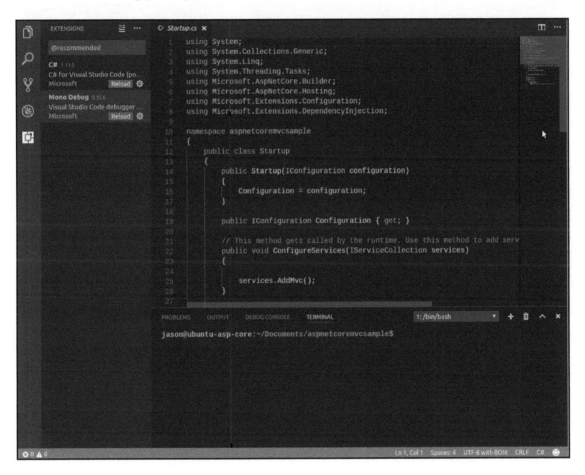

5. Modify the `launch.json` file in the `.vscode` folder and set the debugger to **.NET Core Launch (web)**:

6. Set a breakpoint somewhere in the code and start debugging by either pressing *F5* or clicking on the green flash in the **Debugging** viewlet. Try hitting the breakpoint; everything should work correctly:

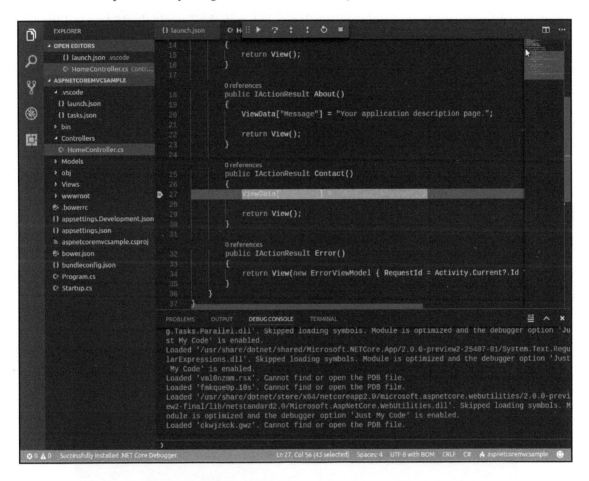

Creating your first ASP.NET Core 2.0 application in Linux

To create and run your first sample application using only the Terminal window in Linux, you have to do the following steps:

1. If the .NET Core 2.0 SDK is not yet installed, then download and install .NET Core Preview 2 from `https://www.microsoft.com/net/core/preview` for your Linux distribution. Here is an example of how to do that for Ubuntu:

```
sudosh -c 'echo "deb [arch=amd64]
 https://apt-mo.trafficmanager.net/repos/dotnet-release/
  xenial main" > /etc/apt/sources.list.d/dotnetdev.list'
sudo apt-key adv --keyserver hkp://keyserver.ubuntu.com:80
 --recv-keys 417A0893
sudo apt-get update
sudo apt-get install dotnet-sdk-2.0.0-preview2-006497
```

2. Create a folder for your sample application, `mkdir ~/Documents/aspnetcoremvcsample`.

3. Move into the created folder, `cd ~/Documents/aspnetcoremvcsample`.

4. Create a new web application based on the ASP.NET Core 2.0 MVC web application template, `dotnet new mvc`:

5. Run the sample application by executing `dotnet run`:

```
jason@ubuntu-asp-core: ~/Documents/aspnetcoremvcsample
 Installing NuGet.Frameworks 4.0.0.
 Installing Microsoft.Build 15.3.0-preview-000388-01.
 Installing System.Diagnostics.TraceSource 4.0.0.
 Installing Microsoft.Build.Framework 15.3.0-preview-000388-01.
 Installing Microsoft.Build.Tasks.Core 15.3.0-preview-000388-01.
 Installing Microsoft.Build.Utilities.Core 15.3.0-preview-000388-01.
 Installing System.Text.Encoding.CodePages 4.0.1.
 Installing System.Diagnostics.Contracts 4.0.1.
 Installing System.Collections.Immutable 1.2.0.
 Installing System.Collections.NonGeneric 4.0.1.
 Installing System.Diagnostics.FileVersionInfo 4.0.0.
 Installing System.Diagnostics.Process 4.1.0.
 Restore completed in 2.06 sec for /home/jason/Documents/aspnetcoremvcsample/a
spnetcoremvcsample.csproj.


Restore succeeded.

jason@ubuntu-asp-core:~/Documents/aspnetcoremvcsample$ dotnet run
Hosting environment: Production
Content root path: /home/jason/Documents/aspnetcoremvcsample
Now listening on: http://localhost:5000
Application started. Press Ctrl+C to shut down.
```

6. Open a browser and go to `http://localhost:5000`:

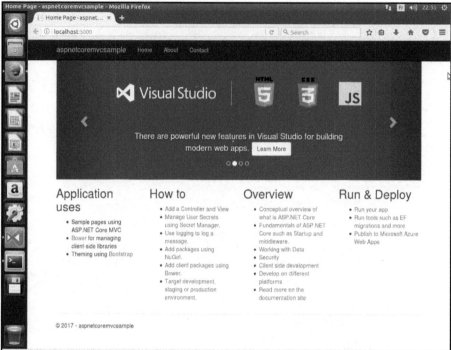

Summary

In this chapter, you have learned how to set up your development environment to be able to work with ASP.NET Core 2.0. You have seen how to install either Visual Studio 2017 or Visual Studio Code.

You then created your first ASP.NET Core 2.0 web application in both development environments, and you have even built a project in Linux to showcase the cross-platform capabilities.

In the next chapter, we will talk about how to set up a continuous integration pipeline by using Visual Studio Team Services, including work items and Git branches, as well as build and release pipelines.

3

Creating a Continuous Integration Pipeline in VSTS

Building great applications is not a trivial task. On the contrary, it is a difficult and complex endeavor in which many actors need to efficiently work together to create applications that correspond to high-end user expectations.

Today, everything moves very fast and **time-to-market** is very important for success. This chapter is going to introduce methods, processes, and tools to help you optimize your development processes, thus building high-quality software with short release cycles.

Traditionally, building software is done by planning whole software projects from beginning to end, writing detailed specifications, developing and testing (often in a rush), while hoping that everything will work as expected (V-model).

Sometimes this approach works and sometimes it does not. When it does not work, developers implement features while only testing manually, with the objective of adding unit tests later. Then, at the end of the project, they have to speed up to assure on-time delivery and often run out of time.

This leads to projects with significant technical, functional, and quality flaws, with a high number of bugs and tremendous maintenance effort resulting in long release cycles. In the worst case, end users will not like the delivered features, thus the final product could be considered a complete failure.

There is a better way of doing things, something people have been talking about for some time now, and that you surely have already heard of—Agile methodologies!

Agile methodologies, when combined with **continuous integration** (**CI**) and **continuous deployment** (**CD**), provide solutions for building better software with a fast time-to-market, lower maintenance costs, better overall quality, and higher customer satisfaction.

While this book is not about Agile methodologies as such, we recommend familiarizing yourself with the subject, and we are going to explain all of the tools and processes that accompany and surround it.

In this chapter, we will cover the following topics:

- Continuous integration, continuous deployment, and build and release pipelines
- Using **Visual Studio Team Services** (**VSTS**) for continuous integration and continuous deployment
- Creating a free VSTS subscription and your first VSTS project
- Organizing your work via work items
- Using Git as a version control system
- Creating a VSTS build pipeline
- Creating a VSTS release pipeline

Continuous integration, continuous deployment, and build and release pipelines

When using continuous integration, development teams write code, which, after a code review, gets integrated into a version control system, from where it is built and tested automatically. This normally happens multiple times a day. Thus, a development team can detect problems and bugs quickly and fix them as early as possible, enabling what is commonly called **Fail Fast**.

Continuous deployment is a natural extension of continuous integration, since it assures that every application modification after being built and tested is releasable. It consists of automatically upgrading development, testing, staging, and production systems.

A pipeline defines a complete development and release workflow. It contains all of the steps required for conception, development, quality assurance, and testing, until the delivery of the final product. It includes continuous integration and continuous deployment processes for building high-quality applications in an industrialized way.

Note that you can separate your development process into two different pipelines, a build and a release pipeline, or have only one single pipeline that does it all, depending on your specific needs.

There are various technologies and tools that help you to implement an efficient, productive, fully-automated, and industrialized software development process based on continuous integration and continuous deployment. We are going to use Visual Studio Team Services in the following examples.

Using VSTS for continuous integration and continuous deployment

If you need to collaboratively work together and share code, plan and manage your user stories and development tasks, track progress of your features and bugs, all in an Agile environment, then VSTS is one of the solutions you can find in the cloud, and perhaps even the best.

It supports many different programming languages (C#, Java, JavaScript, and more), various development tools (Visual Studio, Eclipse, and more) and is scalable to any team size.

Additionally, it is free of charge for up to five users in a private team project, which is very helpful for trying out the examples shown in this book.

VSTS provides the following main features:

- **Work items and the Kanban board**: Plan and assign work and tasks
- **Source code management**: Share code in a version control system
- **Testing**: Create and execute test plans containing test cases
- **Package store**: Put your own NuGet packages in a store
- **Build pipeline**: Build code for creating application packages
- **Release pipeline**: Deploy application packages to different release targets

For further information on VSTS and all of its features, please go to
`https://www.visualstudio.com/team-services/features`.

Creating a free VSTS subscription and your first VSTS project

We will now explain how to create your own free VSTS subscription and your first project. You are going to use it later to try out and understand the examples illustrated within this book:

1. Go to `https://www.visualstudio.com/team-services` and click on the **Get Started for free** button:

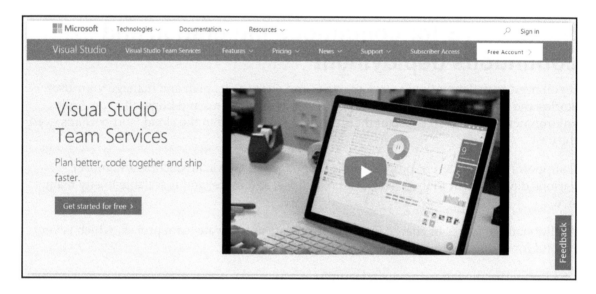

2. Log in with your work, school, or personal Microsoft account:

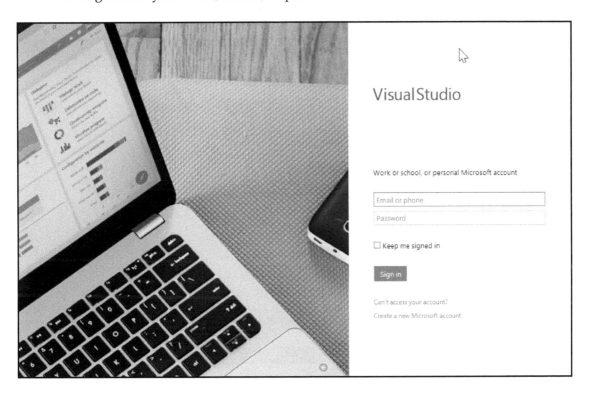

3. If you are connecting for the first time, enter additional information such as your name, your country, and your email address, then click on **Continue**:

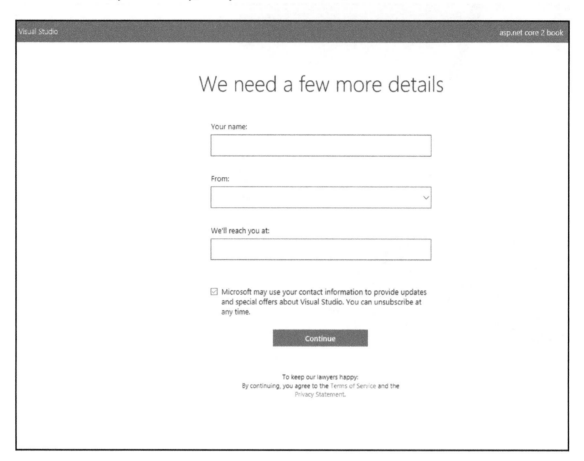

4. Now that your account is created, let's create a new project. For our example, select **Git** as version control, click on **Change Details**, then choose **Work item process—Scrum**:

5. Your new project gets generated, and you are now ready to create your first work items and Git repositories, as shown later in the book.

Organizing your work via work items

Work items are used to plan, assign, track, and more generally speaking, organize your work during a software development project. They help to better understand what needs to be done and give insights on the status of your project.

Some common work item usages are:

- Create, prioritize, and track user stories for application features
- Create and track development tasks necessary to implement user stories
- Create, prioritize, and track application bugs
- Determine application quality and application release dates
- Display progress of user stories, tasks, and bugs in a single Kanban board

As you have seen before, you can choose the work item process during VSTS project creation. This choice defines the standard **work item types** (**WITs**) available.

There are more than 14 WITs by default and you can create your own custom WITs for advanced scenarios. Most of the time, you will not need to create your own custom WITs.

Possible work item process choices are:

- Scrum, if your team uses the Scrum methodology and if you want to track your **product backlog items** (**PBI**) on a Kanban board
- Agile, if your team practices an Agile methodology but does not want to comply with specific Scrum constraints and terminologies
- CMMI, if your team follows a more formal development tasks follow-up, you can track requests, changes, risks, and reviews

Here is a list of WITs depending on the work item process:

Domain	Scrum	Agile	CMMI
Product planning	PBI Bug	User story Bug	Requirement Change Bug
Portfolio	Epic Feature	Epic Feature	Epic Feature
Task and sprint planning	Task	Task	Task
Bug backlog management	Bug	Bug	Bug
Issue and risk management	Impediment	Issue	Issue Risk Review

In our example, we have chosen the **Scrum** process. Product owners create epics, features, and product backlog items (the equivalent to user stories). During the sprint planning development, tasks are defined and linked to product backlog items. Everything is visible to the whole team via a Kanban board in the cloud:

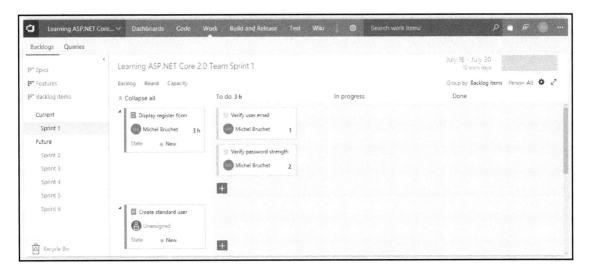

Testers create and execute test cases by using the VSTS web portal or Microsoft Test Manager. They create and assign bugs and code defects and blocking issues can be tracked:

VSTS allows you to hierarchically organize your work. You can drill up, drill down, reorder, and modify parent items as well as use filters in hierarchical views.

 For even more information, go to
https://www.visualstudio.com/en-us/docs/work/backlogs/create-you
r-backlog.

Let's look at the different elements in more detail. An epic can be described as a large user story with a large amount of work. It must be broken down into features and smaller product backlog items to be able to fully understand its requirements and then implement it efficiently during multiple sprints:

Features decompose epics into smaller apprehensible parts. They consist of a group of product backlog items that correspond to the detailed expected functionalities:

A product backlog item is a unit of work that has business value and that is small enough to be completed during a single sprint. If you cannot finish it in a single sprint, then it has to be considered a feature and must be decomposed further:

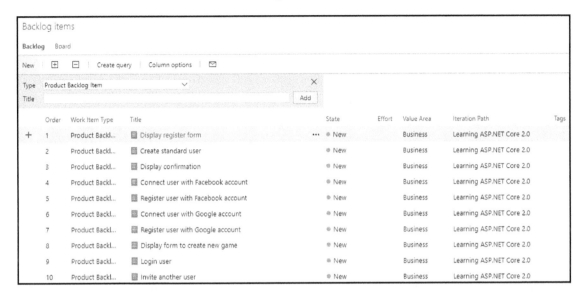

Tasks describe the development work necessary for implementing the expected product backlog item functionalities during the sprint. They are linked to product backlog items for trackability and to be able to automatically calculate project advancement.

Bugs contain issues that have been raised and that need to be resolved during a sprint. They are linked to their corresponding product backlog items:

After defining epics, features, and product backlog items, you can do your sprint planning and decide what needs to be done in which iteration. Additionally, the Kanban board provides a great visual representation for better understanding:

The working capacity for each team member can be defined for each sprint and a work detail's report allows you to follow their work achievements in real time:

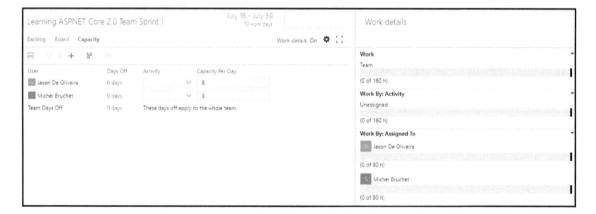

Furthermore, each work item has a state that changes over time. The state allows you to track work achievements and filter work items for better understanding and detecting issues.

The following figure shows the various default work item states depending on the work item process:

	Scrum	**Agile**	**CMMI**
Work Item States	New Approved Committed Done Removed	New Active Resolved Closed Removed	Proposed Active Resolved Closed

You can query for work items, create graphs, and publish them to your VSTS project home page. This is a very useful feature if you need to retrieve specific work items or need to get a holistic view of your project:

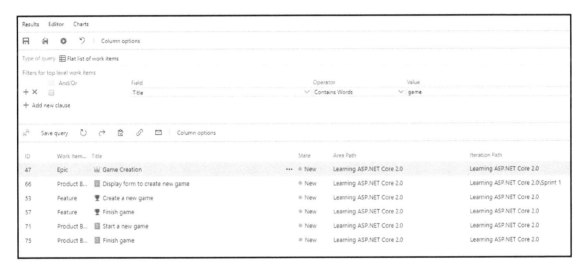

Using Git as a version control system

Git has had some considerable success over the last few years. It has become the preferred distributed version control system among the developer community.

There is a great integration between VSTS and Git, and you have some powerful and productive features at your disposal (`https://www.visualstudio.com/en-us/docs/work/backlogs/connect-work-items-to-git-dev-ops`):

- Git branches can be created from within your backlog or Kanban board
- Git feature branches can easily be created for multiple work items directly from the VSTS website
- Pull requests and commits are automatically linked to corresponding work items
- Build **Summary** page shows work items, which are linked to a commit, as associated work items

Let's see how to create a new Git repository, clone it locally, use it within Visual Studio 2017, and create your first commit:

1. In your VSTS project, click in the top menu on **Code**, then click on the **Clone in Visual Studio** button:

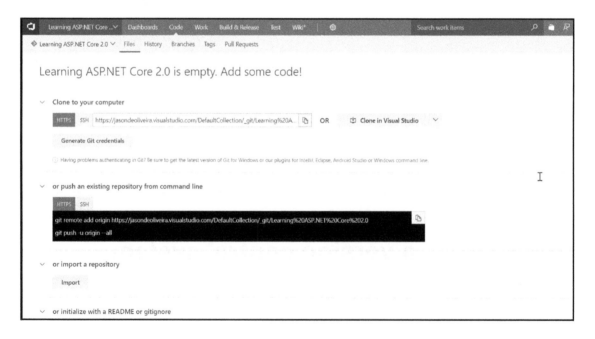

2. A new window will be displayed; select **Microsoft Visual Studio Web Protocol Handler Selector**:

3. Visual Studio 2017 is started automatically and you can authenticate with your work, school, or personal Microsoft account:

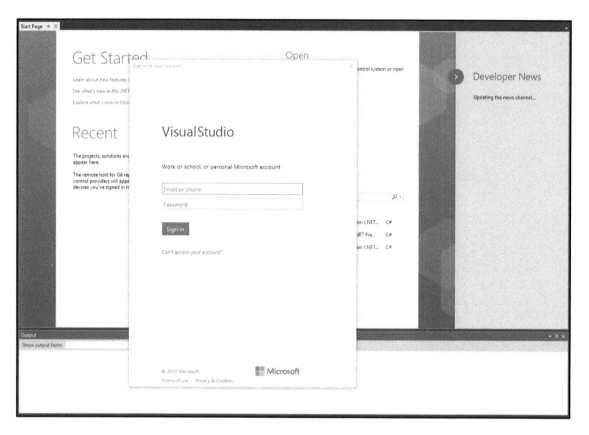

4. Choose the destination folder for your local Git repository and click on the **Clone** button to start the download:

5. Go to **Team Explorer - Home** and click on **Settings**:

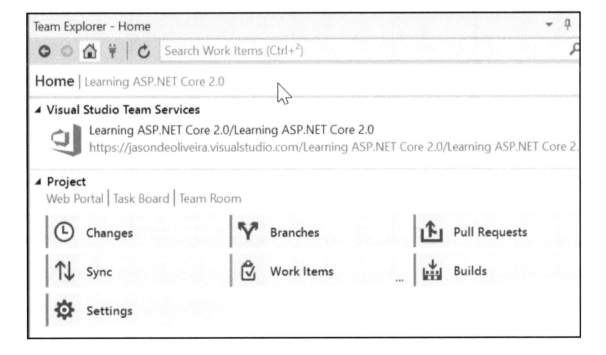

6. In **Team Explorer - Settings**, click on **Repository Settings**:

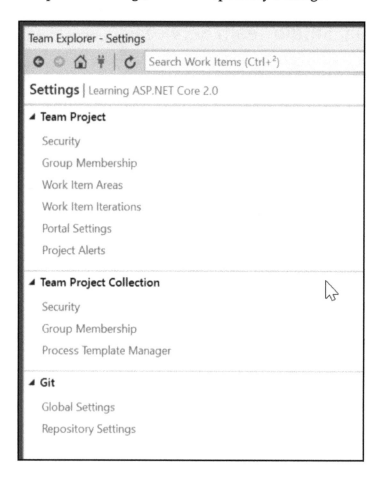

7. In the **Ignore & Attributes Files** section, click on **Add** for each file:

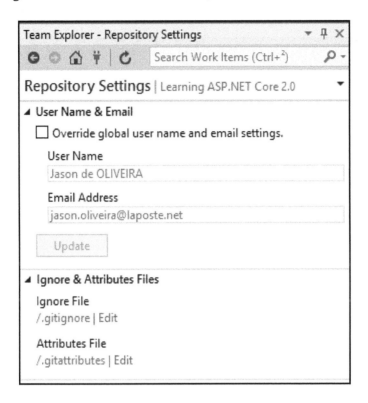

8. Return to **Team Explorer - Home**, and this time click on **Changes**, enter a comment for your first commit, and click on the **Commit Staged** button:

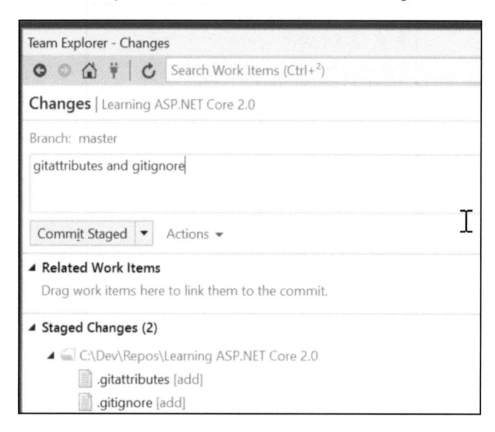

9. Your first commit has been created locally; click on the **Sync** link to push it to the server:

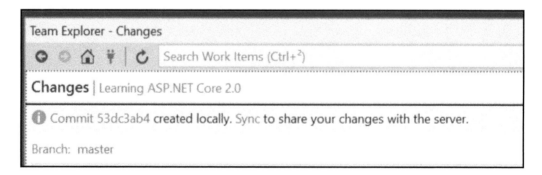

10. Go to the VSTS website and click on **Code** in the upper menu; you can see that your created files have been uploaded:

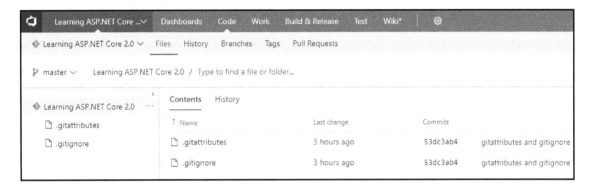

That's it! You have created and initialized your Git repository. It's as easy as that! From here, you have multiple paths you can follow. For instance, leaving everything in the same branch is not really a very good idea, especially when you have to maintain multiple versions of your application.

 You can get some guidance for different branching strategies from
https://www.visualstudio.com/en-us/articles/git-branching-guidan
ce.

Using feature branches

The philosophy behind feature branches is that the first thing you have to do each time you begin working on a new VSTS feature (or even VSTS product backlog item), is create a new, so-called feature branch.

You then work in this branch completely isolated until you are ready to push your tested and validated modifications to your master branch (or in more sophisticated environments, your development branch). Until it is pushed, it will not interfere with your other features, neither will it cause bugs or lower the overall quality.

If a project deadline approaches and you have not finished all of the planned features in time, you do not need to stress anymore! Why? Because you can integrate only the features that are ready for release. You will have a product with fewer features, but you can be confident that those are going to work as expected without any risks.

Let's look at how to create a feature branch using Visual Studio 2017 and Git:

1. Open Visual Studio 2017, go to the **Team Explorer** tab, and click on the **Branches** button:

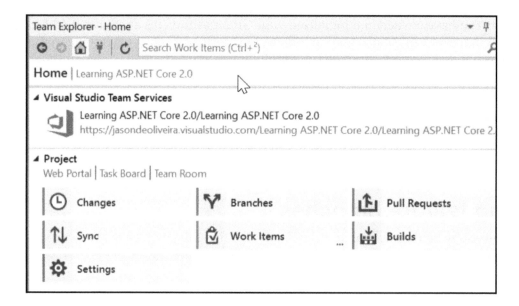

2. In **Team Explorer - Branches**, click on the **New Branch** link:

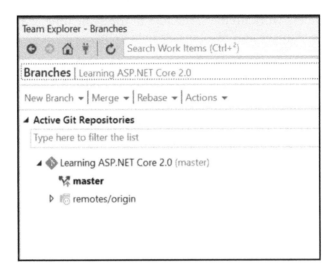

3. Enter a new feature branch name (use the FEA- prefix), and click on the **Create Branch** button:

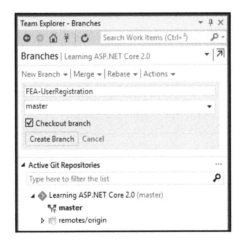

Merging changes and resolving conflicts

Sometimes, team members work on the same files at the same time, leading to conflicts. Let's see how to merge changes and resolve conflicts in this case:

1. Create a text file called `HelloWorld.txt` and add it to your local repository. Push the file to the server, and update the file both on the server and in your local repository.

2. If you try to push the `HelloWorld.txt` file that has been modified both locally and in the remote repository, you get an error message and the push fails:

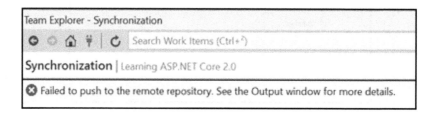

3. When looking in the output window, you get additional information:

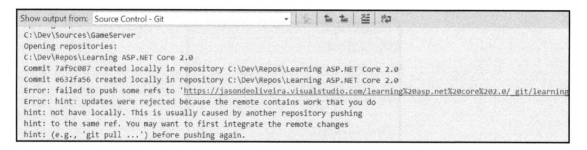

4. Click on the **Pull** link and you will get the remote changes, which will result in a conflict between your local copy and the remote one. Click either on the **Resolve the conflicts** or **Conflicts** link:

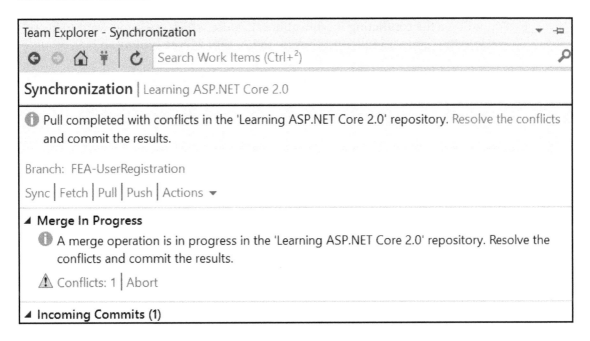

5. You will see a list of conflicting files. Click on the conflict you want to resolve and click on the **Merge** button:

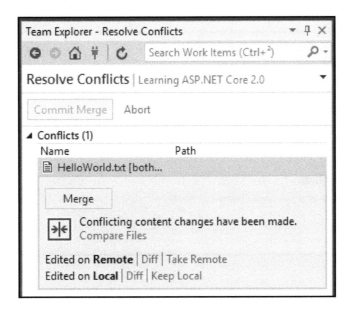

6. You will see the conflicting modifications. Choose which ones you want to keep (the left, the right, or both) and click on the **Accept Merge** button:

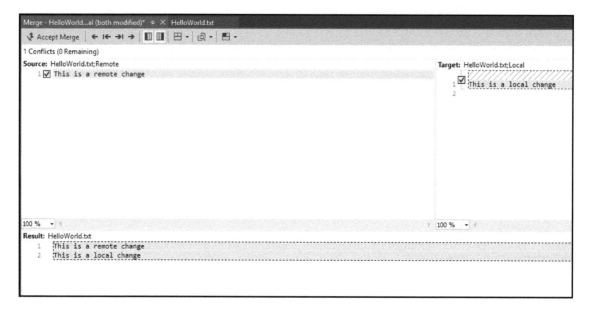

7. Back in the **Team Explorer**, click on the **Commit Merge** button:

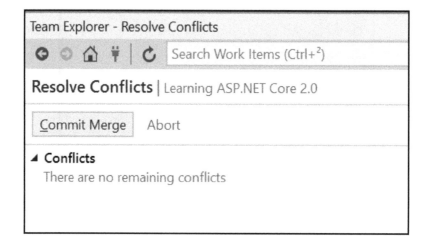

8. Enter a comment and click on the **Commit Staged** button to finalize and commit the merge locally:

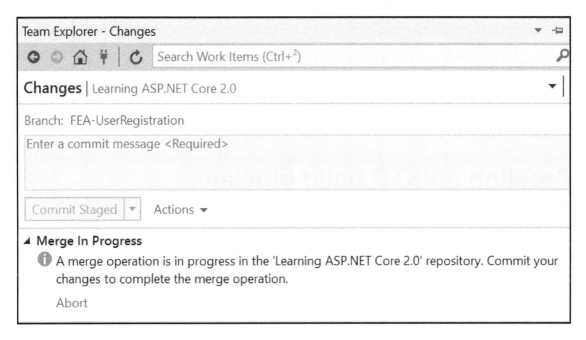

9. After the commit has been created locally, click on the **Sync** link and then on the **Push** link:

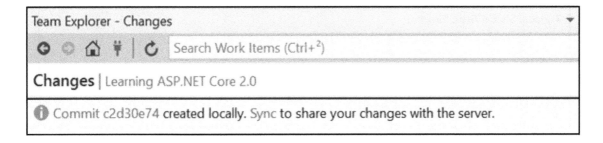

10. You should now see that the changes have been uploaded to the remote repository:

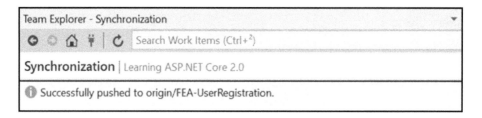

Creating a VSTS build pipeline

After having planned and organized your work and created your Git repository, you should now configure a VSTS build pipeline, which will allow you to do continuous integration of your application:

1. Open Visual Studio 2017 and go to the **Team Explorer** tab, then click on the **Builds** button:

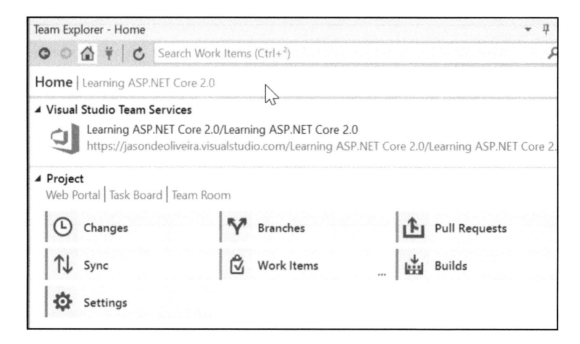

2. Next, click on the **New Build Definition** link:

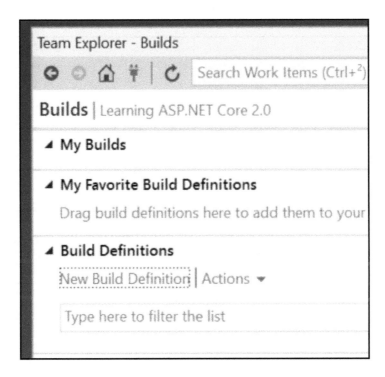

3. The VSTS website is opened and you are presented with a choice of build definition templates, select the **ASP.NET Core** template:

4. In the new build definition, enter a name and select your default agent queue. We recommend using **Hosted VS2017**:

5. For choosing a source repository, click on **Get sources**. For our example, we use the default values (**This project, Branch: master, Clean: false**):

6. To enable continuous integration, click on **Triggers** in the build definition menu, then click on the **Enable this trigger** button:

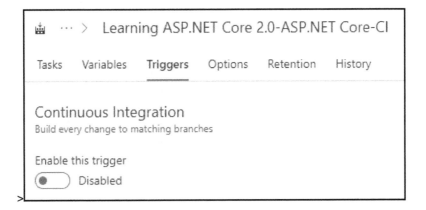

7. After verifying that the Git repository and master branch have been selected, correctly click on the **Save** or **Save & queue** button. The configuration has been finished and a build will automatically be triggered each time code is committed to the repository:

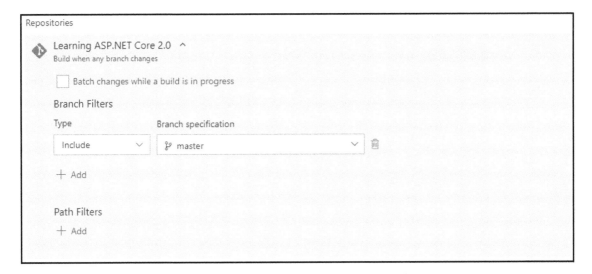

Creating a VSTS release pipeline

Your application gets integrated continuously and you have already seen some great benefits, such as detecting and fixing bugs and issues much faster. Let's not stop there; improving your development process even further is much easier than you think!

We will now see how to adopt the continuous deployment of your application by creating a VSTS release pipeline:

1. Open the VSTS website, click on **Build & Release** in the upper menu, click on **Releases** and then on the **New definition** button, and select the **Empty** definition template:

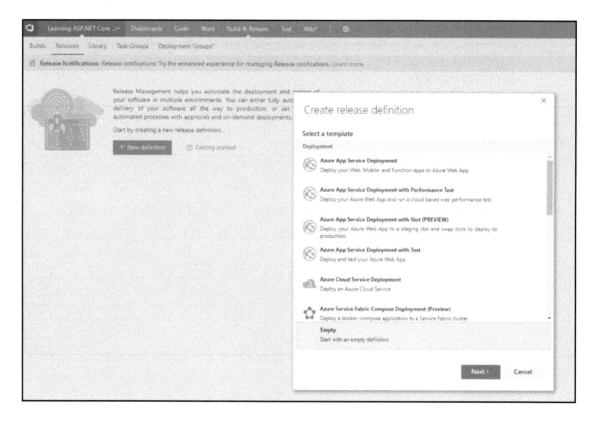

2. You can now select the **Project** and the **Source (Build definition)** and enable the continuous deployment, then click on the **Create** button:

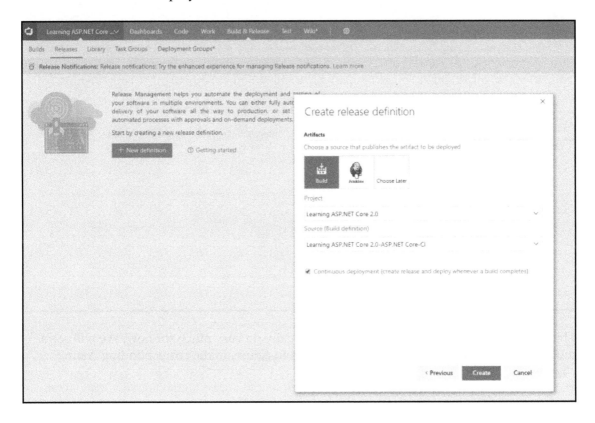

3. The release definition gets created and you can see it in the list:

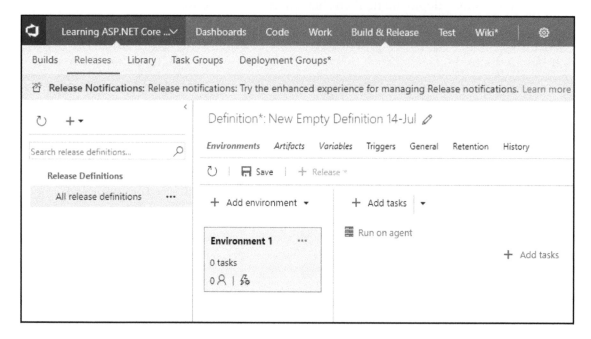

The shown sample release definition does not really do very much for now. We will see a much more advanced version later that deploys to Azure, in the corresponding Azure chapters.

Summary

In this chapter, you have learned about continuous integration, continuous deployment, and build and release pipelines, what the benefits are, and how to implement them using VSTS.

You have created a new VSTS subscription and initialized a new project. We then explored some of the basic concepts, such as work items and Git for source control. At the end, we illustrated how to configure a VSTS build pipeline, as well as a VSTS release pipeline, via a practical example.

In the next two chapters, we will explain the basic concepts of ASP.NET Core 2.0 including the Startup class, using middleware, routing, error handling, and many others.

4
Basic Concepts of ASP.NET Core 2.0 - Part 1

In the last three chapters, you have seen what ASP.NET Core 2.0 is about from a global point of view, as well as set up your development environment, including Visual Studio 2017 (or Visual Studio Code) and a continuous integration and continuous delivery VSTS pipeline with a Git repository.

This is all really interesting, but very theoretical. Now, it is time to do something practical, time to go right into the action, time to build something by yourself!

In this chapter, we are going to build an application to showcase the basic concepts of the ASP.NET Core 2.0 Framework. During the following chapters, we will constantly be improving this application, while using and illustrating the various features of ASP.NET Core 2.0 and the technologies surrounding it.

In this chapter, we will cover the following topics:

- The `Startup` and `Program` classes
- Creating pages and services
- Using Bower and layout pages
- Applying dependency injection
- Using the built-in middlewares
- Creating your own middlewares
- Working with static files
- Using routing, URL redirection, and URL rewriting
- Error handling and model validation

Building the Tic-Tac-Toe game

Let's do something fun! Let's build the *Tic-Tac-Toe* game, also known as noughts and crosses or Xs and Os. Players will choose who takes the Xs and who takes the Os. Then, they will be taking turns to mark spaces in a 3×3 grid, one mark per turn. The player who succeeds in placing three of his marks in a horizontal, vertical, or diagonal row wins the game.

Players must enter their emails and names for registration to create an account before being able to start a game. They will receive a game score after each match, which is going to be added to their total score.

A leaderboard provides information on player rankings and top scores.

For creating a game, a player must send an invitation to another player, then a specific waiting page is displayed for him until another player has responded. The other player, after reception of the invitation email, can then confirm the request and join the game. When the two players are online, the game starts.

As explained in the last chapter, we can use VSTS and its work items to organize and schedule the implementation of the *Tic-Tac-Toe* application. For that, we have to create epics, features, and product backlog items, and then do a sprint planning for prioritizing and deciding what has to be implemented first.

As you can see in the following screenshot, we have decided to work on five product backlog items in the first sprint and have added them to the sprint backlog:

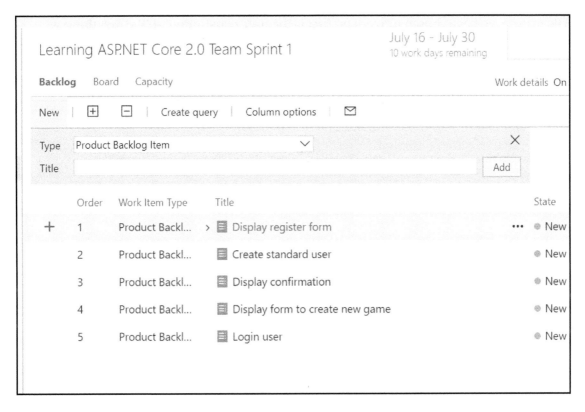

Do you remember what needs to be done next, before implementing any of the new features? You don't remember? Maybe features branches ring a bell?

In the last chapter, we showed the best practices for creating developments, which are isolated and easier to maintain and release. They consist of creating a feature branch in the Git repository for every new feature that you want to add to your application.

Thus, every developer can work on his specific features within his specific feature branch until he has decided that it is ready to be released.

At the end, all of the features ready for release are merged into a development (or release or master) branch. Then integration tests are done, and, if everything is working as expected, a new application version is delivered.

The feature we have chosen to work on first is the user registration, so the first thing we have to do is create a feature branch called **FEA-UserRegistration**. If you do not know how to do that, you can go to Chapter 3, *Creating a Continuous Integration Pipeline in VSTS*, and get a full step-by-step procedure with thorough explanations:

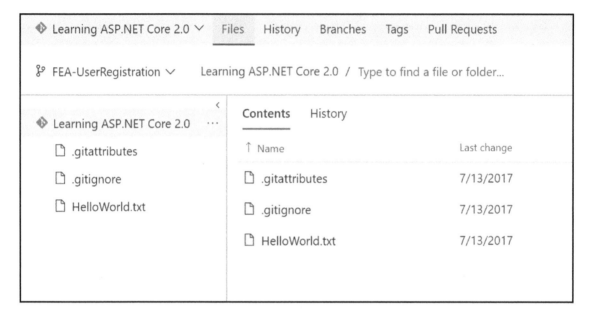

Conceiving and implementing your first Tic-Tac-Toe feature

Before we can implement the user registration feature, we have to understand it and decide how everything should work. We have to define the user stories and workflows. For that, we need to analyze the *Tic-Tac-Toe* game description mentioned previously in more detail.

As explained previously, a user can only create and join games if he has a user account. To create this account, he has to enter his first name, his last name, his email address, and a new password. The system then verifies if the entered email address has already been registered. A given email address can only be registered once. If the email address is new, the user account gets generated, if the email address is known, an error must be displayed.

Let's look at the user registration process and the different components that have to interact for implementing it:

1. There is a home page with a link for user registration, where a new user must click on **Register** for creating his player account. Clicking on the user registration link redirects the user to a dedicated **Registration Page**.

2. The **Registration Page** contains a **Registration Form**, where the user must enter his personal information and then confirm it.

3. A JavaScript client validates the form, submits and sends the data to a **Communication Middleware**, then waits for a result.

4. The **Communication Middleware** receives the request and routes it to a **Registration Service**.

5. The **Registration Service** receives the request, verifies data integrity, checks if the email has already been used for registration, and either registers the user or returns an error message.

6. The **Communication Middleware** receives the result and routes it to the waiting JavaScript client.

7. The JavaScript client redirects the user so that he can start playing games if the result is a success, and it displays an error message if the result is a failure.

The following sequence diagram shows the user registration process. It is easier and quicker to comprehend with a more visual representation:

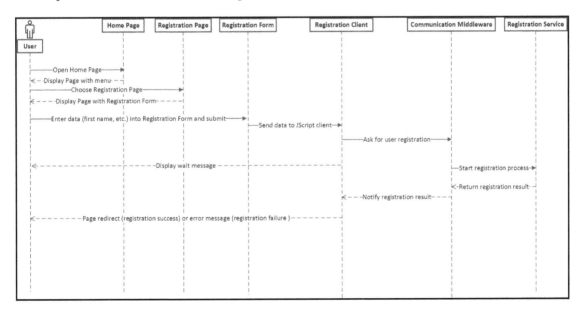

To get started, we need to create a new empty ASP.NET Core 2.0 Web Application, which will be used for adding various components and packages in this chapter and during the rest of the book. We will then add new concepts and functionalities progressively, which will allow you to really understand what is going on and how everything works:

1. Start Visual Studio 2017 and click on **File** | **New** | **Project**.
2. In the **.NET Core** section choose **ASP.NET Core Web Application**, enter the application name, the location of your repository and the solution name, then click on **OK**:

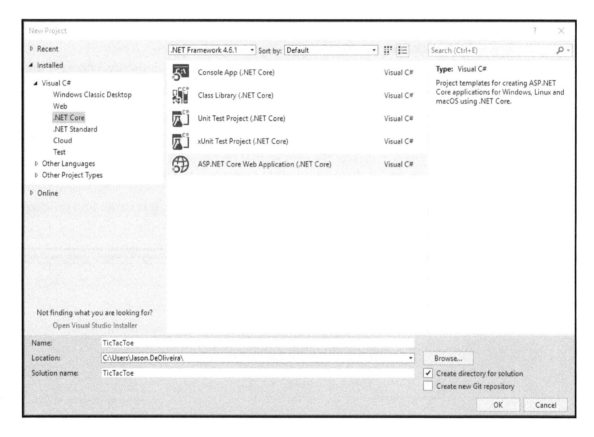

Note that if you have not created a Git repository for your application code yet, you can do it here by ticking the Create new Git repository checkbox.

3. Choose the **Empty** template:

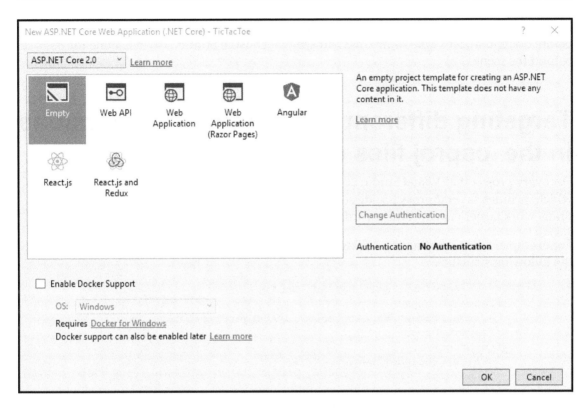

4. A new empty ASP.NET Core 2.0 Web Application project will be generated, containing only the `Program.cs` and `Startup.cs` files:

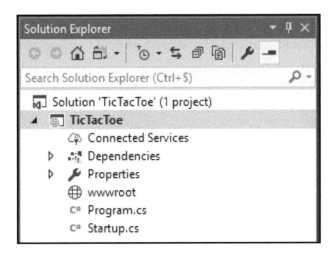

Great, we have created our project and are now ready to implement our first feature! But before doing that, let's take some time and see what Visual Studio 2017 has done for us behind the scenes.

Targeting different .NET Framework versions in the .csproj files of your projects

For every project that Visual Studio 2017 generates, it creates a corresponding `.csproj` file, which includes several project-wide settings such as the referenced assemblies, the .NET Framework target versions, the included files and folders, as well as multiple others.

For example, when opening the ASP.NET Core 2.0 project you created before, you can see the following structure:

```
<Project Sdk="Microsoft.NET.Sdk.Web">
  <PropertyGroup>
    <TargetFramework>netcoreapp2.0</TargetFramework>
  </PropertyGroup>
  <ItemGroup>
    <Folder Include="wwwroot\" />
  </ItemGroup>
  <ItemGroup>
    <PackageReference Include="Microsoft.AspNetCore.All"
     Version="2.0.0-preview2-final" />
  </ItemGroup>
</Project>
```

You can see the `TargetFramework` setting, which allows you to define what .NET Framework versions should be included and used for building and executing the source code.

In our example, it has been set to `netcoreapp2.0`, the specific value for using the .NET Core 2.0 Framework:

```
<TargetFramework>netcoreapp2.0</TargetFramework>
```

Note that you can refer to multiple .NET Framework versions within your library projects. In this case, you have to replace the `TargetFramework` element with the `TargetFrameworks` element.

For instance, if you want to cross-target .NET Core 2.0 and .NET 4.7, you have to use the following settings:

`<TargetFrameworks>netcoreapp2.0;net47</TargetFrameworks>`

When executing your application in **Debug** mode by hitting the *F5* key, you can see that multiple folders and files have been created in the application's `Debug` folder (`\bin\Debug`):

If you change the `.csproj` file and add other target frameworks, you will see that additional folders will get generated. The DLLs for each specific .NET Framework version are then put into the corresponding folders. The following example uses the `TargetFrameworks` settings for .NET Core and .NET 4.7:

Name	Date modified	Type	Size
net47	23/07/2017 21:19	File folder	
netcoreapp2.0	23/07/2017 21:16	File folder	

Using the Microsoft.AspNetCore.All metapackage

When looking in the **Solution Explorer** in the **Dependencies** | **NuGet** section, you can see something very interesting, specific to ASP.NET Core 2.0 projects: the Microsoft.AspNetCore.All metapackage:

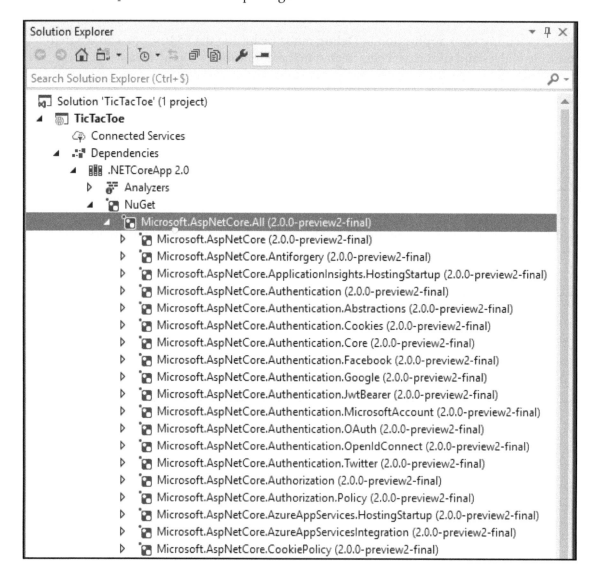

The `Microsoft.AspNetCore.All` project dependency was added automatically when you created your ASP.NET Core 2.0 Web Application. This is done by default for this type of project.

However, `Microsoft.AspNetCore.All` is not a standard NuGet package, since it does not contain any code or DLLs. Instead, it acts as a metapackage, referencing other packages it depends on. To be more specific, it includes all of the packages for ASP.NET Core and Entity Framework Core, together with their internal and external dependencies, and takes advantage of the .NET Core runtime store.

In the example, you can see that a wide variety of packages are retrieved, such as Application Insights, Authentication, Authorization, Azure App Services, and many others.

In older versions of .NET Core (version 1.0 and 1.1), you had to add those NuGet packages all by yourself. Now that Microsoft has created the concept of the ASP.NET Core metapackage, you can find everything in one place.

Furthermore, package trimming excludes binaries, which are not used, so that they are not published when deploying your applications.

Working with the Program class

The `Program` class is the main entry point for ASP.NET Core 2.0 applications. In fact, ASP.NET Core 2.0 applications are very similar to standard .NET Framework console applications in this regard. Both have a `Main` method that is executed when running the application. Even the basic signature of the `Main` method, which accepts an array of strings as arguments, is the same, as you can see in the following code. To no surprise, this is due to the fact that an ASP.NET Core application is, in reality, a console application hosting a web application:

```
using Microsoft.AspNetCore;
using Microsoft.AspNetCore.Hosting;

namespace TicTacToe
{
  public class Program
  {
    public static void Main(string[] args)
    {
        BuildWebHost(args).Run();
    }
```

```
public static IWebHost BuildWebHost(string[] args) =>
    WebHost.CreateDefaultBuilder(args)
        .UseStartup<Startup>()
        .Build();
    }
}
```

Normally, you do not need to touch the `Program` class in any way. By default, everything necessary to run your application is already there and preconfigured.

However, you might want to activate some of the more advanced functionalities.

For instance, you could enable the capture of errors during server startup and display an error page. In this case, you just have to use the following instruction:

```
WebHost.CaptureStartupErrors(true);
```

By default, this setting is not enabled, which means that in case of errors, the host will just exit. This might not be the desired behavior and we recommend changing this parameter accordingly.

Two other useful parameters working together are `PreferHostingUrls` and `UseUrls`. You can indicate whether the host should listen on the standard URLs defined by `Microsoft.AspNetCore.Hosting.Server.IServer`or-specific URLs you have provided. The URLs can have different formats depending on your needs, such as:

- IPV4 address with host and port (for example, `https://192.168.57.12:5000`)
- IPV6 address with port (for example, `https://[0:0:0:0:0:ffff:4137:270a]:5500`)
- Hostname (for example, `https://mycomputer:90`)
- Localhost (for example, `https://localhost:443`)
- Unix socket (for example, `http://unix:/run/dan-live.sock`)

Here is an example of how you could set those parameters:

```
WebHost.PreferHostingUrls(true);
WebHost.UseUrls("http://localhost:5000");
```

Finally, you can enable the integration of your applications with Application Insights, an extensible application performance management service that allows monitoring your applications during runtime and detecting performance anomalies, as well as diagnosing issues and understanding what users do, by setting the following parameter:

```
WebHost.UseApplicationInsights();
```

Here is an example of a `Program` class, which includes all of the concepts shown previously:

```
public class Program
{
  public static void Main(string[] args)
  {
    BuildWebHost(args).Run();
  }

  public static IWebHost BuildWebHost(string[] args) =>
    WebHost.CreateDefaultBuilder(args)
        .CaptureStartupErrors(true)
        .UseStartup<Startup>()
        .PreferHostingUrls(true)
        .UseUrls("http://localhost:5000")
        .UseApplicationInsights()
        .Build();
}
```

Working with the Startup class

Another autogenerated element, which exists in all types of ASP.NET Core 2.0 projects, is the `Startup` class. As you have seen previously, the `Program` class mainly handles everything around the hosting environment. The `Startup` class is all about the preloading and configuration of your services and middlewares. Those two classes are the foundations of all ASP.NET Core 2.0 applications.

Let's look at the basic structure of the `Startup` class to get a better understanding of what is provided and how to make best use of its functionalities:

```
using Microsoft.AspNetCore.Builder;
using Microsoft.AspNetCore.Hosting;
using Microsoft.AspNetCore.Http;
using Microsoft.Extensions.DependencyInjection;

namespace TicTacToe
{
  public class Startup
  {
    public void ConfigureServices(IServiceCollection services)
    {
    }
```

```
public void Configure(IApplicationBuilder app,
 IHostingEnvironment env)
{
  if (env.IsDevelopment())
  {
    app.UseDeveloperExceptionPage();
  }

  app.Run(async (context) =>
  {
    await context.Response.WriteAsync("Hello World!");
  });
}
}
}
```

There are two methods which should require your attention, since you will work with them quite often:

- The `ConfigureServices` method, called by the runtime and used to add services to the container
- The `Configure` method used to configure the HTTP pipeline

We said at the beginning of the chapter that we wanted more practical work, so let's get back to our *Tic-Tac-Toe* game and see how to use the `Startup` class in a real example!

We are going to use MVC for implementing the application, but since you have used the empty **ASP.NET Core 2.0 Web Application** template, nothing has been added by Visual Studio 2017 during project generation. You have to add everything by yourself; what a wonderful opportunity for a better understanding of how everything works!

The first thing to do is to add MVC to the services configuration. You do that by using the `ConfigureServices` method and just adding the MVC middleware:

```
public void ConfigureServices(IServiceCollection services)
{
  services.AddMvc();
}
```

You might say that this was too easy, so what's the catch? There is no catch! Everything in ASP.NET Core 2.0 was developed around simplicity, clarity, and developer productivity.

You can see this again when configuring your MVC middleware and setting the routing path (we will explain routing in more detail later):

```
app.UseMvc(routes =>
```

```
  {
    routes.MapRoute(
      name: "default",
      template: "{controller=Home}/{action=Index}/{id?}");
  });
```

Again, very clear and short instructions that make our lives as developers easier and more productive. It is a really good time to be a developer!

In the next step, you need to enable the usage of static content within your ASP.NET Core 2.0 application for being able to use HTML, CSS, JavaScript, and images.

Do you know how to do that? Yes, you are right, you need to add another middleware. You do that just like before by calling the corresponding app method:

```
app.UseStaticFiles();
```

As a developer, you need to be able to analyze and understand HTML, CSS, and JavaScript behavior and problems quickly. For that, ASP.NET Core 2.0 includes a very handy feature called **Browser Link**. When enabled, it establishes a dedicated communication channel between Visual Studio 2017 for improved developer productivity.

Enabling Browser Link is really easy:

```
app.UseBrowserLink();
```

Following is an example of a `Startup.cs` class you could use for the *Tic-Tac-Toe* game after having configured the various service settings seen previously:

```
public class Startup
{
  public void ConfigureServices(IServiceCollection services)
  {
    services.AddMvc();
  }

  public void Configure(IApplicationBuilder app,
   IHostingEnvironment env)
  {
    if (env.IsDevelopment())
    {
      app.UseDeveloperExceptionPage();
      app.UseBrowserLink();
    }
    else
    {
      app.UseExceptionHandler("/Home/Error");
```

```
    }

    app.UseStaticFiles();

    app.UseMvc(routes =>
    {
      routes.MapRoute(
        name: "default",
          template: "{controller=Home}/{action=Index}/{id?}");
    });
  }
}
```

Preparing the basic project structure

You surely want to see something running and to build the *Tic-Tac-Toe* game. Now that we have defined how everything should work from a functional point of view, we need to start by creating the basic project structure for the application.

For ASP.NET Core 2.0 web applications, it is best practice to have the following project structure for your projects:

- A Controllers folder, containing all of the controllers of your application.
- A Services folder, containing all the services of your application (for example, external communication services).
- A Views folder, containing all of the views of your application. This folder should contain a single Shared subfolder as well as one folder per controller.
- A _ViewImports.cshtml file, to define some namespaces to be available in all views.
- A _ViewStart.cshtml file, to define some code to be executed at the start of each view rendering (for example, set the layout page for all views).
- A _Layout.cshtml file, to define a common layout for all of your views.

Let's create the project structure:

1. Start Visual Studio 2017, open the *Tic-Tac-Toe* ASP.NET Core 2.0 project you have created, create three new folders called `Controllers`, `Services`, and `Views`, and create a subfolder called `Shared` in the `Views` folder:

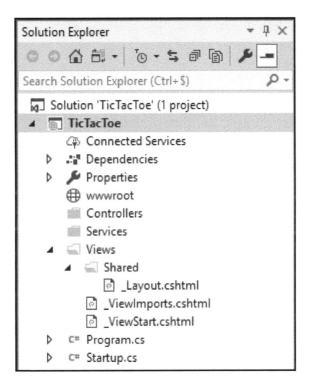

2. Create a new view page called `_ViewImports.cshtml` in the `Views` folder:

```
@using TicTacToe
@addTagHelper*, Microsoft.AspNetCore.Mvc.TagHelpers
```

3. Create a new view page called `_ViewStart.cshtml` in the `Views` folder:

```
@{ Layout = "~/Views/Shared/_Layout.cshtml"; }
```

4. Right-click on the `Views/Shared` folder, select **Add | New Item**, enter `Layout` in the search box, select **MVC View Layout Page**, and click on **Add**:

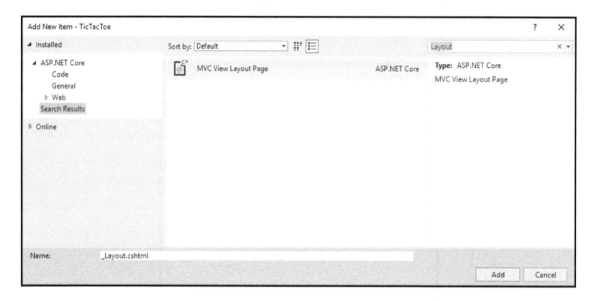

 Note that the layout page concept will be detailed a little bit later in this chapter, but don't worry too much, it is not a very complicated concept.

Creating the Tic-Tac-Toe home page

Since the basic project structure is now in place, we need to implement the different components that need to work together to provide the *Tic-Tac-Toe* game web application:

1. Update the `Program.cs` and `Startup.cs` files, as explained previously.
2. Add a new controller, right-click within the **Solution Explorer** on the `Controllers` folder, then select **Add** | **Controller**:

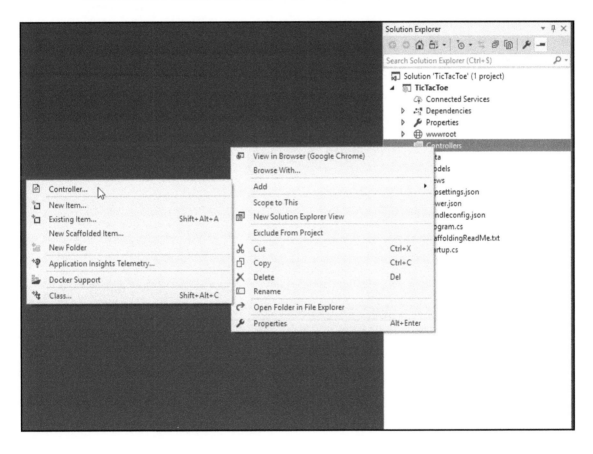

3. In the **Add Scaffold** pop-up window, choose **MVC Controller - Empty** and name your new controller `HomeController`:

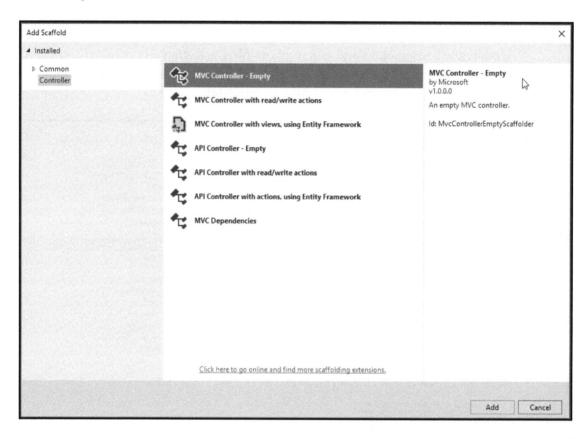

4. Your MVC home controller gets autogenerated, containing a single method. You now need to add a corresponding view by right-clicking on the `Index` method name and selecting **Add View** from the menu:

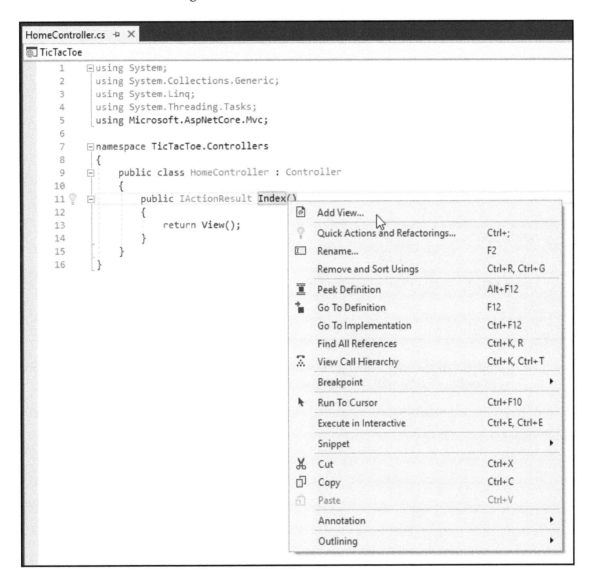

5. The **Add View** window helps to define what needs to be generated. Leave the default empty template and enable the usage of the layout page we are going to modify in the next section of this chapter:

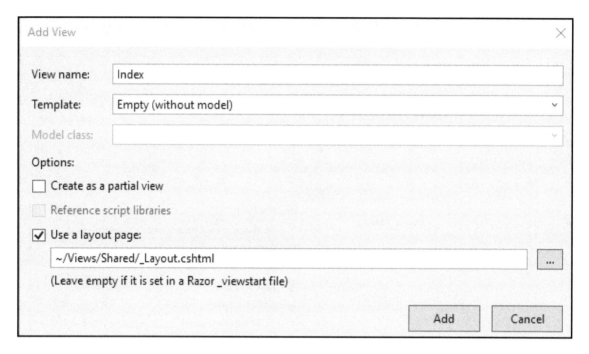

6. Congratulations, your view gets autogenerated and you can test your application by pressing *F5*. We will finalize it later in this chapter:

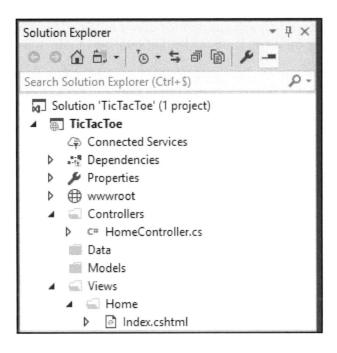

Giving your web pages a more modern look by using Bower and layout pages

In the last section, you saw how to create a basic web page. Knowing how to do that technically is one thing, but creating web applications that succeed is not only about the technical implementation, it is also about how to make your application visually appealing and user-friendly. While this book is not about web design and user experiences, we want to give you some quick and easy means for building better web applications in this regard.

For that, we advise using Bower (`https://bower.io`), the self-proclaimed *Package Manager of the Web*, in conjunction with ASP.NET Core layout pages.

Bower has had some remarkable success in the web development community in the last few years. It helps to install client-side packages with static content such as HTML, CSS, JavaScript, fonts, and images, including their dependencies.

There is some great integration and support for Bower in Visual Studio 2017; you just have to configure it correctly for using it efficiently. Let's see how to do that:

1. Right-click on the Tic-Tac-Toe project, select **Add | New Item**, enter Bower in the search box, select **Bower Configuration File**, and click on **Add**:

2. Adding the **Bower Configuration File** should have added a bower.json file. Update this file with the following content:

```json
{
    "name": "asp.net",
    "private": true,
    "dependencies": {
        "bootstrap": "3.3.6",
        "jquery": "2.2.0",
        "jquery-validation": "1.14.0",
        "jquery-validation-unobtrusive": "3.2.6"
    }
}
```

3. Adding the **Bower Configuration File** should have added a `.bowerrc` file. Update this file and define the directory where the assets should be placed:

```
{
    "directory": "wwwroot/lib"
}
```

4. Right-click on the `bower.json` file and click on **Restore Packages**:

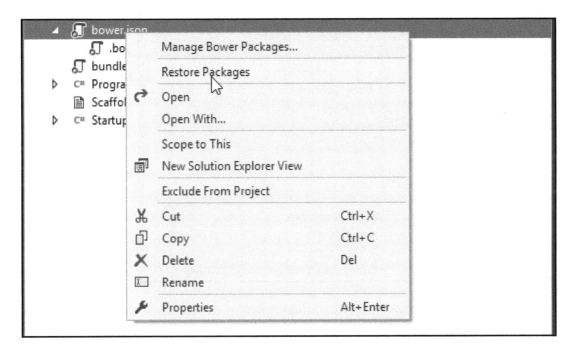

5. The client-side packages (bootstrap, jquery, and more) are downloaded into the folder you have defined (wwwroot/lib). The static content can now be used within your application:

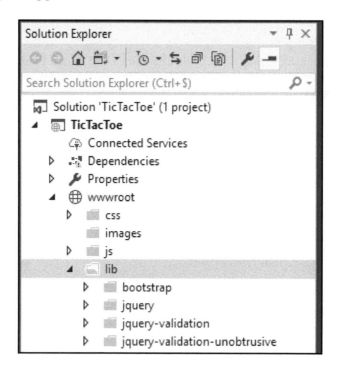

6. In the wwwroot folder, create a folder called css. Add a new style sheet called site.css within this folder:

```css
body {
  padding-top: 50px;
  padding-bottom: 20px;
}

/* Set padding to keep content from hitting the edges */
.body-content {
  padding-left: 15px;
  padding-right: 15px;
}

/* Set width on the form input elements since they're 100% wide
   by default */
input,
select,
```

```css
textarea {
  max-width: 280px;
}

/* styles for validation helpers */
.field-validation-error {
  color: #b94a48;
}

.field-validation-valid {
  display: none;
}

input.input-validation-error {
  border: 1px solid #b94a48;
}

input[type="checkbox"].input-validation-error {
  border: 0 none;
}

.validation-summary-errors {
  color: #b94a48;
}

.validation-summary-valid {
  display: none;
}
```

A successful web application should have a common layout with a consistent user experience when navigating from page to page. This is key for user adoption and user satisfaction. ASP.NET Core layout pages are the right solution for that.

They can be used for defining templates for views in your web applications. All of your views can either use the same template, or different templates can be used depending on your specific needs.

We are going to use the updated layout page, as shown here, for our sample application:

```html
<!DOCTYPE html>
<html>
<head>
  <meta charset="utf-8" />
  <meta name="viewport" content="width=device-width,
   initial-scale=1.0" />
  <title>@ViewData["Title"] - TicTacToe</title>
```

```
<environment include="Development">
  <link rel="stylesheet"
  href="~/lib/bootstrap/dist/css/bootstrap.css" />
  <link rel="stylesheet" href="~/css/site.css" />
</environment>
<environment exclude="Development">
  <link rel="stylesheet"
  href="https://ajax.aspnetcdn.com/ajax/bootstrap
  /3.3.7/css/bootstrap.min.css"
  asp-fallback-href="~/lib/bootstrap/dist/css/bootstrap.min.css"
  asp-fallback-test-class="sr-only"
  asp-fallback-test-property="position" asp-fallback-test-
   value="absolute" />
  <link rel="stylesheet" href="~/css/site.min.css"
   asp-append-version="true" />
</environment>
</head>
<body>
  <nav class="navbar navbar-inverse navbar-fixed-top">
    <div class="container">
    <div class="navbar-header">
     <button type="button" class="navbar-toggle"
       data-toggle="collapse" data-target=".navbar-collapse">
      <span class="sr-only">Toggle navigation</span>
      <span class="icon-bar"></span>
      <span class="icon-bar"></span>
      <span class="icon-bar"></span>
     </button>
     <a asp-area="" asp-controller="Home" asp-action="Index"
      class="navbar-brand">Tic-Tac-Toe</a>
    </div>
    <div class="navbar-collapse collapse">
     <ul class="nav navbar-nav">
       <li><a asp-area="" asp-controller="Home"
         asp-action="Index">Home</a></li>
       <li><a asp-area="" asp-controller="Home"
         asp-action="About">About</a></li>
       <li><a asp-area="" asp-controller="Home"
         asp-action="Contact">Contact</a></li>
     </ul>
    </div>
    </div>
  </nav>
  <div class="container body-content">
    @RenderBody()
    <hr />
    <footer>
      <p>&copy; 2017 - TicTacToe</p>
```

```
      </footer>
   </div>

   <environment include="Development">
    <script src="~/lib/jquery/dist/jquery.js"></script>
    <script src="~/lib/bootstrap/dist/js/bootstrap.js"></script>
    <script src="~/js/site.js" asp-append-version="true"></script>
   </environment>
   <environment exclude="Development">
    <script src="https://ajax.aspnetcdn.com/ajax/jquery/
     jquery-2.2.0.min.js"
     asp-fallback-src="~/lib/jquery/dist/jquery.min.js"
     asp-fallback-test="window.jQuery"
      crossorigin="anonymous"
      integrity="sha384-K+ctZQ+LL8q6tP7I94W+qzQsfRV2a+
      AfHIi9k8z8l9ggpc8X+Ytst4yBo/hH+8Fk">
    </script>
    <script src="https://ajax.aspnetcdn.com/ajax/bootstrap/
     3.3.7/bootstrap.min.js"
     asp-fallback-src="~/lib/bootstrap/dist/js/bootstrap.min.js"
     asp-fallback-test="window.jQuery&&window.jQuery
      .fn&&window.jQuery.fn.modal"
     crossorigin="anonymous"
     integrity="sha384-Tc5IQib027qvyjSMfHjOMaLkfuWVxZxUPnCJA
      712mCWNIpG9mGCD8wGNIcPD7Txa">
    </script>
    <script src="~/js/site.min.js" asp-append-version="true">
    </script>
   </environment>

   @RenderSection("Scripts", required: false)
  </body>
  </html>
```

Before creating the user registration page in the next section, let's update the home page created previously to show some basic information on the *Tic-Tac-Toe* game, while using the layout page shown previously:

```
@{
  ViewData["Title"] = "Home Page";
  Layout = "~/Views/Shared/_Layout.cshtml";
}
<div class="row">
<div class="col-lg-12">
  <h2>Tic-Tac-Toe</h2>
  <div class="alert alert-info">
    <p>Tic-Tac-Toe is a two-player turn-based game.</p>
```

```
    <p>Two players will choose who takes the Xs and who
        takes the Os. They will then be taking turns and
        mark spaces in a 3×3 grid by putting their marks,
        one mark per turn.</p>
    <p>A player who succeeds in placing three of his
        marks in a horizontal, vertical, or diagonal row
        wins the game.</p>
</div>
<p>
    <h3>Register by clicking <a asp-controller="UserRegistration"
        asp-view="Index">here</a></h3>
</p>
</div>
</div>
```

When starting the application, you will see the new home page design:

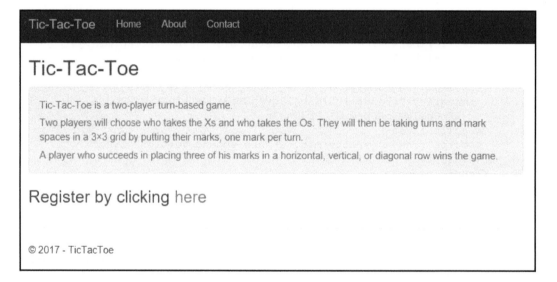

Creating the Tic-Tac-Toe user registration page

You will now integrate the second component, the user registration page with its form, which will allow new users to register to play the *Tic-Tac-Toe* game.

1. Add a new folder called Models to the project.
2. Add a new model by right-clicking on the Models folder in your project and selecting **Add** | **Class**, and name it UserModel:

```
public class UserModel
{
    public Guid Id { get; set; }
    public string FirstName { get; set; }
    public string LastName { get; set; }
    public string Email { get; set; }
    public string Password { get; set; }
    public bool IsEmailConfirmed { get; set; }
    public System.DateTime? EmailConfirmationDate { get; set; }
    public int Score { get; set; }
}
```

3. Add a new controller and call it `UserRegistrationController` (if you do not know how to do this, then refer to the *Creating the Tic-Tac-Toe home page* section).
4. Right-click on the method called `Index` and choose **Add View**. This time, select the **Create** template, choose as **Model** the `UserModel` as mentioned in the previous point, and enable the usage of the layout page:

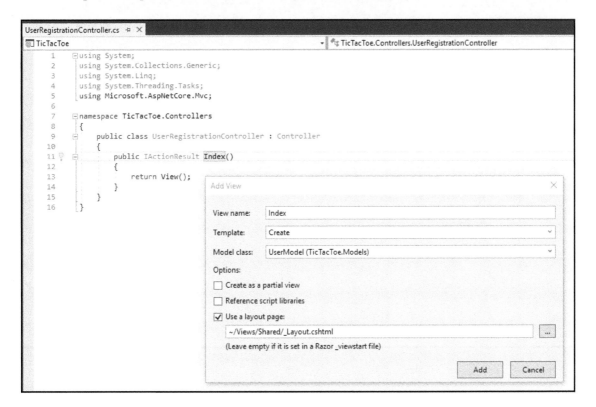

Note that you can leave the layout page empty if you want to use the `_ViewStart.cshtml` file in the `Shared` folder to define a unified common layout for all your views.

The `_ViewStart.cshtml` file is used to share settings between views, while the `_ViewImports` file is used to share `using` namespaces and inject dependency injection instances. Visual Studio 2017 includes two templates for these files.

5. Remove the autogenerated `Id`, `IsEmailConfirmed`, `EmailConfirmationDate`, and `Score` elements from the view; we do not need them for the user registration form.
6. The view is now ready; display it by pressing on *F5* and clicking on the registration link on the home page:

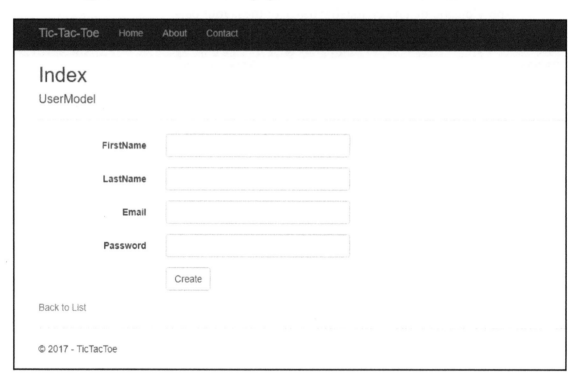

Using dependency injection for encouraging loose coupling within your applications

One of the biggest problems when developing applications is inter-component dependencies. These dependencies make it hard to maintain and evolve your components individually because modifications might badly impact other dependent components. But be assured, there are mechanisms that allow those dependencies to be broken up, one of them being **dependency injection** (**DI**).

Dependency injection allows components to work together, while providing loose coupling. A component only needs to know the contract implemented by another component to work with it. With a DI container, components are not directly instantiated nor are static references used for finding an instance of another component. Instead, it is the responsibility ⬚⬚⬚⬚⬚⬚⬚⬚⬚⬚ retrieve the correct instance during runtime.

When a comp⬚⬚⬚⬚⬚⬚⬚ DI in mind, it is very evolutive by default and is not dependent or ⬚⬚⬚⬚⬚⬚s or behaviors. For example, an authentication service can use prov⬚⬚⬚⬚⬚ h that uses DI, and if new providers are added, existing ones will not⬚⬚⬚

ASP.NET C⬚⬚⬚⬚⬚ simple built-in DI container, which supports constructor injection. T⬚⬚⬚⬚⬚⬚ble for the container, you have to add it within the `Configure`⬚⬚⬚⬚⬚ he `Startup` class. Without knowing it, you have already done that b⬚⬚⬚

```
p⬚⬚⬚⬚⬚eServices(IServiceCollection services)
{
```

In fact, y⬚⬚⬚⬚⬚e thing for your own custom services, you have to declare them wi⬚⬚⬚⬚ is really easy to do when you know what you are doing!

Howev⬚⬚⬚⬚⬚ways of injecting your services and you need to choose which one bes⬚⬚⬚ ls:

⬚⬚⬚n: Creates an instance for each time the method is called (for ⬚⬚⬚ services):

```
⬚⬚⬚Transient<IExampleService, ExampleService>();
```

- **Scoped injection**: Creates an instance once per request pipeline (for example, stateful services):

```
services.AddScoped<IExampleService, ExampleService>();
```

- **Singleton injection**: Creates one single instance for the whole application:

```
services.AddSingleton<IExampleService, ExampleService>();
```

Note that you should add the instances for your services by yourself if you do not want the container to automatically dispose of them. The container will call the `Dispose` method of each service instance it creates by itself.

Here is an example of how to instantiate your services by yourself:
```
services.AddSingleton(new ExampleService());
```

Now that you understand how to use DI, let's apply your knowledge and create the next component for our sample application.

Creating the Tic-Tac-Toe user service

We have created a home page as well as a user registration page. Users can click on the register link and fill out a registration form, but the form data is not yet processed in any way. We are going to add a user service that will have the responsibility of processing user-related tasks, such as user registration requests. Furthermore, you are going to apply some of the ASP.NET Core 2.0 DI mechanisms seen previously:

1. Add a new class called `UserService.cs` to the `Services` folder.
2. Add a new method for user registration, with the model created in the last section as a parameter:

```
public class UserService
{
  public Task<bool>RegisterUser(UserModel userModel)
  {
    return Task.FromResult(true);
  }
}
```

3. Right-click on the class and choose **Quick Actions and Refactorings**, then click on **Extract Interface**:

4. Leave all of the default values in the pop-up window and click on **OK**:

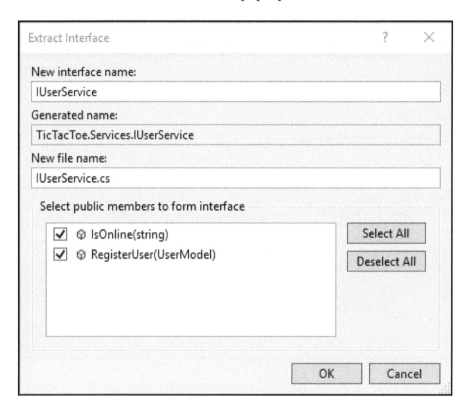

5. Visual Studio 2017 will generate a new file called `IUserService.cs` containing the extracted interface definition, as shown here:

```
public interface IUserService
{
   Task<bool>RegisterUser(UserModeluserModel);
}
```

6. Update the `UserRegistrationController` created previously and apply the constructor injection mechanism:

```
public class UserRegistrationController : Controller
{
   private IUserService _userService;
   public UserRegistrationController(IUserService userService)
   {
     _userService = userService;
```

```
    }
    public IActionResult Index()
    {
      return View();
    }
  }
```

7. Add some simple code for processing the user registration within the UserRegistrationController (we are adding validation later in the chapter):

```
[HttpPost]
public async Task<IActionResult> Index(UserModel userModel)
{
  await _userService.RegisterUser(userModel);
  return Content($"User {userModel.FirstName}
   {userModel.LastName} has been registered sucessfully");
}
```

8. Go to the Startup class and declare the UserService within the ConfigureServices method to make it available to the application:

```
public void ConfigureServices(IServiceCollection services)
{
  services.AddMvc();
  services.AddSingleton<IUserService, UserService>();
}
```

9. Test your application by pressing *F5*, filling out the registration page, and then clicking on **OK**. You should get the following output:

Very good, you have already created multiple components of the *Tic-Tac-Toe* application, very good progress! Please stay sharp, since the next section is very important, as it explains middlewares in detail.

Working with middlewares

As you have seen before, the `Startup` class is responsible for adding and configuring middlewares in your ASP.NET Core 2.0 applications. But what is middleware? When and how do you use it and how do you create your own middlewares? Those are all the questions we are going to discuss now.

Essentially, multiple middlewares compose the functionalities of your ASP.NET Core 2.0 applications. Even the most basic functionalities such as serving up static content are performed by them, as you might have noticed by now.

Middlewares are part of the ASP.NET Core 2.0 request pipeline for handling requests and responses. When they are chained together, they can pass incoming requests from one to another and perform actions before and after the next middleware is called within the pipeline:

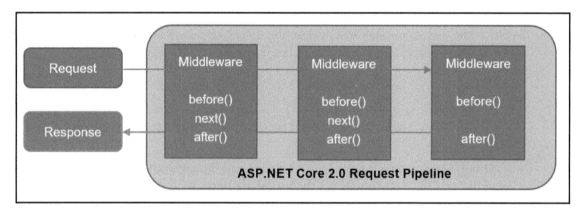

Using middlewares allows your applications to be more flexible and evolutive, since you can add and remove middlewares easily in the `Configure` method of the `Startup` class.

Furthermore, the order in which you call the middlewares in the `Configure` method is the order in which they are going to get invoked. It is advised to call middlewares in the following order to assure better performance, functionality, and security:

1. Exception handling middlewares.
2. Static files middlewares.
3. Authentication middlewares.
4. MVC middlewares.

If you do not call them in this order, you might get some unexpected behavior and even errors, since middleware actions might be applied too late or too early within the request pipeline.

For example, if you do not call the **Exception Handling Middleware** first, you might not catch all of the exceptions that occur before its invocation. Another example is when you call the **Response Compression Middleware** after the **Static Files Middleware**. In this case, your static files will not be compressed, which might not be the desired behavior. So, take care of the ordering of your middleware calls; it can make a huge difference.

The following are some of the built-in middlewares you can use in your applications (the list is not exhaustive; there are many more):

Authentication	OAuth 2 and OpenID authentication, based on the newest version of IdentityModel
CORS	Cross-origin resource sharing protection, based on HTTP headers
Response caching	HTTP response caching
Response compression	HTTP responses gzip compression
Routing	HTTP request routing framework
Session	Basic local and distributed session object management
Static files	HTML, CSS, JavaScript, and image support including directory browsing
URL rewriting	URL SEO optimization and rewriting

The built-in middlewares will be sufficient for the most basic requirements and standard use cases, but you will surely need to create your own middlewares. There are two ways of doing that: creating them inline in the Startup class or creating them within a self-contained class.

Let's look at how to define inline middlewares first; here are the methods available:

- Run
- Map
- MapWhen
- Use

The Run method is used to add middleware and immediately return a response, thus short-circuiting the request pipeline. It does not call any of the following middlewares and ends the request pipeline. It is therefore advised to place it at the end of your middleware calls (see middleware ordering, discussed previously).

The Map method allows for executing a certain branch and adding the corresponding middleware if the request path starts with a specific path, which means you can effectively branch the request pipeline.

The MapWhen method provides basically the same concept of branching the request pipeline and adding a specific middleware, but with control over the branching conditions, since it is based on the result of a Func<HttpContext, bool> predicate.

The Use method adds middleware and allows either calling the next middleware in line or short-circuiting the request pipeline. However, if you want to pass on the request after executing a specific action, you have to call the next middleware manually by using next.Invoke with the current context as a parameter.

Here are some examples of how to use these extension methods:

```
private static void ApiPipeline(IApplicationBuilder app)
{
  app.Run(async context =>
  {
    await context.Response.WriteAsync("Branched to Api Pipeline.");
  });
}

private static void WebPipeline(IApplicationBuilder app)
{
  app.MapWhen(context =>
  {
    return context.Request.Query.ContainsKey("usr");
  }, UserPipeline);

  app.Run(async context =>
  {
```

```
    await context.Response.WriteAsync("Branched to Web Pipeline.");
  });
}

private static void UserPipeline(IApplicationBuilder app)
{
  app.Run(async context =>
  {
    await context.Response.WriteAsync("Branched to User Pipeline.");
  });
}

public void Configure(IApplicationBuilder app, IHostingEnvironmentenv)
{
  app.Map("/api", ApiPipeline);
  app.Map("/web", WebPipeline);

  app.Use(next =>async context =>
  {
    await context.Response.WriteAsync("Called Use.");
    await next.Invoke(context);
  });

  app.Run(async context =>
  {
    await context.Response.WriteAsync("Finished with Run.");
  });
}
```

As shown before, you can create your middlewares inline, but this is not recommended for more advanced scenarios. We advise you to put your middlewares in self-contained classes in this case, and the process for doing so is really easy. Middleware is just a class with a certain structure, which is exposed via an extension method.

Let's create a basic communication middleware for the *Tic-Tac-Toe* application:

1. Create a new folder called Middlewares within your project, then add a new class called CommunicationMiddleware.cs, using the following code:

```
public class CommunicationMiddleware
{
  private readonly RequestDelegate _next;
  private readonly IUserService _userService;

  public CommunicationMiddleware(RequestDelegate next,
    IUserService userService)
  {
```

```
    _next = next;
    _userService = userService;
  }

  public async Task Invoke(HttpContext context)
  {
    await _next.Invoke(context);
  }
}
```

2. Create a new folder called `Extensions` within your project, then add a new class called `CommunicationMiddlewareExtension.cs`, with the following code:

```
public static class CommunicationMiddlewareExtension
{
  public static IApplicationBuilder
   UseCommunicationMiddleware(this IApplicationBuilder app)
  {
    return app.UseMiddleware<CommunicationMiddleware>();
  }
}
```

3. Add a using directive for `TicTacToe.Extensions` in the `Startup` class, then add the **Communication Middleware** in the `Configure` method:

```
using TicTacToe.Extensions;
...
public void Configure(IApplicationBuilder app,
 IHostingEnvironment env)
{
  ...
  app.UseCommunicationMiddleware();
  app.UseMvc(routes =>
  {
    routes.MapRoute(
     name: "default",
     template: "{controller=Home}/{action=Index}/{id?}");
  });
}
```

4. Set some breakpoints in the **Communication Middleware** implementation and start the application by pressing *F5*. You will see that the breakpoints will be hit if everything is working correctly:

```
CommunicationMiddleware.cs  ⊕  ✕
⬛ TicTacToe                                          ▾  ⁂ TicTacToe.Middlewares.CommunicationMiddleware
      1      □using Microsoft.AspNetCore.Http;
      2       using System;
      3       using System.Collections.Generic;
      4       using System.Linq;
      5       using System.Threading;
      6       using System.Threading.Tasks;
      7       using TicTacToe.Services;
      8
      9      □namespace TicTacToe.Middlewares
     10       {
     11      □    public class CommunicationMiddleware
     12            {
     13                private readonly RequestDelegate _next;
     14                private readonly IUserService _userService;
     15
     16      □        public CommunicationMiddleware(RequestDelegate next, IUserService userService)
     17                {
     18                    _next = next;
     19                    _userService = userService;
     20                }
     21
     22      □        public async Task Invoke(HttpContext context)
     23                {
     24                    await _next.Invoke(context);
     25                    return;
     26                }
     27            }
     28       }
     29
```

This is just a basic example of how to create your own middleware; there are no functional changes visible between this section and the others. You are going to further implement the various functionalities for finalizing the *Tic-Tac-Toe* application in the next chapters, and the communication middleware seen in this chapter is going to do some real work shortly.

Working with static files

When working with web applications, most of the time, you have to work with HTML, CSS, JavaScript, and images, which are considered static files by ASP.NET Core 2.0.

Access to these files is not available by default, but you saw what needs to be done to allow static files to be used within your applications at the beginning of the chapter. In fact, you must add and configure the corresponding middleware in the `Startup` class to be able to serve static files:

```
app.UseStaticFiles();
```

Note that by default all static files served by this middleware are public and anyone can access them. If you need to protect some of your files, you need to either store them outside the wwwroot folder or you need to use the FileResult controller action, which supports the authorization middleware.

Furthermore, directory browsing is disabled by default for security reasons. You can, however, activate it easily if you need to allow users to see folders and files:

1. Add the DirectoryBrowsingMiddleware in the ConfigureService method of the Startup class right after calling the AddMvc() method:

   ```
   services.AddDirectoryBrowser();
   ```

2. From within the Configure method of the Startup class, call the UseDirectoryBrowser method (after calling the UseCommunicationMiddleware method) to activate directory browsing:

   ```
   app.UseDirectoryBrowser();
   ```

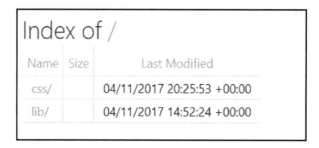

3. Remove the call to the UseDirectoryBrowser method from the Startup class; we do not need it for the sample application

Using routing, URL redirection, and URL rewriting

When building applications, routing is used for mapping incoming requests to route handlers (URL matching) and for generating URLs for the responses (URL generation).

The routing capabilities of ASP.NET Core 2.0 combine and unify the routing capabilities of MVC and Web API that have existed before. They have been rebuilt from the ground up to create a common routing framework with all of the various features in a single place, available to all types of ASP.NET Core 2.0 projects.

Let's look at how routing works internally to better understand how it can be useful in your applications and how to apply it to our *Tic-Tac-Toe* example.

For each received request, a matching route is retrieved, based on the request URL. Routes are processed in the order they appear within the route collection.

To be more specific, incoming requests are dispatched to the corresponding handlers. Most of the time this is done based on data in the URL, but you could also use any data in your requests for more advanced scenarios.

If you are using the MVC middleware, you can define and create your routes in the `Startup` class, as shown at the beginning of the chapter. This is the easiest way for getting started with URL matching and URL generation:

```
app.UseMvc(routes =>
{
  routes.MapRoute(
    name: "default",
    template: "{controller=Home}/{action=Index}/{id?}");
});
```

There is also a dedicated routing middleware that you can use for working with routing in your applications, which you have seen in the previous section on middleware. You just have to add it in the `Startup` class:

```
public void ConfigureServices(IServiceCollection services)
{
  services.AddRouting();
}
```

Here is an example of how to use it to call the UserRegistration service in the Startup class:

```
public void ConfigureServices(IServiceCollection services)
{
  services.AddMvc();
  services.AddSingleton<IUserService, UserService>();
  services.AddRouting();
}
public void Configure(IApplicationBuilder app, IHostingEnvironment env)
{
  if (env.IsDevelopment())
  {
    app.UseDeveloperExceptionPage();
    app.UseBrowserLink();
  }
  else
  {
    app.UseExceptionHandler("/Home/Error");
  }
  app.UseStaticFiles();
  var routeBuilder = new RouteBuilder(app);
  routeBuilder.MapGet("CreateUser", context =>
  {
    var firstName = context.Request.Query["firstName"];
    var lastName = context.Request.Query["lastName"];
    var email = context.Request.Query["email"];
    var password = context.Request.Query["password"];
    var userService =
      context.RequestServices.GetService<IUserService>();
    userService.RegisterUser(new UserModel { FirstName = firstName,
     LastName = lastName, Email = email, Password = password });
    return context.Response.WriteAsync($"User {firstName}
     {lastName} has been sucessfully created.");
  });
  var newUserRoutes = routeBuilder.Build();
  app.UseRouter(newUserRoutes);
  app.UseCommunicationMiddleware();
  app.UseMvc(routes =>
  {
    routes.MapRoute(
    name: "default",
    template: "{controller=Home}/{action=Index}/{id?}");
  });
  app.UseStatusCodePages("text/plain",
  "HTTP Error - Status Code: {0}");
}
```

If you call it with some query string parameters, you will get the following result:

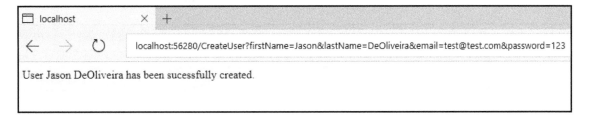

Another important middleware is the **URL Rewriting Middleware**. It provides URL redirection and URL rewriting functionalities. However, there is a crucial difference between both that you need to understand.

URL redirection requires a round-trip to the server and is done on the client side. The client first receives a moved permanently 301 or moved temporary 302 HTTP status code, which indicates the new redirection URL to be used. Then, the client calls the new URL to retrieve the requested resource, so it will be visible to the client.

URL rewriting, on the other hand, is purely server side. The server will internally retrieve the requested resource from a different resource address. The client will not know that the resource has been served from another URL, as it is not visible to the client.

Coming back to the *Tic-Tac-Toe* application, we can use URL rewriting to give a more meaningful URL for registering new users. Instead of using UserRegistration/Index, we can use a much shorter URL, such as /NewUser:

```
var options = new RewriteOptions()
  .AddRewrite("NewUser", "/UserRegistration/Index", false);
app.UseRewriter(options);
```

Here, the user thinks that the page has been served from /NewUser, while in reality it has been served from /UserRegistration/Index without the user noticing:

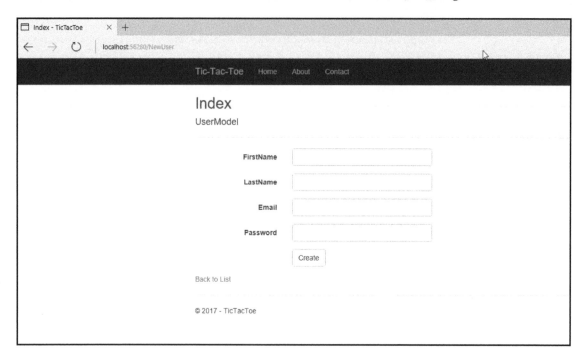

Adding error handling to your applications

When developing applications, the question is not if errors and bugs will occur, but when they will occur. Building applications is a very complex task and it is nearly impossible to think about all of the cases that might occur during runtime. And even if you think you have thought about everything, then the environment is not behaving as expected, for example, a service is not available or processing a request is taking much more time than expected.

You have two solutions to this problem, which need to be applied at the same time—unit tests and error handling. Unit tests will assure the correct behavior during development time from an application point of view, while error handling helps you to be prepared during runtime for environmental issues. We are going to look at how to add efficient error handling to your ASP.NET Core 2.0 applications in this section.

By default, if there is no error handling at all and if an exception occurs, your application will just stop, users will not be able to use it anymore, and in the worst case scenario, there will be an interruption of service.

The first thing to do during development time is to activate the default development exception page; it displays detailed information on exceptions that occur. You have already seen how to do this at the beginning of the chapter:

```
if (env.IsDevelopment())
{
  app.UseDeveloperExceptionPage();
}
```

On the default development exception page, you can deep dive into the raw exception details for analyzing the stack trace. You have multiple tabs that allow you to look at query string parameters, client-side cookies, and request headers.

Those are some powerful indicators for better understanding what has happened and why it has happened. They should help you pinpoint problems and resolve issues more quickly during development time.

The following is an example of what happens if an exception has occurred:

However, it is not recommended to use the default development exception page in production environments because it contains too much information about your system, which could be used to compromise your system.

For production environments, it is advised to configure a dedicated error page with static content. In the following example, you can see that the default development exception page is used during development time and that a specific error page is displayed if the application is configured to run in a non-development environment:

```
if (env.IsDevelopment())
{
  app.UseDeveloperExceptionPage();
  app.UseBrowserLink();
}
else
{
  app.UseExceptionHandler("/Home/Error");
}
```

By default, no information is displayed in case of HTTP error codes between 400 and 599. This includes, for example, 404 (not found) and 500 (internal server error). Users will just see a blank page, which is not very user-friendly.

You should activate the specific UseStatusCodePages middleware in the Startup class. It will help you to customize what needs to be displayed in this case. Meaningful information will help users to better understand what happens within your applications and will lead to better customer satisfaction.

The most basic configuration could be to just display a text message:

```
app.UseStatusCodePages("text/plain", "HTTP Error - Status Code: {0}");
```

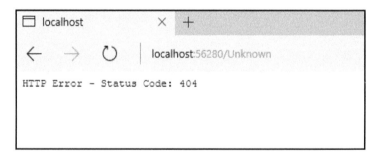

But, you can go even further. For instance, you can redirect to specific error pages for specific HTTP error status codes.

The following example shows how to send a moved temporary 302 (found) HTTP status code to the client and then redirect them to a specific error page:

```
app.UseStatusCodePagesWithRedirects("/error/{0}");
```

This example shows how to return the original HTTP status code to the client and then redirect them to a specific error page:

```
app.UseStatusCodePagesWithReExecute("/error/{0}");
```

You can disable HTTP status code pages for specific requests as shown here:

```
var statusCodePagesFeature =
  context.Features.Get<IStatusCodePagesFeature>();
if (statusCodePagesFeature != null)
{
  statusCodePagesFeature.Enabled = false;
}
```

Now that we have seen how to handle errors on the outside, let's look at how to handle them on the inside, within your applications.

If we go back to the `UserRegisterController` implementation, we can see that it has multiple flaws. What if the fields have not been filled in correctly or not at all? What if the model definition has not been respected? For now, we do not require anything and we do not validate anything.

Let's fix that and see how to build an application that is more robust:

1. Update the `UserModel`, use decorators to set some properties as required, and require a certain data type:

```
public class UserModel
{
  public Guid Id { get; set; }
  [Required()]
  public string FirstName { get; set; }
  [Required()]
  public string LastName { get; set; }
  [Required(), DataType(DataType.EmailAddress)]
  public string Email { get; set; }
```

```
            [Required(), DataType(DataType.Password)]
            public string Password { get; set; }
            public bool IsEmailConfirmed { get; set; }
            public System.DateTime? EmailConfirmationDate { get; set; }
            public int Score { get; set; }
        }
```

2. Update the specific `Index` method within the `UserRegistrationController`, then add the `ModelState` validation code:

```
[HttpPost]
public async Task<IActionResult> Index(UserModel userModel)
{
  if (ModelState.IsValid)
  {
    await _userService.RegisterUser(userModel);
    return Content($"User {userModel.FirstName}
     {userModel.LastName} has been registered sucessfully");
  }
  return View(userModel);
}
```

3. If you do not fill the required fields or you give an incorrect email address and click on **OK**, you will now get a corresponding error message:

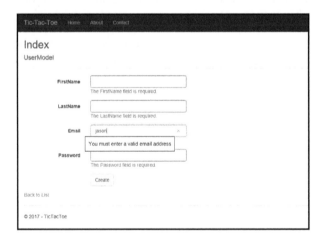

Summary

In this chapter, you have learned about some of the basic concepts of ASP.NET 2.0. There was much to understand and much to see, and we hope you have had some fun trying everything out by yourself. You have surely made some tremendous progress!

At the beginning, you created the *Tic-Tac-Toe* project; then, you started implementing its different components. We explored the `Program` and `Startup` classes, saw how to use Bower and layout pages, learned how to apply dependency injection, and used static files.

Furthermore, we introduced middleware and routing for more advanced scenarios. At the end, we illustrated how to add efficient error handling to your applications via a practical example.

In the next chapter, we will continue and introduce additional concepts such as WebSockets, globalization, localization, and configuration, as well as building once and running on multiple environments.

5
Basic Concepts of ASP.NET Core 2.0 - Part 2

The previous chapter gave you some insights into the various functionalities and features you have at your disposal when using ASP.NET Core 2.0 for building efficient and more maintainable web applications. We have explained some of the basic concepts and you have seen multiple examples of how to apply them to a real-world application called *Tic-Tac-Toe*.

You have progressed quite nicely so far, since you have assimilated how ASP.NET Core 2.0 applications are internally structured, how to configure them correctly, and how to extend them with custom behaviors, which is key for building your own applications in the future.

But let's not stop there! You are now going to discover how to best implement the missing components, evolve the existing ones even further, and add client-side code to allow you to have a fully-running end-to-end *Tic-Tac-Toe* application at the end of this chapter.

In this chapter, we will cover the following topics:

- Optimizing client-side development using JavaScript, bundling, and minification
- Working with WebSockets for real-time communication scenarios
- Taking advantage of session and user cache management
- Applying globalization and localization for multi-lingual user interfaces
- Configuring your applications and services
- Using logging and telemetry for monitoring and supervision purposes
- Implementing advanced dependency injection concepts
- Building once and running on multiple environments

Client-side development using JavaScript

In the previous chapter, you created a home page and a user registration page using the MVC pattern. You implemented a controller (`UserRegistrationController`) as well as a corresponding view for processing user registration requests. You then added a service (`UserService`) and middleware (`CommunicationMiddleware`), but we have just started, so they are not finished yet.

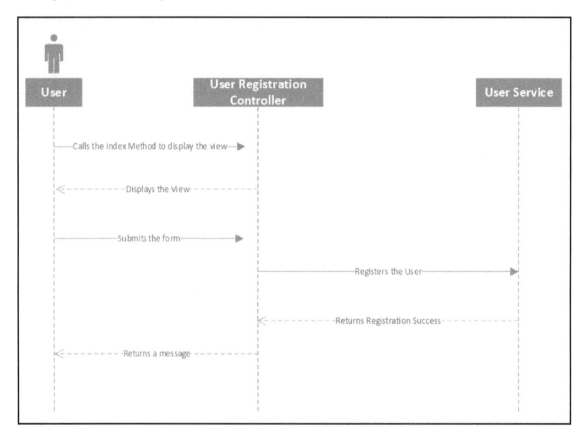

When comparing with the initial workflow of the *Tic-Tac-Toe* application, we can see that there are still multiple things missing, such as the whole client-side part, really working with the **Communication Middleware,** as well as multiple other features we still need to implement.

Let's start by working on the client-side part and see how to apply more advanced techniques. Then, you will learn how to optimize everything as best as possible.

If you remember, last time, we stopped after a user had submitted his data to the registration form, which was sent to the `UserService`. We then just displayed a plain text message, as follows:

But, the processing is not finished here. We need to add the whole email confirmation process using client-side development and JavaScript, and that is what we are going to do next:

1. Start Visual Studio 2017 and open the *Tic-Tac-Toe* project. Add a new method called `EmailConfirmation` to the `UserRegistrationController`:

    ```
    [HttpGet]
    public IActionResult EmailConfirmation (string email)
    {
      ViewBag.Email = email;
      return View();
    }
    ```

2. Right-click on the `EmailConfirmation` method and generate the corresponding view and update it with some meaningful information:

    ```
    @{
        ViewData["Title"] = "EmailConfirmation";
        Layout = "~/Views/Shared/_Layout.cshtml";
    }
    <h2>EmailConfirmation</h2>
    An email has been sent to @ViewBag.Email, please confirm your
    email address by clicking on the provided link.
    ```

3. Go to the `UserRegistrationController` and modify the `Index` method to redirect to the `EmailConfirmation` method from the previous step instead of returning the text message:

    ```
    [HttpPost]
    public async Task<IActionResult> Index(UserModel userModel)
    {
    ```

```
      if (ModelState.IsValid)
      {
        await _userService.RegisterUser(userModel);
        return RedirectToAction(nameof(EmailConfirmation),
        new { userModel.Email });
      }
      else
      {
        return View(userModel);
      }
    }
```

4. Start the application by pressing *F5* and register a new user and verify that the new **EmailConfirmation** page is displayed correctly:

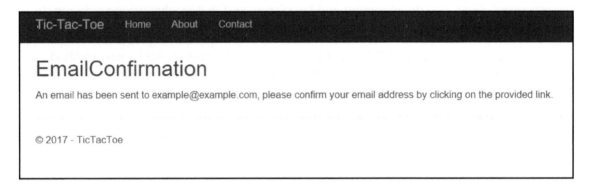

Very good, you have implemented the first set of modifications necessary to finalize the user registration process. In the next part, we need to check that the user has confirmed his email address. Let's see how to do that next:

1. Add two new methods, `GetUserByEmail` and `UpdateUser`, to the `IUser` interface. These will be used for handling the email confirmation updates:

```
public interface IUserService
{
  Task<bool> RegisterUser(UserModel userModel);
  Task<UserModel> GetUserByEmail(string email);
  Task UpdateUser(UserModel user);
}
```

2. Implement the new methods, use a static `ConcurrentBag` to persist the `UserModel`, and modify the `RegisterUser` method in the `UserService`, as follows:

```
public class UserService : IUserService
{
  private static  ConcurrentBag<UserModel> _userStore;

  static UserService()
  {
    _userStore = new ConcurrentBag<UserModel>();
  }

  public Task<bool> RegisterUser(UserModel userModel)
  {
    _userStore.Add(userModel);
    return Task.FromResult(true);
  }

  public Task<UserModel> GetUserByEmail(string email)
  {
    return Task.FromResult(_userStore.FirstOrDefault(
     u => u.Email == email));
  }

  public  Task UpdateUser(UserModel userModel)
  {
    _userStore = new ConcurrentBag<UserModel>
    (_userStore.Where(u => u.Email != userModel.Email))
    {
      userModel
    };
    return Task.CompletedTask;
  }
}
```

3. Add a new model called `GameInvitationModel`. This will be used for game invitations after successful user registration:

```
public class GameInvitationModel
{
  public Guid Id { get; set; }
  public string EmailTo { get; set; }
  public string InvitedBy { get; set; }
  public bool IsConfirmed { get; set; }
  public DateTime ConfirmationDate { get; set; }
}
```

4. Add a new controller called `GameInvitationController` and update its `Index` method for automatically setting the `InvitedBy` property:

```
public class GameInvitationController : Controller
{
  private IUserService _userService;
  public GameInvitationController(IUserService userService)
  {
    _userService = userService;
  }

  [HttpGet]
  public async Task<IActionResult> Index(string email)
  {
    var gameInvitationModel = new GameInvitationModel {
      InvitedBy = email };
    return View(gameInvitationModel);
  }
}
```

5. Generate a corresponding view by right-clicking on the `Index` method, while selecting the **Create** template and using as the **Model class** the `GameInvitationModel` from before:

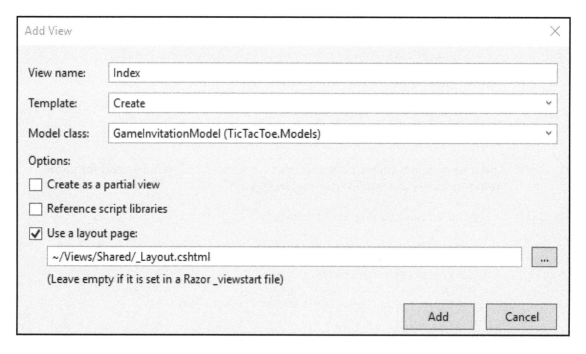

6. Modify the auto-generated view, remove all unnecessary input controls, and leave only the `EmailTo` input control:

```
@model TicTacToe.Models.GameInvitationModel
@{
    ViewData["Title"] = "Index";
}
<h4>GameInvitationModel</h4>
<hr />
<div class="row">
  <div class="col-md-4">
    <form asp-action="Index">
      <input type="hidden" asp-for="Id" />
      <input type="hidden" asp-for="InvitedBy" />
      <div asp-validation-summary="ModelOnly"
       class="text-danger"></div>
      <div class="form-group">
        <label asp-for="EmailTo" class="control-label"></label>
        <input asp-for="EmailTo" class="form-control" />
        <span asp-validation-for="EmailTo"
         class="text-danger"></span>
      </div>
      <div class="form-group">
        <input type="submit" value="Create"
         class="btn btn-default" />
      </div>
    </form>
  </div>
</div>
```

7. Now, update the `EmailConfirmation` method in the
   `UserRegistrationController`. The user has to be redirected to the
   `GameInvitationController` after his email has been confirmed, and, as you
   can see, we are going to simulate the effective confirmation in the code for now:

```
[HttpGet]
public async Task<IActionResult> EmailConfirmation(string email)
{
  var user = await _userService.GetUserByEmail(email);
  if (user?.IsEmailConfirmed == true)
    return RedirectToAction("Index", "GameInvitation",
    new { email = email });

  ViewBag.Email = email;
  user.IsEmailConfirmed = true;
  user.EmailConfirmationDate = DateTime.Now;
  await _userService.UpdateUser(user);
  return View();
}
```

8. Start the application by pressing *F5*, register a new user, and verify that the **Email Confirmation** page is displayed as before. In Microsoft Edge, press *F5* to reload the page, and if everything is working as expected, you should now be redirected to the **Game Invitation** page:

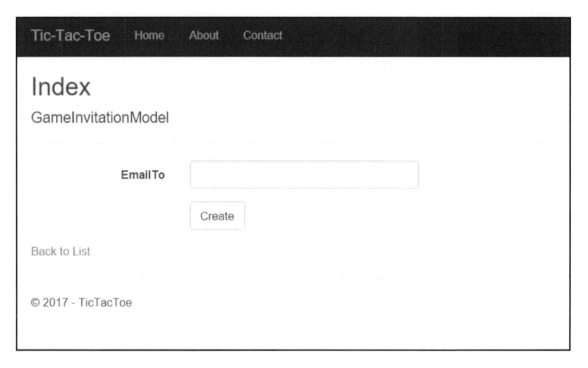

Great, some more progress! Everything is working up until the game invitation now, but unfortunately, there is still user intervention necessary. The user has to manually refresh the **Email Confirmation** page by pressing *F5* until his email has been confirmed; only then is he redirected to the **Game Invitation** page.

The entire refresh process must be automated and optimized in the next step. Your options are:

- Place a HTML meta refresh tag in the head section of the page
- Use simple JavaScript, which does the refresh programmatically
- Implement **XMLHttpRequest** (**XHR**) using jQuery

HTML3 has introduced the meta refresh tag for automatically refreshing pages after a certain amount of time. However, this method is not advisable because it creates a high server load, and a security setting in Microsoft Edge may completely deactivate it and some ad blockers will stop it from working. So, if you use it, you cannot be sure that it is going to work correctly.

Using simple JavaScript might very well automate the page refresh programmatically, but it has mainly the same flaws and is, therefore, neither recommended.

XHR is what we are really looking for, as it provides exactly what we need for our *Tic-Tac-Toe* application. It allows for:

- Updating web pages without reloading them
- Requesting and receiving data from the server even after page load
- Sending data to the server in the background

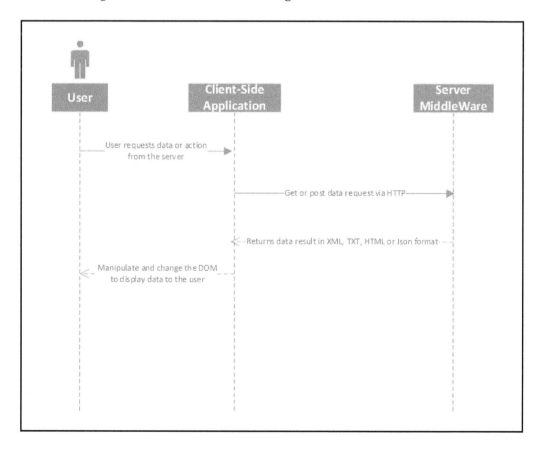

You are now going to use XHR for automating and optimizing the client-side implementation of the user registration email confirmation processing. The steps for doing so are as follows:

1. Create a new folder called `app` in the `wwwroot` folder (this folder will contain all the client-side code in the following steps) and create a subfolder within this folder called `js`.

2. Add a new JavaScript file called `scripts1.js` in the `wwwroot/app/js` folder, with the following content:

```
var interval;
function EmailConfirmation(email) {
  interval = setInterval(() => {
    CheckEmailConfirmationStatus(email);
  }, 5000);
}
```

3. Add a new JavaScript file called `scripts2.js` in the `wwwroot/app/js` folder, with the following content:

```
function CheckEmailConfirmationStatus(email) {
  $.get("/CheckEmailConfirmationStatus?email=" + email,
    function (data) {
      if (data === "OK") {
        if (interval !== null)
        clearInterval(interval);
        alert("ok");
      }
  });
}
```

4. Open the layout page in the `Views\Shared\_Layout.cshtml` file and add a new `Development` environment element before the closing `body` tag (it is best practice to put it there):

```
<environment include="Development">
  <script src="~/app/js/scripts1.js"></script>
  <script src="~/app/js/scripts2.js"></script>
</environment>
```

5. Update the `Invoke` method in the **Communication Middleware** and add a new method called `ProcessEmailConfirmation`, which is going to simulate the email confirmation:

```
public async Task Invoke(HttpContext context)
```

```
{
  if (context.Request.Path.Equals(
    "/CheckEmailConfirmationStatus"))
  {
    await ProcessEmailConfirmation(context);
  }
  else
  {
    await _next?.Invoke(context);
  }
}

private async Task ProcessEmailConfirmation(
 HttpContext context)
{
  var email = context.Request.Query["email"];
  var user = await _userService.GetUserByEmail(email);

  if (string.IsNullOrEmpty(email))
  {
    await context.Response.WriteAsync("BadRequest:Email is
      required");
  }
  else if (
    (await _userService.GetUserByEmail(email)).IsEmailConfirmed)
  {
    await context.Response.WriteAsync("OK");
  }
  else
  {
    await context.Response.WriteAsync(
      "WaitingForEmailConfirmation");
    user.IsEmailConfirmed = true;
    user.EmailConfirmationDate = DateTime.Now;
    _userService.UpdateUser(user).Wait();

  }
}
```

6. Update the `EmailConfirmation` view by adding at the bottom of the page a call to the JavaScript `EmailConfirmation` function from the previous step:

```
@section Scripts
{
  <script>
    $(document).ready(function () {
      EmailConfirmation('@ViewBag.Email');
```

```
          });
        </script>
    }
```

7. Update the `EmailConfirmation` method in the
   `UserRegistrationController`. Since the **Communication Middleware** is now
   going to simulate the effective email confirmation, remove the following lines:

   ```
   user.IsEmailConfirmed = true;
   user.EmailConfirmationDate = DateTime.Now;
   await _userService.UpdateUser(user);
   ```

8. Start the application by pressing *F5* and register a new user. You will see a
   JavaScript alert box returning `WaitingForEmailConfirmation`, and after some
   time, another with **OK**:

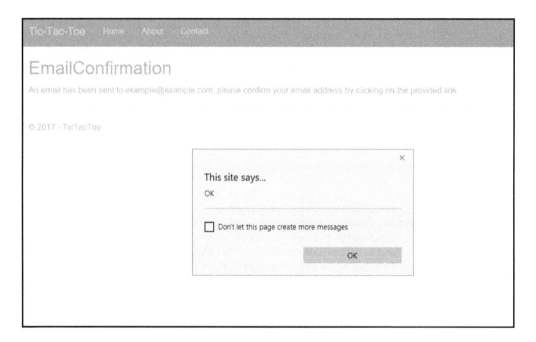

9. Now, you have to update the `CheckEmailConfirmationStatus` method in the
   `scripts2.js` file to redirect in case of a confirmed email. For that, remove the
   `alert("OK");` instruction and add the following instruction in its place:

   ```
   window.location.href = "/GameInvitation?email=" + email;
   ```

10. Start the application by pressing *F5* and register a new user. Everything should be automated and you should automatically be redirected to the **Game Invitation** page at the end:

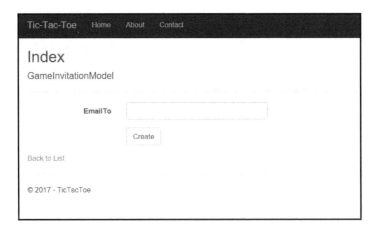

 Note that if you still see the alert box even though you have updated the project in Visual Studio, you might have to delete the cached data in your browser to have the JavaScript refreshed correctly in your browser and see the new behavior.

Optimizing your web applications and using bundling and minification

As you saw in `Chapter 4`, *Basic Concepts of ASP.NET Core 2.0 - Part 1*, we have chosen the community-proven Bower as a client-side package manager. We have left the `bower.json` file untouched, which means that we have restored the four default packages and added some references within the ASP.NET Core 2.0 Layout Page to use them:

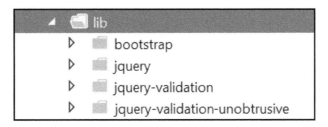

In today's world of modern web application development, it is best practice to separate client-side JavaScript code and CSS style sheets into multiple files during development. But, having so many files may lead to performance and bandwidth problems during runtime in production environments.

That is why during the build process, everything must be optimized before generating the final release packages, which means that JavaScript and CSS files must be bundled and minified. TypeScript and CoffeeScript files must be transcompiled into JavaScript.

Bundling and minification are two techniques you can use for improving the overall page load performance of your web applications. Bundling allows for combining multiple files into a single file, whereas minification optimizes the code of your JavaScript and CSS files for smaller payloads. They work together to reduce the number of server requests as well as the overall request size.

ASP.NET Core 2.0 supports different solutions for bundling and minification:

- Visual Studio extension **Bundler & Minifier**
- Gulp
- Grunt

Let's see how to bundle and minify multiple JavaScript files in the *Tic-Tac-Toe* project by using the Visual Studio extension **Bundler & Minifier** together with the `bundleconfig.json` file:

1. In the top menu select **Tools | Extensions and Updates**, click on **Online**, enter `Bundler & Minifier` in the search box, select **Bundler & Minifier,** and finally, click on **Download**:

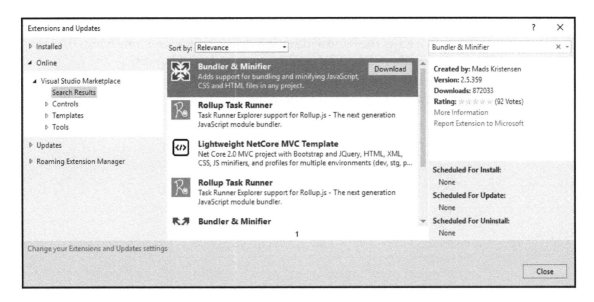

2. Close Visual Studio; the installation will continue. Next, click on **Modify**:

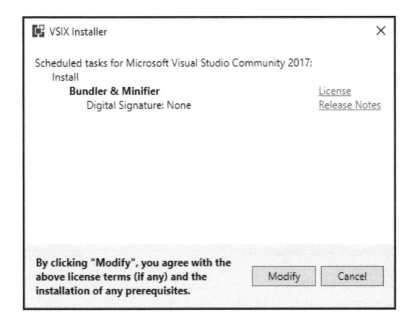

3. Restart Visual Studio. You are now going to optimize the number of opened connections as well as the bandwidth usage by bundling and minifying. For that, add a new JSON file called `bundleconfig.json` to the project.

4. Update the `bundleconfig.json` file for bundling the two JavaScript files into a single one called `site.js` and for minifying the `site.css` and `site.js` files:

```json
[
  {
    "outputFileName": "wwwroot/css/site.min.css",
    "inputFiles": [
      "wwwroot/css/site.css"
    ]
  },
  {
    "outputFileName": "wwwroot/js/site.js",
    "inputFiles": [
      "wwwroot/app/js/scripts1.js",
      "wwwroot/app/js/scripts2.js"
    ],
    "sourceMap": true,
    "includeInProject": true
  },
  {
    "outputFileName": "wwwroot/js/site.min.js",
    "inputFiles": [
      "wwwroot/js/site.js"
    ],
    "minify": {
      "enabled": true,
      "renameLocals": true
    },
    "sourceMap": false
  }
]
```

5. Right-click on the project and select **Bundler & Minifier** | **Update Bundles**:

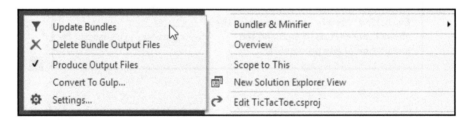

6. When looking in the **Solution Explorer**, you can see that two new files called `site.min.css` and `site.min.js` have been generated.

7. When looking in the **Task Runner Explorer**, you can see the bundling and minifying process you have configured for the project:

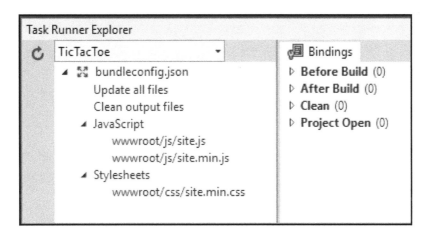

8. Right-click on **Update all files** and select **Run**. You can now see and understand what the process is doing in more detail:

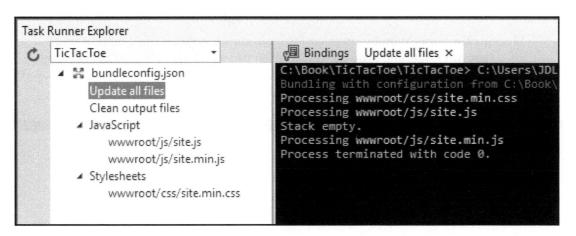

9. Schedule the process for execution after each build by right-clicking on **Update all files** and selecting **Bindings | After build**. A new file called `bundleconfig.json.bindings` gets generated, and if you remove the `wwwroot/js` folder and rebuild the project, the files are auto-generated.

10. To see the newly-generated files in action, go to the **Debug** tab in the project settings and set the ASPNETCORE_ENVIRONMENT variable to Staging and save:

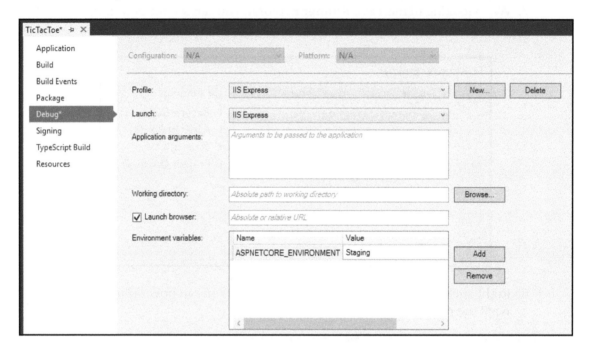

11. Start the application by pressing *F5*, open the Developer Tools by pressing *F12* in Microsoft Edge, and redo the registration process. You will see that only the bundled and minified site.min.css and site.min.js files have been loaded and that load times are faster:

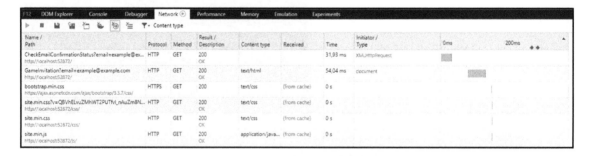

OK, now that we know how to implement the client side and benefit from bundling and minification in modern web application development, let's return to the *Tic-Tac-Toe* game and optimize it even further and add the missing components.

Working with WebSockets for real-time communication scenarios

At the end of the previous section, everything was working fully automated as expected. However, there is still some room for additional improvements.

As it is, the client side sends periodical requests to the server side to see if the email confirmation status has changed. This may lead to a lot of requests to see if there has been a status change or not.

Furthermore, the server side cannot inform the client side as soon as an email has been confirmed, since it has to wait for a client request to respond to.

In this section, you will learn about the concepts of WebSockets (`https://docs.microsoft.com/en-us/aspnet/core/fundamentals/websockets`), and how they will allow you to further optimize your client-side implementations.

WebSockets enables persistent two-way communication channels over TCP, which is especially interesting for applications that need to run real-time communication scenarios (chat, stock tickers, games, and more). And it just so happens that our application is a game, which is one of the main application types that largely benefit from working directly with a socket connection.

Note that you could also consider SignalR as an alternative. At the time of writing this book, the SignalR Core version was not yet available. However, it could be available after publication, so you should look it up and use it instead if it is available. It will provide a better solution for real-time communication scenarios and encapsulate some of the functionalities missing from WebSockets you might have implemented for yourself manually.

You can look it up at `https://github.com/aspnet/SignalR`.

Let's optimize the client-side implementation of the *Tic-Tac-Toe* application by using WebSockets for real-time communication:

1. Go to the Tic-Tac-Toe `Startup` class in the `Configure` method and add the **WebSockets Middleware** just before the **Communication Middleware** and the **MVC Middleware** (remember that the middleware invocation order is important for assuring correct behavior):

```
app.UseWebSockets();
app.UseCommunicationMiddleware();
...
```

2. Update the **Communication Middleware** and add two new methods called `SendStringAsync` and `ReceiveStringAsync` for WebSockets communication:

```
private static Task SendStringAsync(WebSocket socket,
  string data, CancellationToken ct = default(CancellationToken))
{
  var buffer = Encoding.UTF8.GetBytes(data);
  var segment = new ArraySegment<byte>(buffer);
  return socket.SendAsync(segment, WebSocketMessageType.Text,
    true, ct);
}

private static async Task<string> ReceiveStringAsync(
  WebSocket socket, CancellationToken ct =
  default(CancellationToken))
{
  var buffer = new ArraySegment<byte>(new byte[8192]);
  using (var ms = new MemoryStream())
  {
    WebSocketReceiveResult result;
    do
    {
      ct.ThrowIfCancellationRequested();

      result = await socket.ReceiveAsync(buffer, ct);
      ms.Write(buffer.Array, buffer.Offset, result.Count);
    }
    while (!result.EndOfMessage);

    ms.Seek(0, SeekOrigin.Begin);
    if (result.MessageType != WebSocketMessageType.Text)
      throw new Exception("Unexpected message");

    using (var reader = new StreamReader(ms, Encoding.UTF8))
```

```
    {
      return await reader.ReadToEndAsync();
    }
  }
}
```

3. Update the **Communication Middleware** and add a new method called `ProcessEmailConfirmation` for email confirmation processing via WebSockets:

```
public async Task ProcessEmailConfirmation(HttpContext context,
  WebSocket currentSocket, CancellationToken ct, string email)
{
  UserModel user = await _userService.GetUserByEmail(email);
  while (!ct.IsCancellationRequested &&
   !currentSocket.CloseStatus.HasValue &&
   user?.IsEmailConfirmed == false)
  {
    if (user.IsEmailConfirmed)
    {
      await SendStringAsync(currentSocket, "OK", ct);
    }
    else
    {
      user.IsEmailConfirmed = true;
      user.EmailConfirmationDate = DateTime.Now;

      await _userService.UpdateUser(user);
      await SendStringAsync(currentSocket, "OK", ct);
    }

    Task.Delay(500).Wait();
    user = await _userService.GetUserByEmail(email);
  }
}
```

4. Update the `Invoke` method in the **Communication Middleware** and add calls to the WebSockets-specific methods from the previous step, while still keeping the standard implementations for browsers that do not support WebSockets:

```
public async Task Invoke(HttpContext context)
{
  if (context.WebSockets.IsWebSocketRequest)
  {
    var webSocket =
      await context.WebSockets.AcceptWebSocketAsync();
    var ct = context.RequestAborted;
```

```
    var json = await ReceiveStringAsync(webSocket, ct);
    var command = JsonConvert.DeserializeObject<dynamic>(json);

    switch (command.Operation.ToString())
    {
      case "CheckEmailConfirmationStatus":
      {
        await ProcessEmailConfirmation(context, webSocket,
         ct, command.Parameters.ToString());
        break;
      }
    }
  }
  else if (context.Request.Path.Equals(
   "/CheckEmailConfirmationStatus"))
  {
    await ProcessEmailConfirmation(context);
  }
  else
  {
    await _next?.Invoke(context);
  }
}
```

5. Modify the `scripts1.js` file and add some WebSockets-specific code for opening and working with sockets:

```
var interval;
function EmailConfirmation(email) {
  if (window.WebSocket) {
    alert("Websockets are enabled");
    openSocket(email, "Email");
  }
  else {
    alert("Websockets are not enabled");
    interval = setInterval(() => {
      CheckEmailConfirmationStatus(email);
    }, 5000);
  }
}
```

6. Modify the `scripts2.js` file and add some WebSockets-specific code for opening and working with sockets and redirecting to the **Game Invitation** page if the email has been confirmed:

```
function CheckEmailConfirmationStatus(email) {
  $.get("/CheckEmailConfirmationStatus?email=" + email,
```

```
   function (data) {
     if (data === "OK") {
       if (interval !== null)
        clearInterval(interval);
        window.location.href = "/GameInvitation?email=" + email;
     }
   });
}

var openSocket = function (parameter, strAction) {
  if (interval !== null)
   clearInterval(interval);

  var protocol = location.protocol === "https:" ?
   "wss:" : "ws:";
  var operation = "";
  var wsUri = "";

  if (strAction == "Email") {
    wsUri = protocol + "//" + window.location.host +
     "/CheckEmailConfirmationStatus";
    operation = "CheckEmailConfirmationStatus";
  }

  var socket = new WebSocket(wsUri);
  socket.onmessage = function (response) {
    console.log(response);
    if (strAction == "Email" && response.data == "OK") {
      window.location.href = "/GameInvitation?email=" +
       parameter;
    }
  };

  socket.onopen = function () {
    var json = JSON.stringify({
      "Operation": operation,
      "Parameters": parameter
    });

    socket.send(json);
  };

  socket.onclose = function (event) {
  };
};
```

7. When you start the application and proceed with the user registration, you will get the information if WebSockets is supported. If it is, you will get redirected to the **Game Invitation** page like before, but with the benefit of a much faster processing time:

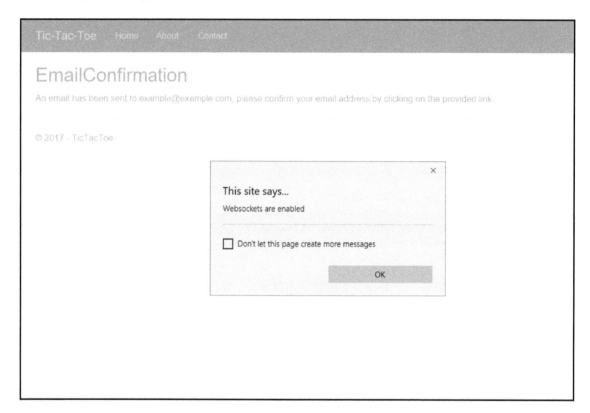

That concludes our trip into client-side development and optimization under ASP.NET Core 2.0 for the moment. You are now going to see how to further extend and finalize the *Tic-Tac-Toe* application with additional ASP.NET Core concepts that will help you in your daily work building multi-lingual, production-ready web applications.

Taking advantage of session and user cache management

As a web developer, you might know that HTTP is a stateless protocol, which means that by default there is not a notion of sessions as such. Each request is handled independently and no values are retained between different requests.

Nonetheless, there are different methods for working with data. You can work with query strings, submit form data, or you can use cookies to store data on the client. However, all of those mechanisms are more or less manual and need to be managed by yourself.

If you are an experienced ASP.NET developer, you will be familiar with the concepts of session state and session variables. Those variables are stored on the web server and you can access them during different user requests for having a central place to store and receive data. Session state is ideal for storing user data specific to a session, without the need for permanent persistence.

Note that it is best practice to not store any sensitive data in session variables due to security reasons. Users might not close their browsers; thus, session cookies might not be cleared (also, some browsers keep session cookies alive).

Also, a session might not be restricted to a single user, other users might continue with the same session, which could provide security risks.

ASP.NET Core 2.0 provides session state and session variables by using a dedicated **Session Middleware**. Basically, there are two distinct types of session providers:

- In-memory session providers (locally to a single server)
- Distributed session providers (shared between multiple servers)

Let's see how to activate the in-memory session provider in the *Tic-Tac-Toe* application for storing the user interface culture and language:

1. Open the layout page in the `Views\Shared\_Layout.cshtml` file and add a new **User Interface Language Drop-Down** to the menu after the other menu items. This will allow users to select between English and French:

```
<li class="dropdown">
  <a class="dropdown-toggle" data-toggle="dropdown"
    href="#">Settings<span class="caret"></span></a>
  <ul class="dropdown-menu multi-level">
```

```
<li class="dropdown-submenu">
  <a class="dropdown-toggle" data-toggle="dropdown"
   href="#">Select your language (@ViewBag.Language)
   <span class="caret"></span></a>
  <ul class="dropdown-menu">
    <li @(ViewBag.Language == "EN" ? "active" : "")>
      <a asp-controller="Home" asp-action="SetCulture"
       asp-route-culture="EN">English</a></li>
    <li @(ViewBag.Language == "FR" ? "active" : "")>
      <a asp-controller="Home" asp-action="SetCulture"
       asp-route-culture="FR">French</a></li>
  </ul>
</li>
</ul>
</li>
```

2. Open the `HomeController` and add a new method called `SetCulture`. This will contain the code for storing the user culture settings in a **Session Variable**:

```
public IActionResult SetCulture(string culture)
{
  Request.HttpContext.Session.SetString("culture", culture);
  return RedirectToAction("Index");
}
```

3. Update the `Index` method of `HomeController` for retrieving the culture from the **Culture Session Variable**:

```
public IActionResult Index()
{
  var culture =
    Request.HttpContext.Session.GetString("culture");
  ViewBag.Language = culture;
  return View();
}
```

4. Got to the `wwwroot/css/site.css` file and add some new CSS classes for a more modern look for the **User Interface Language Drop-Down**:

```
.dropdown-submenu {
  position: relative;
}

.dropdown-submenu > .dropdown-menu {
  top: 0;
  left: 100%;
  margin-top: -6px;
```

```css
  margin-left: -1px;
  -webkit-border-radius: 0 6px 6px 6px;
  -moz-border-radius: 0 6px 6px;
  border-radius: 0 6px 6px 6px;
}

.dropdown-submenu:hover > .dropdown-menu {
  display: block;
}

.dropdown-submenu > a:after {
  display: block;
  content: " ";
  float: right;
  width: 0;
  height: 0;
  border-color: transparent;
  border-style: solid;
  border-width: 5px 0 5px 5px;
  border-left-color: #ccc;
  margin-top: 5px;
  margin-right: -10px;
}

.dropdown-submenu:hover > a:after {
  border-left-color: #fff;
}

.dropdown-submenu.pull-left {
  float: none;
}

.dropdown-submenu.pull-left > .dropdown-menu {
  left: -100%;
  margin-left: 10px;
  -webkit-border-radius: 6px 0 6px 6px;
  -moz-border-radius: 6px 0 6px 6px;
  border-radius: 6px 0 6px 6px;
}
```

5. Add the built-in **Session Middleware** of ASP.NET Core 2.0 in the
   ConfigureServices method of the Startup class:

```csharp
services.AddSession(o =>
{
  o.IdleTimeout = TimeSpan.FromMinutes(30);
});
```

6. Activate the **Session Middleware** in the `Configure` method of the `Startup` class by adding it just after the **Static Files Middleware**:

```
app.UseStaticFiles();
app.UseSession();
```

7. Update the `Index` method in the `GameInvitationController`, set the email session variable:

```
[HttpGet]
public async Task<IActionResult> Index(string email)
{
    var gameInvitationModel = new GameInvitationModel {
        InvitedBy = email };
    HttpContext.Session.SetString("email", email);
    return View(gameInvitationModel);
}
```

8. Start the application by pressing *F5*. You should see the new **User Interface Language Drop-Down** with the options to select between English and French:

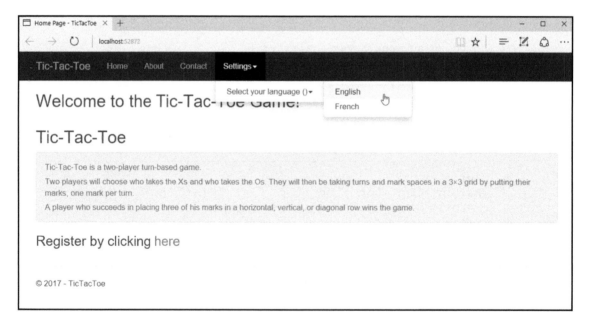

Good, you have seen how to activate and use session state. However, most of the time you will have multiple web servers, not just one, especially in today's cloud environments. So, how do you store session state out of memory in a distributed cache?

Well, that is easy, you just have to register additional services within the Startup class. These additional services will provide this functionality. Here are some examples:

- Distributed Memory Cache:

  ```
  services.AddDistributedMemoryCache();
  ```

- Distributed SQL Server Cache:

  ```
  services.AddDistributedSqlServerCache(o =>
  {
    o.ConnectionString = _configuration["DatabaseConnection"];
    o.SchemaName = "dbo";
    o.TableName = "sessions";
  });
  ```

- Distributed Redis Cache:

  ```
  services.AddDistributedRedisCache(o =>
  {
    o.Configuration = _configuration["CacheRedis:Connection"];
    o.InstanceName = _configuration["CacheRedis:InstanceName"];
  });
  ```

We have added a new **User Interface Language Drop-Down** in this section, but you have not yet seen how to handle multiple languages within your applications. There's no time to lose; let's see how to do that and use the drop-down and session variable for changing the user interface language on-the-fly in the following section.

Applying globalization and localization for multi-lingual user interfaces

Sometimes your applications achieve success, sometimes even very considerable success, and so you want to provide them internationally to a wider audience and deploy them at a larger scale. But too bad, you cannot do that easily, because you have not thought of localizing your applications from the beginning, and now you have to modify your already-running application with the risk of regressions and destabilizations.

Do not fall into this trap! Think about your target audience and future deployment strategy from the start!

Localizing your applications should be considered from the beginning of your projects, especially since it is very easy and straightforward to do when using the ASP.NET Core 2.0 Framework. It provides existing services and middlewares for this purpose.

Building applications which support different languages and cultures for display, input, and output is called globalization, whereas adapting a globalized application to a specific culture is called localization.

There are three different methods for localizing ASP.NET Core 2.0 web applications:

- The String Localizer
- The View Localizer
- Localizing Data Annotations

In this section, you will learn about the concepts of globalization and localization and how they will allow you to further optimize your websites for internationalization.

 For additional information on globalization and localization, please visit `https://docs.microsoft.com/en-us/aspnet/core/fundamentals/locali` `zation`.

So, how do you get started? Well, first of all, let's look at how to make the *Tic-Tac-Toe* application localizable, by using the String Localizer:

1. Go to the `Services` folder and add a new service called `CultureProviderResolverService`. This will retrieve the culture setting by looking at the `Culture` query string, the `Culture` cookie, and the `Culture` session variable (created in the previous section of this chapter).

2. Implement the `CultureProviderResolverService` by inheriting it from the `RequestCultureProvider` and overriding its specific methods:

```
public class CultureProviderResolverService :
 RequestCultureProvider
{
  private static readonly char[] _cookieSeparator = new[] {'|' };
  private static readonly string _culturePrefix = "c=";
  private static readonly string _uiCulturePrefix = "uic=";

  public override async Task<ProviderCultureResult>
   DetermineProviderCultureResult(HttpContext httpContext)
  {
    if (GetCultureFromQueryString(httpContext,
```

```
    out string culture))
  return new ProviderCultureResult(culture, culture);

  else if (GetCultureFromCookie(httpContext, out culture))
  return new ProviderCultureResult(culture, culture);

  else if (GetCultureFromSession(httpContext, out culture))
  return new ProviderCultureResult(culture, culture);

  return await NullProviderCultureResult;
}

private bool GetCultureFromQueryString(
 HttpContext httpContext, out string culture)
{
  if (httpContext == null)
  {
    throw new ArgumentNullException(nameof(httpContext));
  }

  var request = httpContext.Request;
  if (!request.QueryString.HasValue)
  {
    culture = null;
    return false;
  }

  culture = request.Query["culture"];
  return true;
}

private bool GetCultureFromCookie(HttpContext httpContext,
 out string culture)
{
  if (httpContext == null)
  {
    throw new ArgumentNullException(nameof(httpContext));
  }

  var cookie = httpContext.Request.Cookies["culture"];
  if (string.IsNullOrEmpty(cookie))
  {
    culture = null;
    return false;
  }

  culture = ParseCookieValue(cookie);
  return !string.IsNullOrEmpty(culture);
```

```csharp
        }

        public static string ParseCookieValue(string value)
        {
          if (string.IsNullOrWhiteSpace(value))
          {
            return null;
          }

          var parts = value.Split(_cookieSeparator,
           StringSplitOptions.RemoveEmptyEntries);
          if (parts.Length != 2)
          {
            return null;
          }

          var potentialCultureName = parts[0];
          var potentialUICultureName = parts[1];

          if (!potentialCultureName.StartsWith(_culturePrefix) ||
           !potentialUICultureName.StartsWith(_uiCulturePrefix))
          {
            return null;
          }

          var cultureName =
            potentialCultureName.Substring(_culturePrefix.Length);
          var uiCultureName =
            potentialUICultureName.Substring(_uiCulturePrefix.Length);
          if (cultureName == null && uiCultureName == null)
          {
            return null;
          }

          if (cultureName != null && uiCultureName == null)
          {
            uiCultureName = cultureName;
          }

          if (cultureName == null && uiCultureName != null)
          {
            cultureName = uiCultureName;
          }

          return cultureName;
        }

        private bool GetCultureFromSession(HttpContext httpContext,
```

```
  out string culture)
{
  culture = httpContext.Session.GetString("culture");
  return !string.IsNullOrEmpty(culture);
}
}
```

3. Add the **Localization Service** at the top of the ConfigureServices method in the Startup class:

```
public void ConfigureServices(IServiceCollection services)
{
  services.AddLocalization(options => options.ResourcesPath =
    "Localization");
  ...
}
```

4. Add the **Localization Middleware** to the Configure method in the Startup class and define the supported cultures:

> Note that the order of adding **middlewares** is important, as you have already seen. You have to add the **Localization Middleware** just before the **MVC Middleware**.

```
...
var supportedCultures =
  CultureInfo.GetCultures(CultureTypes.AllCultures);
var localizationOptions = new RequestLocalizationOptions
{
  DefaultRequestCulture = new RequestCulture("en-US"),
  SupportedCultures = supportedCultures,
  SupportedUICultures = supportedCultures
};

localizationOptions.RequestCultureProviders.Clear();
localizationOptions.RequestCultureProviders.Add(new
 CultureProviderResolverService());

app.UseRequestLocalization(localizationOptions);

app.UseMvc(...);
```

Note that you can use different methods to change the culture of your applications during runtime:

Query strings: Provide the culture in the URI

Cookies: Store the culture in a cookie

Browser: Browser page language settings

Custom: Implement your own provider (shown in this example)

5. In the **Solution Explorer**, add a new folder called Localization (it will be used to store the resource files), create a subfolder called Controllers, then within this folder, add a new resource file called GameInvitationController.resx.

Note that you can put your resource files either into subfolders (for example, Controllers, Views, and more) or directly name your files accordingly (for example, Controllers.GameInvitationController.resx, Views.Home.Index.resx, and more). However, we advise you to use the folder approach for clarity, readability, and better organization of your files.

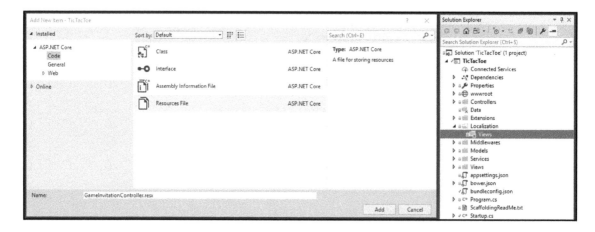

If you have errors when using your resource files with .NET Core, right-click on each file and select **Properties**. Then, check in each file that the **Build Action** is set to **Content** instead of **Embedded Resource**. There are bugs that should have been fixed by the final release, but if they are not, you can use this handy work-around to make everything work as expected.

6. Open the GameInvitationController.resx resource file and add a new GameInvitationConfirmationMessage in English:

Name	▲ Value
GameInvitationConfirmationMessage	You have invited {0} for the next game.

7. In the same Controllers folder, add a new resource file for the French translations called GameInvitationController.fr.resx:

Name	▲ Value
GameInvitationConfirmationMessage	Vous avez invité {0} pour la prochaine partie.

8. Go to the GameInvitationController, add the stringLocalizer, and update the constructor implementation:

```
private IStringLocalizer<GameInvitationController>
 _stringLocalizer;
private IUserService _userService;
public GameInvitationController(IUserService userService,
 IStringLocalizer<GameInvitationController> stringLocalizer)
{
  _userService = userService;
  _stringLocalizer = stringLocalizer;
}
```

9. Add a new Index method to the GameInvitationController. This will return a localized message depending on the application locale settings:

```
[HttpPost]
public IActionResult Index(
```

```
GameInvitationModel gameInvitationModel)
{
   return Content(_stringLocalizer[
   "GameInvitationConfirmationMessage",
    gameInvitationModel.EmailTo]);
}
```

10. Start the application in English (the default culture), then, register a new user until you get the following text message, which should be in English:

11. Change the application language to French by using the **User Interface Language Drop-Down**, then register a new user until you get the following text message, which should now be in French:

That's it, you have seen how to localize any type of string within your applications, which can be useful for some of your specific application use cases. However, this is not the recommended approach when working with views.

The ASP.NET Core 2.0 Framework provides some powerful features for localizing views. You are going to use the View Localizer approach in the next example:

1. Update the `ConfigureServices` method in the `Startup` class and add the **View Localization Service** to the **MVC Service** declaration:

   ```
   services.AddMvc().AddViewLocalization(
     LanguageViewLocationExpanderFormat.Suffix,
     options => options.ResourcesPath = "Localization");
   ```

2. Modify the `Views/ViewImports.cshtml` file and add the **View Localizer** functionalities so that they will be available for all views:

   ```
   @using Microsoft.AspNetCore.Mvc.Localization
   @inject IViewLocalizer Localizer
   ```

3. Open the **Home Page View** and add a new title, which is going to be localized further, as follows:

   ```
   <h2>@Localizer["Title"]</h2>
   ```

4. In the **Solution Explorer** go to the `Localization` folder and create a subfolder called `Views`, then, add two new resource files called `Home.Index.resx` and `Home.Index.fr.resx` to this folder:

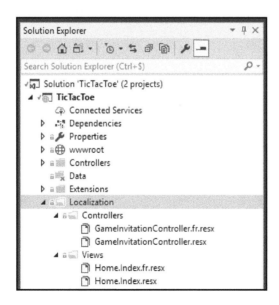

5. Open the `Home.Index.resx` file and add an entry for the English title:

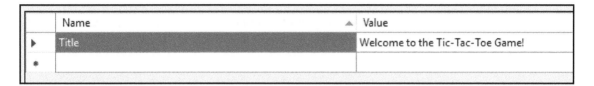

6. Open the `Home.Index.fr.resx` file and add an entry for the French title:

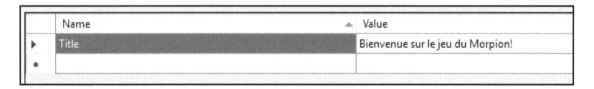

7. Start the application and set the user interface language drop-down to English:

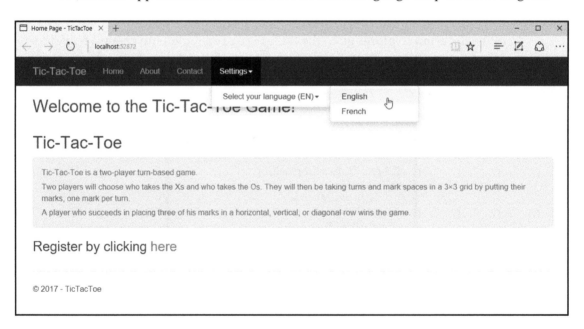

8. Change the application language to French using the **User Interface Language Drop-Down**. The title should now be displayed in French:

You have seen how to easily localize your views, but how do you localize forms that are using Data Annotations within your views? Let's look at that in more detail; you will be surprised at what the ASP.NET Core 2.0 Framework has to offer in this case!

We are going to completely localize the user registration form in the following examples:

1. In the **Solution Explorer**, go to the `Localization/Views` folder, add two new resource files called `UserRegistration.Index.resx` and `UserRegistration.Index.fr.resx`.

2. Open the `UserRegistration.Index.resx` file and add a `Title` and a `SubTitle` element with English translations:

Name	Value
Title	User Registration
▶ SubTitle	User Record
∗	

3. Open the `UserRegistration.Index.fr.resx` file and add a `Title` and a `SubTitle` element with French translations:

Name	Value
Title	Inscription de l'utilisateur
SubTitle	Fiche Utilisateur
∗	

4. Update the **User Registration Index View** to use the **View Localizer**:

```
@model TicTacToe.Models.UserModel
@{
    ViewData["Title"] = Localizer["Title"];
}
<h2>@ViewData["Title"]</h2>
<h4>@Localizer["SubTitle"]</h4>
<hr />
<div class="row">
...
```

5. Start the application, set the language to French using the **User Interface Language Drop-Down**, and then go to the **User Registration** page. The titles should be displayed in French. Click on **Create** without entering anything in the input fields and see what happens:

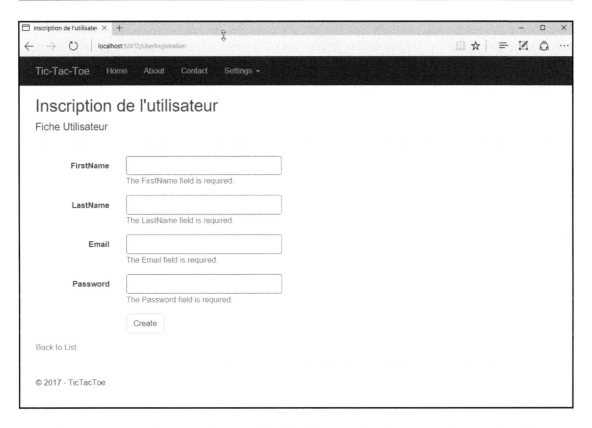

Something is missing here. You have added localization for the page title as well as the subtitle of the **User Registration** page, but we are still missing some localizations for the form. But what are we missing?

You surely have seen for yourself that the error messages are not localized and translated yet. We are using the Data Annotation framework for error handling and form validation, so how do you localize Data Annotation validation error messages? That is what you are going to see now:

1. Add the **Data Annotation Localization Service** to the **MVC Service** declaration in the `ConfigureServices` method of the `Startup` class:

```
services.AddMvc().AddViewLocalization(
    LanguageViewLocationExpanderFormat.Suffix, options =>
    options.ResourcesPath = "Localization")
    .AddDataAnnotationsLocalization();
```

2. Go to the `Localization` folder and create a subfolder called `Models`, then add two new resource files called `UserModel.resx` and `UserModel.fr.resx`.

3. Update the `UserModel.resx` file with English translations:

Name	Value
Email	E-Mail
EmailRequired	The e-mail is required.
FirstName	First Name
FirstNameRequired	The first name is required.
LastName	Last Name
LastNameRequired	The last name is required.
Password	Password
PasswordRequired	The password is required.

4. Update the `UserModel.fr.resx` file with French translations:

Name		Value
Email		E-Mail
▶ EmailRequired		L'e-mail est obligatoire.
FirstName		Prénom
FirstNameRequired		Le prénom est obligatoire.
LastName		Nom
LastNameRequired		Le nom est obligatoire.
Password		Mot de passe
PasswordRequired		Le mot de passe est obligatoire.
✳		

5. Update the `UserModel` implementation to be able to use the resource files from above:

```
public class UserModel
{
    public Guid Id { get; set; }

    [Display(Name = "FirstName")]
    [Required(ErrorMessage = "FirstNameRequired")]
    public string FirstName { get; set; }

    [Display(Name = "LastName")]
    [Required(ErrorMessage = "LastNameRequired")]
    public string LastName { get; set; }

    [Display(Name = "Email")]
    [Required(ErrorMessage = "EmailRequired"),
     DataType(DataType.EmailAddress)]
    [EmailAddress]
    public string Email { get; set; }

    [Display(Name = "Password")]
    [Required(ErrorMessage = "PasswordRequired"),
     DataType(DataType.Password)]
    public string Password { get; set; }
    public bool IsEmailConfirmed { get; set; }
    public System.DateTime? EmailConfirmationDate { get; set; }
    public int Score { get; set; }
}
```

6. Rebuild the solution and start the application. You will see that the whole **User Registration** page, including the error messages, is now completely translated when changing the user interface language to French:

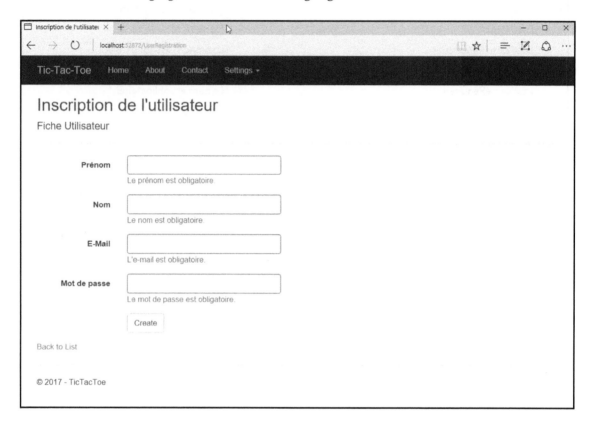

You have seen how to localize strings, views, and even error messages using Data Annotations. For that, you have used the built-in features of ASP.NET Core 2.0, since they contain everything for developing multi-lingual localizable web applications. The next section is going to give you some insights on how to configure your applications and services.

Configuring your applications and services

In the previous sections, you have further advanced by adding missing components to the user registration process and even localizing parts of the *Tic-Tac-Toe* application. However, you have always simulated the email confirmation by setting the user confirmation programmatically in code. In this section, we will modify this part to really send emails to newly-registered users and make everything fully configurable.

First, you are going to add a new **Email Service**, which will be used to send emails to users who have freshly registered on the website:

1. Within the `Services` folder, add a new service called `EmailService`, and implement a default `SendEmail` method (we will update it later):

```
public class EmailService
{
  public Task SendEmail(string emailTo, string subject,
   string message)
  {
    return Task.CompletedTask;
  }
}
```

2. Extract the `IEmailService` interface:

3. Add the new **Email Service** to the `ConfigureServices` method of the `Startup` class (we want a single application instance, so add it as **Singleton**):

```
services.AddSingleton<IEmailService, EmailService>();
```

4. Update the `UserRegistrationController` to be able to access the `EmailService` created in the previous step:

```
readonly IUserService _userService;
readonly IEmailService _emailService;
public UserRegistrationController(IUserService userService,
 IEmailService emailService)
{
  _userService = userService;
  _emailService = emailService;
}
```

5. Update the `EmailConfirmation` method in the `UserRegistrationController` for calling the `SendEmail` method of the `EmailService`:

```
[HttpGet]
public async Task<IActionResult> EmailConfirmation(string email)
{
  var user = await _userService.GetUserByEmail(email);
  var urlAction = new UrlActionContext
  {
    Action = "ConfirmEmail",
    Controller = "UserRegistration",
    Values = new { email },
    Protocol = Request.Scheme,
    Host = Request.Host.ToString()
  };

  var message = $"Thank you for your registration on our web
   site, please click here to confirm your email " +
   $"{Url.Action(urlAction)}";

  try
  {
    _emailService.SendEmail(email,
      "Tic-Tac-Toe Email Confirmation", message).Wait();
  }
  catch (Exception e)
  {
  }
```

```
    if (user?.IsEmailConfirmed == true)
     return RedirectToAction("Index", "GameInvitation",
      new { email = email });

    ViewBag.Email = email;

    return View();
}
```

Great, you have an **Email Service** now, but your work is not finished yet. You need to be able to configure the service for setting environment-specific parameters (SMTP server name, port, SSL, and more) and then send the emails. Nearly all of the services you create in the future will have some kind of configuration, which should be configurable from the outside of your code.

ASP.NET Core 2.0 has a built-in Configuration API for this purpose. It provides various functionalities for reading configuration data from multiple sources during application runtime. *Name-value* pairs, which can be grouped into multi-level hierarchies, are used for configuration data persistence. Furthermore, the configuration data can be automatically deserialized into **plain old C# objects** (**POCO**), which contain only private members and properties.

The following configuration sources are supported:

- Configuration files (JSON, XML, and even classic INI files)
- Environment variables
- Command-line arguments
- In-memory .NET objects
- Encrypted user stores
- Azure Key Vault
- Custom providers

 For more information on the Configuration API, please visit `https://docs.microsoft.com/en-us/aspnet/core/fundamentals/configuration?tabs=basicconfiguration`.

Let's see how to make the **Email Service** quickly configurable by using the ASP.Net Core 2.0 Configuration API together with a JSON configuration file:

1. Add a new `appsettings.json` configuration file to the project and add the following custom section. This will be used to configure the **Email Service**:

```
"Email": {
  "MailType": "SMTP",
  "MailServer": "localhost",
  "MailPort": 25,
  "UseSSL": false,
  "UserId": "",
  "Password": "",
  "RemoteServerAPI": "",
  "RemoteServerKey": ""
}
```

2. In the **Solution Explorer,** create a new folder called `Options` at the root of the project. Add a new POCO called `EmailServiceOptions` to this folder, and implement private members as well as public properties for the options seen previously:

```
public class EmailServiceOptions
{
  public string MailType { get; set; }
  public string MailServer { get; set; }
  public string MailPort { get; set; }
  public string UseSSL { get; set; }
  public string UserId { get; set; }
  public string Password { get; set; }
  public string RemoteServerAPI { get; set; }
  public string RemoteServerKey { get; set; }

  public EmailServiceOptions()
  {

  }

  public EmailServiceOptions(string mailType,
   string mailServer, string mailPort, string useSSL,
   string userId, string password, string remoteServerAPI,
   string remoteServerKey)
  {
    MailType = mailType;
    MailServer = mailServer;
    MailPort = mailPort;
```

```
        UseSSL = useSSL;
        UserId = userId;
        Password = password;
        RemoteServerAPI = remoteServerAPI;
        RemoteServerKey = remoteServerKey;
    }
}
```

3. Update the `EmailService` implementation, add the `EmailServiceOptions`, and add a parameterized constructor to the class:

```
private EmailServiceOptions _emailServiceOptions;
public EmailService(IOptions<EmailServiceOptions>
 emailServiceOptions)
{
  _emailServiceOptions = emailServiceOptions.Value;
}
```

4. Add a new constructor to the `Startup` class to allow you to configure your **Email Service**:

```
public IConfiguration _configuration { get; }
public Startup(IConfiguration configuration)
{
  _configuration = configuration;
}
```

5. Update the `ConfigureServices` method of the `Startup` class:

```
services.Configure<EmailServiceOptions>
 (_configuration.GetSection("Email"));
services.AddSingleton<IEmailService, EmailService>();
```

6. Update the `SendEmail` method in the `EmailService`. Use the **Email Service Options** to retrieve the settings from the configuration file:

```
public Task SendEmail(string emailTo, string subject,
 string message)
{
  using (var client =
    new SmtpClient(_emailServiceOptions.MailServer,
    int.Parse(_emailServiceOptions.MailPort)))
  {
    if (bool.Parse(_emailServiceOptions.UseSSL) == true)
      client.EnableSsl = true;

    if (!string.IsNullOrEmpty(_emailServiceOptions.UserId))
```

```
        client.Credentials =
            new NetworkCredential(_emailServiceOptions.UserId,
            _emailServiceOptions.Password);

        client.Send(new MailMessage("example@example.com",
            emailTo, subject, message));
    }
    return Task.CompletedTask;
}
```

7. Put a breakpoint into the `EmailService` constructor and start the application in Debug mode by pressing *F5* and verify that the **Email Service Options** values have been retrieved correctly from the configuration file. If you have an SMTP server, you can also verify that the email has really been sent:

```
12  ⊟      public class EmailService : IEmailService
13         {
14             private EmailServiceOptions _emailServiceOptions;
15  ⊟         public EmailService(IOptions<EmailServiceOptions> emailServiceOptions)
16             {
17 ○               _emailServiceOptions = emailServiceOptions.Value;
18             }
19
20  ⊟         public Task SendEmail(string em ⌨  emailServiceOptions  {Microsoft.Extensions.Options.OptionsManager<TicTacToe.Options.EmailServiceOptions>}  ▣
21             {                                  ⌨  Value                  {TicTacToe.Options.EmailServiceOptions}
22  ⊟             using (var client = new SmtpC⌨ MailPort       🔍 ▾ "25"
23                 {                              ⌨ MailServer     🔍 ▾ "localhost"      Server, int.Parse(_emailServiceOptions.MailPort)))
24                     if (bool.Parse(_emailServi⌨ MailType       🔍 ▾ "SMTP"
25                         client.EnableSsl = tru⌨ Password       🔍 ▾ ""
26                                                 ⌨ RemoteServerAPI 🔍 ▾ ""
27                     if (!string.IsNullOrEmpty(⌨ RemoteServerKey 🔍 ▾ ""
28                         client.Credentials = new⌨ UseSSL         🔍 ▾ "False"  viceOptions.UserId, _emailServiceOptions.Password);
29                                                 ⌨ UserId         🔍 ▾ ""
30                     client.Send(new MailMessage("example@example.com", emailTo, subject, message));
31                 }
32                 return Task.CompletedTask;
33             }
34
35         }
```

You have seen how to configure your applications and services by using the built-in Configuration API of ASP.NET Core 2.0, which allows you to write less code and to be much more productive, while providing a far more elegant and more maintainable solution in the end.

Using logging

When you are developing your applications, you use one of the well-known integrated development environments such as Visual Studio 2017 or Visual Studio Code, as described in the beginning chapters of the book. You do this every day, and most of the things you do become reflexes and you do them automatically after some time.

It is natural for you to be able to debug your applications and understand what is happening during runtime, by using the advanced debugging features of Visual Studio 2017, for example. Looking up variable values, seeing what methods get called in what order, understanding what instances are injected, and capturing exceptions, are key to building applications that are robust and respond to business needs.

Then, when deploying your applications to production environments, you suddenly miss all of those features. Rarely will you find a production environment where Visual Studio is installed, but, errors and unexpected behaviors will happen and you will need to be able to understand and fix them as fast as possible.

That is where logging and telemetry come into play. By instrumenting your applications and logging when entering and when leaving methods, as well as important variable values or any kind of information you consider important during runtime, you will be able to go to the application log and see what is happening in the production environment in case of problems.

In the previous section, we added an **Email Service** for sending emails and configured it using external configuration files. What if the configured SMTP server is not responding? What if we forgot to update the server settings from development to production? Well, for now, we will just get an exception message displayed in the browser:

In this section, we are going to show you how to use logging and exception handling for providing a better, more industrialized solution to this type of problem.

ASP.NET Core 2.0 provides built-in support for logging to the following targets:

- Azure AppServices dairy
- Console
- Windows Event Source
- Trace
- Debugger output
- Application Insights

But files, databases, and logging services are not supported by default. If you want to send your logs to these targets, you need to use a third-party logger solution such as log4net, Serilog, NLog, Apache, ELMAH, or Loggr.

You can also easily create your own provider by implementing the `ILoggerProvider` interface, which is what you are going to see here:

1. Add a new **Class Library (.NET Core)** project to the solution and call it `TicTacToe.Logging` (delete the autogenerated `Class1.cs` file):

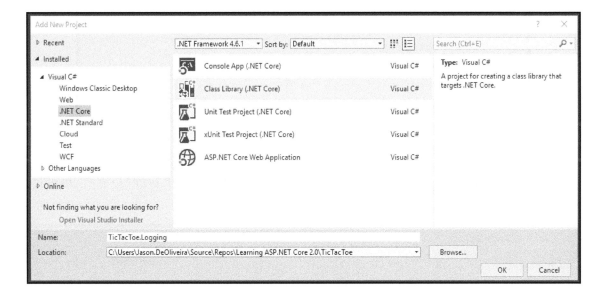

2. Add the NuGet packages `Microsoft.Extensions.Logging` and `Microsoft.Extensions.Logging.Configuration` via the **NuGet Package Manager**:

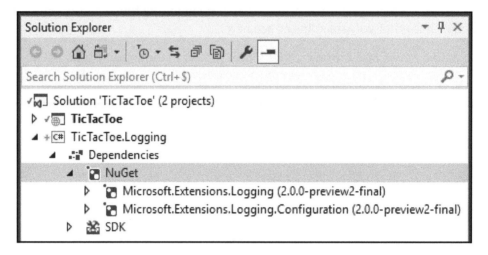

3. Add a project reference in the **TicTacToe Web Application** project for being able to use assets from the `TicTacToe.Logging` class library:

4. Add a new class called `LogEntry`. This will contain the log data:

```
internal class LogEntry
{
  public int EventId { get; internal set; }
  public string Message { get; internal set; }
  public string LogLevel { get; internal set; }
  public DateTime CreatedTime { get; internal set; }
}
```

5. Add a new class called `FileLoggerHelper`. This will be used for file operations:

```
internal class FileLoggerHelper
{
  private string fileName;

  public FileLoggerHelper(string fileName)
  {
    this.fileName = fileName;
  }

  static ReaderWriterLock locker = new ReaderWriterLock();

  internal void InsertLog(LogEntry logEntry)
  {
    var directory = System.IO.Path.GetDirectoryName(fileName);

    if (!System.IO.Directory.Exists(directory))
     System.IO.Directory.CreateDirectory(directory);

    try
    {
      locker.AcquireWriterLock(int.MaxValue);
      System.IO.File.AppendAllText(fileName,
        $"{logEntry.CreatedTime} {logEntry.EventId}
        {logEntry.LogLevel} {logEntry.Message}" +
        Environment.NewLine);
    }
    finally
    {
      locker.ReleaseWriterLock();
    }
  }

}
```

6. Add a new class called `FileLogger` and implement the `ILogger` interface:

```
public sealed class FileLogger : ILogger
{
  private string _categoryName;
  private Func<string, LogLevel, bool> _filter;
  private string _fileName;
  private FileLoggerHelper _helper;

  public FileLogger(string categoryName, Func<string, LogLevel,
   bool> filter, string fileName)
  {
    _categoryName = categoryName;
    _filter = filter;
    _fileName = fileName;
    _helper = new FileLoggerHelper(fileName);
  }

  public IDisposable BeginScope<TState>(TState state)
  {
    return null;
  }

  public void Log<TState>(LogLevel logLevel, EventId eventId,
   TState state, Exception exception, Func<TState, Exception,
   string> formatter)
  {
    if (!IsEnabled(logLevel))
    {
      return;
    }

    if (formatter == null)
    {
      throw new ArgumentNullException(nameof(formatter));
    }

    var message = formatter(state, exception);

    if (string.IsNullOrEmpty(message))
    {
      return;
    }
    if (exception != null)
    {
      message += "\n" + exception.ToString();
    }
```

```
   var logEntry = new LogEntry
   {
     Message = message,
     EventId = eventId.Id,
     LogLevel = logLevel.ToString(),
     CreatedTime = DateTime.UtcNow
   };

   _helper.InsertLog(logEntry);
 }

 public bool IsEnabled(LogLevel logLevel)
 {
   return (_filter == null || _filter(_categoryName, logLevel));
 }
}
```

7. Add a new class called `FileLoggerProvider` and implement the `ILoggerProvider` interface. This will be injected later:

```
public class FileLoggerProvider : ILoggerProvider
{
  private readonly Func<string, LogLevel, bool> _filter;
  private string _fileName;

  public FileLoggerProvider(Func<string, LogLevel,
   bool> filter, string fileName)
  {
    _filter = filter;
    _fileName = fileName;
  }

  public ILogger CreateLogger(string categoryName)
  {
    return new FileLogger(categoryName, _filter, _fileName);
  }

  public void Dispose()
  {
  }
}
```

8. To simplify calling the **File Logging Provider** from the web application, we need to add a static class called `FileLoggerExtensions` (with configuration section, filename, and log verbosity level as parameters):

```
public static class FileLoggerExtensions
{
  const long DefaultFileSizeLimitBytes = 1024 * 1024 * 1024;
  const int DefaultRetainedFileCountLimit = 31;

  public static ILoggingBuilder AddFile(this ILoggingBuilder
   loggerBuilder, IConfigurationSection configuration)
  {
    if (loggerBuilder == null)
    {
      throw new ArgumentNullException(nameof(loggerBuilder));
    }

    if (configuration == null)
    {
      throw new ArgumentNullException(nameof(configuration));
    }

    var minimumLevel = LogLevel.Information;

    var levelSection = configuration["Logging:LogLevel"];

    if (!string.IsNullOrWhiteSpace(levelSection))
    {
      if (!Enum.TryParse(levelSection, out minimumLevel))
      {
        System.Diagnostics.Debug.WriteLine("The minimum level
          setting `{0}` is invalid", levelSection);
        minimumLevel = LogLevel.Information;
      }
    }

    return loggerBuilder.AddFile(configuration[
      "Logging:FilePath"], (category, logLevel) =>
      (logLevel >= minimumLevel), minimumLevel);
  }

  public static ILoggingBuilder AddFile(this ILoggingBuilder
   loggerBuilder, string filePath, Func<string, LogLevel,
   bool> filter, LogLevel minimumLevel = LogLevel.Information)
  {
    if (String.IsNullOrEmpty(filePath)) throw
     new ArgumentNullException(nameof(filePath));
```

```
    var fileInfo = new System.IO.FileInfo(filePath);

    if (!fileInfo.Directory.Exists)
      fileInfo.Directory.Create();

    loggerBuilder.AddProvider(new FileLoggerProvider(filter,
     filePath));

    return loggerBuilder;
  }

  public static ILoggingBuilder AddFile(this ILoggingBuilder
   loggerBuilder, string filePath,
   LogLevel minimumLevel = LogLevel.Information)
  {
    if (String.IsNullOrEmpty(filePath)) throw
     new ArgumentNullException(nameof(filePath));

    var fileInfo = new System.IO.FileInfo(filePath);

    if (!fileInfo.Directory.Exists)
      fileInfo.Directory.Create();

    loggerBuilder.AddProvider(new FileLoggerProvider((category,
     logLevel) => (logLevel >= minimumLevel), filePath));

    return loggerBuilder;
  }
}
```

9. In the **TicTacToe Web Project**, add two new options called
   `LoggingProviderOption` and `LoggingOptions` to the `Options` folder:

```
public class LoggingProviderOption
{
  public string Name { get; set; }
  public string Parameters { get; set; }
  public int LogLevel { get; set; }
}
public class LoggingOptions
{
  public LoggingProviderOption[] Providers { get; set; }
}
```

10. In the **TicTacToe Web Project**, add a new extension called `ConfigureLoggingExtension` to the `Extensions` folder:

```
using Microsoft.Extensions.Configuration;
using Microsoft.Extensions.Logging;
using TicTacToe.Logging;
...
public static class ConfigureLoggingExtension
{
  public static ILoggingBuilder AddLoggingConfiguration(this
   ILoggingBuilder loggingBuilder, IConfiguration configuration)
  {
    var loggingOptions = new LoggingOptions();
    configuration.GetSection("Logging").Bind(loggingOptions);

    foreach (var provider in loggingOptions.Providers)
    {
      switch (provider.Name.ToLower())
      {
        case "console":
        {
          loggingBuilder.AddConsole();
          break;
        }
        case "file":
        {
          string filePath = System.IO.Path.Combine(
            System.IO.Directory.GetCurrentDirectory(), "logs",
            $"TicTacToe_{System.DateTime.Now.ToString(
              "ddMMyyHHmm")}.log");
          loggingBuilder.AddFile(filePath,
           (LogLevel)provider.LogLevel);
          break;
        }
        default:
        {
          break;
        }
      }
    }

    return loggingBuilder;
  }
}
```

11. Go to the `Program` class of the **TicTacToe Web Application** project, update the `BuildWebHost` method, and call the extension from before:

```
public static IWebHost BuildWebHost(string[] args) =>
  WebHost.CreateDefaultBuilder(args)
    .CaptureStartupErrors(true)
    .UseStartup<Startup>()
    .PreferHostingUrls(true)
    .UseUrls("http://localhost:5000")
    .UseApplicationInsights()
    .ConfigureLogging((hostingcontext, logging) =>
    {
      logging.AddLoggingConfiguration(
        hostingcontext.Configuration);
    })
    .Build();
```

Don't forget to add the following using statement at the beginning of the class:
```
using TicTacToe.Extensions;
```

12. Add a new section called `Logging` to the `appsettings.json` file:

```
"Logging": {
  "Providers": [
    {
      "Name": "Console",
      "LogLevel": "1"
    },
    {
      "Name": "File",
      "LogLevel": "2"
    }
  ],
  "MinimumLevel": 1
}
```

13. Start the application and verify that a new log file has been created in a folder called `logs` within the application folder:

This is the first step, easy and quickly done. You now have a log file to which you can write your logs. You will see that it is just as easy to use the integrated logging functionalities to create logs from anywhere within your ASP.NET Core 2.0 applications (`Controllers`, `Services`, and more).

Let's quickly add some logs to the *Tic-Tac-Toe* application:

1. Update the `UserRegistrationController` constructor implementation:

```
readonly IUserService _userService;
readonly IEmailService _emailService;
readonly ILogger<UserRegistrationController> _logger;
public UserRegistrationController(IUserService userService,
 IEmailService emailService, ILogger<UserRegistrationController>
 logger)
{
  _userService = userService;
  _emailService = emailService;
  _logger = logger;
}
```

2. Update the `EmailConfirmation` method in the `UserRegistrationController` and add a log at the start of the method:

```
_logger.LogInformation($"##Start## Email confirmation
 process for {email}");
```

3. Update the **Email Service** implementation, add a logger to its constructor, and add a new `SendMail` method:

```
public class EmailService : IEmailService
{
  private EmailServiceOptions _emailServiceOptions;
  readonly ILogger<EmailService> _logger;
  public EmailService(IOptions<EmailServiceOptions>
   emailServiceOptions, ILogger<EmailService> logger)
  {
    _emailServiceOptions = emailServiceOptions.Value;
    _logger = logger;
  }

  public Task SendEmail(string emailTo, string subject,
   string message)
  {
    try
    {
      _logger.LogInformation($"##Start sendEmail## Start
       sending Email to {emailTo}");

      using (var client =
        new SmtpClient(_emailServiceOptions.MailServer,
        int.Parse(_emailServiceOptions.MailPort)))
      {
        if (bool.Parse(_emailServiceOptions.UseSSL) == true)
            client.EnableSsl = true;

        if (!string.IsNullOrEmpty(_emailServiceOptions.UserId))
            client.Credentials =
             new NetworkCredential(_emailServiceOptions.UserId,
             _emailServiceOptions.Password);

            client.Send(new MailMessage("example@example.com",
             emailTo, subject, message));
      }
    }
    catch (Exception ex)
    {
      _logger.LogError($"Cannot send email {ex}");
    }

    return Task.CompletedTask;
  }
}
```

4. Open the generated log file and analyze its contents:

```
8/3/2017 8:15:10 PM 1 Information Executing action method TicTacToe.Controllers.UserRegistrationController.Index (TicTacToe) with arguments (TicTacToe.Models.UserModel) -
ModelState is Valid
8/3/2017 8:15:10 PM 1 Information Executing RedirectResult, redirecting to /UserRegistration/EmailConfirmation?Email=example@example.com.
8/3/2017 8:15:10 PM 2 Information Executed action TicTacToe.Controllers.UserRegistrationController.Index (TicTacToe) in 3.0544ms
03/08/2017 20:15:10 2 Information Request finished in 5.7796ms 302
03/08/2017 20:15:10 1 Information Request starting HTTP/1.1 GET http://localhost:52872/UserRegistration/EmailConfirmation?Email=example@example.com
8/3/2017 8:15:10 PM 1 Information Executing action method TicTacToe.Controllers.UserRegistrationController.EmailConfirmation (TicTacToe) with arguments
(example@example.com) - ModelState is Valid
8/3/2017 8:15:10 PM 0 Information ##Start## Email confirmation process for example@example.com
8/3/2017 8:15:10 PM 0 Information ##Start## Sending email to :example@example.com subject:Tic-Tac-Toe Email Confirmation message:Thank you for your registration on our
web site, please click here to confirm your email HTTP/1.1://localhost:52872/UserRegistration/ConfirmEmail?email=example@example.com
8/3/2017 8:15:11 PM 0 Error ##Failed## Sending email to example@example.com failed, reason:System.Net.Mail.SmtpException: Failure sending mail. --->
System.Net.Internals.SocketExceptionFactory+ExtendedSocketException: No connection could be made because the target machine actively refused it 127.0.0.1:25
   at System.Net.Sockets.Socket.DoConnect(EndPoint endPointSnapshot, SocketAddress socketAddress)
   at System.Net.Sockets.Socket.Connect(EndPoint remoteEP)
   at System.Net.Sockets.TcpClient.Connect(IPEndPoint remoteEP)
   at System.Net.Sockets.TcpClient.Connect(String hostname, Int32 port)
--- End of stack trace from previous location where exception was thrown ---
   at System.Runtime.ExceptionServices.ExceptionDispatchInfo.Throw()
   at System.Net.Sockets.TcpClient.Connect(String hostname, Int32 port)
   at System.Net.Mail.SmtpConnection.GetConnection(String host, Int32 port)
   at System.Net.Mail.SmtpTransport.GetConnection(String host, Int32 port)
   at System.Net.Mail.SmtpClient.GetConnection()
   at System.Net.Mail.SmtpClient.Send(MailMessage message)
   --- End of inner exception stack trace ---
   at System.Net.Mail.SmtpClient.Send(MailMessage message)
   at TicTacToe.Services.EmailService.SendEmail(String emailTo, String subject, String message) in C:\Users\Jason.DeOliveira\Source\Repos\Learning ASP.NET Core
2.0\TicTacToe\TicTacToe\Services\EmailService.cs:line 65
8/3/2017 8:15:11 PM 0 Information ##End## Sending email to :example@example.com subject:Tic-Tac-Toe Email Confirmation message:Thank you for your registration on our web
site, please click here to confirm your email HTTP/1.1://localhost:52872/UserRegistration/ConfirmEmail?email=example@example.com
8/3/2017 8:15:11 PM 1 Information Executing ViewResult, running view at path /Views/UserRegistration/EmailConfirmation.cshtml.
8/3/2017 8:15:11 PM 2 Information Executed action TicTacToe.Controllers.UserRegistrationController.EmailConfirmation (TicTacToe) in 1047.9871ms
03/08/2017 20:15:11 2 Information Request finished in 1051.5675ms 200 text/html; charset=utf-8
03/08/2017 20:15:13 1 Information Request starting HTTP/1.1 GET http://localhost:52872/GameInvitationConfirmation
03/08/2017 20:15:13 2 Information Request finished in 3.1004ms 101
```

Implementing advanced dependency injection concepts

In the previous chapter, you saw how **dependency injection** (**DI**) works and how to use the constructor injection method. But, if you need to inject many instances during runtime, this method can be quite cumbersome and can make it complicated to understand and maintain your code.

Therefore, you can use a more advanced technique of DI called **method injection**. This allows accessing instances directly from within your code.

In the following example, you are going to add a new service for handling game invitations and update the *Tic-Tac-Toe* application for being able to send emails for contacting other users to join a game, while using method injection:

1. Add a new service called `GameInvitationService` in the `Services` folder for managing game invitations (adding, updating, removing, and more):

```
public class GameInvitationService
{
  private static ConcurrentBag<GameInvitationModel>
   _gameInvitations;
  public GameInvitationService()
  {
    _gameInvitations = new ConcurrentBag<GameInvitationModel>();
  }

  public Task<GameInvitationModel> Add(GameInvitationModel
   gameInvitationModel)
  {
    gameInvitationModel.Id = Guid.NewGuid();
    _gameInvitations.Add(gameInvitationModel);
    return Task.FromResult(gameInvitationModel);
  }
  public Task Update(GameInvitationModel gameInvitationModel)
  {
    _gameInvitations = new ConcurrentBag<GameInvitationModel>
    (_gameInvitations.Where(x => x.Id != gameInvitationModel.Id))
    {
      gameInvitationModel
    };
    return Task.CompletedTask;
  }

  public Task<GameInvitationModel> Get(Guid id)
  {
    return Task.FromResult(_gameInvitations.FirstOrDefault(
     x => x.Id == id));
  }
}
```

2. Extract the `IGameInvitationService` interface:

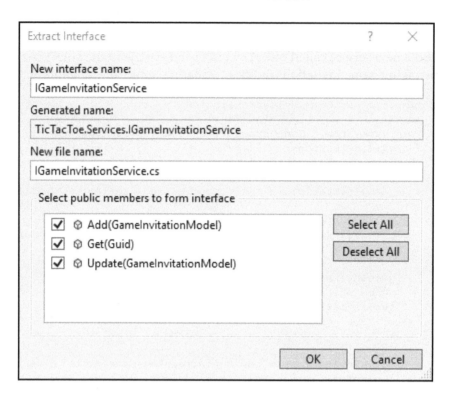

3. Add the new **Game Invitation Service** to the `ConfigureServices` method of the `Startup` class (we want a single application instance, so add it as Singleton):

```
services.AddSingleton<IGameInvitationService,
  GameInvitationService>();
```

4. Update the `Index` method in the `GameInvitationController` and inject an instance of the **Game Invitation Service** via method injection by using the `RequestServices` provider:

```
[HttpPost]
public IActionResult Index(GameInvitationModel
  gameInvitationModel, [FromServices]IEmailService emailService)
{
  var gameInvitationService =
    Request.HttpContext.RequestServices.GetService
      <IGameInvitationService>();
  if (ModelState.IsValid)
```

```
    {
      emailService.SendEmail(gameInvitationModel.EmailTo,
       _stringLocalizer["Invitation for playing a Tic-Tac-Toe game"],
       _stringLocalizer[$"Hello, you have been invited to play
        the Tic-Tac-Toe game by {0}. For joining the game,
        please click here {1}", gameInvitationModel.InvitedBy,
        Url.Action("GameInvitationConfirmation",
        "GameInvitation", new { gameInvitationModel.InvitedBy,
         gameInvitationModel.EmailTo }, Request.Scheme,
         Request.Host.ToString())]);
      var invitation =
       gameInvitationService.Add(gameInvitationModel).Result;
      return RedirectToAction("GameInvitationConfirmation",
       new { id = invitation.Id });
    }
    return View(gameInvitationModel);
}
```

 Don't forget to add the following using statement at the beginning of the
class: `using Microsoft.Extensions.DependencyInjection;`,
otherwise the `.GetService<IGameInvitationService>();` method
cannot be used and you will get build errors.

5. Add a new method called `GameInvitationConfirmation` to the
   `GameInvitationController`:

```
[HttpGet]
public IActionResult GameInvitationConfirmation(Guid id,
 [FromServices]IGameInvitationService gameInvitationService)
{
  var gameInvitation = gameInvitationService.Get(id).Result;
  return View(gameInvitation);
}
```

6. Create a new view for the `GameInvitationConfirmation` method you added
   previously. This will display a waiting message to the user:

```
@model TicTacToe.Models.GameInvitationModel
@{
    ViewData["Title"] = "GameInvitationConfirmation";
    Layout = "~/Views/Shared/_Layout.cshtml";
}
<h1>@Localizer["You have invited {0} to play a Tic-Tac-Toe game
 with you, please wait until the user is connected",
 Model.EmailTo]</h1>
@section Scripts{
```

```
      <script>
        $(document).ready(function () {
          GameInvitationConfirmation('@Model.Id');
        });
      </script>
    }
```

7. Add a new method called `GameInvitationConfirmation` to the `scripts1.js` file. You can use the same basic structure we have used for the existing `EmailConfirmation` method:

```javascript
function GameInvitationConfirmation(id) {
  if (window.WebSocket) {
    alert("Websockets are enabled");
    openSocket(id, "GameInvitation");
  }
  else {
    alert("Websockets are not enabled");
    interval = setInterval(() => {
      CheckGameInvitationConfirmationStatus(id);
    }, 5000);
  }
}
```

8. Add a method called `CheckGameInvitationConfirmationStatus` to the `scripts2.js` file. You can use the same basic structure we have used for the existing `CheckEmailConfirmationStatus` method:

```javascript
function CheckGameInvitationConfirmationStatus(id) {
  $.get("/GameInvitationConfirmation?id=" + id, function (data) {
    if (data.result === "OK") {
      if (interval !== null)
        clearInterval(interval);
      window.location.href = "/GameSession/Index/" + id;
    }
  });
}
```

9. Update the `openSocket` method in the `scripts2.js` file and add the specific Game Invitation case:

```javascript
var openSocket = function (parameter, strAction) {
  if (interval !== null)
  clearInterval(interval);

  var protocol = location.protocol === "https:" ? "wss:" : "ws:";
```

```
var operation = "";
var wsUri = "";
if (strAction == "Email") {
  wsUri = protocol + "//" + window.location.host +
    "/CheckEmailConfirmationStatus";
  operation = "CheckEmailConfirmationStatus";
}
else if (strAction == "GameInvitation") {
  wsUri = protocol + "//" + window.location.host +
    "/GameInvitationConfirmation";
  operation = "CheckGameInvitationConfirmationStatus";
}

var socket = new WebSocket(wsUri);
socket.onmessage = function (response) {
  console.log(response);
  if (strAction == "Email" && response.data == "OK") {
    window.location.href = "/GameInvitation?email=" + parameter;
  }
  else if (strAction == "GameInvitation") {
    var data = $.parseJSON(response.data);

    if (data.Result == "OK")
      window.location.href = "/GameSession/Index/" + data.Id;
  }
};

socket.onopen = function () {
  var json = JSON.stringify({
    "Operation": operation,
    "Parameters": parameter
  });

  socket.send(json);
};

socket.onclose = function (event) {
};
};
```

10. Add a new method called `ProcessGameInvitationConfirmation` in the
    Communication Middleware. This will process **Game Invitation Requests**
    without using WebSockets, for browsers not supporting it:

```
private async Task ProcessGameInvitationConfirmation(HttpContext
  context)
{
```

```
var id = context.Request.Query["id"];
if (string.IsNullOrEmpty(id))
  await context.Response.WriteAsync("BadRequest:Id is required");

var gameInvitationService =
  context.RequestServices.GetService<IGameInvitationService>();
var gameInvitationModel =
  await gameInvitationService.Get(Guid.Parse(id));

if (gameInvitationModel.IsConfirmed)
  await context.Response.WriteAsync(
   JsonConvert.SerializeObject(new
 {
   Result = "OK",
   Email = gameInvitationModel.InvitedBy,
   gameInvitationModel.EmailTo
 }));
 else
 {
   await context.Response.WriteAsync(
     "WaitGameInvitationConfirmation");
 }
}
```

Don't forget to add the following using statement at the beginning of the class:
`using Microsoft.Extensions.DependencyInjection;`

11. Add a new method called `ProcessGameInvitationConfirmation` with additional parameters to the **Communication Middleware**. This will process **Game Invitation Requests** while using WebSockets for browsers supporting it:

```
private async Task
 ProcessGameInvitationConfirmation(HttpContext context,
 WebSocket webSocket, CancellationToken ct, string parameters)
{
  var gameInvitationService =
    context.RequestServices.GetService<IGameInvitationService>();
  var id = Guid.Parse(parameters);
  var gameInvitationModel = await gameInvitationService.Get(id);
  while (!ct.IsCancellationRequested &&
         !webSocket.CloseStatus.HasValue &&
          gameInvitationModel?.IsConfirmed == false)
  {
    await SendStringAsync(webSocket,
     JsonConvert.SerializeObject(new
```

```
    {
      Result = "OK",
      Email = gameInvitationModel.InvitedBy,
      gameInvitationModel.EmailTo,
      gameInvitationModel.Id
    }), ct);

    Task.Delay(500).Wait();

    gameInvitationModel = await gameInvitationService.Get(id);
  }
}
```

12. Update the `Invoke` method in the **Communication Middleware**. This has to work with email confirmations and game invitation confirmations from now on, with and without WebSockets:

```
public async Task Invoke(HttpContext context)
{
  if (context.WebSockets.IsWebSocketRequest)
  {
    ...
    switch (command.Operation.ToString())
    {
      ...
      case "CheckGameInvitationConfirmationStatus":
      {
        await ProcessGameInvitationConfirmation(context,
          webSocket, ct, command.Parameters.ToString());
        break;
      }
    }
  }
  else if (context.Request.Path.Equals(
    "/CheckEmailConfirmationStatus"))
  {
    await ProcessEmailConfirmation(context);
  }
  else if (context.Request.Path.Equals(
    "/CheckGameInvitationConfirmationStatus"))
  {
    await ProcessGameInvitationConfirmation(context);
  }
  else
  {
    await _next?.Invoke(context);
  }
```

```
}
```

In this section, you have seen how to use method injection in your ASP.NET Core 2.0 web applications. This is the preferred method for injecting your services and you should use it whenever applicable.

Also, you have advanced well with the implementation of the *Tic-Tac-Toe* game. Mostly everything around user registration, email confirmation, game invitation, and game invitation confirmation has now been implemented.

Building once and running on multiple environments

After building your applications, you have to think about deploying them to different environments. As you have already seen in the previous section on configuration, you can use configuration files for changing the configuration of your services and even your application.

In the case of multiple environments, you have to duplicate the `appsettings.json` file for each environment and name it accordingly, `appsettings.{EnvironmentName}.json`.

ASP.NET Core 2.0 will automatically retrieve the configuration settings in hierarchical order, first from the common `appsettings.json` file and then from the corresponding `appsettings.{EnvironmentName}.json` file, while adding or replacing values if necessary.

However, developing conditional code that uses different components based on different deployment environments and configurations, seems to be complicated at first. In traditional applications, you must create a lot of code to handle all of the different cases by yourself and then maintain it.

In ASP.NET Core 2.0, you have a vast number of internal functionalities at your disposal to achieve this goal. You can then simply use environment variables (development, staging, production, and more) for indicating a specific runtime environment, thus configuring your application for that environment.

As you will see during this section, you can use specific method names and even class names to use existing injection and override mechanisms, provided by ASP.NET Core 2.0 out of the box, for configuring your applications.

In the following example, we are adding an environment-specific component to the application (SendGrid), which only has to be used if the application is deployed to a specific production environment (Azure):

1. Add the **SendGrid NuGet Package** to the project. This will be used for future Azure production deployments of the *Tic-Tac-Toe* application:

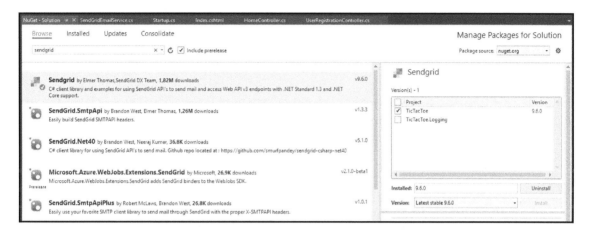

2. Add a new service called SendGridEmailService within the Services folder. This will be used for sending emails via SendGrid. Have it inherit the IEmailService interface and implement the specific SendEmail method:

```
public class SendGridEmailService : IEmailService
{
  private EmailServiceOptions _emailServiceOptions;
  private ILogger<EmailService> _logger;
  public SendGridEmailService(IOptions<EmailServiceOptions>
    emailServiceOptions, ILogger<EmailService> logger)
  {
    _emailServiceOptions = emailServiceOptions.Value;
    _logger = logger;
  }

  public Task SendEmail(string emailTo, string subject,
    string message)
  {
    _logger.LogInformation($"##Start## Sending email via
      SendGrid to :{emailTo} subject:{subject} message:{message}");
    var client =
      new SendGrid.SendGridClient(
        _emailServiceOptions.RemoteServerAPI);
```

```
            var sendGridMessage =
              new SendGrid.Helpers.Mail.SendGridMessage
            {
              From = new SendGrid.Helpers.Mail.EmailAddress(
              _emailServiceOptions.UserId)
            };
            sendGridMessage.AddTo(emailTo);
            sendGridMessage.Subject = subject;
            sendGridMessage.HtmlContent = message;
            client.SendEmailAsync(sendGridMessage);
            return Task.CompletedTask;
        }
    }
```

3. Add a new extension method for being able to more easily declare specific **Email Services** for specific environments. For that, go to the `Extensions` folder and add a new `EmailServiceExtension`:

```
    public static class EmailServiceExtension
    {
      public static IServiceCollection AddEmailService(
        this IServiceCollection services, IHostingEnvironment
        hostingEnvironment, IConfiguration configuration)
      {
        services.Configure<EmailServiceOptions>
        (configuration.GetSection("Email"));
        if (hostingEnvironment.IsDevelopment() ||
            hostingEnvironment.IsStaging())
        {
          services.AddSingleton<IEmailService, EmailService>();
        }
        else
        {
          services.AddSingleton<IEmailService, SendGridEmailService>();
        }
        return services;
      }
    }
```

4. Update the `Startup` class to use the created assets from before. For better readability and maintainability, we will go even further and create a dedicated `ConfigureServices` method for each environment we have to support, remove the existing `ConfigureServices` method, and add the following environment-specific `ConfigureServices` methods:

```
    public IConfiguration _configuration { get; }
```

```
public IHostingEnvironment _hostingEnvironment { get; }
public Startup(IConfiguration configuration,
 IHostingEnvironment hostingEnvironment)
{
  _configuration = configuration;
  _hostingEnvironment = hostingEnvironment;
}
public void ConfigureCommonServices(IServiceCollection services)
{
  services.AddLocalization(options =>
   options.ResourcesPath = "Localization");
  services.AddMvc().AddViewLocalization(
   LanguageViewLocationExpanderFormat.Suffix, options =>
    options.ResourcesPath =
     "Localization").AddDataAnnotationsLocalization();
  services.AddSingleton<IUserService, UserService>();
  services.AddSingleton<IGameInvitationService,
   GameInvitationService>();
  services.Configure<EmailServiceOptions>
   (_configuration.GetSection("Email"));
  services.AddEmailService(_hostingEnvironment, _configuration);
  services.AddRouting();
  services.AddSession(o =>
  {
    o.IdleTimeout = TimeSpan.FromMinutes(30);
  });
}

public void ConfigureDevelopmentServices(
 IServiceCollection services)
{
  ConfigureCommonServices(services);
}

public void ConfigureStagingServices(
 IServiceCollection services)
{
  ConfigureCommonServices(services);
}

public void ConfigureProductionServices(
 IServiceCollection services)
{
  ConfigureCommonServices(services);
}
```

Note that you could also apply the same approach to the `Configure` method in the `Startup` class. For that, you just remove the existing `Configure` method and add new methods for the environments you would like to support, such as `ConfigureDevelopment`, `ConfigureStaging`, and `ConfigureProduction`. The best practice would be to combine all of the common code into a `ConfigureCommon` method and call it from the other methods, as shown below for the specific `ConfigureServices` methods.

5. Start the application by pressing *F5* and verify that everything is still running correctly. You should see that the added methods will automatically be used and that the application is fully functional.

That was easy and straightforward! No specific conditional code for the environments, nothing complicated to evolve and to maintain, just very clear and easy-to-understand methods that contain the environment name they have been developed for. A very clean solution to the problem of building once and running on multiple environments.

But, that is not all! What if we told you that you do not need to have a single Startup class? What if you could have a dedicated Startup class for each environment with only the code applicable to its context? That would be great, right? Well, that is exactly what ASP.NET Core 2.0 provides.

To be able to use dedicated Startup classes for each environment, you just have to update the Program class, the main entry point for ASP.NET Core 2.0 applications. You change a single line in the `BuildWebHost` method for passing the assembly name `.UseStartup("TicTacToe")` instead of `.UseStartup<Startup>()`, and then you can use this fantastic feature:

```
public static IWebHost BuildWebHost(string[] args) =>
   WebHost.CreateDefaultBuilder(args)
     .CaptureStartupErrors(true)
     .UseStartup("TicTacToe")
     .PreferHostingUrls(true)
     .UseUrls("http://localhost:5000")
     .UseApplicationInsights()
     .Build();
   }
 }
```

Now, you can add dedicated Startup classes for the different environments, such as `StartupDevelopment`, `StartupStaging`, and `StartupProduction`. As with the method approach before, they will be automatically used; nothing else needs to be done on your side. Just update the `Program` class, implement your environment-specific Startup classes, and it works. ASP.NET Core 2.0 really makes our lives much easier by providing these useful features.

Summary

In this chapter, you have learned some more advanced concepts of ASP.NET Core 2.0 and implemented some of the missing components of the *Tic-Tac-Toe* application.

At the beginning, you created the client-side parts of the *Tic-Tac-Toe* web application using JavaScript. We have explored how to optimize your web applications by using bundling and minification, as well as WebSockets for real-time communication scenarios.

Furthermore, you have seen how to benefit from the integrated user and session handling, which was shown in an easy-to-understand example.

Then, we introduced globalization and localization for multi-lingual user interfaces, application and service configuration, as well logging to better understand what is happening within your applications during runtime.

At the end, we illustrated via a practical example how to build your applications once and then adapt them to different environments by using the concepts of multiple `ConfigureServices` and `Configure` methods, as well as multiple `Startup` classes depending on deployment targets.

In the next chapter, we will talk about ASP.NET Core MVC, Razor in MVC (areas, layouts, partial views, and more), Razor Pages, and the View Engine.

6
Creating MVC Applications

Most of today's modern web applications are based on the **Model View Controller** pattern, also commonly called **MVC**. You should have noticed that we have also used it in the previous chapters for building the foundations of the *Tic-Tac-Toe* sample application.

So, you have already worked with it in multiple places, without even knowing what was happening in the background and why it was important to apply this specific pattern.

An initial pre-version of ASP.NET MVC was released in 2007. It was conceived and designed by Scott Guthrie, who also co-created ASP.NET as such, as well as Phil Haack, who led the development team. The first packaged official version was ASP.NET MVC 1, which was released in 2009.

Since then, the ASP.NET MVC framework has proven itself over the years, until effectively becoming the market standard. Microsoft has successfully evolved it into an industrialized and efficient framework with high developer productivity.

There are many examples of web applications that take full advantage of the multiple features MVC has to offer. Two great examples are Stack Overflow and CodePlex. They provide information to developers and have a very high user base, with the need to scale to thousands, or even millions, of users at the same time.

In this chapter, we will cover the following topics:

- Understanding the Model View Controller pattern
- Creating dedicated layouts for multiple devices
- Using View Pages, Partial Views, View Components, and Tag Helpers
- Dividing web application into multiple Areas
- Applying advanced concepts such as view engines, unit tests, and integration tests

Understanding the Model View Controller pattern

The MVC pattern separates applications into three main layers—models, views, and controllers. One of the benefits of this pattern is the separation of concerns, also called the **Single Responsibility Principle** (**SRP**), which makes it possible to develop, debug, and test application features independently.

When using the MVC pattern, a user request is routed to a Controller, which will use a Model for retrieving data and performing actions. The Controller selects a corresponding view for display to the user, while providing it with the necessary data from the Model.

There is less impact if a layer (for example, Views) changes, since it is now loosely coupled to the other layers of your applications (for example, controllers and models).

It is also much easier to test the different layers of your applications. In the end, you will have better maintainability and more robust code by using this pattern:

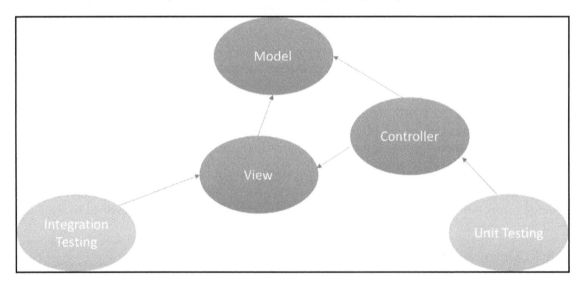

Models

A Model contains the logical data structures as well as the data of your applications, independent from their visual representations. In the context of ASP.NET Core 2.0, it also supports localization and validation, as you have seen in the previous chapters.

Models can be created in the same project with your views and controllers or in a dedicated project for the better organization. Scaffolding uses models for auto-generating views. Furthermore, models can be used to bind forms to entity objects automatically.

In terms of data persistence, various data storage targets can be used. In the case of databases, you should be using Entity Framework, which will be introduced in one of the following chapters of this book. Models are serialized when working with Web APIs.

Views

A View provides the visual representation and user interface elements for your applications. When using ASP.NET Core 2.0, views are written using HMTL and Razor markup. They generally have a `.cshtml` file extension.

A View either contains a complete web page, a web page part (called partial view), or a layout. In ASP.NET Core 2.0, a View can be separated into logical subdivisions with their own behaviors, which are called View Components.

Additionally, Tag Helpers allow you to centralize and encapsulate HTML code in a single tag and use it across all your applications. ASP.NET Core 2.0 already includes many existing Tag Helpers for improving developer productivity.

Controllers

A Controller manages the interactions between models and views. It provides the logical behavior and business logic for your applications. It chooses which View has to be rendered for a specific user request.

Generally speaking, since controllers provide the main application entry point, this means that they are controlling how applications should respond to user requests.

Unit tests

The main goal of unit tests is to validate the business logic within controllers. Normally, unit tests are put into their own external unit tests projects, while multiple test frameworks are available (XUnit, NUnit, or MSTest).

As described previously, since everything is completely decoupled when using the MVC pattern, you can test your controllers at any point independently from the other parts of your applications by using unit tests.

Integration tests

End-to-end validation of application functionalities is done via integration tests. They check that everything is working as expected from an application user point of view. Therefore, controllers and their corresponding views are tested together.

As with unit tests, integration tests are normally put into their own testing projects and you can use a variety of testing frameworks (XUnit, NUnit, or MSTest). You will, however, also need to use a web server automation toolkit for this type of test.

Creating dedicated layouts for multiple devices

Modern web applications use web page layouts to provide a consistent and coherent style. It is best practice to use HTML in combination with CSS to define this layout. In ASP.NET Core 2.0, the common web page layout definition is centralized in a layout page. This page includes all the common user interface elements, such as the header, the menu, the sidebar, and the footer.

Furthermore, common CSS and JavaScript files are referenced in the layout page, so that they can be used throughout your whole application. This allows you to reduce code in your views, thus helping you to apply the **DRY** (**Don't Repeat Yourself**) principle.

We have been using a layout page since the very early versions of the *Tic-Tac-Toe* sample application. It was first introduced when we added it in a previous chapter. We have used it since to give our application a modern look, as you can see here:

Let's look at the layout page in more detail, to understand what it is and how to take advantage of its features for creating dedicated layouts for multiple devices with different form factors (PCs, telephones, tablets, and more).

In Chapter 4, *Basic Concepts of ASP.NET Core 2.0 - Part 1*, we added a layout page called `_Layout.cshtml` within the `Views\Shared` folder. When opening this page and analyzing its content, you can see that it contains common elements applicable to all the pages within your application (header, menu, footer, CSS, JavaScripts, and more):

```
_Layout.cshtml  ⊟ ✕
   1        <!DOCTYPE html>
   2       ⊟<html>
   3       ⊞<head>...</head>
  19       ⊟<body>
  20        ⊟    <nav class="navbar navbar-inverse navbar-fixed-top">
  21        ⊟        <div class="container">
  22        ⊞            <div class="navbar-header">...</div>
  31        ⊞            <div class="navbar-collapse collapse">...</div>
  50                 </div>
  51             </nav>
  52        ⊟    <div class="container body-content">
  53                 @RenderBody()
  54                 <hr />
  55        ⊟        <footer>
  56                     <p>&copy; 2017 - TicTacToe</p>
  57                 </footer>
  58             </div>
  59
  60        ⊞    <environment>...</environment>
  67        ⊞    <environment>...</environment>
  82
  83             @RenderSection("Scripts", required: false)
  84         </body>
  85         </html>
  86
```

The common head section within the layout page contains CSS links but also SEO tags such as title, description, and keywords. As you have already seen before, ASP.NET Core 2.0 provides a neat feature, which allows you to include environment-specific content automatically via environment tags (development, staging, production, and more).

Bootstrap has become a quasi-standard for rendering `menu` and `navbar` components, which is why we have also used it for the *Tic-Tac-Toe* application.

It is best practice to put common JavaScript files at the bottom of your layout page; they can also be included depending on ASP.NET Core environment tags.

You can use the `Views\_ViewStart.cshtml` file to define the layout page for all your pages in a central place. Or, if you want to set a specific layout page manually, you can set it at the top of your page:

```
@{
    Layout = "_Layout";
}
```

To better structure your layout pages, you can define sections for organizing where certain page elements, including common script sections, should be placed. An example is the script section you can see within the layout page, which we added in one of the first examples of the *Tic-Tac-Toe* application. By default, it has been put at the bottom of the page by adding a dedicated meta tag:

```
RenderSection: @RenderSection("Scripts", required: false)
```

You can also define sections in your views for adding files or client-side scripts. We have already done that in the context of the **Email Confirmation** View, where you have added a section for calling the client-side JavaScript `EmailConfirmation` method:

```
@section Scripts{
    <script>
        $(document).ready(function () {
            EmailConfirmation('@ViewBag.Email');
        });
    </script>
}
```

Enough with all this theoretical talk, let's get practical and do something ourselves! Let's see how to optimize the *Tic-Tac-Toe* application for mobile devices:

1. We want to change the display specifically for mobile devices, so start Visual Studio 2017, go to the **Solution Explorer**, create a new folder called `Filters`, then add a new file called `DetectMobileFilter`:

    ```
    public class DetectMobileFilter : IActionFilter
    {
        static Regex MobileCheck = new Regex(@"android|
            (android|bb\d+|meego).+mobile|avantgo|bada\/|
            blackberry|blazer|compal|elaine|fennec|hiptop|
            iemobile|ip(hone|od)|iris|kindle|lge|maemo|
            midp|mmp|mobile.+firefox|netfront|
            opera m(ob|in)i|palm( os)?|phone|p(ixi|re)\/|
    ```

```
      plucker|pocket|psp|series(4|6)0|symbian|
      treo|up\.(browser|link)|vodafone|wap|windows (ce|phone)|
      xda|xiino", RegexOptions.IgnoreCase | RegexOptions.Multiline
      | RegexOptions.Compiled);
  static Regex MobileVersionCheck = new Regex(@"1207|
      6310|6590|3gso|4thp|50[1-6]i|770s|802s|a
      wa|abac|ac(er|oo|s\-)|ai(ko|rn)|al(av|ca|co)|
      amoi|an(ex|ny|yw)|aptu|ar(ch|go)|as(te|us)|
      attw|au(di|\-m|r |s)|avan|be(ck|ll|nq)|bi(lb|rd)|
      bl(ac|az)|br(e|v)w|bumb|bw\-(n|u)|c55\/|capi|ccwa|cdm\-|
      cell|chtm|cldc|cmd\-|co(mp|nd)|craw|da(it|ll|ng)|dbte|dc\-s|
      devi|dica|dmob|do(c|p)o|ds(12|\-d)|el(49|ai)|em(l2|ul)|
      er(ic|k0)|esl8|ez([4-7]0|os|wa|ze)|fetc|fly(\-|_)|g1
      u|g560|gene|gf\-5|g\-mo|go(\.w|od)|gr(ad|un)|haie|hcit|
      hd\-(m|p|t)|hei\-|hi(pt|ta)|hp( i|ip)|hs\-c|ht(c(\-| |
      _|a|g|p|s|t)|tp)|hu(aw|tc)|i\-(20|go|ma)|i230|iac( |\-|
      \/)|ibro|idea|ig01|ikom|im1k|inno|ipaq|iris|
      ja(t|v)a|jbro|jemu|jigs|kddi|keji|kgt( |\/)|klon|kpt |kwc\-|
      kyo(c|k)|le(no|xi)|lg( g|\/(k|l|u)|50|54|\-[a-w])|
      libw|lynx|m1\-w|m3ga|m50\/|ma(te|ui|xo)|mc(01|21|ca)|m\-cr|
      me(rc|ri)|mi(o8|oa|ts)|mmef|mo(01|02|bi|de|do|t(\-| |
      o|v)|zz)|mt(50|p1|v )|mwbp|mywa|n10[0-2]|n20[2-3]|
      n30(0|2)|n50(0|2|5)|n7(0(0|1)|10)|ne((c|m)\-|on|
      tf|wf|wg|wt)|nok(6|i)|nzph|o2im|op(ti|wv)|oran|
      owg1|p800|pan(a|d|t)|pdxg|pg(13|\-([1-8]|c))|phil|
      pire|pl(ay|uc)|pn\-2|po(ck|rt|se)|prox|psio|pt\-g|qa\-a|
      qc(07|12|21|32|60|\-[2-7]|i\-)|qtek|r380|r600|raks|rim9|
      ro(ve|zo)|s55\/|sa(ge|ma|mm|ms|ny|va)|sc(01|h\-|oo|p\-)|
      sdk\/|se(c(\-|0|1)|47|mc|nd|ri)|sgh\-|shar|sie(\-|m)|sk\-0|
      sl(45|id)|sm(al|ar|b3|it|t5)|so(ft|ny)|sp(01|h\-|v\-|v )|
      sy(01|mb)|t2(18|50)|t6(00|10|18)|ta(gt|lk)|tcl\-|tdg\-|
      tel(i|m)|tim\-|t\-mo|to(pl|sh)|ts(70|m\-|m3|m5)|
      tx\-9|up(\.b|g1|si)|utst|v400|v750|veri|vi(rg|te)|
      vk(40|5[0-3]|\-v)|vm40|voda|vulc|vx(52|53|60|
      61|70|80|81|83|85|98)|w3c(\-| )|webc|whit|wi(g|nc|nw)|
      wmlb|wonu|x700|yas\-|your|zeto|zte\-",
      RegexOptions.IgnoreCase | RegexOptions.Multiline |
      RegexOptions.Compiled);

  public static bool IsMobileUserAgent(
   ActionExecutedContext context)
  {
    string userAgent = (context.HttpContext.Request.Headers
      as FrameRequestHeaders)?.HeaderUserAgent;
    if (context.HttpContext != null && userAgent != null)
    {

      if (userAgent.Length < 4)
```

```
            return false;

    if (MobileCheck.IsMatch(userAgent) ||
      MobileVersionCheck.IsMatch(userAgent.Substring(0, 4)))
        return true;
    }
  return false;
  }


  public void OnActionExecuted(ActionExecutedContext context)
  {
    var viewResult = (context.Result as ViewResult);
    if(viewResult == null)
        return;
    if (IsMobileUserAgent(context))
    {
      viewResult.ViewData["Layout"] =
       "~/Views/Shared/_LayoutMobile.cshtml";
    }
    else
    {
      viewResult.ViewData["Layout"] =
       "~/Views/Shared/_Layout.cshtml";
    }
  }


  public void OnActionExecuting(ActionExecutingContext context)
  {
  }
}
```

2. Duplicate the existing `Views/Shared/_Layout.cshtml` file and rename the copy `_LayoutMobile.cshtml`.

3. Update the **Home Page Index View**, remove the existing layout definition and display a different title depending on the device by adding two dedicated sections called `Desktop` and `Mobile`:

```
@{
    ViewData["Title"] = "Home Page";
}
<div class="row">
  <div class="col-lg-12">
    @section Desktop {<h2>@Localizer["DesktopTitle"]</h2>}
    @section Mobile {<h2>@Localizer["MobileTitle"]</h2>}
    <div class="alert alert-info">
  ...
```

Note that you must also update all the other views of the application (GameInvitation/GameInvitationConfirmation, GameInvitation/Index, Home/Index, UserRegistration/EmailConfirmation, UserRegistration/Index) with the section tags from the preceding code for now:

```
@section Desktop{<h2>@Localizer["DesktopTitle"]</h2>}

@section Mobile {<h2>@Localizer["MobileTitle"]</h2>}
```

If you do not add them in your other views, you will get errors in the next steps. However, this is only a temporary solution; we will see later in the chapter how to address this problem more effectively by using conditional statements.

4. Update the **Resource Files**. Here is an example for the English **Home Page Index Resource File**; you should also add the French translations:

Name	Value
DesktopTitle	Welcome to the Tic-Tac-Toe Desktop Game!
MobileTitle	Welcome to the Tic-Tac-Toe Mobile Game!

5. Modify the `Views/Shared/_Layout.cshtml` file by replacing the `@RenderBody()` element with the following instructions; the `Desktop` section should be displayed and the `Mobile` section should be ignored:

```
@RenderSection("Desktop", required: false)
@{IgnoreSection("Mobile");}
@RenderBody()
```

6. Modify the `Views/Shared/_LayoutMobile.cshtml` file by replacing the `@RenderBody()` element with the following instructions; the `Mobile` section should be displayed and the `Desktop` section should be ignored:

```
@RenderSection("Mobile", required: false)
@{IgnoreSection("Desktop");}
@RenderBody()
```

7. Go to the `Views/_ViewStart.cshtml` file and change the **Layout** assignment for all your web pages to be able to use the layout definitions from the preceding code:

```
@{Layout = Convert.ToString(ViewData["Layout"]);}
```

8. In the last step, update the `Startup` class and add the `DetectMobileFilter` to the MVC service registration as a parameter:

```
services.AddMvc(o =>
  o.Filters.Add(typeof(DetectMobileFilter)))...
```

9. Start the *Tic-Tac-Toe* application normally in Microsoft Edge:

10. Open the Developer Tools by clicking on *F12*, go to the **Emulation** tab and select a mobile device, then reload the *Tic-Tac-Toe* application; it will be displayed as if you had opened it on the device:

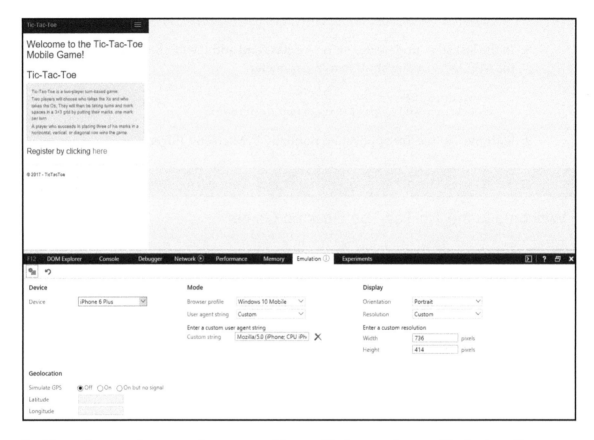

In this section, you have seen how to provide specific layouts for specific devices. You are now going to see how to apply other advanced ASP.NET Core 2.0 MVC features for better productivity and better applications.

Using View Pages, Partial Views, View Components, and Tag Helpers

ASP.NET Core 2.0 and Razor, when coupled with Visual Studio 2017, provide several functionalities for creating your MVC views. In this section, you will see how those functionalities can help you to be more productive.

You can, for instance, create views by using the Visual Studio 2017 integrated scaffolding features, which you have already done in previous chapters multiple times. It allows you to automatically generate the following types of views:

- View Pages
- Partial Views

Would you like to understand what they are and how to use Visual Studio 2017 to work with them efficiently? Stay sharp since we are now going to explain everything in detail.

Using View Pages

View Pages are used to render results based on actions and for giving responses to HTTP requests. In an MVC approach, they define and encapsulate the visible part of your applications—the presentation layer. Furthermore, they use the `.cshtml` file extension and are stored in the `Views` folder of the application by default.

The Visual Studio 2017 scaffolding features provide different View Page templates, as you can see here:

- **Create**: Generate a form for inserting data
- **Edit**: Generate a form for updating data
- **Delete**: Generate a form for displaying a record with a button to confirm deletion
- **Details**: Generate a form for displaying a record with two buttons, one for going to edit form and one for going to delete displayed record page
- **List**: Generate an HTML table for showing a list of objects
- **Empty**: Generate an empty page without using any models

If you cannot use Visual Studio 2017 for generating your Page Views, you might as well implement them manually by adding them to the `Views` folder yourself. In this case, you have to respect the MVC conventions. So add them in a corresponding sub-folder, while matching the action name, for allowing ASP.NET to find your manually created views.

Let's create the Leaderboard for the *Tic-Tac-Toe* game and see all of this in action:

1. Open the **Solution Explorer,** go to the `Views` folder and create a new sub-folder called `Leaderboard`, right-click on the folder and select **Add** | **New Item** | **MVC View Page** in the wizard, and click on the **Add** button:

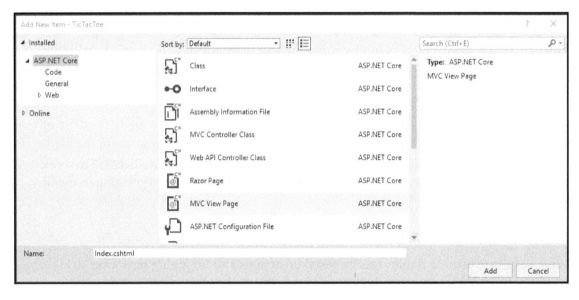

2. Open the created file and clear its content, associate the **Leaderboard** View with the **User Model** by adding the following instruction to the top of the page:

```
@model IEnumerable<TicTacToe.Models.UserModel>
```

3. It is best practice to set its title variable to display it in the SEO tags:

```
@{ViewData["Title"] = "Index";}
```

4. Add new two sections, `Desktop` and `Mobile`, by using the `@section` meta tag, and the last updated time by using the `@()` meta tag:

```
<div class="row">
  <div class="col-lg-12">
    @section Desktop {<h2>@Localizer["DesktopTitle"] (
      Last updated @(System.DateTime.Now))</h2>}
    @section Mobile {<h2>@Localizer["MobileTitle"] (
      Last updated @(System.DateTime.Now))</h2>}
  </div>
</div>
```

5. Add the English and French resource files for the **Leaderboard** View and define localizations for the `DesktopTitle` and `MobileTitle`.

6. Right-click on the `Controllers` folder and select **Add** | **Class**, name it `LeaderboardController.cs`, and click on the **Add** button:

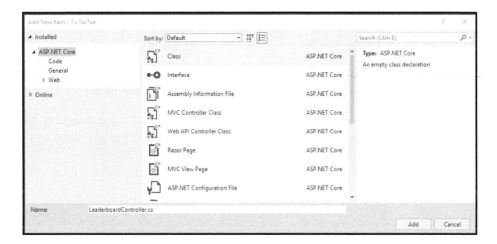

7. Update the **Leaderboard** Controller implementation:

```
public class LeaderboardController : Controller
{
  public IActionResult Index()
  {
    return View();
  }
}
```

Note that Razor matches views with actions as follows:
`<actionname>.cshtml` or `<actionname>.<culture>.cshtml` in the `Views/<controllername>` folder

8. Update the `_Layout.cshtml` and `_LayoutMobile.cshtml` files in the `Views/Shared` folder, and add an ASP.NET Tag Helper for calling the new **Leaderboard** View within the `navbar` menu just after the `Home` element:

```
<li><a asp-area="" asp-controller="Leaderboard"
   asp-action="Index">Leaderboard</a></li>
```

9. Start the application and display the new **Leaderboard** View:

Now that you know the basics, let's look at some more advanced techniques when using Razor, such as code blocks, control structures, and conditional statements.

Code blocks, @{ }, are used for setting or calculating variables and for formatting data. You have already used them in the _ViewStart.cshtml file in one of the previous examples to define which specific layout page should be used:

```
@{
    Layout = Convert.ToString(ViewData["Layout"]);
}
```

Control structures provide everything necessary for working with loops. You could use @for, @foreach, @while, and @do for repeating elements, for example. They act exactly the same as their C# equivalents.

We are now going to use them for implementing the **Leaderboard** View:

1. Add a new HTML table to the **Leaderboard** View, while using the previously mentioned control structures:

```
@model IEnumerable<TicTacToe.Models.UserModel>
@{ViewData["Title"] = "Index";}
<div class="row">
    <div class="col-lg-12">
        @section Desktop {<h2>@Localizer["DesktopTitle"] (
        Last updated @(System.DateTime.Now))</h2>}
        @section Mobile {<h2>@Localizer["MobileTitle"] (
        Last updated @(System.DateTime.Now))</h2>}
        <table class="table table-striped">
            <thead>
                <tr>
                    <th>Name</th>
                    <th>Email</th>
                    <th>Score</th>
                </tr>
            </thead>
```

```
            <tbody>
                @foreach (var user in Model)
            {
                <tr>
                    <td>@user.FirstName  @user.LastName</td>
                    <td>@user.Email</td>
                    <td>@user.Score.ToString()</td>
                </tr>
            }
            </tbody>
        </table>
    </div>
</div>
```

2. Add a new `GetTopUsers` method to the `IUserService` interface for retrieving the top users for display within the **Leaderboard** View:

```
Task<IEnumerable<UserModel>> GetTopUsers(int numberOfUsers);
```

3. Implement the new `GetTopUsers` method within the `UserService`:

```
public Task<IEnumerable<UserModel>>
 GetTopUsers(int numberOfUsers)
{
    return Task.Run(() =>
      (IEnumerable<UserModel>)_userStore.OrderBy(x =>
      x.Score).Take(numberOfUsers).ToList());
}
```

4. Update the **Leaderboard** Controller to call the new method:

```
public class LeaderboardController : Controller
{
    private IUserService _userService;
    public LeaderboardController(IUserService userService)
    {
        _userService = userService;
    }

    public async Task<IActionResult> Index()
    {
        var users = await _userService.GetTopUsers(10);
        return View(users);
    }
}
```

5. Press *F5* and start the application, register multiple users, and display the
Leaderboard:

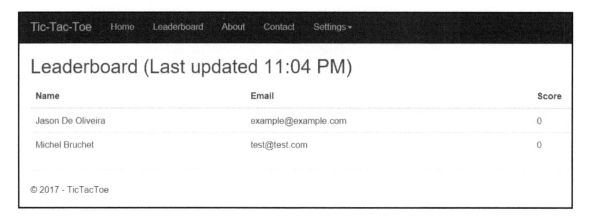

Conditional Statements such as @if, @else if, @else, and @switch allow rendering
elements conditionally. They also work exactly the same as their C# counterparts.

As mentioned before, you need to define the Desktop and Mobile sections in all of your
views:

```
@section Desktop { }
@section Mobile { }
```

For example, if you remove them temporarily from the **Leaderboard Index View** and try to
display it while the ASPNETCORE_ENVIRONMENT variable is set to Development so that the
Developer Exception page is activated, you will get the following error message:

An unhandled exception occurred while processing the request.

InvalidOperationException: The layout page '/Views/Shared/_Layout.cshtml' cannot find the section 'MobileTitle' in the content page '/Views/Leaderboard/Index.cshtml'.

Microsoft.AspNetCore.Mvc.Razor.RazorPage.IgnoreSection(string sectionName)

Stack   Query   Cookies   Headers

InvalidOperationException: The layout page '/Views/Shared/_Layout.cshtml' cannot find the section 'MobileTitle' in the content page '/Views/Leaderboard/Index.cshtml'.

Microsoft.AspNetCore.Mvc.Razor.RazorPage.IgnoreSection(string sectionName)

AspNetCore._Views_Shared__Layout_cshtml+<<ExecuteAsync>b__47_7>d.MoveNext() in **_Layout.cshtml**

   56.   IgnoreSection("MobileTitle");

System.Runtime.ExceptionServices.ExceptionDispatchInfo.Throw()

System.Runtime.CompilerServices.TaskAwaiter.HandleNonSuccessAndDebuggerNotification(Task task)

Microsoft.AspNetCore.Razor.Runtime.TagHelpers.TagHelperExecutionContext+<SetOutputContentAsync>d__30.MoveNext()

System.Runtime.ExceptionServices.ExceptionDispatchInfo.Throw()

System.Runtime.CompilerServices.TaskAwaiter.HandleNonSuccessAndDebuggerNotification(Task task)

This is because we changed the `Layout` and `Mobile` layout pages for the application in one of the previous steps and used an `IgnoreSection` instruction. Unfortunately, sections must always be declared when using `IgnoreSection` instructions.

But now that you know that conditional statements exist, you can already see a better solution, right? Yes, exactly; we have to wrap the `IgnoreSection` instruction with a conditional `if` statement within the two layout pages.

Here is how you need to update the layout page using the `IsSectionDefined` method:

```
@RenderSection("Desktop", required: false)
@if(IsSectionDefined("Mobile")){IgnoreSection("Mobile");}
@RenderBody()
```

Here is how you need to update the `Mobile` layout page:

```
@RenderSection("Mobile", required: false)
@if(IsSectionDefined("Desktop")){IgnoreSection("Desktop");}
@RenderBody()
```

Start the application and you will see that everything is now working as expected, but this time with a much cleaner, more elegant, and easier-to-understand solution; that is, using the built-in functionalities of ASP.NET Core 2.0 and Razor.

For additional information on Razor please visit:
https://docs.microsoft.com/en-us/aspnet/core/mvc/views/razor

Using Partial Views

You have seen how to create View Pages using Razor, but sometimes you have to repeat elements within all or some of your View Pages. Wouldn't it be helpful if you could create reusable components within your views for this case? Unsurprisingly, ASP.NET Core 2.0 does implement this feature by default, by providing so-called Partial Views.

Partial Views are rendered within calling View Pages. Like standard View Pages, they also have the .cshtml file extension. You can define them once and then use them within all your View Pages. What a great way to optimize your code by reducing code duplication, which leads to better quality and less maintenance!

You are going to see how to benefit from that right now, by optimizing the Layout and Mobile layout pages to use a single menu:

1. Go to the Views/Shared folder and add a new **MVC View Page** called _Menu.cshtml, it will be used as the **Menu Partial View**:

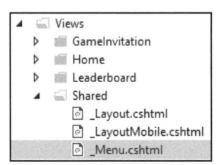

2. Copy the nav bar from one of the layout pages and paste it into the **Menu Partial View**:

```
<nav class="navbar navbar-inverse navbar-fixed-top">
...
</nav>
```

3. Replace the `nav` bar with `@Html.Partial("_Menu")` in both layout pages.
4. Start the application and validate that everything is still working as before. You should not see any differences, but that is a good thing; you have encapsulated and centralized the menu in a Partial View now.

Using View Components

You have seen how to create reusable components by using Partial Views, which can be called from any View Pages within your applications, and applied this concept to the top menu of the *Tic-Tac-Toe* application. But sometimes, even this feature is not enough.

Sometimes you need something more powerful, something more flexible, that you can use throughout your whole web application and maybe even for multiple web applications. That is where View Components come into play.

View Components are used for complex use cases that require some code running on the server (for example, Login Panel, Tag Cloud, and Shopping Cart), where Partial Views are too limited to be used, and where you need to be able to test functionalities extensively.

You are going to add a View Component for managing game sessions in the following example; you will see that it is very similar to a standard Controller implementation:

1. Add a new model called `TurnModel` to the `Models` folder:

```
public class TurnModel
{
  public Guid Id { get; set; }
  public Guid UserId { get; set; }
  public UserModel User { get; set; }
  public int X { get; set; }
  public int Y { get; set; }
}
```

2. Add a new model called `GameSessionModel` to the `Models` folder:

```
public class GameSessionModel
{
  public Guid Id { get; set; }
  public Guid UserId1 { get; set; }
  public Guid UserId2 { get; set; }
  public UserModel User1 { get; set; }
  public UserModel User2 { get; set; }
  public IEnumerable<TurnModel> Turns { get; set; }
```

```
    public UserModel Winner { get; set; }
    public UserModel ActiveUser { get; set; }
    public Guid WinnerId { get; set; }
    public Guid ActiveUserId { get; set; }
    public bool TurnFinished { get; set; }
}
```

3. Add a new service called `GameSessionService` to the `Services` folder, implement it, and extract the `IGameSessionService` interface:

```
public class GameSessionService
{
  private static ConcurrentBag<GameSessionModel> _sessions;
  static GameSessionService()
  {
    _sessions = new ConcurrentBag<GameSessionModel>();
  }

  public Task<GameSessionModel> GetGameSession(Guid gameSessionId)
  {
    return Task.Run(() => _sessions.FirstOrDefault(
     x => x.Id == gameSessionId));
  }
}
```

4. Register the `GameSessionService` within the `Startup` class, as you have already done with all the other services:

```
services.AddSingleton<IGameSessionService, GameSessionService>();
```

5. Go to the **Solution Explorer**, create a new folder called `Components`, then add a new class called `GameSessionViewComponent.cs`:

```
[ViewComponent(Name = "GameSession")]
public class GameSessionViewComponent : ViewComponent
{
  IGameSessionService _gameSessionService;
  public GameSessionViewComponent(IGameSessionService
   gameSessionService)
  {
    _gameSessionService = gameSessionService;
  }

  public async Task<IViewComponentResult> InvokeAsync(Guid
   gameSessionId)
  {
    var session =
```

```
      await _gameSessionService.GetGameSession(gameSessionId);
    return View(session);
  }
}
```

6. Go to the **Solution Explorer** and create a new folder called `Components` within the `Views/Shared` folder. Within this folder create a new folder called `GameSession` for the `GameSessionViewComponent`, then add a new View called `default.cshtml`:

```
@using Microsoft.AspNetCore.Http
@model TicTacToe.Models.GameSessionModel
@{
  var email = Context.Session.GetString("email");
}
@if (Model.ActiveUser?.Email == email)
{
  <table>
    @for (int rows = 0; rows < 3; rows++)
    {
      <tr style="height:150px;">
        @for (int columns = 0; columns < 3; columns++)
        {
          <td style="width:150px; border:1px solid #808080">
            @{
              var position = Model.Turns?.FirstOrDefault(
                turn => turn.X == columns && turn.Y == rows);

              if (position != null)
              {
                if (position.User?.Email == "Player1")
                {
                  <i class="glyphicon glyphicon-unchecked"
                    style="width:100%;height:100%"></i>
                }
                else
                {
                  <i class="glyphicon glyphicon-remove-circle"
                    style="width:100%;height:100%"></i>
                }
              }
              else
              {
                <a asp-action="SetPosition"
                  asp-controller="GameSession"
                  asp-route-id="@Model.Id"
                  asp-route-email="@email"
```

```
                class="btn btn-default"
                style="width:150px; min-height:150px; ">
                 
              </a>
          }
        }
        </td>
      }
    </tr>
  }
  </table>
}
else
{
  <div class="alert">
    <i class="glyphicon glyphicon-alert">Please wait until
      the other user has finished his turn.</i>
  </div>
}
```

 We advise using the following syntax for putting all Partial Views for your View Components in their corresponding folders:
`Views\Shared\Components\<ViewComponentName>\<ViewName>`

7. Update the `_ViewImports.cshtml` file to use the View Component:

```
@addTagHelper *, TicTacToe
```

8. Create a new folder called `GameSession` within the `Views` folder, then add a new View called `Index`:

```
@model TicTacToe.Models.GameSessionModel
@section Desktop
{
  <h1>Game Session @Model.Id</h1>
  <h2>Started at @(DateTime.Now.ToShortTimeString())</h2>
  <div class="alert alert-info">
    <table class="table">
      <tr>
        <td>User 1:</td>
        <td>@Model.User1?.Email (<i class="glyphicon
        glyphicon-unchecked"></i>)</td>
      </tr>
      <tr>
        <td>User 2:</td>
        <td>@Model.User2?.Email (<i class="glyphicon
```

```
        glyphicon-remove-circle"></i>)</td>
      </tr>
    </table>
  </div>
}
@section Mobile{
  <h1>Game Session @Model.Id</h1>
  <h2>Started at @(DateTime.Now.ToShortTimeString())</h2>
  User 1: @Model.User1?.Email <i class="glyphicon
  glyphicon-unchecked"></i><br />
  User 2: @Model.User2?.Email (<i class="glyphicon
  glyphicon-remove-circle"></i>)
}
<vc:game-session game-session-id="@Model.Id"></vc:game-session>
```

9. Add a public constructor to the `GameSessionService` for getting an instance of **User Service**:

```csharp
private IUserService _UserService;
public GameSessionService(IUserService userService)
{
  _UserService = userService;
}
```

10. Add a method to the `GameSessionService` for creating game sessions, and update the **Game Session Service Interface**:

```csharp
public async Task<GameSessionModel> CreateGameSession(
 Guid invitationId, string invitedByEmail,
 string invitedPlayerEmail)
{
  var invitedBy =
   await _UserService.GetUserByEmail(invitedByEmail);
  var invitedPlayer =
   await _UserService.GetUserByEmail(invitedPlayerEmail);

  GameSessionModel session = new GameSessionModel
  {
    User1 = invitedBy,
    User2 = invitedPlayer,
    Id = invitationId,
    ActiveUser = invitedBy
  };

  _sessions.Add(session);
  return session;
}
```

11. Add a new Controller called `GameSessionController` within the `Controllers` folder, and implement a new `Index` method:

```
public class GameSessionController : Controller
{
  private IGameSessionService _gameSessionService;
  public GameSessionController(IGameSessionService
   gameSessionService)
  {
    _gameSessionService = gameSessionService;
  }

  public async Task<IActionResult> Index(Guid id)
  {
    var session = await _gameSessionService.GetGameSession(id);
    if (session == null)
    {
      var gameInvitationService =
        Request.HttpContext.RequestServices
        .GetService<IGameInvitationService>();
      var invitation = await gameInvitationService.Get(id);
      session =
        await _gameSessionService.CreateGameSession(
          invitation.Id,invitation.InvitedBy,
          invitation.EmailTo);
    }
    return View(session);
  }
}
```

Note that for calling `RequestServices.GetService<T>();` you must also add `using Microsoft.Extensions.DependencyInjection;` as you have already done in other examples.

12. Start the application, register a new user, and invite another user to play a game, wait for the new **Game Session** page to be displayed:

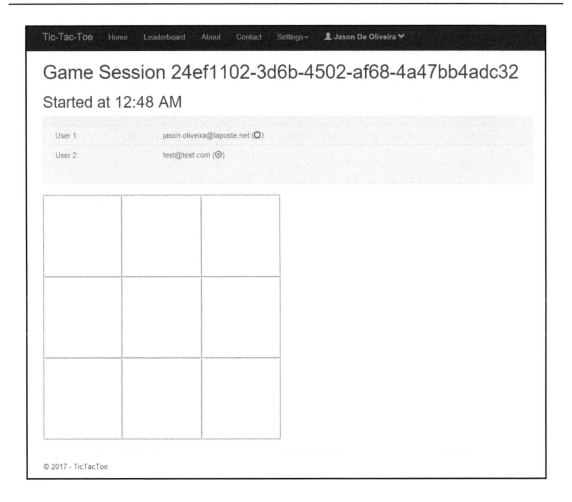

Using Tag Helpers

Tag Helpers are a new feature of ASP.NET Core 2.0, which allow server-side code to be used when creating and rendering HTML elements. They can be compared to already existing and well-known HTML helpers for rendering HTML content.

ASP.NET Core 2.0 already provides many built-in Tag Helpers, such as `ImageTagHelper` and `LabelTagHelper` that you can use within your applications.

When creating your own Tag Helpers, you can target HTML elements based on an element name, an attribute name, or a parent tag. You can then use standard HTML tags in your views, while presentation logic written in C# is applied on the web server.

Additionally, you can even create custom tags as you will see in this section about creating a Gravatar tag. You will use this within the *Tic-Tac-Toe* application:

1. Open the **Solution Explorer** and create a new folder called `TagHelpers`, then add a new class called `GravatarTagHelper.cs`.

2. Implement the `GravatarTagHelper.cs` class; it will be used to connect to the Gravatar online service for retrieving account photos for users:

```
[HtmlTargetElement("Gravatar")]
public class GravatarTagHelper : TagHelper
{
  private ILogger<GravatarTagHelper> _logger;
  public GravatarTagHelper(ILogger<GravatarTagHelper> logger)
  {
    _logger = logger;
  }
  public string Email { get; set; }
  public override void Process(TagHelperContext context,
   TagHelperOutput output)
  {
    byte[] photo = null;
    if (CheckIsConnected())
    {
      photo = GetPhoto(Email);
    }
    else
    {
      photo = File.ReadAllBytes(Path.Combine(
        Directory.GetCurrentDirectory(),
        "wwwroot", "images", "no-photo.jpg"));
    }

    string base64String = Convert.ToBase64String(photo);
    output.TagName = "img";
    output.Attributes.SetAttribute("src",
     $"data:image/jpeg;base64,{base64String}");
  }

  private bool CheckIsConnected()
  {
    try
    {
      using (var httpClient = new HttpClient())
      {
        var gravatarResponse = httpClient.GetAsync(
          "http://www.gravatar.com/avatar/").Result;
```

```
      return (gravatarResponse.IsSuccessStatusCode);
    }
  }
  catch (Exception ex)
  {
    _logger?.LogError($"Cannot check the gravatar
     service status: {ex}");
    return false;
  }
}

private byte[] GetPhoto(string email)
{
  var httpClient = new HttpClient();
  return httpClient.GetByteArrayAsync(
   new Uri($"http://www.gravatar.com/avatar/
   {HashEmailForGravatar(email)}")).Result;
}

private static string HashEmailForGravatar(string email)
{
  var md5Hasher = MD5.Create();
  byte[] data = md5Hasher.ComputeHash(
   Encoding.ASCII.GetBytes(email.ToLower()));

  var stringBuilder = new StringBuilder();
  for (int i = 0; i < data.Length; i++)
  {
    stringBuilder.Append(data[i].ToString("x2"));
  }
  return stringBuilder.ToString();
}
}
```

3. Open the `Views/_ViewImports.cshtml` file and verify that the `addTagHelper` instruction is existing; if not, add it to the file:

```
@addTagHelper *, TicTacToe
```

4. Update the `Index` method in the `GameInvitationController`, store the user email, and display the name (first name and last name) in a session variable:

```
[HttpGet]
public async Task<IActionResult> Index(string email)
{
  var gameInvitationModel = new GameInvitationModel {
   InvitedBy = email, Id = Guid.NewGuid() };
```

```
        Request.HttpContext.Session.SetString("email", email);
        var user = await _userService.GetUserByEmail(email);
        Request.HttpContext.Session.SetString("displayName",
         $"{user.FirstName} {user.LastName}");
        return View(gameInvitationModel);
    }
```

5. Add a new model called `AccountModel` to the `Models` folder:

```
public class AccountModel
{
    public string Email { get; set; }
    public string DisplayName { get; set; }
}
```

6. Add a new Partial View called `_Account.cshtml` in the `Views/Shared` folder:

```
@model TicTacToe.Models.AccountModel
<li class="dropdown">
  <a href="#" class="dropdown-toggle" data-toggle="dropdown">
    <span class="glyphicon glyphicon-user"></span>
    <strong>@Model.DisplayName</strong>
    <span class="glyphicon glyphicon-chevron-down"></span>
  </a>
<ul class="dropdown-menu" id="connected-dp">
<li>
 <div class="navbar-login">
  <div class="row">
   <div class="col-lg-4">
    <p class="text-center">
      <Gravatar email="@Model.Email"></Gravatar>
    </p>
   </div>
   <div class="col-lg-8">
    <p class="text-left"><strong>@Model.DisplayName</strong></p>
    <p class="text-left small"><a asp-action="Index"
      asp-controller="Account">@Model.Email</a></p>
   </div>
  </div>
 </div>
</li>
<li class="divider"></li>
<li>
  <div class="navbar-login navbar-login-session">
   <div class="row">
    <div class="col-lg-12">
     <p>
```

```
        <a href="#" class="btn btn-danger btn-block">Log off</a>
      </p>
    </div>
  </div>
 </div>
</li>
</ul>
</li>
```

7. Add a new CSS class to the `wwwroot/css/site.css` file:

```
#connected-dp {
  min-width: 350px;
}
```

Note that you might need to empty your browser cache or force a refresh for the application to update the `site.css` file within your browser.

8. Update the **Menu Partial View**, and retrieve the user display name and email at the top of the page:

```
@using Microsoft.AspNetCore.Http;
@{
  var email = Context.Session.GetString("email");
  var displayName = Context.Session.GetString("displayName");
}
```

9. Update the **Menu Partial View**, and add the new **Account Partial View** from before, located just after the **Settings** element in the menu:

```
<li>
@if (!string.IsNullOrEmpty(email))
{
  Html.RenderPartial("_Account",
   new TicTacToe.Models.AccountModel {
    Email = email, DisplayName = displayName });
}
</li>
```

10. Create an account on Gravatar with your email and upload a photo, start the *Tic-Tac-Toe* application, and register with the same email. You should now see a new dropdown with a photo and display name in the top menu:

 Note that you have to be online for this to work. If you want to test your code offline, you should put a photo in the `wwwroot\images` folder called `no-photo.jpg`; otherwise, you will get an error since no offline photo can be found.

Easy to understand and easy to use, but when to use View Components and when to use Tag Helpers? The following simple rules should help you decide when to use which of the explained concepts:

- View Components are used whenever you need templates for views, for rendering a group of elements, and associating server code with it.
- Tag Helpers are used to append behavior to a single HTML element, instead of a group of elements.

Dividing web applications into multiple Areas

Sometimes, when working with larger web applications, it can be interesting to logically separate them into multiple smaller, functional units. Each unit can then have its own controllers, views, and models, which makes it easier to understand, manage, evolve, and maintain them over time.

ASP.NET Core 2.0 provides some simple mechanisms based on the folder structure for dividing web applications into multiple functional units, also called **Areas**.

For example, to separate the standard Area from the more advanced administration Area within your applications. The standard Area could then even enable anonymous access on some pages, while asking for authentication and authorization on others, whereas the administration Area would always require authentication and authorization on all pages.

The following conventions and restrictions apply to Areas:

- An Area is a subdirectory under the `Areas` folder
- An Area contains at least the two subfolders: `Controllers` and `Views`
- An Area may contain specific layout pages as well as dedicated `_ViewImport.cshtml` and `_ViewStart.cshtml` files
- You have to register a specific route, which enables Areas within its routing definition, to be able to use Areas in your applications
- It is recommended to use the following format for Area URLs: `http://<Host>/<AreaName>/<ControllerName>/<ActionName>`
- The Tag Helper `asp-area` can be used for appending an Area to a URL

Let's look at how to create a specific Administration Area for Account Management:

1. Open the **Solution Explorer** and create a new folder called `Areas`, right-click on the folder and select **Add | Area**, enter `Account` as **Area name**, and click on the **Add** button:

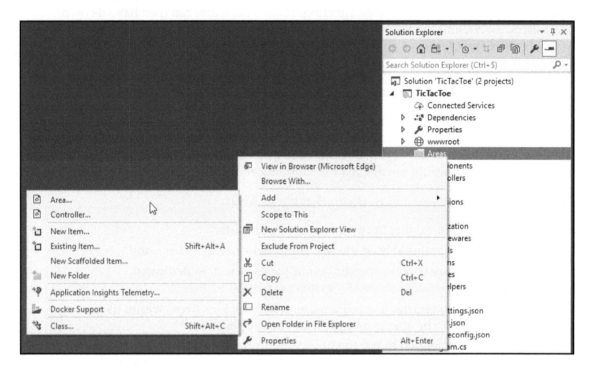

2. Scaffolding will create a dedicated folder structure for the **Account Area**:

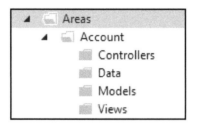

3. Add a new route for `Areas` to the `UseMVC` declaration within the `Configure` method of the `Startup` class:

```
app.UseMvc(routes =>
{
  routes.MapRoute(name: "areaRoute",
   template: "{area:exists}/{controller=Home}/{action=Index}");

  routes.MapRoute(name: "default",
   template: "{controller=Home}/{action=Index}/{id?}");
});
```

4. Right-click on the `Controllers` folder within the **Account Area** and add a new Controller called `HomeController`:

```
[Area("Account")]
public class HomeController : Controller
{
  private IUserService _userService;
  public HomeController(IUserService userService) {
    _userService = userService;
  }
  public async Task<IActionResult> Index() {
    var email = HttpContext.Session.GetString("email");
    var user = await _userService.GetUserByEmail(email);
    return View(user);
  }
}
```

5. Add a new folder called `Home` in the `Account/Views` folder, and add a View called `Index` in this new folder:

```
@model TicTacToe.Models.UserModel
<h3>Account Details</h3>
<div class="container">
  <div class="row">
    <div class="col-xs-12 col-sm-6 col-md-6">
      <div class="well well-sm">
        <div class="row">
          <div class="col-sm-6 col-md-4">
            <Gravatar email="@Model.Email"></Gravatar>
          </div>
          <div class="col-sm-6 col-md-8">
            <h4>@($"{Model.FirstName} {Model.LastName}")</h4>
            <p>
             <i class="glyphicon glyphicon-envelope"></i> 
```

```
            <a href="mailto:@Model.Email">@Model.Email</a>
            </p>
            <p>
             <i class="glyphicon glyphicon-calendar">
             </i> @Model.EmailConfirmationDate
            </p>
           </div>
          </div>
         </div>
        </div>
       </div>
```

6. Update the **Account Partial View**, and add a link to display the preceding view (just after the existing Log off link):

```
<a class="btn btn-default btn-block" asp-action="Index"
    asp-controller="Account">View Details</a>
```

7. Start the application, register a new user, and call the new Area by clicking on the **Account Details** link in the account dropdown:

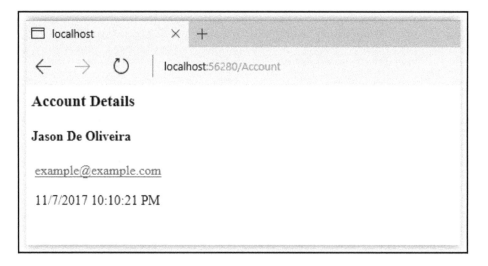

We will stop the implementation of the Administration Area here and come back to it in Chapter 9, *Securing ASP.NET Core 2.0 Applications*, where you will see how to secure access to it.

Applying advanced concepts

Now that we have seen all the basic features of ASP.NET Core 2.0 MVC, let's look at some of the more advanced features, which can help you during your daily work as a developer.

You will also learn how to use Visual Studio 2017 for testing your applications and thus providing better quality for your users.

Using view engines

When ASP.NET Core 2.0 uses server-side code for rendering HTML, it uses a View Engine. By default, when building standard views with their associated .cshtml files, you use the Razor View Engine with the Razor syntax, for example.

By convention, this engine is able to work with views, which are located within the Views folder. Since it is built-in and the default engine, it is bound automatically to the HTTP Request Pipeline without you doing anything for it to work.

If you need to use Razor for rendering files that are located outside of the Views folder and don't come directly from the HTTP Request Pipeline, such as email templates for example, you cannot use the default Razor View Engine. Instead, you need to define your own View Engine and make it responsible for generating the HTML code in this case.

In the following example, we will explain how you can use Razor for rendering an email based on an email template, which is not coming from the HTTP Request Pipeline:

1. Open the **Solution Explorer** and create a new folder called ViewEngines, add a new class called EmailViewEngine.cs, and extract its interface, IEmailViewEngine:

```
public class EmailViewEngine
{
  private readonly IRazorViewEngine _viewEngine;
  private readonly ITempDataProvider _tempDataProvider;
  private readonly IServiceProvider _serviceProvider;

  public EmailViewEngine(
    IRazorViewEngine viewEngine,
    ITempDataProvider tempDataProvider,
    IServiceProvider serviceProvider)
  {
    _viewEngine = viewEngine;
    _tempDataProvider = tempDataProvider;
```

```
      _serviceProvider = serviceProvider;
    }
    private IView FindView(ActionContext actionContext,
     string viewName)
    {
      var getViewResult =
        _viewEngine.GetView(executingFilePath: null,
          viewPath: viewName, isMainPage: true);
      if (getViewResult.Success)
      {
        return getViewResult.View;
      }
      var findViewResult = _viewEngine.FindView(actionContext,
        viewName, isMainPage: true);
      if (findViewResult.Success)
      {
        return findViewResult.View;
      }
      var searchedLocations =
        getViewResult.SearchedLocations.Concat(
          findViewResult.SearchedLocations);
      var errorMessage = string.Join(
       Environment.NewLine,
        new[] { $"Unable to find view '{viewName}'. The following
        locations were searched:" }.Concat(searchedLocations));

      throw new InvalidOperationException(errorMessage);
    }

    public async Task<string> RenderEmailToString<TModel>(string
     viewName, TModel model)
    {
      var actionContext = GetActionContext();
      var view = FindView(actionContext, viewName);
      if (view == null)
      {
        throw new InvalidOperationException(string.Format(
          "Couldn't find view '{0}'", viewName));
      }

      using (var output = new StringWriter())
      {
        var viewContext = new ViewContext(
          actionContext,
          view,
          new ViewDataDictionary<TModel>(
            metadataProvider: new EmptyModelMetadataProvider(),
            modelState: new ModelStateDictionary())
```

```
        {
          Model = model
        },
        new TempDataDictionary(
          actionContext.HttpContext,
          _tempDataProvider),
        output,
        new HtmlHelperOptions());

      await view.RenderAsync(viewContext);
      return output.ToString();
    }
  }
   private ActionContext GetActionContext()
   {
     var httpContext = new DefaultHttpContext
     {
       RequestServices = _serviceProvider
     };
     return new ActionContext(httpContext, new RouteData(),
      new ActionDescriptor());
   }
 }
```

2. Create a new folder called `Helpers`, and add a new class called `EmailViewRenderHelper.cs`:

```
public class EmailViewRenderHelper
{
  IHostingEnvironment _hostingEnvironment;
  IConfiguration _configurationRoot;
  IHttpContextAccessor _httpContextAccessor;

  public async Task<string> RenderTemplate<T>(string template,
   IHostingEnvironment hostingEnvironment, IConfiguration
   configurationRoot, IHttpContextAccessor httpContextAccessor,
   T model) where T:class
  {
    _hostingEnvironment = hostingEnvironment;
    _configurationRoot = configurationRoot;
    _httpContextAccessor = httpContextAccessor;
    var renderer =
      httpContextAccessor.HttpContext.RequestServices
      .GetRequiredService<IEmailViewEngine>();
    return await renderer.RenderEmailToString<T>(template,
     model);
  }
```

```
    }
```

3. Add a new service called `EmailTemplateRenderService` in the `Services` folder and extract its interface, `IEmailTemplateRenderService`:

```
public class EmailTemplateRenderService
{
    private IHostingEnvironment _hostingEnvironment;
    private IConfiguration _configuration;
    private IHttpContextAccessor _httpContextAccessor;

    public EmailTemplateRenderService(IHostingEnvironment
     hostingEnvironment, IConfiguration configuration,
     IHttpContextAccessor httpContextAccessor)
    {
      _hostingEnvironment = hostingEnvironment;
      _configuration = configuration;
      _httpContextAccessor = httpContextAccessor;
    }

    public async Task<string> RenderTemplate<T>(string
     templateName, T model, string host) where T : class
    {
      var html = await new EmailViewRenderHelper()
        .RenderTemplate(templateName, _hostingEnvironment,
        _configuration, _httpContextAccessor, model);
      var targetDir =
        Path.Combine(Directory.GetCurrentDirectory(),
        "wwwroot", "Emails");

      if (!Directory.Exists(targetDir))
        Directory.CreateDirectory(targetDir);

      string dateTime = DateTime.Now.ToString("ddMMHHyyHHmmss");
      var targetFileName = Path.Combine(targetDir,
        templateName.Replace("/", "_").Replace("\\", "_") + "." +
        dateTime + ".html");
      html = html.Replace("{ViewOnLine}",
        $"{host.TrimEnd('/')}/Emails/{Path.GetFileName
        (targetFileName)}");
      html = html.Replace("{ServerUrl}", host);
      File.WriteAllText(targetFileName, html);
      return html;
    }
}
```

4. Register the `EmailViewEngine` and `EmailTemplateRenderService` in the `Startup` class:

```
services.AddTransient<IEmailTemplateRenderService,
 EmailTemplateRenderService>();
services.AddTransient<IEmailViewEngine, EmailViewEngine>();
```

 Note that it is required to register the `EmailViewEngine` and the `EmailTemplateRenderService` as transient because of the HTTP Context Accessor injection.

5. Add a new layout page in the `Views/Shared` folder called `_LayoutEmail.cshtml`:

```
<!DOCTYPE html>
<html>
<head>
  <meta charset="utf-8" />
  <meta name="viewport" content="width=device-width,
   initial-scale=1.0" />
  <title>@ViewData["Title"] - TicTacToe</title>

  <environment include="Development">
    <link rel="stylesheet"
     href="~/lib/bootstrap/dist/css/bootstrap.css" />
    <link rel="stylesheet" href="~/css/site.css" />
  </environment>
  <environment exclude="Development">
    <link rel="stylesheet"
     href="https://ajax.aspnetcdn.com/ajax/bootstrap/3.3.7/
     css/bootstrap.min.css"
     asp-fallback-href="~/lib/bootstrap/dist/css/bootstrap.min.css"
     asp-fallback-test-class="sr-only"
     asp-fallback-test-property="position"
     asp-fallback-test-value="absolute" />
    <link rel="stylesheet" href="~/css/site.min.css"
     asp-append-version="true" />
  </environment>
</head>
<body>
  <div class="container body-content">
    @RenderBody()
    <hr />
    <footer>
      <p>&copy; 2017 - TicTacToe</p>
```

```
        </footer>
      </div>

      <environment include="Development">
        <script src="~/lib/jquery/dist/jquery.js"></script>
        <script src="~/lib/bootstrap/dist/js/bootstrap.js"></script>
        <script src="~/js/site.js" asp-append-version="true"></script>
      </environment>
      <environment exclude="Development">
        <script src="https://ajax.aspnetcdn.com/
         ajax/jquery/jquery-2.2.0.min.js"
         asp-fallback-src="~/lib/jquery/dist/jquery.min.js"
         asp-fallback-test="window.jQuery"
         crossorigin="anonymous"
         integrity="sha384-K+ctZQ+LL8q6tP7I94W+qzQsfRV2a+
           AfHIi9k8z8l9ggpc8X+Ytst4yBo/hH+8Fk">
        </script>
        <script src="https://ajax.aspnetcdn.com/ajax/bootstrap/
         3.3.7/bootstrap.min.js"
         asp-fallback-src="~/lib/bootstrap/dist/js/bootstrap.min.js"
         asp-fallback-test="window.jQuery && window.jQuery.fn
           && window.jQuery.fn.modal"
         crossorigin="anonymous"
         integrity="sha384-Tc5IQib027qvyjSMfHjOMaLkfuWVxZxUPnCJA7
           l2mCWNIpG9mGCD8wGNIcPD7Txa">
        </script>
        <script src="~/js/site.min.js"
         asp-append-version="true"></script>
      </environment>

      @RenderSection("Scripts", required: false)
    </body>
    </html>
```

6. Add a new model called `UserRegistrationEmailModel` to the `Models` folder:

```
public class UserRegistrationEmailModel
{
  public string Email { get; set; }
  public string DisplayName { get; set; }
  public string ActionUrl { get; set; }
}
```

7. Create a new sub-folder called `EmailTemplates` in the `Views` folder and add a new view called `UserRegistrationEmail`:

```
@model TicTacToe.Models.UserRegistrationEmailModel
@{
  ViewData["Title"] = "View";
  Layout = "_LayoutEmail";
}
<h1>Welcome @Model.DisplayName</h1>
  Thank you for registering on our website. Please click <a
    href="@Model.ActionUrl">here</a> to confirm your email.
```

8. Update the `EmailConfirmation` method within the `UserRegistrationController` for using the new **Email View Engine** before sending any emails:

```
var userRegistrationEmail = new UserRegistrationEmailModel
{
  DisplayName = $"{user.FirstName} {user.LastName}",
  Email = email,
  ActionUrl = Url.Action(urlAction)
};

var emailRenderService =
  HttpContext.RequestServices.GetService
  <IEmailTemplateRenderService>();
var message =
  await emailRenderService.RenderTemplate(
    "EmailTemplates/UserRegistrationEmail",
    userRegistrationEmail, Request.Host.ToString());
```

 Note that for calling `RequestServices.GetService<T>();`, you must also add `using Microsoft.Extensions.DependencyInjection;` as you have already done in other examples.

9. Start the application and register a new user, open the `UserRegistrationEmail`, and analyze its content (look in the `wwwroot/Emails` folder):

> **Welcome Jason De Oliveira**
>
> Thank you for registering on our website. Please click here to confirm your email.
>
> © 2017 - TicTacToe

 Note that a View Engine can be used for rendering email content, as seen in the preceding example, but it can also be used for rendering views outside of the `Views` folder, for rendering views from within a database, or for using the themes folder as in ASP.NET 4.

You have seen many concepts and many code examples throughout the various chapters of this book, but we have not yet talked about how to ensure excellent quality and maintainability for your applications. The next section is going to shed some light on this subject, since it is dedicated to application testing.

Providing better quality by creating unit tests and integration tests

Building high-quality applications and satisfying application users is a difficult endeavor. Even more, shipping products that have technical and functional flaws can lead to enormous problems during the maintenance phase of your applications.

The worst-case scenario is that, since maintenance is so demanding on time and resources, you will not be able to evolve your applications as quickly as possible to lower your time-to-market, and you will be unable to provide exciting new features. But rest assured that your competition is not waiting! They will surpass you and you will lose market share and market leadership.

But how can you succeed? How can you reduce the time to detect bugs and functional problems? You have to test your code and your applications! And you have to do that as much as possible and as soon as possible. It is common knowledge that fixing a bug during development time is cheaper and quicker, whereas fixing a bug during production takes more time and money.

Having a low **Mean Time To Repair** (**MTTR**) for bugs can make a big difference when it comes to becoming a future market'leader within your specific markets.

Let's continue with the development of the *Tic-Tac-Toe* application and then see how to carefully test it in more detail:

1. Add a new method called `AddTurn` to the `GameSessionService` and update the **Game Session Service Interface**:

```
public async Task<GameSessionModel> AddTurn(Guid id,
  string email, int x, int y) {
  var gameSession = _sessions.FirstOrDefault(session =>
   session.Id == id);
  List<Models.TurnModel> turns;
  if (gameSession.Turns != null && gameSession.Turns.Any())
    turns = new List<Models.TurnModel>(gameSession.Turns);
  else
    turns = new List<TurnModel>();

  turns.Add(new TurnModel
  {
    User = await _UserService.GetUserByEmail(email),
    X = x,
    Y = y
  });

  if (gameSession.User1?.Email == email)
    gameSession.ActiveUser = gameSession.User2;
  else
    gameSession.ActiveUser = gameSession.User1;

  gameSession.TurnFinished = true;
  _sessions = new ConcurrentBag<GameSessionModel>
  (_sessions.Where(u => u.Id != id))
  {
    gameSession
  };
  return gameSession;
}
```

2. Add a new method called `SetPosition` to `GameSessionController`:

```
public async Task<IActionResult> SetPosition(Guid id,
  string email, int x, int y)
{
  var gameSession =
    await _gameSessionService.GetGameSession(id);
```

```
await _gameSessionService.AddTurn(gameSession.Id, email,
 x, y);
return View("Index", gameSession);
}
```

3. Add a new model called `InvitationEmailModel` to the `Models` folder:

```
public class InvitationEmailModel
{
  public string DisplayName { get; set; }
  public UserModel InvitedBy { get; set; }
  public DateTime InvitedDate { get; set; }
  public string ConfirmationUrl { get; set; }
}
```

4. Add a new View called `InvitationEmail` to the `Views/EmailTemplates` folder:

```
@model TicTacToe.Models.InvitationEmailModel
@{
  ViewData["Title"] = "View";
  Layout = "_LayoutEmail";
}
<h1>Welcome @Model.DisplayName</h1>
You have been invited by @($"{Model.InvitedBy.FirstName}
{Model.InvitedBy.LastName}") for playing the Tic-Tac-Toe game.
Please click <a href="@Model.ConfirmationUrl">here</a> for
joining the game.
```

5. Update the `Index` method in the `GameInvitationController` for using the **Invitation Email Template** mentioned previously:

```
[HttpPost]
public async Task<IActionResult> Index(
 GameInvitationModel gameInvitationModel,
 [FromServices]IEmailService emailService)
{
  var gameInvitationService =
    Request.HttpContext.RequestServices.GetService
    <IGameInvitationService>();
  if (ModelState.IsValid)
  {
    try
    {
      var invitationModel = new InvitationEmailModel
      {
        DisplayName = $"{gameInvitationModel.EmailTo}",
```

```
        InvitedBy =
         await _userService.GetUserByEmail(
          gameInvitationModel.InvitedBy),
          ConfirmationUrl = Url.Action("ConfirmGameInvitation",
         "GameInvitation", new { id = gameInvitationModel.Id },
          Request.Scheme, Request.Host.ToString()),
          InvitedDate = gameInvitationModel.ConfirmationDate
      };

     var emailRenderService =
      HttpContext.RequestServices.GetService
      <IEmailTemplateRenderService>();
     var message =
      await emailRenderService.RenderTemplate
      <InvitationEmailModel>("EmailTemplates/InvitationEmail",
       invitationModel, Request.Host.ToString());
      await emailService.SendEmail(
       gameInvitationModel.EmailTo, _stringLocalizer[
       "Invitation for playing a Tic-Tac-Toe game"], message);
    }
    catch
    {

    }

    var invitation =
     gameInvitationService.Add(gameInvitationModel).Result;
    return RedirectToAction("GameInvitationConfirmation",
     new { id = gameInvitationModel.Id });
   }
   return View(gameInvitationModel);
  }
```

6. Add a new method called `ConfirmGameInvitation`
   to `GameInvitationController`:

```
[HttpGet]
public IActionResult ConfirmGameInvitation (Guid id,
[FromServices]IGameInvitationService gameInvitationService)
{
  var gameInvitation = gameInvitationService.Get(id).Result;
  gameInvitation.IsConfirmed = true;
  gameInvitation.ConfirmationDate = DateTime.Now;
  gameInvitationService.Update(gameInvitation);
  return RedirectToAction("Index", "GameSession", new { id = id });
}
```

7. Start the application and verify that everything is working as expected, including the various emails and steps for starting a new game.

Now that we have implemented all this new code, how do we test it? How do we ensure that it is working as expected? You could start the application in debug mode and verify manually that all variables are set correctly and that the application flow is correct, but that would be very tedious and not very efficient.

How could you do it better? Well, by using unit tests and integration tests, which we will introduce in the following sections.

Adding unit tests

Unit tests allow you to individually verify the behavior of your various technical components and ensure that they are working as expected. They also help you to quickly identify regressions and analyze the overall impact of new developments.

Visual Studio 2017 includes powerful features for unit testing. The **Test Explorer** helps you to run unit tests as well as view and analyze test results. For that, you can either use the built-in Microsoft testing framework or additional frameworks such as NUnit or xUnit.

Furthermore, you can automatically execute unit tests after each build, so developers can react quickly if something is not working as expected.

Refactoring code can be done without fearing regressions, since unit tests ensure that everything is still working as before. No more excuses for not having the best code quality possible!

You could even go further and apply **Test Driven Development** (**TDD**), which is where you write unit tests before writing implementations. Additionally, unit tests become some sort of design document and functional specifications in this case.

 This book is about ASP.NET Core 2.0, so we will not go into too much detail about unit tests. It is, however, advised to dig deeper and familiarize yourself with all the different unit test concepts for building better applications.

We are now going to see how easy it is to use xUnit, the preferred unit testing framework for ASP.NET Core:

1. Add a new project of **xUnit Test Project (.NET Core)** type called
   `TicTacToe.UnitTests` to the **TicTacToe Solution**:

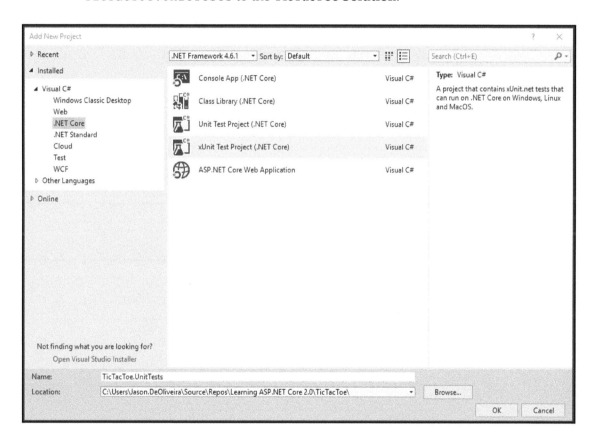

2. Update the **xUnit** and **Microsoft.NET.Test.SDK** NuGet packages to the latest versions using the **NuGet Package Manager**:

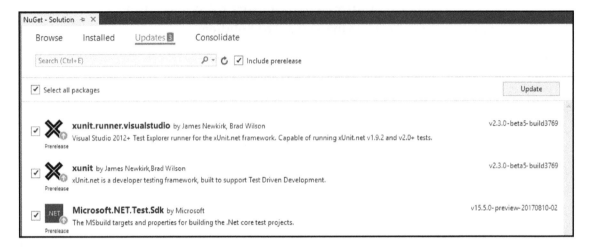

3. Add references to the `TicTacToe` and `TicTacToe.Logging` projects:

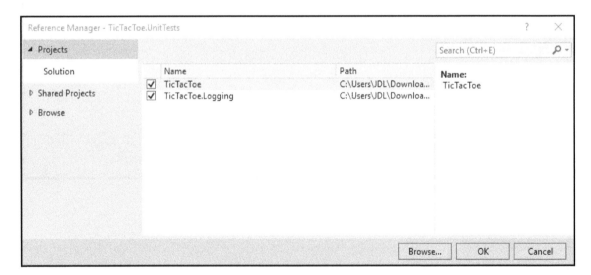

4. Delete the autogenerated class, add a new class called `FileLoggerTests.cs` for testing a regular class, and implement a new method called `ShouldCreateALogFileAndAddEntry`:

```
public class FileLoggerTests
{
  [Fact]
  public void ShouldCreateALogFileAndAddEntry()
  {
    var fileLogger = new FileLogger(
      "Test", (category, level) => true,
      Path.Combine(Directory.GetCurrentDirectory(),
      "testlog.log"));
    var isEnabled = fileLogger.IsEnabled(LogLevel.Information);
    Assert.True(isEnabled);
  }
}
```

5. Add another new class called `UserServiceTests.cs` for testing a service, and implement a new method called `ShouldAddUser`:

```
public class UserServiceTests
{
  [Theory]
  [InlineData("test@test.com", "test", "test", "test123!")]
  [InlineData("test1@test.com", "test1", "test1", "test123!")]
  [InlineData("test2@test.com", "test2", "test2", "test123!")]
  public async Task ShouldAddUser(string email,
   string firstName, string lastName, string password)
  {
    var userModel = new UserModel
    {
      Email = email,
      FirstName = firstName,
      LastName = lastName,
      Password = password
    };

    var userService = new UserService();
    var userAdded = await userService.RegisterUser(userModel);
    Assert.True(userAdded);
  }
}
```

6. Open **Test Explorer** via **Test** I **Windows** I **Test Explorer** and then choose to **Run All**, to ensure that all the tests execute successfully:

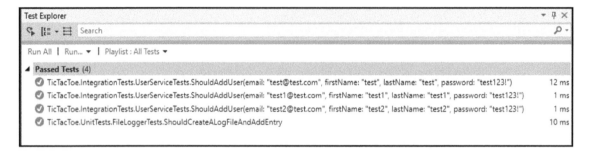

Unit tests are great and really important, but also somewhat limited. They only test each technical component separately, which is the main goal of this type of test. The idea behind unit tests is to quickly get a glimpse of the current status of all your technical components, one-by-one, without slowing down the continuous integration process. They do not test applications under real production conditions, since external dependencies are mocked. Instead, they are intended to run quickly and ensure that each method being tested creates no unintended side effects in other methods or classes.

If you stop here, you will not be able to find the maximum bugs possible during the development phase. You have to go even further and test all components together in a real environment; this is where integration tests come into play.

Adding integration tests

Integration tests are a logical extension to unit tests. They test the integration between multiple technical components within your applications in a real environment with access to external data sources (such as Databases, Web Services, and Caches).

The goal of this type of test is to ensure that everything is working well together and providing the expected functionalities when combining the various technical components together for creating application behavior.

Furthermore, integration tests should always have clean-up steps, so that they can run repeatedly without error and will not leave any artifacts behind in databases or file systems. In the following example, you will understand how to apply integration tests to the *Tic-Tac-Toe* application:

1. Add a new project of **xUnit Test Project (.NET Core)** type called `TicTacToe.IntegrationTests` to the **TicTacToe Solution**, update the NuGet packages and add references to the `TicTacToe` and `TicTacToe.Logging` projects as previously shown for the **Unit Tests Project**.

2. Add the `Microsoft.AspNetCore.TestHost` NuGet package to be able to create fully-automated integration tests using xUnit:

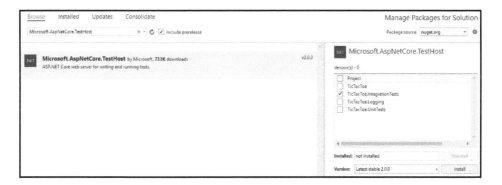

3. Delete the autogenerated class, add a new class called `IntegrationTests.cs`, and implement a new method called `ShouldGetHomePageAsync`:

```
using Microsoft.Extensions.DependencyInjection;
using System.Reflection;
using System.Linq;
using Microsoft.CodeAnalysis;
...
public class IntegrationTests
{
  private readonly TestServer _testServer;
  private readonly HttpClient _httpClient;
  public IntegrationTests()
  {
    string applicationBasePath =
     Path.GetFullPath(Path.Combine(
      Directory.GetCurrentDirectory(),
      @"..\..\..\..\TicTacToe"));
    Directory.SetCurrentDirectory(applicationBasePath);
    Environment.SetEnvironmentVariable(
```

```
                    "ASPNETCORE_ENVIRONMENT", "Development");
            var builder = new WebHostBuilder()
             .UseKestrel()
             .UseContentRoot(applicationBasePath)
             .UseStartup<Startup>()
             .ConfigureServices(services =>
            {
              services.Configure((RazorViewEngineOptions options) =>
              {
                var previous = options.CompilationCallback;
                options.CompilationCallback = (context) =>
                {
                  previous?.Invoke(context);
                  var assembly =
                    typeof(Startup).GetTypeInfo().Assembly;
                  var assemblies =
                    assembly.GetReferencedAssemblies().Select(x =>
                     MetadataReference.CreateFromFile(
                      Assembly.Load(x).Location)).ToList();
                    assemblies.Add(MetadataReference.CreateFromFile(
                     Assembly.Load(new AssemblyName(
                      "mscorlib")).Location));
                    assemblies.Add(MetadataReference.CreateFromFile(
                     Assembly.Load(new AssemblyName(
                      "System.Private.Corelib")).Location));
                    assemblies.Add(MetadataReference.CreateFromFile(
                     Assembly.Load(new AssemblyName("netstandard,
                     Version = 2.0.0.0, Culture = neutral,
                     PublicKeyToken = cc7b13ffcd2ddd51")).Location));
                    assemblies.Add(MetadataReference.CreateFromFile(
                     Assembly.Load(new AssemblyName(
                      "System.Linq")).Location));
                    assemblies.Add(MetadataReference.CreateFromFile(
                     Assembly.Load(new AssemblyName(
                      "System.Threading.Tasks")).Location));
                    assemblies.Add(MetadataReference.CreateFromFile(
                     Assembly.Load(new AssemblyName(
                      "System.Runtime")).Location));
                    assemblies.Add(MetadataReference.CreateFromFile(
                     Assembly.Load(new AssemblyName(
                      "System.Dynamic.Runtime")).Location));
                    assemblies.Add(MetadataReference.CreateFromFile(
                     Assembly.Load(new AssemblyName(
                      "Microsoft.AspNetCore.Razor.Runtime")).Location));
                    assemblies.Add(MetadataReference.CreateFromFile(
                     Assembly.Load(new AssemblyName(
                      "Microsoft.AspNetCore.Mvc")).Location));
                    assemblies.Add(MetadataReference.CreateFromFile(
```

```
                Assembly.Load(new AssemblyName(
                "Microsoft.AspNetCore.Razor")).Location));
              assemblies.Add(MetadataReference.CreateFromFile(
                Assembly.Load(new AssemblyName(
                "Microsoft.AspNetCore.Mvc.Razor")).Location));
              assemblies.Add(MetadataReference.CreateFromFile(
                Assembly.Load(new AssemblyName(
                "Microsoft.AspNetCore.Html.Abstractions")).Location));
              assemblies.Add(MetadataReference.CreateFromFile(
                Assembly.Load(new AssemblyName(
                "System.Text.Encodings.Web")).Location));
              context.Compilation =
                context.Compilation.AddReferences(assemblies);
          };
        });
      });

    _testServer = new TestServer(builder)
    {
      BaseAddress = new Uri("http://localhost:5000")

    };
    _httpClient = _testServer.CreateClient();
  }

  [Fact]
  public async Task ShouldGetHomePageAsync()
  {
    var response = await _httpClient.GetAsync("/");
    response.EnsureSuccessStatusCode();
    var responseString = await
      response.Content.ReadAsStringAsync();
    Assert.Contains("Welcome to the Tic-Tac-Toe Desktop Game!",
      responseString);
  }
}
```

4. Run the tests in **Test Explorer** and ensure that they execute successfully:

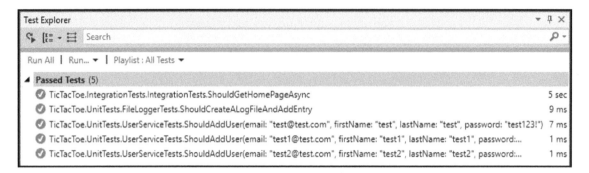

Now that you have seen how to test your applications in the previous examples, you can continue to add additional unit and integration tests to fully understand these concepts and to build a testing coverage that will allow you to provide high-quality applications.

Summary

In this chapter, you learned about the MVC pattern, its different components and layers, and how important it is for building great ASP.NET Core 2.0 web applications.

You saw how to use layout pages and the features surrounding it to create device-specific layouts and thus adapting your user interfaces to the devices they will be running on.

Furthermore, you have used View Pages to build the visible part, the presentation layer, of your web applications.

Then we looked at Partial Views, View Components, and Tag Helpers to better encapsulate and reuse your presentation logic throughout the different views of your applications.

At the end, we illustrated advanced concepts such as the View Engine, as well as units tests and integration tests for creating high-quality applications with a low **MTTR** for your bugs.

In the next chapter, we will talk about the ASP.NET Core 2.0 Web API framework and how to build, test, and deploy Web API applications.

7
Creating Web API Applications

You do not know it yet, but this chapter is the chapter you have been waiting for! It is very special for multiple reasons.

First, we will finish the gaming part and you will be able to start playing the *Tic-Tac-Toe* game. Yes, at last, the whole application will run and you will be able to compete against other users. Very exciting!

Second, you will see how to integrate your applications with other systems and services. This is very important, since applications are no longer isolated silos. Instead, they communicate with each other and continuously exchange data for providing even more value to customers. How do you do that? You provide interoperable Web APIs, which allow for plugging components, sometimes based on completely different technologies, together!

Third, using Web APIs will not only allow you to integrate with other systems; it will also help you to build more flexible and reusable application components, which you can then combine for creating new applications responding to more advanced use cases.

The APIs you will be creating in this chapter are not only usable by the MVC Web frontend you have been working on, but also by new mobile frontends you might build in the future. This will allow you to reach even more customers. You will be able to provide omnichannel experiences to your customers, where they start using one device and finish on another.

In this chapter, we will cover the following topics:

- Applying Web API concepts and best practices
- Building RPC-style Web APIs
- Building REST-style Web APIs
- Building HATEOAS-style Web APIs

Applying Web API concepts and best practices

ASP.NET Core 2.0 combines the best features of ASP.NET MVC and Web APIs together into a single framework. This makes complete sense, since they provide many similar functionalities.

Before this merger, developers had to rewrite code when they needed to expose data in different formats via MVC and Web APIs. They had to work with multiple frameworks and concepts at the same time. Fortunately, this entire process has been completely streamlined in ASP.NET Core 2.0, as you will see during this chapter.

The following diagram illustrates how client HTTP requests are handled by ASP.NET Core 2.0 concerning Web APIs and MVC:

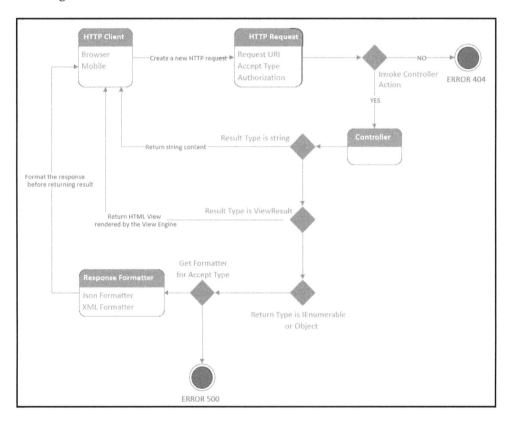

Web APIs normally use either JSON or XML as a response format. JSON would be the preferred format, since it has become quasi-standard on the market and everybody is using it due to its simplicity and efficiency.

Furthermore, filters and middlewares can be used with Web APIs, since ASP.NET Core 2.0 manages Web APIs the same way it does for standard MVC Controllers. This can be quite handy in some use cases and developers can apply their skills more widely.

In general, there are three different styles for creating Web APIs when using ASP.NET Core 2.0:

- RPC-style
- REST-style
- HATEOAS-style

 Note that it is also possible to use SOAP for creating Web APIs, but it is not recommended. Instead, SOAP should be used in the context of standard web services, which is why it is not shown in the following examples.

We will present each style in more detail and you will see some practical examples, which will help you decide on your own integration strategy.

Building RPC-style Web APIs

The **RPC**-style is based on the **Remote Procedure Call** paradigms, which have existed for a long time now (since the early 1980s). It is based on including an action name in the URL, which therefore makes it very similar to standard MVC actions.

One of the big advantages of ASP.NET Core 2.0 is that you do not need to separate the MVC parts from the Web API parts. Instead, you can use both in your controller implementations.

Controllers are now capable of rendering View results as well as JSON/XML API responses, which enables easy migrations from one to the other. Additionally, you can use a specific route path or the same route path for your MVC actions.

In the following example, you are going to transform a controller action from an MVC View result into an RPC-style Web API:

1. Add a new method called `ConfirmEmail` to the `UserRegistrationController`; it will be used to confirm the user registration email:

```
[HttpGet]
public async Task<IActionResult> ConfirmEmail(string email)
{
  var user = await _userService.GetUserByEmail(email);
  if (user != null)
  {
    user.IsEmailConfirmed = true;
    user.EmailConfirmationDate = DateTime.Now;
    await _userService.UpdateUser(user);
    return RedirectToAction("Index", "Home");
  }
  return BadRequest();
}
```

2. Update the `ConfirmGameInvitation` method within the `GameInvitationController`, store the email of the invited user in a session variable and register the new user via the user service:

```
[HttpGet]
public async Task<IActionResult> ConfirmGameInvitation(Guid id,
 [FromServices]IGameInvitationService gameInvitationService)
{
  var gameInvitation = await gameInvitationService.Get(id);
  gameInvitation.IsConfirmed = true;
  gameInvitation.ConfirmationDate = DateTime.Now;
  await gameInvitationService.Update(gameInvitation);
  Request.HttpContext.Session.SetString("email",
   gameInvitation.EmailTo);
  await _userService.RegisterUser(new UserModel
  {
    Email = gameInvitation.EmailTo, EmailConfirmationDate =
      DateTime.Now, IsEmailConfirmed =true
  });
  return RedirectToAction("Index", "GameSession", new { id });
}
```

3. Update the table element in `GameSessionViewComponent` in the `Views/Shared/Components/GameSession/default.cshtml` file:

```
@using Microsoft.AspNetCore.Http
@model TicTacToe.Models.GameSessionModel
@{
  var email = Context.Session.GetString("email");
}
<div id="gameBoard">
  <table>
    @for (int rows = 0; rows < 3; rows++)
    {
      <tr style="height:150px;">
        @for (int columns = 0; columns < 3; columns++)
        {
          <td style="width:150px; border:1px
            solid #808080" id="@($"c_{rows}_{columns}")">
            @{
                var position = Model.Turns?.FirstOrDefault(
                  turn => turn.X == columns && turn.Y == rows);
                if (position != null)
                {
                  if (position.User == Model.User1)
                  {
                    <i class="glyphicon glyphicon-unchecked"
                        style="width:100%;height:100%"></i>
                  }
                  else
                  {
                    <i class="glyphicon glyphicon-remove-circle"
                        style="width:100%;height:100%"></i>
                  }
                }
                else
                {
                  <a class="btn btn-default btn-SetPosition"
                      style="width:150px; min-height:150px;"
                      data-X="@columns" data-Y="@rows">
                       
                  </a>
                }
            }
          </td>
        }
      </tr>
    }
  </table>
```

```
    </div>
    <div class="alert" id="divAlertWaitTurn">
      <i class="glyphicon glyphicon-alert">Please wait until the
        other user has finished his turn.</i>
    </div>
```

4. Add a new JavaScript file within the `wwwroot\app\js` folder called `GameSession.js`; it will be used to call the Web API. Add a temporary alert box for testing purposes:

```javascript
function SetGameSession(gdSessionId, strEmail) {
  window.GameSessionId = gdSessionId;
  window.EmailPlayer = strEmail;
}

$(document).ready(function () {
  $(".btn-SetPosition").click(function () {
    var intX = $(this).attr("data-X");
    var intY = $(this).attr("data-Y");
    SendPosition(window.GameSessionId, window.EmailPlayer,
      intX, intY);
  })
})

function SendPosition(gdSession, strEmail, intX, intY) {
  var port = document.location.port ? (":" +
   document.location.port) : "";
  var url = document.location.protocol + "//" +
   document.location.hostname + port +
   "/restApi/v1/SetGamePosition/" + gdSession;
  var obj = {
    "Email": strEmail, "x": intX, "y": intY
  };

  var json = JSON.stringify(obj);
  $.ajax({
    'url': url,
    'accepts': "application/json; charset=utf-8",
    'contentType': "application/json",
    'data': json,
    'dataType': "json",
    'type': "POST",
    'success': function (data) {
      alert(data);
    }
  });
}
```

5. Add the preceding new JavaScript file to the `bundleconfig.json` file, for bundling it together with the other files into the `site.js` file:

```json
{
  "outputFileName": "wwwroot/js/site.js",
  "inputFiles": [
    "wwwroot/app/js/scripts1.js",
    "wwwroot/app/js/scripts2.js",
    "wwwroot/app/js/GameSession.js"
  ],
  "sourceMap": true,
  "includeInProject": true
},
```

6. Add a new property called `Email` to the `TurnModel` model:

```csharp
public string Email { get; set; }
```

7. Update the `SetPosition` method within `GameSessionController` and expose it as a Web API for being able to receive Ajax calls from the JavaScript `SendPosition` function previously implemented:

```csharp
[Produces("application/json")]
[HttpPost("/restapi/v1/SetGamePosition/{sessionId}")]
public async Task<IActionResult> SetPosition(
  [FromRoute]Guid sessionId)
{
  if (sessionId != Guid.Empty)
  {
    using (var reader = new StreamReader(Request.Body,
      Encoding.UTF8, true, 1024, true))
    {
      var bodyString = reader.ReadToEnd();
      if (string.IsNullOrEmpty(bodyString))
        return BadRequest("Body is empty");

      var turn =
        JsonConvert.DeserializeObject<TurnModel>(bodyString);

      turn.User =
        await HttpContext.RequestServices.GetService
        <IUserService>().GetUserByEmail(turn.Email);
      turn.UserId = turn.User.Id;
      if (turn == null)
        return BadRequest("You must pass a TurnModel
          object in your body");
```

```
                      var gameSession =
                       await _gameSessionService.GetGameSession(sessionId);

                      if (gameSession == null)
                        return BadRequest($"Cannot find Game Session {sessionId}");

                      if (gameSession.ActiveUser.Email != turn.User.Email)
                        return BadRequest($"{turn.User.Email} cannot play
                        this turn");

                      gameSession =
                       await _gameSessionService.AddTurn(
                       gameSession.Id, turn.User.Email, turn.X, turn.Y);
                      if (gameSession != null &&
                          gameSession.ActiveUser.Email != turn.User.Email)
                        return Ok(gameSession);
                      else
                        return BadRequest("Cannot save turn");
                    }
                  }
                  return BadRequest("Id is empty");
              }
```

Note that it is best practice to prefix Web APIs with a meaningful name
and a version number (for example, /restapi/v1) as well as to support
JSON and XML.

8. Update the **Game Session Index View** in the Views folder and call the JavaScript
SetGameSession function with the corresponding parameters:

```
@using Microsoft.AspNetCore.Http
@model TicTacToe.Models.GameSessionModel
@{
  var email = Context.Session.GetString("email");
}
@section Desktop
{
  <h1>Game Session @Model.Id</h1>
  <h2>Started at @(DateTime.Now.ToShortTimeString())</h2>
  <div class="alert alert-info">
    <table class="table">
      <tr>
        <td>User 1:</td>
        <td>@Model.User1?.Email (<i class="glyphicon
          glyphicon-unchecked"></i>)</td>
      </tr>
```

```
      <tr>
        <td>User 2:</td>
        <td>@Model.User2?.Email (<i class="glyphicon
          glyphicon-remove-circle"></i>)</td>
      </tr>
    </table>
  </div>
}
@section Mobile{
  <h1>Game Session @Model.Id</h1>
  <h2>Started at @(DateTime.Now.ToShortTimeString())</h2>
  User 1: @Model.User1?.Email <i class="glyphicon
    glyphicon-unchecked"></i><br />
  User 2: @Model.User2?.Email (<i class="glyphicon
    glyphicon-remove-circle"></i>)
}
<h3>User Email @email</h3>
<h3>Active User <span id="activeUser">
 @Model.ActiveUser?.Email</span></h3>
<vc:game-session game-session-id="@Model.Id"></vc:game-session>
@section Scripts{
  <script>
    SetGameSession("@Model.Id", "@email");
  </script>
}
```

9. Update the `ProcessEmailConfirmation` method for WebSockets in the
   Communication Middleware:

```
public async Task ProcessEmailConfirmation(HttpContext context,
 WebSocket currentSocket, CancellationToken ct, string email)
{
  var user = await _userService.GetUserByEmail(email);
  while (!ct.IsCancellationRequested &&
   !currentSocket.CloseStatus.HasValue &&
    user?.IsEmailConfirmed == false)
  {
    await SendStringAsync(currentSocket,
     "WaitEmailConfirmation", ct);
    await Task.Delay(500);
    user = await _userService.GetUserByEmail(email);
  }

  if (user.IsEmailConfirmed)
  {
    await SendStringAsync(currentSocket, "OK", ct);
  }
```

```
        }
```

10. Update the `ProcessGameInvitationConfirmation` method for WebSockets in the **Communication Middleware**:

```
private async Task ProcessGameInvitationConfirmation(
 HttpContext context, WebSocket webSocket,
 CancellationToken ct, string parameters)
{
  var gameInvitationService =
   context.RequestServices.GetService<IGameInvitationService>();
  var id = Guid.Parse(parameters);
  var gameInvitationModel =
   await gameInvitationService.Get(id);
  while (!ct.IsCancellationRequested &&
         !webSocket.CloseStatus.HasValue &&
          gameInvitationModel?.IsConfirmed == false)
  {
    await Task.Delay(500);
    gameInvitationModel = await gameInvitationService.Get(id);
    await SendStringAsync(webSocket, "WaitForConfirmation", ct);
  }

  if (gameInvitationModel.IsConfirmed)
  {
    await SendStringAsync(webSocket,
     JsonConvert.SerializeObject(new
    {
      Result = "OK",
      Email = gameInvitationModel.InvitedBy,
      gameInvitationModel.EmailTo,
      gameInvitationModel.Id
    }), ct);
  }
}
```

11. Update the `CheckGameInvitationConfirmationStatus` method in the `scripts2.js` JavaScript file; it has to verify the returned data now:

```
function CheckGameInvitationConfirmationStatus(id) {
  $.get("/GameInvitationConfirmation?id=" + id, function (data) {
    if (data.result === "OK") {
      if (interval !== null) {
        clearInterval(interval);
      }
      window.location.href = "/GameSession/Index/" + id;
    }
```

```
    });
  }
```

12. Update the `Process` method in the **Gravatar Tag Helper** and handle the case where no photo exists correctly:

```
public override void Process(TagHelperContext context,
 TagHelperOutput output)
{
  byte[] photo = null;
  if (CheckIsConnected())
  {
    photo = GetPhoto(Email);
  }
  else
  {
    string filePath =
     Path.Combine(Directory.GetCurrentDirectory(),
     "wwwroot", "images", "no-photo.jpg");
    if (File.Exists(filePath))
      photo = File.ReadAllBytes(filePath);
  }

  if(photo != null && photo.Length > 0)
  {
    output.TagName = "img";
    output.Attributes.SetAttribute("src",
     $"data:image/jpeg;base64,{Convert.ToBase64String(photo)}");
  }
}
```

13. Update the `Add` method in `GameInvitationService`:

```
public Task<GameInvitationModel> Add(
 GameInvitationModel gameInvitationModel)
{
  _gameInvitations.Add(gameInvitationModel);
  return Task.FromResult(gameInvitationModel);
}
```

14. Update the **Desktop Layout Page** and **Mobile Layout Page**; cleanup by removing the development `environment` tag containing `script1.js` and `script2.js` at the bottom of both pages.

15. Update the `scripts1.js` JavaScript file and clean up by removing all the alert boxes that display whether WebSockets are enabled.

16. Start the application, register a new user, start a game session by inviting another user, click on a cell, and you will now see a JavaScript alert box:

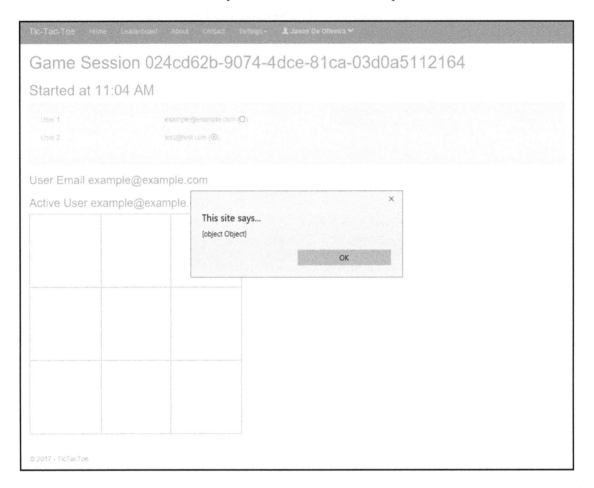

Very well; you have seen how to transform the existing `GameSessionController` action into an RPC-style Web API. Since all the different ASP.NET web frameworks have been centralized into a single framework in ASP.NET Core 2.0, this can be done easily and quickly without re-writing code or changing too much in your existing code.

In the next step, we will see how to add a new method to the RPC-style Web API for checking if the turn for the current user has been finished and thus the next user can start his turn:

1. Add a new property called `TurnNumber` to the `GameSessionModel` for tracking the current turn number:

   ```
   public int TurnNumber { get; set; }
   ```

2. Add a new property called `IconNumber` to the `TurnModel` for being able to define what icon (X or O) needs to be used for display later:

   ```
   public string IconNumber { get; set; }
   ```

3. Add a new method called `GetGameSession` to the `GameSessionController`; it will be exclusive to Web API calls:

   ```
   [Produces("application/json")]
   [HttpGet("/restapi/v1/GetGameSession/{sessionId}")]
   public async Task<IActionResult> GetGameSession(Guid sessionId)
   {
     if (sessionId != Guid.Empty)
     {
       var session =
        await _gameSessionService.GetGameSession(sessionId);

       if (session != null)
       {
         return Ok(session);
       }
       else
       {
         return NotFound($"can not found session {sessionId}");
       }
     }
     else
     {
       return BadRequest("session id is null");
     }
   }
   ```

4. Update the `AddTurn` method in `GameSessionService`, so that it calculates the `IconNumber` and `TurnNumber`:

   ```
   public async Task<GameSessionModel> AddTurn(Guid id,
     string email, int x, int y)
   ```

```
{
  List<Models.TurnModel> turns;
  var gameSession = _sessions.FirstOrDefault(
   session => session.Id == id);
  if (gameSession.Turns != null && gameSession.Turns.Any())
    turns = new List<Models.TurnModel>(gameSession.Turns);
  else
    turns = new List<TurnModel>();

  turns.Add(new TurnModel
  {
    User = await _UserService.GetUserByEmail(email),
     X = x,
     Y = y,
     IconNumber = email == gameSession.User1?.Email ? "1" : "2"
  });

  gameSession.Turns = turns;
  gameSession.TurnNumber = gameSession.TurnNumber + 1;
  if (gameSession.User1?.Email == email)
    gameSession.ActiveUser = gameSession.User2;
  else
    gameSession.ActiveUser = gameSession.User1;

  gameSession.TurnFinished = true;
  _sessions = new ConcurrentBag<GameSessionModel>
   (_sessions.Where(u => u.Id != id))
  {
    gameSession
  };
  return gameSession;
}
```

5. Update the **Game Session Index View**, use images, and add the possibility to enable and disable the gameboard:

```
@using Microsoft.AspNetCore.Http
@model TicTacToe.Models.GameSessionModel
@{
  var email = Context.Session.GetString("email");
}
@section Desktop
{
  <h1>Game Session @Model.Id</h1>
  <h2>Started at @(DateTime.Now.ToShortTimeString())</h2>
  <div class="alert alert-info">
  <table class="table">
```

```
    <tr>
      <td>User 1:</td>
      <td>@Model.User1?.Email (<i class="glyphicon
       glyphicon-unchecked"></i>)</td>
    </tr>
    <tr>
      <td>User 2:</td>
      <td>@Model.User2?.Email (<i class="glyphicon
       glyphicon-remove-circle"></i>)</td>
    </tr>
  </table>
  </div>


}
@section Mobile{
 <h1>Game Session @Model.Id</h1>
 <h2>Started at @(DateTime.Now.ToShortTimeString())</h2>
 User 1: @Model.User1 <i class="glyphicon
  glyphicon-unchecked"></i><br />
 User 2: @Model.User2 (<i class="glyphicon
  glyphicon-remove-circle"></i>)
}
<h3>User Email @email</h3>
<h3>Active User <span id="activeUser">
 @Model.ActiveUser?.Email</span></h3>
<vc:game-session game-session-id="@Model.Id"></vc:game-session>
@section Scripts{
  <script>
  SetGameSession("@Model.Id", "@email");
  EnableCheckTurnIsFinished();
  @if(email != Model.ActiveUser?.Email)
  {
    <text>DisableBoard(@Model.TurnNumber);</text>
  }
  else
  {
    <text>EnableBoard(@Model.TurnNumber);</text>
  }
  </script>
}
```

6. Add a new JavaScript file called `CheckTurnIsFinished.js` to the `wwwroot\app\js` folder; update the `bundleconfig.json` file accordingly:

```
function EnableCheckTurnIsFinished() {
  interval = setInterval(() => {
    CheckTurnIsFinished();
```

```
   }, 2000);
}

function CheckTurnIsFinished() {
  var port = document.location.port ? (":" +
   document.location.port) : "";
  var url = document.location.protocol + "//" +
   document.location.hostname + port +
   "/restapi/v1/GetGameSession/" + window.GameSessionId;

  $.get(url, function (data) {
    if (data.turnFinished === true &&
     data.turnNumber >= window.TurnNumber) {
      CheckGameSessionIsFinished();
      ChangeTurn(data);
    }
  });
}

function ChangeTurn(data) {
  var turn = data.turns[data.turnNumber-1];
  DisplayImageTurn(turn);

  $("#activeUser").text(data.activeUser.email);
  if (data.activeUser.email !== window.EmailPlayer) {
    DisableBoard(data.turnNumber);
  }
  else {
    EnableBoard(data.turnNumber);
  }
}

function DisableBoard(turnNumber) {
  var divBoard = $("#gameBoard");
  divBoard.hide();
  $("#divAlertWaitTurn").show();
  window.TurnNumber = turnNumber;
}

function EnableBoard(turnNumber) {
  var divBoard = $("#gameBoard");
  divBoard.show();
  $("#divAlertWaitTurn").hide();
  window.TurnNumber = turnNumber;
}

function DisplayImageTurn(turn) {
  var c = $("#c_" + turn.y + "_" + turn.x);
```

```
    var css;

    if (turn.iconNumber === "1") {
    css = 'glyphicon glyphicon-unchecked';
  }
  else {
    css = 'glyphicon glyphicon-remove-circle';
  }

  c.html('<i class="' + css + '"></i>');
}
```

7. Update the `SetGameSession` method in the `GameSession.js` JavaScript file; set the `TurnNumber` to zero by default:

```
function SetGameSession(gdSessionId, strEmail) {
  window.GameSessionId = gdSessionId;
  window.EmailPlayer = strEmail;
  window.TurnNumber = 0;
}
```

8. Update the `SendPosition` method in the `GameSession.js` JavaScript file and remove the temporary testing alert box added before; we don't need it anymore, and the game will be fully functional at the end of this section:

```
function SendPosition(gdSession, strEmail, intX, intY) {
  var port = document.location.port ? (":" +
   document.location.port) : "";
  var url = document.location.protocol + "//" +
   document.location.hostname + port +
   "/restApi/v1/SetGamePosition/" + gdSession;
  var obj = {
    "Email": strEmail, "x": intX, "y": intY
  };

  var json = JSON.stringify(obj);
  $.ajax({
    'url': url,
    'accepts': "application/json; charset=utf-8",
    'contentType': "application/json",
    'data': json,
    'dataType': "json",
    'type': "POST"
  });
}
```

9. Add two new methods to the `GameSessionController`, the first one called `CheckGameSessionIsFinished` and the second one called `CheckIfUserHasWon`:

```
[Produces("application/json")]
[HttpGet("/restapi/v1/CheckGameSessionIsFinished/{sessionId}")]
public async Task<IActionResult> CheckGameSessionIsFinished(
 Guid sessionId)
{
  if (sessionId != Guid.Empty)
  {
    var session =
     await _gameSessionService.GetGameSession(sessionId);
    if (session != null)
    {
      if (session.Turns.Count() == 9)
        return Ok("The game was a draw.");

      var userTurns = session.Turns.Where(
        x => x.User == session.User1).ToList();
      var user1Won = CheckIfUserHasWon(session.User1?.Email,
        userTurns);

      if (user1Won)
      {
        return Ok($"{session.User1.Email} has won the game.");
      }
      else
      {
        userTurns = session.Turns.Where(
          x => x.User == session.User2).ToList();
        var user2Won = CheckIfUserHasWon(session.User2?.Email,
          userTurns);

        if (user2Won)
          return Ok($"{session.User2.Email} has won the game.");
        else
          return Ok("");
      }
    }
    else
    {
      return NotFound($"Cannot find session {sessionId}.");
    }
  }
  else
  {
```

```
      return BadRequest("SessionId is null.");
   }
}

private bool CheckIfUserHasWon(string email,
 List<TurnModel> userTurns)
{
  if (userTurns.Any(x => x.X == 0 && x.Y == 0) &&
    userTurns.Any(x => x.X == 1 && x.Y == 0) &&
    userTurns.Any(x => x.X == 2 && x.Y == 0))
   return true;
  else if (userTurns.Any(x => x.X == 0 && x.Y == 1) &&
    userTurns.Any(x => x.X == 1 && x.Y == 1) &&
    userTurns.Any(x => x.X == 2 && x.Y == 1))
   return true;
  else if (userTurns.Any(x => x.X == 0 && x.Y == 2) &&
    userTurns.Any(x => x.X == 1 && x.Y == 2) &&
    userTurns.Any(x => x.X == 2 && x.Y == 2))
   return true;
  else if (userTurns.Any(x => x.X == 0 && x.Y == 0) &&
    userTurns.Any(x => x.X == 0 && x.Y == 1) &&
    userTurns.Any(x => x.X == 0 && x.Y == 2))
   return true;
  else if (userTurns.Any(x => x.X == 1 && x.Y == 0) &&
    userTurns.Any(x => x.X == 1 && x.Y == 1) &&
    userTurns.Any(x => x.X == 1 && x.Y == 2))
   return true;
  else if (userTurns.Any(x => x.X == 2 && x.Y == 0) &&
    userTurns.Any(x => x.X == 2 && x.Y == 1) &&
    userTurns.Any(x => x.X == 2 && x.Y == 2))
   return true;
  else if (userTurns.Any(x => x.X == 0 && x.Y == 0) &&
    userTurns.Any(x => x.X == 1 && x.Y == 1) &&
    userTurns.Any(x => x.X == 2 && x.Y == 2))
   return true;
  else if (userTurns.Any(x => x.X == 2 && x.Y == 0) &&
    userTurns.Any(x => x.X == 1 && x.Y == 1) &&
    userTurns.Any(x => x.X == 0 && x.Y == 2))
   return true;
  else
    return false;
}
```

10. Add a new JavaScript file called `CheckGameSessionIsFinished.js` to the `wwwroot\app\js` folder and update the `bundleconfig.json` file accordingly:

```
function CheckGameSessionIsFinished() {
```

```
var port = document.location.port ? (":" +
document.location.port) : "";
var url = document.location.protocol + "//" +
document.location.hostname + port +
"/restapi/v1/CheckGameSessionIsFinished/" +
window.GameSessionId;

$.get(url, function (data) {
  debugger;
  if (data.indexOf("won") > 0 || data == "The game
  was a draw.") {
    alert(data);
    window.location.href = document.location.protocol +
    "//" + document.location.hostname + port;
  }
});
}
```

11. Start the game, register a new account, open the confirmation email, confirm it, send a game invitation email, confirm the game invitation, and start playing. Everything should be working now, and you should be able to play the game until a user has won or until the game is a draw:

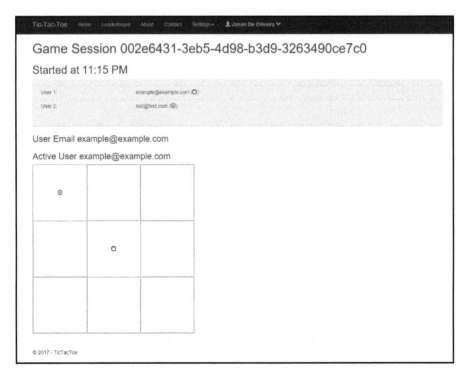

This has been the RPC-style, which is very close to standard MVC Controller actions. In the next sections, you will see a completely different approach, which is based on resources and resource management.

Congratulations; you have now finished the implementation and created a beautiful, modern, browser-based game, in which two users can play against each other.

Prepare yourself, since you are going to see more advanced techniques and discover how to provide Web APIs for interoperability using two of the most famous API communication styles called REST and HATEOAS.

To play the game, you can either use two separate private browser windows or use two distinct browsers such as Chrome, Edge, or Firefox. For testing your Web APIs, it is advised to install and use Postman, but you could also use any other HTTP REST-compatible client, such as Fiddler, or even Firefox via its advanced features.

Building REST-style Web APIs

The REST-style was invented by Roy Fiedling in the 2000s and is one of the best ways to provide interoperability between systems that are based on multiple technologies, whether it be in your network or on the internet.

Furthermore, the REST approach is not a technology by itself, but instead some best practices for efficiently using the HTTP protocol.

Instead of adding a new layer like SOAP or XML-RPC, REST uses different elements of the HTTP protocol for providing its services:

- The URI identifies a resource
- The HTTP Verb identifies an action
- The response is not the resource, but only a representation of the resource
- The client authentication is passed as parameter in the header of requests

Unlike the RPC-style, the main purpose is no longer to provide actions, but is instead to manage and manipulate resources.

To get even more information on the concepts and ideas behind REST, you should read the dissertation of Roy Fiedling, which you can find at http://www.ics.uci.edu/~fielding/pubs/dissertation/top.htm.

As you can see in the following diagram, there are mainly three types of resources in the *TicTacToe* application:

- **Users**
- **Game Invitations**
- **Game Sessions**

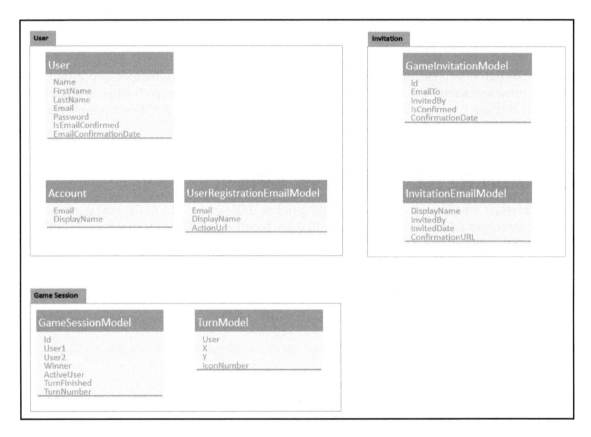

We are now going to illustrate how to use the REST-style for building a Game Invitation REST API:

1. Add two new methods called `All` and `Delete` to the `GameInvitationService` and update the **Game Invitation Service Interface** accordingly:

```
public Task<IEnumerable<GameInvitationModel>> All()
{
```

```
        return Task.FromResult<IEnumerable<GameInvitationModel>>
          (_gameInvitations.ToList());
    }

    public Task Delete(Guid id)
    {
        _gameInvitations = new ConcurrentBag<GameInvitationModel>
          (_gameInvitations.Where(x => x.Id != id));
        return Task.CompletedTask;
    }
```

2. Add a new API Controller called `GameInvitationApiController`, right-click on the `Controllers` folder and select **Add** | **Controller**, and then choose the **API Controller with read/write actions** template:

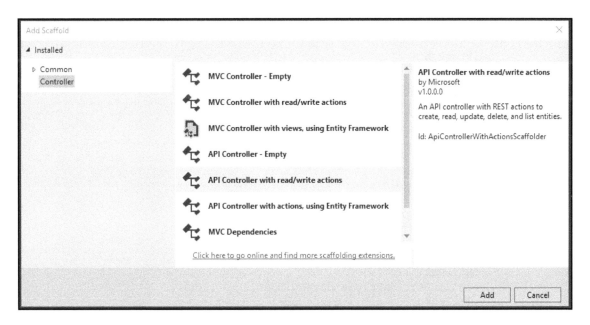

3. Remove the auto-generated code and replace it with the following REST API implementation; you will see how straightforward it is:

```
[Produces("application/json")]
[Route("restapi/v1/GameInvitation")]
public class GameInvitationApiController : Controller
{
    private IGameInvitationService _gameInvitationService;
    private IUserService _userService;
    public GameInvitationApiController(IGameInvitationService
```

```
  gameInvitationService, IUserService userService)
{
  _gameInvitationService = gameInvitationService;
  _userService = userService;
}

[HttpGet]
public async Task<IEnumerable<GameInvitationModel>> Get()
{
  return await _gameInvitationService.All();
}

[HttpGet("{id}", Name = "Get")]
public async Task<GameInvitationModel> Get(Guid id)
{
  return await _gameInvitationService.Get(id);
}

[HttpPost]
public IActionResult Post([FromBody]GameInvitationModel
 invitation)
{
  if (!ModelState.IsValid)
    return BadRequest(ModelState);

  var invitedPlayer =
    _userService.GetUserByEmail(invitation.EmailTo);
  if (invitedPlayer == null) return BadRequest();

    _gameInvitationService.Add(invitation);
    return Ok();
}

[HttpPut("{id}")]
public IActionResult Put(Guid id,
 [FromBody]GameInvitationModel invitation)
{
  if (!ModelState.IsValid)
    return BadRequest(ModelState);

  var invitedPlayer =
   _userService.GetUserByEmail(invitation.EmailTo);
  if (invitedPlayer == null) return BadRequest();

  _gameInvitationService.Update(invitation);
  return Ok();
}
```

```
[HttpDelete("{id}")]
public void Delete(Guid id)
{
  _gameInvitationService.Delete(id);
}
}
```

 Note that for learning purposes, we have just given a very basic example of what you could implement. Normally, you should provide the same functionalities as in your controller implementations (sending emails, confirming emails, verifying data, etc.) and some advanced error handling.

4. Start the application, install and start **Postman** for doing some manual tests on the new REST API you are now providing, and send an **HTTP GET Request** to `http://<yourhost>/restapi/v1/GameInvitation`. There will be no game invitations, since you have not created any yet:

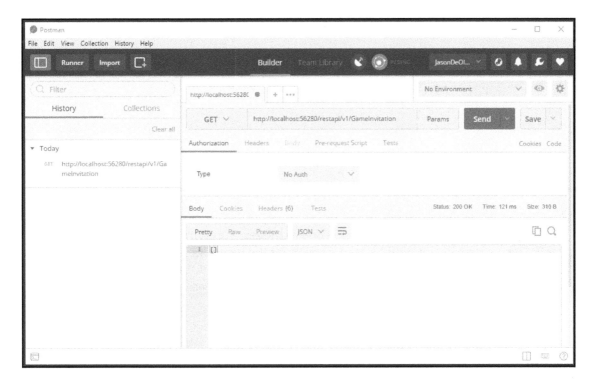

5. Create a new **Game Invitation**, send an **HTTP POST Request** to
   `http://<yourhost>/restapi/v1/GameInvitation`, click on **Body**, select **raw**
   and **JSON**, and use `"id":"7223160d-6243-498b-9d35-81b8c947b5ca"`,
   `"EmailTo":"example@example.com"`, and
   `"InvitedBy":"test@test.com"` as parameters:

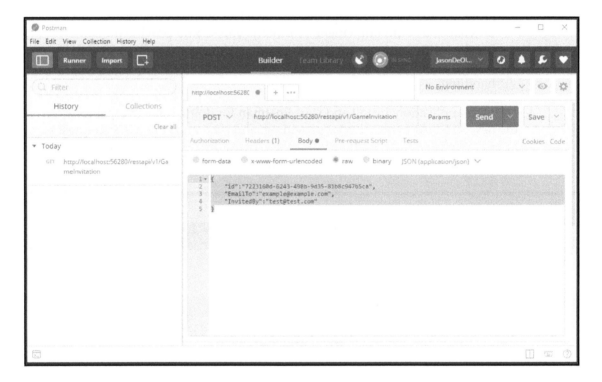

Note that we have added the automatic creation of a user if it does not
exist for testing purposes in one of the previous chapters. In a real worked
scenario, you will have to implement the user registration Web APIs and
call them before the Game Invitation Web APIs. Otherwise, you will get a
bad request, since we have added some code to assure data coherence and
integrity.

6. You can retrieve the **Game Invitation** either by sending an **HTTP GET Request** to `http://<yourhost>/restapi/v1/GameInvitation` or, more specifically, by sending an **HTTP GET Request** to `http://<yourhost>/restapi/v1/GameInvitation/7223160d-6243-498b-9d35-81b8c947b5ca`:

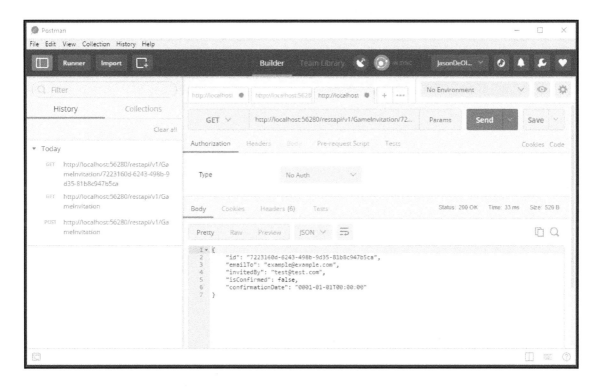

7. Update the **Game Invitation**, send an **HTTP PUT Request** to
   `http://<yourhost>/restapi/v1/GameInvitation/7223160d-6243-498b-9d35-81b8c947b5ca`, click on **Body**, select **raw** and **JSON**, and
   use `"id":"7223160d-6243-498b-9d35-81b8c947b5ca"`,
   `"EmailTo":"updated@updated.com"`, and
   `"InvitedBy":"test@test.com"` as parameters:

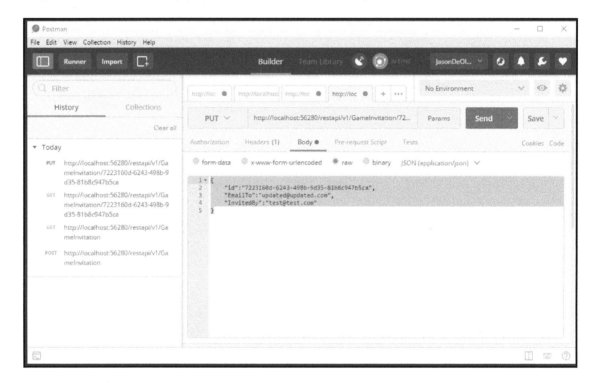

8. Look at the updated **Game Invitation** and send an **HTTP GET Request** to
   `http://<yourhost>/restapi/v1/GameInvitation/7223160d-6243-498b-9d35-81b8c947b5ca`:

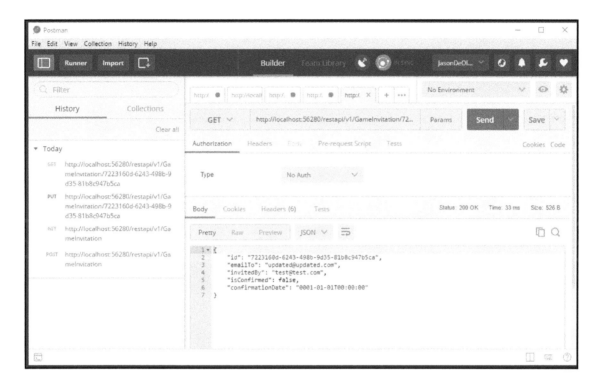

9. Delete the **Game Invitation** and send an **HTTP DELETE Request** to
   `http://<yourhost>/restapi/v1/GameInvitation/7223160d-6243-498b-9d35-81b8c947b5ca`:

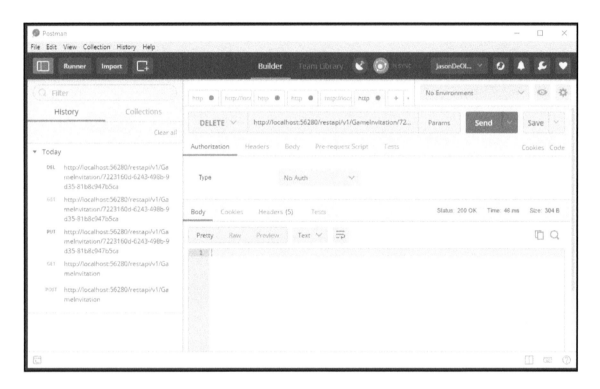

10. Verify the **Game Invitation** deletion and send an **HTTP GET Request** to
    `http://<yourhost>/restapi/v1/GameInvitation`:

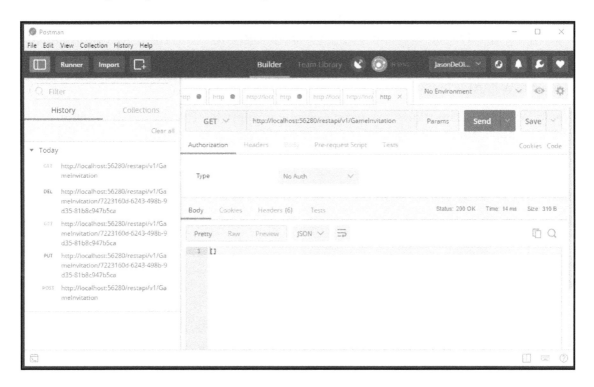

The REST-style is the most common style of Web APIs you can find on the market as of today. It is easy to understand and very well adapted for interoperability use cases.

In the next section, you will see a more advanced style called HATEOAS, which is especially well suited for constantly evolving Web APIs.

Building HATEOAS-style Web APIs

The **HATEOAS (Hypermedia as the Engine of Application State)** style is yet another approach for providing efficient Web APIs. It is, however, completely different from the other two styles presented before. With this approach, clients can dynamically navigate to a needed resource by traversing various hypermedia links, which are provided in the HTTP responses.

The advantage of this style is that the server does not drive application state anymore; instead, it is the hypermedia links returned by the server that oversee that.

Additionally, when compared to the other styles, API changes are much better handled when using this style, since clients do not hardcode URIs to actions (RPC-style) or resources (REST-style) anymore. Instead, they can work with hypermedia links returned by the server with each response, which is an interesting concept that allows for more flexible and evolvable Web APIs.

The following diagram shows an example of how to apply the HATEOAS-style to the *TicTacToe* application:

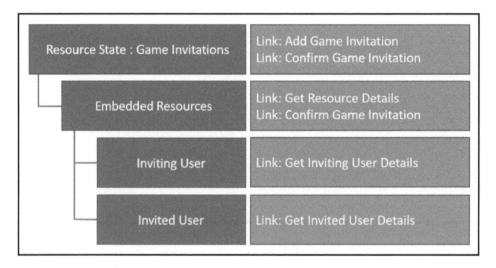

An example JSON representation of this diagram could be:

```
{
  "_links": {
    "self": { "href": "/gameinvitations" },
    "next": { "href": "/gameinvitations?page=2" },
    "find": {
      "href": "/gameinvitations{?Id}",
      "templated": "true"
    }
  },
  "_embedded": {
    "gameinvitations": [
      {
        "_links": {
          "self": { "href": "/gameinvitations/
```

```
        f1eaf6ac-c998-40da-8eb5-198eaa2cc96f" },
      "confirm": { "href": "/gameinvitations/
      f1eaf6ac-c998-40da-8eb5-198eaa2cc96f/confirm" }
    },
    "isConfirmed": "false",
    "confirmDate": "null",
    "emailTo": {
      "self": { "href": "/user/1" }
    },
    "invitedBy": {
      "self": "\"{\"href\":\"/user/2\"}"
    }
  }
]
  }
}
```

Let's see how to technically implement HATEOAS for the Game Invitations of the `TicTacToe` application:

1. Go to the **NuGet Package Manager** and add the `Halcyon.Mvc` package, which will allow you to implement HATEOAS Web APIs more quickly and easily:

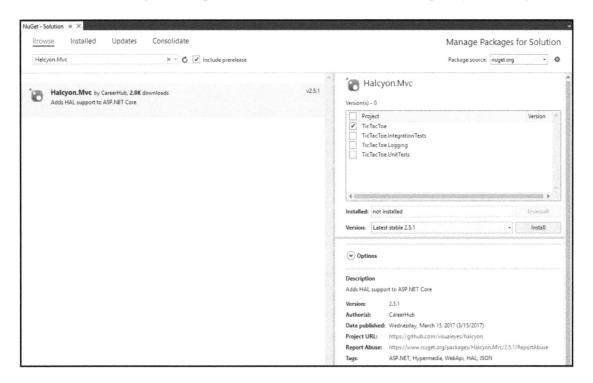

2. Update the `Startup` class, use the **HAL Json Formatter** instead of the **Standard Json Formatter**:

```
services.AddMvc(o =>
{
  o.Filters.Add(typeof(DetectMobileFilter));

  o.OutputFormatters.RemoveType<JsonOutputFormatter>();
  o.OutputFormatters.Add(new JsonHalOutputFormatter(new
   string[] { "application/hal+json",
   "application/vnd.example.hal+json",
   "application/vnd.example.hal.v1+json" }));
}).AddViewLocalization(
   LanguageViewLocationExpanderFormat.Suffix,
   options => options.ResourcesPath =
    "Localization").AddDataAnnotationsLocalization();
```

3. Update the `Get` method in the `GameInvitationAPiController`, use the `Halcyon.Mvc` specific features, and return a `HAL` result:

```
[HttpGet]
public async Task<IActionResult> Get()
{
  var invitations = await _gameInvitationService.All();
  var responseConfig = new HALModelConfig
  {
    LinkBase = $"{Request.Scheme}://{Request.Host.ToString()}",
    ForceHAL = Request.ContentType ==
    "application/hal+json" ? true : false
  };

  var response = new HALResponse(responseConfig);
  response.AddLinks(new Link("self", "/GameInvitation"),
    new Link("confirm", "/GameInvitation/{id}/Confirm"));

  List<HALResponse> invitationsResponses = new List<HALResponse>();
  foreach (var invitation in invitations)
  {
    var rInv = new HALResponse(invitation, responseConfig);

    rInv.AddLinks(new Link("self", "/GameInvitation/" +
     invitation.Id));
    rInv.AddLinks(new Link("confirm",
     $"/GameInvitation/{invitation.Id}/confirm"));

    var invitedPlayer =
     _userService.GetUserByEmail(invitation.EmailTo);
```

```
rInv.AddEmbeddedResource("invitedPlayer", invitedPlayer,
 new Link[]
{
  new Link("self", $"/User/{invitedPlayer.Id}")
});

var invitedBy =
 _userService.GetUserByEmail(invitation.InvitedBy);
rInv.AddEmbeddedResource("invitedBy", invitedBy, new Link[]
{
  new Link("self", $"/User/{invitedBy.Id}")
});

invitationsResponses.Add(rInv);
}

response.AddEmbeddedCollection("invitations",
 invitationsResponses);
return this.HAL(response);
}
```

4. Start the application and Postman, send an **HTTP POST Request** to
   `http://<yourhost>/restapi/v1/GameInvitation` for creating a new Game
   Invitation, click on **Body**, select **raw** and **JSON**, and
   use `"id":"7223160d-6243-498b-9d35-81b8c947b5ca"`,
   `"EmailTo":"example@example.com"`, and
   `"InvitedBy":"test@test.com"` as parameters:

5. Retrieve the **Game Invitation** by sending an **HTTP GET Request** to
   `http://<yourhost>/restapi/v1/GameInvitation` with `Content-Type:`
   `application/hal+json`; you will see that the HTTP response now includes
   HATEOAS links:

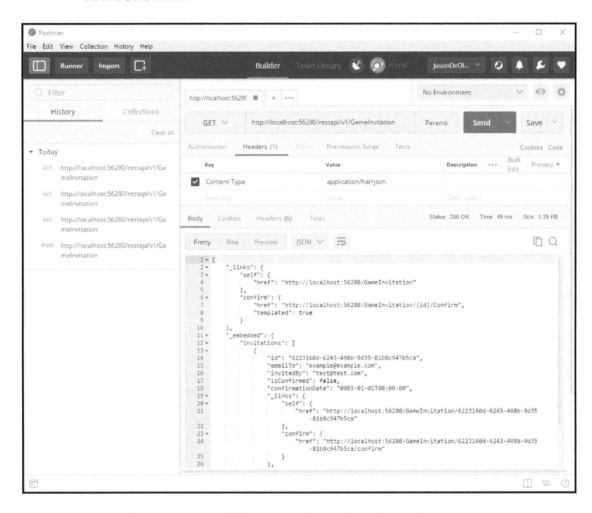

HATEOAS provides some powerful features, which allow for evolving components
independently. Clients can be completely decoupled from the business workflows running
on the server that manages the interaction by using links and other hypermedia artifacts,
such as forms.

Summary

In this chapter, you have learned how to build Web APIs for your applications for integration purposes and for loosely coupled application architectures.

We have explored different styles for your Web APIs, such as RPC, REST, and HATEOAS. Each of those styles has specific advantages and use cases. You have to choose carefully, depending on your specific application needs, since there is not one single style that outclasses the others.

You have seen examples of how to transform existing controller actions into RPC-style Web APIs and how to build REST-style and HATEOAS-style Web APIs from the ground up.

We have used Postman to manually test our Web APIs and you have acquired enough knowledge to apply all of these new concepts to your own environments.

In the next chapter, we will talk about how to access data by using Entity Framework Core 2 in your ASP.NET Core 2.0 applications.

8
Accessing Data using Entity Framework Core 2

We have advanced greatly with the implementation of the *Tic-Tac-Toe* web application, but when you restart the application all the user registration and application data is reset. This is due to the fact that we do not persist any data yet.

To persist data and be able to reload it when the application starts, you have to put it into some kind of persistent storage such as files (XML, JSON, CSV) or databases.

A database would be the best choice, since it provides better performance and more security when compared to simple file storage, which is why we are going to use it in the following examples.

Since ASP.NET 3.0 you can use an ORM framework called Entity Framework for accessing data in databases in a more productive and simple way. ASP.NET Core 2.0 works with a dedicated version of this framework called Entity Framework Core 2.

In this chapter, we will cover the following topics:

- Getting started with Entity Framework Core 2
- Working with Entity Framework Core 2 Data Annotations
- Using Entity Framework Core 2 Migrations
- Creating, reading, updating, and deleting data
- Working with request features

Getting started with Entity Framework Core 2

The Meta package `Microsoft.AspNetCore.All` contains Entity Framework Core 2, including all required packages for working with Microsoft SQL Server and SQLite.

 Note that if you need to work with other databases such as MySQL, you have to download additional packages from NuGet. You can find a list of all currently available Entity Framework Core 2 NuGet packages here: `https://www.nuget.org/packages?page=2&q=Tags%3A%22entity-fr amework-core%22`.

Establishing a connection

To open a session to the database and query and update instances of your entities, you use a `DbContext`, which is based on a combination of the unit of work and repository patterns.

Let's see how to prepare the *Tic-Tac-Toe* application to use Entity Framework Core 2 to connect to an SQL Database by using a `DbContext` and a connection string:

1. Go to the **Solution Explorer**, add a new folder called `Data`, add a new class called `GameDbContext.cs`, and implement a `DbSet` property for each Model (`UserModel`, `TurnModel`, and more):

```
public class GameDbContext : DbContext
{
  public DbSet<GameInvitationModel> GameInvitationModels {
   get; set; }
  public DbSet<GameSessionModel> GameSessionModels { get; set; }
  public DbSet<TurnModel> TurnModels { get; set; }
  public DbSet<UserModel> UserModels { get; set; }

  public GameDbContext(DbContextOptions<GameDbContext>
   dbContextOptions) : base(dbContextOptions)
  {

  }
}
```

2. Register the **Game Db Context** in the `Startup` class and pass the connection string and database provider as parameters within the constructor. You only need a single instance, so use `AddSingleton`:

```
var connectionString =
  _configuration.GetConnectionString("DefaultConnection");
services.AddEntityFrameworkSqlServer()
  .AddDbContext<GameDbContext>((serviceProvider, options) =>
  options.UseSqlServer(connectionString)
  .UseInternalServiceProvider(serviceProvider)
);

var dbContextOptionsbuilder =
  new DbContextOptionsBuilder<GameDbContext>()
  .UseSqlServer(connectionString);
services.AddSingleton(dbContextOptionsbuilder.Options);
```

3. Update the `UserService` to be able to work with the **Game Db Context**; add a new public constructor and a private member for the **Game Db Context** from before:

```
private DbContextOptions<GameDbContext> _dbContextOptions;
public UserService(DbContextOptions<GameDbContext>
 dbContextOptions)
{
  _dbContextOptions = dbContextOptions;
}
```

4. Update the `RegisterUser` method in the `UserService` to use the **Game Db Context**:

```
public async Task<bool> RegisterUser(UserModel userModel)
{
  using(var db = new GameDbContext(_dbContextOptions))
  {
    db.UserModels.Add(userModel);
    await db.SaveChangesAsync();
    return true;
  }
}
```

5. Add a new extension called `ModelBuilderExtensions` in the `Extensions` folder. This will be used to define table name conventions:

```
public static class ModelBuilderExtensions
{
```

```
public static void RemovePluralizingTableNameConvention(
 this ModelBuilder modelBuilder)
{
  foreach (IMutableEntityType entity in
   modelBuilder.Model.GetEntityTypes())
  {
    entity.Relational().TableName = entity.DisplayName();
  }
}
}
```

6. Update the `OnModelCreating` method in the **Game Db Context** to further configure the model that was discovered by convention from the entity types exposed in the `DbSet` properties; call the extension from before to apply the table name conventions:

```
protected override void OnModelCreating(ModelBuilder
 modelBuilder)
{
  modelBuilder.RemovePluralizingTableNameConvention();
}
```

Note that you could also use another method called `OnConfiguring` in the DB Context, to configure the DB Context without using `DbContextOptions`.

7. Add a new class called `GameDbContextFactory` in the `Data` folder. This will be used to instantiate the **Game Db Context** with specific options:

```
public class GameDbContextFactory :
 IDesignTimeDbContextFactory<GameDbContext>
{
  public GameDbContext CreateDbContext(string[] args)
  {
    var optionsBuilder =
     new DbContextOptionsBuilder<GameDbContext>();
    optionsBuilder.UseSqlServer(@"Server=
     (localdb)\MSSQLLocalDB;Database=TicTacToe;
     Trusted_Connection=True;MultipleActiveResultSets=true");
    return new GameDbContext(optionsBuilder.Options);
  }
}
```

If you have already worked with databases, you should be familiar with the concept of connection strings. They contain the configuration (address, username, password, and more) and settings (encryption, protocol, and more) required to be able to connect to a database.

In ASP.NET Core 2.0 you can use an `appSettings.<env>.json` file to configure connection strings. Connection strings are loaded automatically, when using the `ConnectionStrings` section within this file:

```
"ConnectionStrings": {
  "DefaultConnection":
  "Server=(localdb)\\MSSQLLocalDB;Database=TicTacToe;
    Trusted_Connection=True;MultipleActiveResultSets=true"
},
```

As you have seen in the example before, you can use the `GetConnectionString` method to retrieve a connection string during runtime of your ASP.NET Core 2.0 applications:

```
var databaseConnectionString =
  _configuration.GetConnectionString("DefaultConnection");
```

This is everything you need to know to use the **Game Db Context** and the corresponding default connection string stored within the `appsettings.json` configuration file of the *Tic-Tac-Toe* application.

Defining primary keys and foreign keys via Data Annotations

In the next step, you need to modify the existing Models to be able to persist them within an SQL Database. To allow Entity Framework Core 2.0 to create, read, update and delete records, you need to specify a primary key for each Model. You do that by using Data Annotations, which allow you to decorate a property with the `[Key]` decorator.

Here is an example of how to use Data Annotations for the `UserModel`:

```
public class UserModel
{
  [Key]
  public long Id { get; set; }
  ...
}
```

You should apply this to the UserModel, GameInvitationModel, GameSessionModel and TurnModel of the *Tic-Tac-Toe* application. You can reuse existing Id properties and decorate them with the [Key] decorator, or add new ones if a Model does not yet contain an Id property.

Note that it is sometimes required to use composite keys as the identity for your rows in a table. In this case decorate each property with the [Key] decorator. Furthermore, you can use Column[Order=] for defining the position of the property, if you need to order a composite key.

When working with SQL Server (or any other SQL 92 DBMS), the first thing you should think about is the relation between tables. In Entity Framework Core 2, you can specify foreign keys within Models by using the [ForeignKey] decorator.

Concerning the *Tic-Tac-Toe* application, this means that you have to update the GameInvitationModel and add a **Foreign Key** relation to the **User Model Id,** as you can see here:

1. Update the GameInvitationModel; add a foreign key to InvitedByUser:

```
public class GameInvitationModel
{
  [Key]
  public Guid Id { get; set; }
  public string EmailTo { get; set; }

  public string InvitedBy { get; set; }

  [ForeignKey(nameof(InvitedByUserId))]
  public UserModel InvitedByUser { get; set; }
  public Guid InvitedByUserId { get; set; }

  public bool IsConfirmed { get; set; }
  public DateTime ConfirmationDate { get; set; }
}
```

2. Update the GameSessionModel; add a foreign key to UserId1:

```
public class GameSessionModel
{
  [Key]
  public Guid Id { get; set; }
  public Guid UserId1 { get; set; }
  public Guid UserId2 { get; set; }
  [ForeignKey(nameof(UserId1))]
```

```
    public UserModel User1 { get; set; }
    public UserModel User2 { get; set; }
    public IEnumerable<TurnModel> Turns { get; set; }
    public UserModel Winner { get; set; }
    public UserModel ActiveUser { get; set; }
    public Guid WinnerId { get; set; }
    public Guid ActiveUserId { get; set; }
    public bool TurnFinished { get; set; }
    public int TurnNumber { get; set; }
}
```

3. Update the `TurnModel`; add a foreign key to `UserId`:

```
public class TurnModel
{
    [Key]
    public Guid Id { get; set; }
    public Guid UserId { get; set; }
    [ForeignKey(nameof(UserId))]
    public UserModel User { get; set; }
    public int X { get; set; }
    public int Y { get; set; }
    public string Email { get; set; }
    public string IconNumber { get; set; }
}
```

Entity Framework Core 2 maps all properties in a model with a schema representation by default. But some more complex property types are not compatible, which is why you should exclude them from auto-mapping. But how do we do that? Well, by using the `[NotMapped]` decorator. How easy and straightforward is that?

For the *Tic-Tac-Toe* application, it makes no sense to persist the active user for a turn, for example, so you should exclude them from the auto-mapping by using the `[NotMapped]` decorator in the `GameSessionModel`:

```
public class GameSessionModel
{
    [Key]
    public Guid Id { get; set; }
    public Guid UserId1 { get; set; }
    public Guid UserId2 { get; set; }

    [ForeignKey(nameof(UserId1))]
    public UserModel User1 { get; set; }
    public UserModel User2 { get; set; }
    public IEnumerable<TurnModel> Turns { get; set; }
```

```
[NotMapped]
public UserModel Winner { get; set; }

[NotMapped]
public UserModel ActiveUser { get; set; }
public Guid WinnerId { get; set; }
public Guid ActiveUserId { get; set; }
public bool TurnFinished { get; set; }
public int TurnNumber { get; set; }
}
```

For more information on Entity Framework Data Annotations, please visit the following link:

`https://msdn.microsoft.com/en-us/library/jj591583(v=vs.113).aspx`

Okay, now you have decorated all your models by using Entity Framework Core 2 Data Annotations, but you will quickly see that you have two properties, User1 and User2, in the GameSessionModel that point to the same UserModel entity. This results in a circular relationship, and thus will become a problem when working with relational databases for operations such as cascading updates or cascading deletions.

To avoid circular relationships in the example, you need to decorate User1 with the [ForeignKey] decorator and update the OnModelCreating method in the **Game Db Context** to define the Foreign Key for User2. These two modifications will allow you to define the two foreign keys, while avoiding the automatic cascading operations, which would cause problems:

```
protected override void OnModelCreating(ModelBuilder modelBuilder)
{
  modelBuilder.RemovePluralizingTableNameConvention();
  modelBuilder.Entity(typeof(GameSessionModel))
  .HasOne(typeof(UserModel), "User2")
  .WithMany()
  .HasForeignKey("User2Id").OnDelete(DeleteBehavior.Restrict);
}
```

In the last step, you need to fix the unit tests. You might have already seen it; the unit test project does not build anymore if you try compiling the solution. In fact, you need to update the unit tests, since the `UserService` requires an instance of `DbContextOptions` now:

```
var dbContextOptionsBuilder =
  new DbContextOptionsBuilder<GameDbContext>()
    .UseSqlServer(@"Server=(localdb)\MSSQLLocalDB;Database=TicTacToe;
     Trusted_Connection=True;MultipleActiveResultSets=true");

var userService = new UserService(dbContextOptionsBuilder.Options);
```

Using Entity Framework Core 2 Migrations

As you have seen, when developing applications your models might change frequently when refactoring and finalizing your projects. This might lead to a database schema that is out of sync, and which therefore needs to be updated manually by creating an upgrade script.

Fortunately, Entity Framework Core 2 includes a feature called Migrations to help you with this tedious task by automatically keeping your models and the corresponding database schemas in sync.

After you have updated the models, services and controllers to comply to the constraints from above, and have modified the **Game Db Context** accordingly, you are now ready to use Entity Framework Core 2 Migrations:

1. Add a first version of your Db schema called `InitialDbSchema`, open the **NuGet Package Manager** by clicking in the top menu on **Tools | NuGet Package Manager | Package Manager Console**, and execute the `Add-Migration InitialDbSchema` command:

```
Package Manager Console
Package source: All          Default project: TicTacToe
Each package is licensed to you by its owner. NuGet is not responsible for, nor does it grant any licenses to, third-party packages. Some packages may include
dependencies which are governed by additional licenses. Follow the package source (feed) URL to determine any dependencies.

Package Manager Console Host Version 4.4.0.4431

Type 'get-help NuGet' to see all available NuGet commands.

PM> Add-Migration InitialDbSchema
```

2. A new folder called `Migrations` will be automatically added by Visual Studio. It will contain two auto-generated files, which will help you to manage and upgrade your Db Schema in the future:

If your database is accessible from your development environment, you can update it directly from within Visual Studio 2017:

1. Go to the **Package Manager Console** and execute the `Update-Database` command. This will create the database the first time it is used, or update it automatically when you change your models:

2. Go to the **SQL Server Object Explorer** and analyze the Db Schema that Entity Framework 2 Migrations has autogenerated in SQL Server:

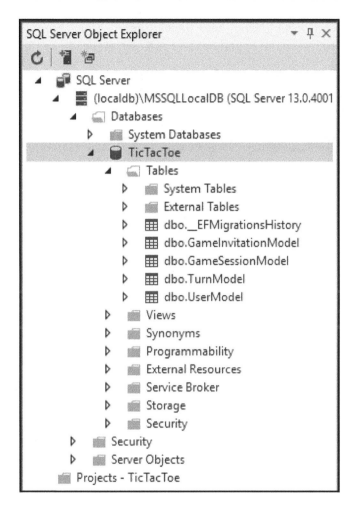

3. Right-click on the __EFMigrationsHistory table and select **View Data** to see how Entity Framework Migrations track Db Schema versions:

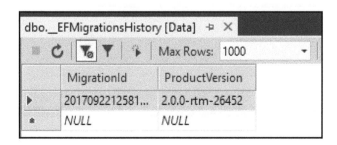

If your database is not accessible from your development environment, (for example, for staging or production), you have to generate an SQL script file:

1. Go to the **Package Manager Console** and execute the `Script-Migration` command to auto-generate an SQL script file, which can be used to create the *Tic-Tac-Toe* application database:

2. Execute the generated SQL script file on the specific environments using your preferred database tools (SQL Server Management Studio, and so on) to create the *Tic-Tac-Toe* application database.

You can also use Entity Framework Core 2 Migration directly from within your code to assure that the database is constantly in sync with your models by calling the `Migrate` method of the `GameDbContext` instance within the `Configure` method of the `Startup` class, as shown here:

1. Update the `Configure` method in the `Startup` class; add the following instructions at the bottom of the method:

```
using (var scope =
 app.ApplicationServices.GetService<IServiceScopeFactory>()
   .CreateScope())
{
  scope.ServiceProvider.GetRequiredService<GameDbContext>()
    .Database.Migrate();
}
```

2. Start the *Tic-Tac-Toe* application by pressing *F5*:

Note that if a table or a property does not exist in the database and if the connection string provides enough access rights, Entity Framework Core 2 will automatically create it.

After having updated the models and the corresponding application database, all model data is now persisted and application state is going to be available even after an application restart. This means that you cannot register already existing emails, you have to add new ones manually, so truncate the database and delete them now.

Creating, reading, updating, and deleting data

In the preceding sections, we have done everything to define the models and get the database up and running in a consistent and coherent way. In this section, you will finally see how to work with data and execute create, read, update, and delete operations.

Let's see how to use `GameDbContext` to work with data:

1. Update the `UserService`; remove the `ConcurrencyBag` and the static constructor, and update the `GetUserByEmail` method:

```
public async Task<UserModel> GetUserByEmail(string email)
{
  using (var db = new GameDbContext(_dbContextOptions))
  {
    return await db.UserModels.FirstOrDefaultAsync(
    x => x.Email == email);
  }
}
```

2. Update the `UpdateUser` method in the `UserService` to see how to update data using the Db Context:

```
public async Task UpdateUser(UserModel userModel)
{
  using (var gameDbContext =
    new GameDbContext(_dbContextOptions))
  {
    gameDbContext.Update(userModel);
    await gameDbContext.SaveChangesAsync();
  }
}
```

3. Update the `GetTopUsers` method within the `UserService` to learn how to build advanced queries with sorting and filtered data using the Db Context:

```
public async Task<IEnumerable<UserModel>> GetTopUsers(
 int numberOfUsers)
{
  using (var gameDbContext =
   new GameDbContext(_dbContextOptions))
  {
    return await gameDbContext.UserModels.OrderByDescending(
     x => x.Score).ToListAsync();
  }
}
```

4. Add a new method called `IsUserExisting` to the `UserService`. This will be used to check if a user exists. Update the `IUserService` interface:

```
public async Task<bool> IsUserExisting(string email)
{
```

```
using (var gameDbContext =
 new GameDbContext(_dbContextOptions))
{
  return await gameDbContext.UserModels.AnyAsync(
   user => user.Email == email);
}
}
```

Now you have seen how to configure your applications to use Entity Framework Core 2 and all of its useful and interesting features. It provides a great way of abstracting complexity and removing time-consuming tasks from you daily life as a developer. You do not need to learn any additional languages anymore (SQL, for example); nor do you need to change environments for creating, reading, updating, and deleting records in a database. Everything can be done from within your code and from within Visual Studio to assure high developer productivity and efficiency.

Summary

In this chapter, you have learned how to use Entity Framework Core 2 together with ASP.NET Core 2.0 for working with SQL Server databases.

We have seen how to use a Db Context and connection string to connect to an SQL Server database. We have then updated the models in the *Tic-Tac-Toe* application with primary and foreign key definitions by using Entity Framework Core 2 Data Annotations, as well as overriding the OnModelCreating method within the Db Context.

You have worked with Entity Framework Core 2 Migrations to be able to constantly keep your models in your code consistent with their corresponding database representations.

Furthermore, you have learnt how to insert, update and query data in an easy, productive and efficient way.

In the next chapter, we will talk about how to secure access to your ASP.NET Core 2.0 applications by using the integrated ASP.NET Core 2.0 authorization features.

9

Securing ASP.NET Core 2.0 Applications

In today's world of increasing digital crime and internet fraud, all modern web applications require the implementation of strong security mechanisms for preventing attacks and user identity usurpation.

Until now, we have concentrated on understanding how to build efficient ASP.NET Core 2.0 web applications, without thinking about user authentication, user authorization, or data protection at all, but since the *Tic-Tac-Toe* application is getting more and more sophisticated, we will have to address security issues before finally deploying it to the public.

Building a web application and not thinking about security would be a big failing and could bring down even the greatest and most famous websites. In the case of security breaches and personal data theft, the negative reputation and user confidence impacts could be tremendous, and nobody would want to work with those applications and—more troublesome—companies anymore.

This is a topic that needs to be taken very seriously. You should work with security companies to make code verifications and intrusion tests to ensure that you comply with best practices and high security standards (OWASP10, for example).

Luckily, ASP.NET Core 2.0 contains everything necessary to help you with this complicated, but important, topic. Most of the built-in features do not even require advanced programming or security skills. You will see that it is very easy to understand and implement secure applications by using the ASP.NET Core 2.0 Identity Framework.

In this chapter, we will cover the following topics:

- Adding basic user form authentication
- Adding external provider authentication
- Adding forgotten password and password reset mechanisms
- Working with two-factor authentication
- Implementing authorization

Implementing authentication

Authentication allows applications to identify a specific user. It is not used to manage user access rights, which is the role of authorization, nor is it used to protect data, which is the role of data protection.

There are several methods for authenticating application users, such as:

- Basic user forms authentication, using a login form with login and password boxes
- **Single Sign-On** (**SSO**) authentication, where the user only authenticates once for all their applications within the context of their company
- Social networks external provider authentication (such as Facebook and LinkedIn)
- Certificate or **public key infrastructure** (**PKI**) authentication

ASP.NET Core 2.0 supports all these methods, but in this chapter, we will concentrate on forms authentication with a user login and password, and external provider authentication via Facebook.

In the following examples, you will see how to use those methods for authenticating application users, as well as some more advanced features like email confirmation and password reset mechanisms.

And last but not least, you will see how to implement two-factor authentication using the built-in ASP.NET Core 2.0 Authentication features for your most critical applications.

Let's prepare the implementation of the different authentication mechanisms for the *Tic-Tac-Toe* application:

1. Update the lifetime of the `UserService`, `GameInvitationService`, and `GameSessionService` in the `Startup` class:

   ```
   services.AddTransient<IUserService, UserService>();
   services.AddScoped<IGameInvitationService,
    GameInvitationService>();
   services.AddScoped<IGameSessionService, GameSessionService>();
   ```

2. Update the `Configure` method within the `Startup` class, and call the **Authentication Middleware** directly after the **Static Files Middleware**:

   ```
   app.UseStaticFiles();
   app.UseAuthentication();
   ```

3. Update the `UserModel` to use it with the built-in ASP.NET Core 2.0 Identity authentication features, and remove the `Id` and `Email` properties, which are already provided by the `IdentityUser` class:

   ```
   public class UserModel : IdentityUser<Guid>
   {
     [Display(Name = "FirstName")]
     [Required(ErrorMessage = "FirstNameRequired")]
     public string FirstName { get; set; }
     [Display(Name = "LastName")]
     [Required(ErrorMessage = "LastNameRequired")]
     public string LastName { get; set; }
     [Display(Name = "Password")]
     [Required(ErrorMessage = "PasswordRequired"),
      DataType(DataType.Password)]
     public string Password { get; set; }
     [NotMapped]
     public bool IsEmailConfirmed
     {
       get { return EmailConfirmed; }
     }
     public System.DateTime? EmailConfirmationDate { get; set; }
     public int Score { get; set; }
   }
   ```

Note that in the real world, we would advise also removing the `Password` property. However, we will keep it in the example for clarity and learning purposes.

4. Add a new folder called `Managers`, and add a new manager in the folder called `ApplicationUserManager`:

```
public class ApplicationUserManager : UserManager<UserModel>
{
  private IUserStore<UserModel> _store;
  DbContextOptions<GameDbContext> _dbContextOptions;
  public ApplicationUserManager(
   DbContextOptions<GameDbContext> dbContextOptions,
   IUserStore<UserModel> store, IOptions<IdentityOptions>
   optionsAccessor, IPasswordHasher<UserModel> passwordHasher,
   IEnumerable<IUserValidator<UserModel>> userValidators,
   IEnumerable<IPasswordValidator<UserModel>>
   passwordValidators, ILookupNormalizer keyNormalizer,
   IdentityErrorDescriber errors, IServiceProvider services,
   ILogger<UserManager<UserModel>> logger) :
    base(store, optionsAccessor, passwordHasher,
     userValidators, passwordValidators, keyNormalizer,
     errors, services, logger)
  {
    _store = store;
    _dbContextOptions = dbContextOptions;
  }

  public override async Task<UserModel> FindByEmailAsync(
   string email)
  {
    using (var dbContext = new GameDbContext(_dbContextOptions))
    {
      return await dbContext.Set<UserModel>().FirstOrDefaultAsync(
       x => x.Email == email);
    }
  }

  public override async Task<UserModel> FindByIdAsync(
   string userId)
  {
    using (var dbContext = new GameDbContext(_dbContextOptions))
    {
      Guid id = Guid.Parse(userId);
      return await dbContext.Set<UserModel>().FirstOrDefaultAsync(
       x => x.Id == id);
```

```
    }
}

public override async Task<IdentityResult>
 UpdateAsync(UserModel user)
{
  using (var dbContext = new GameDbContext(_dbContextOptions))
  {
    var current =
      await dbContext.Set<UserModel>().FirstOrDefaultAsync(
      x => x.Id == user.Id);
    current.AccessFailedCount = user.AccessFailedCount;
    current.ConcurrencyStamp = user.ConcurrencyStamp;
    current.Email = user.Email;
    current.EmailConfirmationDate = user.EmailConfirmationDate;
    current.EmailConfirmed = user.EmailConfirmed;
    current.FirstName = user.FirstName;
    current.LastName = user.LastName;
    current.LockoutEnabled = user.LockoutEnabled;
    current.NormalizedEmail = user.NormalizedEmail;
    current.NormalizedUserName = user.NormalizedUserName;
    current.PhoneNumber = user.PhoneNumber;
    current.PhoneNumberConfirmed = user.PhoneNumberConfirmed;
    current.Score = user.Score;
    current.SecurityStamp = user.SecurityStamp;
    current.TwoFactorEnabled = user.TwoFactorEnabled;
    current.UserName = user.UserName;
    await dbContext.SaveChangesAsync();
    return IdentityResult.Success;
  }
}

public override async Task<IdentityResult>
 ConfirmEmailAsync(UserModel user, string token)
{
  var isValide = await base.VerifyUserTokenAsync(user,
   Options.Tokens.EmailConfirmationTokenProvider,
   ConfirmEmailTokenPurpose, token);
  if (isValide)
  {
    using (var dbContext =
      new GameDbContext(_dbContextOptions))
    {
      var current =
        await dbContext.UserModels.FindAsync(user.Id);
      current.EmailConfirmationDate = DateTime.Now;
      current.EmailConfirmed = true;
      await dbContext.SaveChangesAsync();
```

```
        return IdentityResult.Success;
      }
    }
    return IdentityResult.Failed();
  }
}
```

5. Update the `Startup` class, and register the `ApplicationUserManager`:

```
services.AddTransient<ApplicationUserManager>();
```

6. Update the `UserService` to work with the **ApplicationUser Manager**, add two new methods called `GetEmailConfirmationCode` and `ConfirmEmail`, and update the **User Service Interface**:

```
public class UserService
{
  private ILogger<UserService> _logger;
  private ApplicationUserManager _userManager;
  public UserService(ApplicationUserManager userManager,
   ILogger<UserService> logger)
  {
    _userManager = userManager;
    _logger = logger;

    var emailTokenProvider = new EmailTokenProvider<UserModel>();
    _userManager.RegisterTokenProvider("Default",
     emailTokenProvider);
  }

  public async Task<bool> ConfirmEmail(string email, string code)
  {
    var start = DateTime.Now;
    _logger.LogTrace($"Confirm email for user {email}");

    var stopwatch = new Stopwatch();
    stopwatch.Start();

    try
    {
      var user = await _userManager.FindByEmailAsync(email);

      if (user == null)
        return false;

      var result = await _userManager.ConfirmEmailAsync(
       user, code);
```

```
    return result.Succeeded;
  }
  catch (Exception ex)
  {
    _logger.LogError($"Cannot confirm email for user
     {email} - {ex}");
    return false;
  }
  finally
  {
    stopwatch.Stop();
    _logger.LogTrace($"Confirm email for user finished in
    {stopwatch.Elapsed}");
  }
}


public async Task<string> GetEmailConfirmationCode(
 UserModel user)
{
  return
   await _userManager.GenerateEmailConfirmationTokenAsync(user);
}

public async Task<bool> RegisterUser(UserModel userModel)
{
  var start = DateTime.Now;
  _logger.LogTrace($"Start register user
   {userModel.Email} - {start}");

  var stopwatch = new Stopwatch();
  stopwatch.Start();

  try
  {
    userModel.UserName = userModel.Email;
    var result = await _userManager.CreateAsync(userModel,
     userModel.Password);
    return result == IdentityResult.Success;
  }
  catch (Exception ex)
  {
    _logger.LogError($"Cannot register user
     {userModel.Email} - {ex}");
    return false;
  }
  finally
  {
```

```
        stopwatch.Stop();
        _logger.LogTrace($"Start register user {userModel.Email}
        finished at {DateTime.Now} - elapsed
        {stopwatch.Elapsed.TotalSeconds} second(s)");
    }
}

public async Task<UserModel> GetUserByEmail(string email)
{
    return await _userManager.FindByEmailAsync(email);
}

public async Task<bool> IsUserExisting(string email)
{
    return (await _userManager.FindByEmailAsync(email)) != null;
}

public async Task<IEnumerable<UserModel>> GetTopUsers(
  int numberOfUsers)
{
    return await _userManager.Users.OrderByDescending(
      x => x.Score).ToListAsync();
}

public async Task UpdateUser(UserModel userModel)
{
    await _userManager.UpdateAsync(userModel);
}
}
```

 Note that you should also update the `UserServiceTest` class to work with the new constructor. For that, you will also have to create a mock for the `UserManager` class and pass it to the constructor. For the moment, you can just comment the test out and update it later. But don't forget to do it!

7. Update the `EmailConfirmation` method in the `UserRegistrationController`, and use the `GetEmailConfirmationCode` method you have added before to retrieve the email code:

```
var urlAction = new UrlActionContext
{
    Action = "ConfirmEmail",
    Controller = "UserRegistration",
    Values = new { email, code =
     await _userService.GetEmailConfirmationCode(user) },
    Protocol = Request.Scheme,
```

```
    Host = Request.Host.ToString()
};
```

8. Update the `ConfirmEmail` method in the `UserRegistrationController`; it has to call the `ConfirmEmail` method in the `UserService` to finish the email confirmation:

```
[HttpGet]
public async Task<IActionResult> ConfirmEmail(string email,
 string code)
{
  var confirmed = await _userService.ConfirmEmail(email, code);

  if (!confirmed)
    return BadRequest();

  return RedirectToAction("Index", "Home");
}
```

9. Add a new class called `RoleModel` in the `Models` folder, and make it inherit from `IdentityRole<long>`, as it will be used by the built-in ASP.NET Core 2.0 Identity Authentication features:

```
public class RoleModel : IdentityRole<Guid>
{
  public RoleModel()
  {
  }

  public RoleModel(string roleName) : base(roleName)
  {
  }
}
```

10. Update the **Game Db Context**, and add a new DbSet for **Role Models**:

```
public DbSet<RoleModel> RoleModels { get; set; }
```

11. Register the **Authentication Service** and the **Identity Service** in the `Startup` class, then use the new **Role Model** you added before:

```
services.AddIdentity<UserModel, RoleModel>(options =>
{
  options.Password.RequiredLength = 1;
  options.Password.RequiredUniqueChars = 0;
  options.Password.RequireNonAlphanumeric = false;
```

```
      options.Password.RequireUppercase = false;
      options.SignIn.RequireConfirmedEmail = false;
}).AddEntityFrameworkStores<GameDbContext>()
.AddDefaultTokenProviders();

services.AddAuthentication(options => {
  options.DefaultScheme =
    CookieAuthenticationDefaults.AuthenticationScheme;
  options.DefaultSignInScheme =
    CookieAuthenticationDefaults.AuthenticationScheme;
  options.DefaultAuthenticateScheme =
    CookieAuthenticationDefaults.AuthenticationScheme;
}).AddCookie();
```

12. Update the **Communication Middleware**, remove the _userService private member from the class, and update the constructor accordingly:

```
public CommunicationMiddleware(RequestDelegate next)
{
  _next = next;
}
```

13. Update the two ProcessEmailConfirmation methods in the **Communication Middleware**, as they must be asynchronous to work with ASP.NET 2.0 Identity:

```
private async Task ProcessEmailConfirmation(HttpContext
 context, WebSocket currentSocket, CancellationToken ct,
 string email)
{
  var userService =
    context.RequestServices.GetRequiredService<IUserService>();
  var user = await userService.GetUserByEmail(email);
  while (!ct.IsCancellationRequested &&
         !currentSocket.CloseStatus.HasValue &&
          user?.IsEmailConfirmed == false)
  {
    await SendStringAsync(currentSocket,
      "WaitEmailConfirmation", ct);
    await Task.Delay(500);
    user = await userService.GetUserByEmail(email);
  }

  if (user.IsEmailConfirmed)
  {
    await SendStringAsync(currentSocket, "OK", ct);
  }
}
```

```
private async Task ProcessEmailConfirmation(HttpContext context)
{
  var userService =
    context.RequestServices.GetRequiredService<IUserService>();
  var email = context.Request.Query["email"];

  UserModel user = await userService.GetUserByEmail(email);

  if (string.IsNullOrEmpty(email))
  {
    await context.Response.WriteAsync("BadRequest:Email is
    required");
  }
  else if ((await
   userService.GetUserByEmail(email)).IsEmailConfirmed)
  {
    await context.Response.WriteAsync("OK");
  }
}
```

14. Update the `GameInvitationService`, and set the public constructor to static.

15. Remove the following `DbContextOptions` registration from the `Startup` class; it will be replaced by another one in the next step:

```
var dbContextOptionsbuilder =
  new DbContextOptionsBuilder<GameDbContext>()
    .UseSqlServer(connectionString);
services.AddSingleton(dbContextOptionsbuilder.Options);
```

16. Update the `Startup` class, and add a new `DbContextOptions` registration:

```
services.AddScoped(typeof(DbContextOptions<GameDbContext>),
(serviceProvider) =>
{
  return new DbContextOptionsBuilder<GameDbContext>()
    .UseSqlServer(connectionString).Options;
});
```

17. Update the `Configure` method in the `Startup` class, then replace the code that does the database migration at the end of the method:

```
var provider = app.ApplicationServices;
var scopeFactory =
  provider.GetRequiredService<IServiceScopeFactory>();
using (var scope = scopeFactory.CreateScope())
using (var context =
```

```
     scope.ServiceProvider.GetRequiredService<GameDbContext>())
{
  context.Database.Migrate();
}
```

18. Update the `Index` method in `GameInvitationController`:

```
...
var invitation =
  gameInvitationService.Add(gameInvitationModel).Result;
return RedirectToAction("GameInvitationConfirmation",
 new { id = invitation.Id });
...
```

19. Update the `ConfirmGameInvitation` method
    in `GameInvitationController`, and add additional fields to the existing user
    registration:

```
await _userService.RegisterUser(new UserModel
{
  Email = gameInvitation.EmailTo,
  EmailConfirmationDate = DateTime.Now,
  EmailConfirmed = true,
  FirstName = "",
  LastName = "",
  Password = "Azerty123!",
  UserName = gameInvitation.EmailTo
});
```

Note that the automatic creation and registration of the invited user is only
a temporary workaround that we have added to simplify the example
application. In the real world, you will need to handle this case differently
and replace the temporary workaround with a real solution.

20. Update the `CreateGameSession` and `AddTurn` methods
    in `GameSessionService` and re-extract the **Game Session Service Interface**:

```
public async Task<GameSessionModel> CreateGameSession(
 Guid invitationId, UserModel invitedBy,
 UserModel invitedPlayer)
{
  var session = new GameSessionModel
  {
    User1 = invitedBy,
    User2 = invitedPlayer,
    Id = invitationId,
```

```
    ActiveUser = invitedBy
  };
  _sessions.Add(session);
  return session;
}

public async Task<GameSessionModel> AddTurn(Guid id,
 UserModel user, int x, int y)
{
  List<Models.TurnModel> turns;
  var gameSession = _sessions.FirstOrDefault(session =>
   session.Id == id);
  if (gameSession.Turns != null && gameSession.Turns.Any())
    turns = new List<Models.TurnModel>(gameSession.Turns);
  else
    turns = new List<TurnModel>();

  turns.Add(new TurnModel
  {
    User = user,
    X = x,
    Y = y,
    IconNumber = user.Email == gameSession.User1?.Email ? "1" : "2"
  });

  gameSession.Turns = turns;
  gameSession.TurnNumber = gameSession.TurnNumber + 1;
  if (gameSession.User1?.Email == user.Email)
    gameSession.ActiveUser = gameSession.User2;
  else
    gameSession.ActiveUser = gameSession.User1;

  gameSession.TurnFinished = true;
  _sessions = new ConcurrentBag<GameSessionModel>
   (_sessions.Where(u => u.Id != id))
  {
    gameSession
  };
  return gameSession;
}
```

21. Update the `Index` method in `GameSessionController`:

```
public async Task<IActionResult> Index(Guid id)
{
  var session = await _gameSessionService.GetGameSession(id);
  var userService =
```

```
        HttpContext.RequestServices.GetService<IUserService>();

  if (session == null)
  {
    var gameInvitationService =
      Request.HttpContext.RequestServices.GetService
      <IGameInvitationService>();
    var invitation = await gameInvitationService.Get(id);

    var invitedPlayer =
      await userService.GetUserByEmail(invitation.EmailTo);
    var invitedBy =
      await userService.GetUserByEmail(invitation.InvitedBy);

    session =
      await _gameSessionService.CreateGameSession(
        invitation.Id, invitedBy, invitedPlayer);
  }
  return View(session);
}
```

22. Update the `SetPosition` method in `GameSessionController`, and pass a `turn.User` instead of a `turn.User.Email`:

    ```
    gameSession = await _gameSessionService.AddTurn(gameSession.Id,
      turn.User, turn.X, turn.Y);
    ```

23. Update the `OnModelCreating` method in the **Game Db Context**, and add a `WinnerId` foreign key:

    ```
    ...
    modelBuilder.Entity(typeof(GameSessionModel))
     .HasOne(typeof(UserModel), "Winner")
     .WithMany()
     .HasForeignKey("WinnerId").OnDelete(DeleteBehavior.Restrict);
    ...
    ```

24. Update the `GameInvitationConfirmation` method in `GameInvitationController`; it must be asynchronous to work with ASP.NET Core 2.0 Identity:

    ```
    [HttpGet]
    public async Task<IActionResult> GameInvitationConfirmation(
      Guid id, [FromServices]IGameInvitationService
      gameInvitationService)
    {
    ```

```
    return await Task.Run(() =>
    {
      var gameInvitation = gameInvitationService.Get(id).Result;
      return View(gameInvitation);
    });
  }
```

25. Update the `Index` and `SetCulture` methods in `HomeController`; they must be asynchronous to work with ASP.NET Core 2.0 Identity:

```
public async Task<IActionResult> Index()
{
  return await Task.Run(() =>
  {
    var culture =
      Request.HttpContext.Session.GetString("culture");
    ViewBag.Language = culture;
    return View();
  });
}

public async Task<IActionResult> SetCulture(string culture)
{
  return await Task.Run(() =>
  {
    Request.HttpContext.Session.SetString("culture", culture);
    return RedirectToAction("Index");
  });
}
```

26. Update the `Index` method in `UserRegistrationController`; it must be asynchronous to work with ASP.NET 2.0 Identity:

```
public async Task<IActionResult> Index()
{
  return await Task.Run(() =>
  {
    return View();
  });
}
```

27. Open the **Package Manager Console** and execute the `Add-Migration IdentityDb` command.

28. Update the database by executing the `Update-Database` command in the **Package Manager Console**.

29. Start the application and register a new user, then verify that everything is still working as expected.

 Note that you have to use a complex password, such as `Azerty123!`, to be able to finish the user registration successfully now, since you have implemented the integrated features of ASP.NET Core 2.0 Identity in this section, which require complex passwords.

Adding basic user forms authentication

Great! You have registered the Authentication Middleware and prepared the database. In the next step, you are going to implement basic user authentication for the *Tic-Tac-Toe* application.

The following example demonstrates how to modify the user registration and add a simple login form with a user login and password textbox for authenticating users:

1. Add a new Model called `LoginModel` to the `Models` folder:

```
public class LoginModel
{
  [Required]
  public string UserName { get; set; }
  [Required]
  public string Password { get; set; }
  public string ReturnUrl { get; set; }
}
```

2. Add a new folder called `Account` to the `Views` folder, and add a new file called `Login.cshtml` within this new folder; it will contain the **Login View**:

```
@model TicTacToe.Models.LoginModel
<div class="container">
  <div id="loginbox" style="margin-top:50px;" class="mainbox
  col-md-6 col-md-offset-3 col-sm-8 col-sm-offset-2">
    <div class="panel panel-info">
      <div class="panel-heading">
        <div class="panel-title">Sign In</div>
      </div>
      <div style="padding-top:30px" class="panel-body">
        <div style="display:none" id="login-alert"
        class="alert alert-danger col-sm-12"></div>
        <form id="loginform" class="form-horizontal"
        role="form" asp-action="Login" asp-controller="Account">
```

```
<input type="hidden" asp-for="ReturnUrl" />
<div asp-validation-summary="ModelOnly"
 class="text-danger"></div>
<div style="margin-bottom: 25px" class="input-group">
  <span class="input-group-addon"><i class="glyphicon
   glyphicon-user"></i></span>
  <input type="text" class="form-control"
   asp-for="UserName" value="" placeholder="username
   or email">
</div>
<div style="margin-bottom: 25px" class="input-group">
  <span class="input-group-addon"><i class="glyphicon
   glyphicon-lock"></i></span>
  <input type="password" class="form-control"
   asp-for="Password" placeholder="password">
</div>
<div style="margin-top:10px" class="form-group">
  <div class="col-sm-12 controls">
    <button type="submit" id="btn-login" href="#"
     class="btn btn-success">Login</button>
  </div>
</div>
<div class="form-group">
  <div class="col-md-12 control">
    <div style="border-top: 1px solid#888;
     padding-top:15px; font-size:85%">
      Don't have an account?
      <a asp-action="Index"
       asp-controller="UserRegistration">Sign Up Here
      </a>
    </div>
  </div>
</div>
</form>
</div>
</div>
</div>
</div>
```

3. Update the UserService, add a SignInManager private field, and update the constructor:

```
...
private SignInManager<UserModel> _signInManager;
public UserService(ApplicationUserManager userManager,
 ILogger<UserService> logger, SignInManager<UserModel>
 signInManager)
```

```
{
  ...
  _signInManager = signInManager;
  ...
}
...
```

4. Add two new methods, called `SignInUser` and `SignOutUser`, to `UserService` and update the **User Service Interface**:

```
public async Task<SignInResult> SignInUser(
 LoginModel loginModel, HttpContext httpContext)
{
  var start = DateTime.Now;
  _logger.LogTrace($"signin user {loginModel.UserName}");

  var stopwatch = new Stopwatch();
  stopwatch.Start();

  try
  {
    var user =
      await _userManager.FindByNameAsync(loginModel.UserName);
    var isValid =
      await _signInManager.CheckPasswordSignInAsync(user,
        loginModel.Password, true);
    if (!isValid.Succeeded)
    {
      return SignInResult.Failed;
    }

    if (!await _userManager.IsEmailConfirmedAsync(user))
    {
      return SignInResult.NotAllowed;
    }

    var identity = new ClaimsIdentity(
      CookieAuthenticationDefaults.AuthenticationScheme);
    identity.AddClaim(new Claim(
      ClaimTypes.Name, loginModel.UserName));
    identity.AddClaim(new Claim(
      ClaimTypes.GivenName, user.FirstName));
    identity.AddClaim(new Claim(
      ClaimTypes.Surname, user.LastName));
    identity.AddClaim(new Claim(
      "displayName", $"{user.FirstName} {user.LastName}"));
```

```
    if (!string.IsNullOrEmpty(user.PhoneNumber))
    {
      identity.AddClaim(new Claim(ClaimTypes.HomePhone,
      user.PhoneNumber));
    }

    identity.AddClaim(new Claim("Score",
     user.Score.ToString()));

    await httpContext.SignInAsync(
     CookieAuthenticationDefaults.AuthenticationScheme,
     new ClaimsPrincipal(identity),
     new AuthenticationProperties { IsPersistent = false });

    return isValid;
  }
  catch (Exception ex)
  {
    _logger.LogError($"can not sigin user
     {loginModel.UserName} - {ex}");
    throw ex;
  }
  finally
  {
    stopwatch.Stop();
    _logger.LogTrace($"sigin user {loginModel.UserName}
    finished in {stopwatch.Elapsed}");
  }
}

public async Task SignOutUser(HttpContext httpContext)
{
  await _signInManager.SignOutAsync();
  await httpContext.SignOutAsync(new AuthenticationProperties {
   IsPersistent = false });
  return;
}
```

5. Add a new controller called `AccountController` to the `Controllers` folder, and implement three new methods for handling user authentication:

```
public class AccountController : Controller
{
  private IUserService _userService;
  public AccountController(IUserService userService)
  {
    _userService = userService;
```

```
    }

    public async Task<IActionResult> Login(string returnUrl)
    {
      return await Task.Run(() =>
      {
        var loginModel = new LoginModel { ReturnUrl = returnUrl };
        return View(loginModel);
      });
    }

    [HttpPost]
    public async Task<IActionResult> Login(LoginModel loginModel)
    {
      if (ModelState.IsValid)
      {
        var result = await _userService.SignInUser(loginModel,
         HttpContext);

        if (result.Succeeded)
        {
          if (!string.IsNullOrEmpty(loginModel.ReturnUrl))
              return Redirect(loginModel.ReturnUrl);
          else
              return RedirectToAction("Index", "Home");
        }
        else
          ModelState.AddModelError("", result.IsLockedOut ?
           "User is locked" : "User is not allowed");
      }
      return View();
    }

    public IActionResult Logout()
    {
      _userService.SignOutUser(HttpContext).Wait();
      HttpContext.Session.Clear();
      return RedirectToAction("Index", "Home");
    }
  }
```

6. Update the `CheckGameSessionIsFinished` method in the `GameSessionController`:

```
[HttpGet("/restapi/v1/CheckGameSessionIsFinished/{sessionId}")]
public async Task<IActionResult> CheckGameSessionIsFinished(
 Guid sessionId)
```

```
{
  if (sessionId != Guid.Empty)
  {
    var session =
      await _gameSessionService.GetGameSession(sessionId);
    if (session != null)
    {
      if (session.Turns.Count() == 9)
        return Ok("The game was a draw.");

      var userTurns = session.Turns.Where(
        x => x.User.Id == session.User1.Id).ToList();
      var user1Won = CheckIfUserHasWon(session.User1?.Email,
        userTurns);
      if (user1Won)
      {
        return Ok($"{session.User1.Email} has won the game.");
      }
      else
      {
        userTurns = session.Turns.Where(
          x => x.User.Id == session.User2.Id).ToList();
        var user2Won = CheckIfUserHasWon(session.User2?.Email,
          userTurns);

        if (user2Won)
          return Ok($"{session.User2.Email} has won
            the game.");
        else
          return Ok("");
      }
    }
    else
    {
      return NotFound($"Cannot find session {sessionId}.");
    }
  }
  else
  {
    return BadRequest("SessionId is null.");
  }
}
```

7. Update the `Views/Shared/_Menu.cshtml` file, and replace the existing code block at the top of the method:

```
@using Microsoft.AspNetCore.Http;
@{
  var email = User?.Identity?.Name ??
   Context.Session.GetString("email");
  var displayName = User.Claims.FirstOrDefault(
   x => x.Type == "displayName")?.Value ??
   Context.Session.GetString("displayName");
}
```

8. Update the `Views/Shared/_Menu.cshtml` file, to display either a **Display Name Element** for already authenticated users, or a **Login Element** for an authenticated user; for that, replace the last `<li>` element:

```
<li>
  @if (!string.IsNullOrEmpty(email))
  {
    Html.RenderPartial("_Account",
     new TicTacToe.Models.AccountModel { Email = email,
     DisplayName = displayName });
  }
  else
  {
    <a asp-area="" asp-controller="Account"
     asp-action="Login">Login</a>
  }
</li>
```

9. Update the `Views/Shared/_Account.cshtml` file, and replace the **Log Off** and **View Details** links:

```
<a class="btn btn-danger btn-block" asp-controller="Account"
 asp-action="Logout" asp-area="">Log Off</a>
<a class="btn btn-default btn-block" asp-action="Index"
 asp-controller="Home" asp-area="Account">View Details</a>
```

10. Go to the `Views\Shared\Components\GameSession` folder, and update the `default.cshtml` file to improve the visual representation:

```
@using Microsoft.AspNetCore.Http
@model TicTacToe.Models.GameSessionModel
@{
  var email = Context.Session.GetString("email");
}
```

```
<div id="gameBoard">
  <table>
    @for (int rows = 0; rows < 3; rows++)
    {
      <tr style="height:150px;">
        @for (int columns = 0; columns < 3; columns++)
        {
          <td style="width:150px; border:1px solid #808080;
            text-align:center; vertical-align:middle"
            id="@($"c_{rows}_{columns}")">
            @{
              var position = Model.Turns?.FirstOrDefault(
               turn => turn.X == columns && turn.Y == rows);
              if (position != null)
              {
                if (position.User == Model.User1)
                {
                  <i class="glyphicon glyphicon-unchecked"></i>
                }
                else
                {
                  <i class="glyphicon glyphicon-remove-circle"></i>
                }
              }
              else
              {
                <a class="btn btn-default btn-SetPosition"
                  style="width:150px; min-height:150px;"
                  data-X="@columns" data-Y="@rows">
                   
                </a>
              }
            }
          </td>
        }
      </tr>
    }
  </table>
</div>
<div class="alert" id="divAlertWaitTurn">
  <i class="glyphicon glyphicon-alert">Please wait until the
     other user has finished his turn.</i>
</div>
```

11. Start the application, click on the **Login** element in the top menu, and sign in as an existing user (or register as a user if you have not done that before):

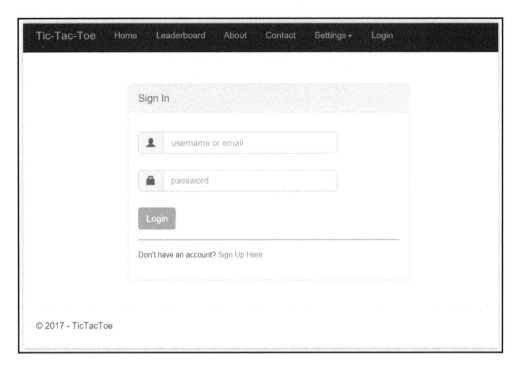

12. Click the **Log Off** button. You should be logged off and get redirected back to the **Home Page**:

Adding external provider authentication

In the following section, we will showcase external provider authentication by using Facebook as an authentication provider.

Here is an overview of the control flow in this case:

1. The user clicks on a dedicated external provider login button.
2. The corresponding controller receives a request indicating which provider is needed, then a challenge is initiated with the external provider.
3. The external provider sends an HTTP callback (POST or GET) with a provider name, a key, and some user claims for the application.
4. The claims are matched with the internal application user.
5. If no internal user can be matched with the claims, the user is either redirected to a specific registration form or is rejected.

 Note that the implementation steps are the same for all external providers if they support OWIN and ASP.NET Core 2.0 Identity, and that you may even create your own providers and integrate them in the same way.

We are now going to implement external provider authentication via Facebook:

1. Update the **Login Form**, and add a button called Login with Facebook directly after the standard **Login Button**:

    ```
    <a id="btn-fblogin" asp-action="ExternalLogin"
     asp-controller="Account" asp-route-Provider="Facebook"
     class="btn btn-primary">Login with Facebook</a>
    ```

2. Update the UserService and **User Service Interface**, then add three new methods called GetExternalAuthenticationProperties, GetExternalLoginInfoAsync, and ExternalLoginSignInAsync:

    ```
    public async Task<AuthenticationProperties>
     GetExternalAuthenticationProperties(string provider,
     string redirectUrl)
    {
      return await Task.FromResult(
       _signInManager.ConfigureExternalAuthenticationProperties(
       provider, redirectUrl));
    }
    ```

```
public async Task<ExternalLoginInfo> GetExternalLoginInfoAsync()
{
  return await _signInManager.GetExternalLoginInfoAsync();
}

public async Task<SignInResult> ExternalLoginSignInAsync(
 string loginProvider, string providerKey, bool isPersistent)
{
  _logger.LogInformation($"Sign in user with external login
   {loginProvider} - {providerKey}");
  return await _signInManager.ExternalLoginSignInAsync(
   loginProvider, providerKey, isPersistent);
}
```

3. Update the `AccountController,` and add two new methods called
   `ExternalLogin` and `ExternalLoginCallBack`:

```
[AllowAnonymous]
public async Task<ActionResult> ExternalLogin(string provider,
 string ReturnUrl)
{
  var redirectUrl = Url.Action(nameof(ExternalLoginCallBack),
   "Account", new { ReturnUrl = ReturnUrl }, Request.Scheme,
    Request.Host.ToString());
  var properties =
    await _userService.GetExternalAuthenticationProperties(
     provider, redirectUrl);
  ViewBag.ReturnUrl = redirectUrl;
  return Challenge(properties, provider);
}

[AllowAnonymous]
public async Task<IActionResult> ExternalLoginCallBack(
 string returnUrl, string remoteError = null)
{
  if (remoteError != null)
  {
    ModelState.AddModelError(string.Empty, $"Error from
     external provider: {remoteError}");
    ViewBag.ReturnUrl = returnUrl;
    return View("Login");
  }

  var info = await _userService.GetExternalLoginInfoAsync();
  if (info == null)
  {
    return RedirectToAction("Login",
```

```
      new { ReturnUrl = returnUrl });
  }

  var result =
   await _userService.ExternalLoginSignInAsync(
     info.LoginProvider, info.ProviderKey, isPersistent: false);
  if (result.Succeeded)
  {
    if (!string.IsNullOrEmpty(returnUrl))
      return Redirect(returnUrl);
    else
      return RedirectToAction("Index", "Home");
  }
  if (result.IsLockedOut)
  {
    return View("Lockout");
  }
  else
  {
    return View("NotFound");
  }
}
```

4. Register the **Facebook Middleware** within the `Startup` class:

```
services.AddAuthentication(options => {
  options.DefaultScheme =
   CookieAuthenticationDefaults.AuthenticationScheme;
  options.DefaultSignInScheme =
   CookieAuthenticationDefaults.AuthenticationScheme;
  options.DefaultAuthenticateScheme =
   CookieAuthenticationDefaults.AuthenticationScheme;
}).AddCookie().AddFacebook(facebook =>
{
  facebook.AppId = "123";
  facebook.AppSecret = "123";
  facebook.ClientId = "123";
  facebook.ClientSecret = "123";
});
```

Note that you must update the Facebook Middleware configuration and register your application in the Facebook developer portal before being able to authenticate logins with a Facebook account.

Please go to `http://developer.facebook.com` for more information.

5. Start the application, click on the **Login with Facebook** button, sign in with your Facebook credentials, and verify that everything is working as expected:

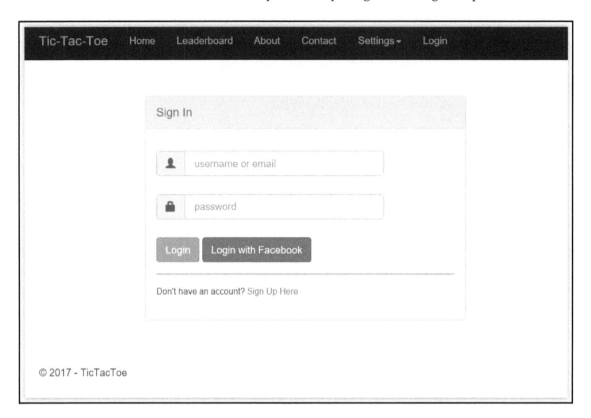

Working with two-factor authentication

The standard security mechanisms you have seen before only require a simple username and password, which makes it increasingly easy for cybercriminals to gain access to confidential data, such as personal and financial details, either by hacking the password or by intercepting user credentials (emails, network sniffing, and such). This data can then be used to commit financial fraud and identity theft.

Two-factor authentication adds an extra layer of security, since it requires not only a username and password, but also a two-factor code that only the user can provide (physical device, software-generated, and so on). This makes it much harder for potential intruders to gain access, and thus helps to prevent identity and data theft.

All major websites provide two-factor authentication as an option, so let's add it to the *Tic-Tac-Toe* application as well:

1. Add a new Model called `TwoFactorCodeModel` to the `Models` folder:

```
public class TwoFactorCodeModel
{
  [Key]
  public long Id { get; set; }
  public Guid UserId { get; set; }
  [ForeignKey("UserId")]
  public UserModel User { get; set; }
  public string TokenProvider { get; set; }
  public string TokenCode { get; set; }
}
```

2. Add a new Model called `TwoFactorEmailModel` to the `Models` folder:

```
public class TwoFactorEmailModel
{
  public string DisplayName { get; set; }
  public string Email { get; set; }
  public string ActionUrl { get; set; }
}
```

3. Register the `TwoFactorCodeModel` within the **Game Db Context** by adding a corresponding `DbSet`:

```
public DbSet<TwoFactorCodeModel> TwoFactorCodeModels { get; set; }
```

4. Open the **NuGet Package Manager Console** and execute the `Add-Migration` `AddTwoFactorCode` command, then update the database by executing the `Update-Database` command.

5. Update the **Application User Manager**, then add three new methods called `SetTwoFactorEnabledAsync`, `GenerateTwoFactorTokenAsync`, and `VerifyTwoFactorTokenAsync`:

```
public override async Task<IdentityResult>
 SetTwoFactorEnabledAsync(UserModel user, bool enabled)
{
  try
  {
    using (var db = new GameDbContext(_dbContextOptions))
    {
      var current = await db.UserModels.FindAsync(user.Id);
```

```
        current.TwoFactorEnabled = enabled;
        await db.SaveChangesAsync();
        return IdentityResult.Success;
      }
    }
    catch (Exception ex)
    {
      return IdentityResult.Failed(new IdentityError {
       Description = ex.ToString() });
    }
  }

public override async Task<string>
 GenerateTwoFactorTokenAsync(UserModel user,
 string tokenProvider)
{
  using (var dbContext = new GameDbContext(_dbContextOptions))
  {
    var emailTokenProvider = new EmailTokenProvider<UserModel>();
    var token = await emailTokenProvider.GenerateAsync(
     "TwoFactor", this, user);
    dbContext.TwoFactorCodeModels.Add(new TwoFactorCodeModel
    {
      TokenCode = token,
      TokenProvider = tokenProvider,
      UserId = user.Id
    });

    if (dbContext.ChangeTracker.HasChanges())
      await dbContext.SaveChangesAsync();

    return token;
  }
}

public override async Task<bool>
 VerifyTwoFactorTokenAsync(UserModel user,
 string tokenProvider, string token)
{
  using (var dbContext = new GameDbContext(_dbContextOptions))
  {
    return await dbContext.TwoFactorCodeModels.AnyAsync(
     x => x.TokenProvider == tokenProvider &&
     x.TokenCode == token && x.UserId == user.Id);
  }
}
```

6. Go to the `Areas/Account/Views/Home` folder, and update the **Index View**:

```
@model TicTacToe.Models.UserModel
@using Microsoft.AspNetCore.Identity
@inject UserManager<TicTacToe.Models.UserModel> UserManager
@{
  var isTwoFactor =
    UserManager.GetTwoFactorEnabledAsync(Model).Result;
  ViewData["Title"] = "Index";
  Layout = "~/Views/Shared/_Layout.cshtml";
}
<h3>Account Details</h3>
<div class="container">
  <div class="row">
    <div class="col-xs-12 col-sm-6 col-md-6">
      <div class="well well-sm">
        <div class="row">
          <div class="col-sm-6 col-md-4">
            <Gravatar email="@Model.Email"></Gravatar>
          </div>
          <div class="col-sm-6 col-md-8">
            <h4>@($"{Model.FirstName} {Model.LastName}")</h4>
            <p>
              <i class="glyphicon glyphicon-envelope">
              </i> <a href="mailto:@Model.Email">
              @Model.Email</a>
            </p>
            <p>
              <i class="glyphicon glyphicon-calendar">
              </i> @Model.EmailConfirmationDate
            </p>
            <p>
              <i class="glyphicon glyphicon-star">
              </i> @Model.Score
            </p>
            <p>
              <i class="glyphicon glyphicon-check"></i>
              <text>Two Factor Authentication </text>
              @if (Model.TwoFactorEnabled)
              {
                <a asp-action="DisableTwoFactor">Disable</a>
              }
              else
              {
                <a asp-action="EnableTwoFactor">Enable</a>
              }
            </p>
```

```
        </div>
      </div>
    </div>
  </div>
 </div>
</div>
```

7. Add a new file called `_ViewImports.cshtml` in the `Areas/Account/Views` folder:

```
@using TicTacToe
@using Microsoft.AspNetCore.Mvc.Localization
@inject IViewLocalizer Localizer
@addTagHelper *, TicTacToe
@addTagHelper *, Microsoft.AspNetCore.Mvc.TagHelpers
```

8. Update the `UserService` and **User Service Interface**, and add two new methods called `EnableTwoFactor` and `GetTwoFactorCode`:

```
public async Task<IdentityResult> EnableTwoFactor(string name,
 bool enabled)
{
  try
  {
    var user = await _userManager.FindByEmailAsync(name);
    user.TwoFactorEnabled = true;
    await _userManager.SetTwoFactorEnabledAsync(user, enabled);
    return IdentityResult.Success;
  }
  catch (Exception ex)
  {
    throw;
  }
}

public async Task<string> GetTwoFactorCode(string userName,
 string tokenProvider)
{
  var user = await GetUserByEmail(userName);
  return await _userManager.GenerateTwoFactorTokenAsync(user,
   tokenProvider);
}
```

9. Update the `SignInUser` method in the `UserService` for supporting two-factor authentication, if it is enabled:

```
public async Task<SignInResult> SignInUser(LoginModel
  loginModel, HttpContext httpContext)
{
  var start = DateTime.Now;
  _logger.LogTrace($"Signin user {loginModel.UserName}");
  var stopwatch = new Stopwatch();
  stopwatch.Start();

  try
  {
    var user =
      await _userManager.FindByNameAsync(loginModel.UserName);
    var isValid =
      await _signInManager.CheckPasswordSignInAsync(user,
        loginModel.Password, true);

    if (!isValid.Succeeded)
    {
      return SignInResult.Failed;
    }

    if (!await _userManager.IsEmailConfirmedAsync(user))
    {
      return SignInResult.NotAllowed;
    }

    if (await _userManager.GetTwoFactorEnabledAsync(user))
    {
      return SignInResult.TwoFactorRequired;
    }

    var identity = new ClaimsIdentity(
      CookieAuthenticationDefaults.AuthenticationScheme);
    identity.AddClaim(new Claim(ClaimTypes.Name,
      loginModel.UserName));
    identity.AddClaim(new Claim(ClaimTypes.GivenName,
      user.FirstName));
    identity.AddClaim(new Claim(ClaimTypes.Surname,
      user.LastName));
    identity.AddClaim(new Claim("displayName",
      $"{user.FirstName} {user.LastName}"));

    if (!string.IsNullOrEmpty(user.PhoneNumber))
    {
```

```
            identity.AddClaim(new Claim(ClaimTypes.HomePhone,
              user.PhoneNumber));
        }
        identity.AddClaim(new Claim("Score",
         user.Score.ToString()));

        await httpContext.SignInAsync(
         CookieAuthenticationDefaults.AuthenticationScheme,
         new ClaimsPrincipal(identity),
         new AuthenticationProperties { IsPersistent = false });

        return isValid;
    }
    catch (Exception ex)
    {
        _logger.LogError($"Ca not sigin user
         {loginModel.UserName} - {ex}");
        throw ex;
    }
    finally
    {
        stopwatch.Stop();
        _logger.LogTrace($"Sigin user {loginModel.UserName}
         finished in {stopwatch.Elapsed}");
    }
}
```

10. Go to the `Areas/Account/Controllers` folder, and update the
    `HomeController`. Update the `Index` method and add two new methods called
    `EnableTwoFactor` and `DisableTwoFactor`:

```
[Authorize]
public async Task<IActionResult> Index()
{
  var user =
    await _userService.GetUserByEmail(User.Identity.Name);
  return View(user);
}

[Authorize]
public IActionResult EnableTwoFactor()
{
  _userService.EnableTwoFactor(User.Identity.Name, true);
  return RedirectToAction("Index");
}

[Authorize]
```

```
public IActionResult DisableTwoFactor()
{
  _userService.EnableTwoFactor(User.Identity.Name, false);
  return RedirectToAction("Index");
}
```

 Note that we will explain the [Authorize] decorator later in this chapter. It is used to add access restrictions to resources.

11. Add a new Model called ValidateTwoFactorModel to the Models folder:

```
public class ValidateTwoFactorModel
{
  public string UserName { get; set; }
  public string Code { get; set; }
}
```

12. Update the AccountController, and add a new method called SendEmailTwoFactor:

```
private async Task SendEmailTwoFactor(string UserName)
{
  var user = await _userService.GetUserByEmail(UserName);
  var urlAction = new UrlActionContext
  {
    Action = "ValidateTwoFactor",
    Controller = "Account",
    Values = new { email = UserName,
    code = await _userService.GetTwoFactorCode(
     user.UserName, "Email") },
    Protocol = Request.Scheme,
    Host = Request.Host.ToString()
  };

  var TwoFactorEmailModel = new TwoFactorEmailModel
  {
    DisplayName = $"{user.FirstName} {user.LastName}",
     Email = UserName,
     ActionUrl = Url.Action(urlAction)
  };
  var emailRenderService =
    HttpContext.RequestServices.GetService
     <IEmailTemplateRenderService>();
  var emailService =
    HttpContext.RequestServices.GetService
```

```
      <IEmailService>();
  var message =
    await emailRenderService.RenderTemplate(
     "EmailTemplates/TwoFactorEmail", TwoFactorEmailModel,
      Request.Host.ToString());
  try
  {
    emailService.SendEmail(UserName, "Tic-Tac-Toe Two Factor
     Code", message).Wait();
  }
  catch
  {
  }
}
```

 Note that for calling `RequestServices.GetService<T>();`, you must also add using `Microsoft.Extensions.DependencyInjection;` as you have done before in other examples.

13. Update the `Login` method in `AccountController`:

```
[HttpPost]
public async Task<IActionResult> Login(LoginModel loginModel)
{
  if (ModelState.IsValid)
  {
    var result = await _userService.SignInUser(loginModel,
     HttpContext);
    if (result.Succeeded)
    {
      if (!string.IsNullOrEmpty(loginModel.ReturnUrl))
        return Redirect(loginModel.ReturnUrl);
      else
        return RedirectToAction("Index", "Home");
    }
    else if (result.RequiresTwoFactor)
    {
      await SendEmailTwoFactor(loginModel.UserName);
      return RedirectToAction("ValidateTwoFactor");
    }
    else
      ModelState.AddModelError("", result.IsLockedOut ? "User
       is locked" : "User is not allowed");
  }

  return View();
```

```
}
```

14. Add a new View called `ValidateTwoFactor` to the `Views/Account` folder:

```
@model TicTacToe.Models.ValidateTwoFactorModel
@{
  ViewData["Title"] = "Validate Two Factor";
  Layout = "~/Views/Shared/_Layout.cshtml";
}
<div class="container">
  <div id="loginbox" style="margin-top:50px;" class="mainbox
  col-md-6 col-md-offset-3 col-sm-8 col-sm-offset-2">
    <div class="panel panel-info">
      <div class="panel-heading">
        <div class="panel-title">Validate Two Factor Code</div>
      </div>
      <div style="padding-top:30px" class="panel-body">
        <div class="text-center">
          <form asp-controller="Account"
           asp-action="ValidateTwoFactor" method="post">
            <div asp-validation-summary="All"></div>
            <div style="margin-bottom: 25px" class="input-group">
              <span class="input-group-addon"><i
               class="glyphicon glyphicon-envelope
               color-blue"></i></span>
              <input id="email" asp-for="UserName"
               placeholder="email address"
               class="form-control" type="email">
            </div>
            <div style="margin-bottom: 25px" class="input-group">
              <span class="input-group-addon"><i
               class="glyphicon glyphicon-lock
               color-blue"></i></span>
              <input id="Code" asp-for="Code"
               placeholder="Enter your code" class="form-control">
            </div>
            <div style="margin-bottom: 25px" class="input-group">
              <input name="submit"
               class="btn btn-lg btn-primary btn-block"
               value="Validate your code" type="submit">
            </div>
          </form>
        </div>
      </div>
    </div>
  </div>
</div>
```

15. Add a new View called `TwoFactorEmail` to the `Views/EmailTemplates` folder:

```
@model TicTacToe.Models.TwoFactorEmailModel
@{
  ViewData["Title"] = "View";
  Layout = "_LayoutEmail";
}
<h1>Welcome @Model.DisplayName</h1>
You have requested a two factor code, please click <a
 href="@Model.ActionUrl">here</a> to continue.
```

16. Update the `UserService` and **User Service Interface**, and add a new method called `ValidateTwoFactor`:

```
public async Task<bool> ValidateTwoFactor(string userName,
 string tokenProvider, string token, HttpContext httpContext)
{
  var user = await GetUserByEmail(userName);
  if (await _userManager.VerifyTwoFactorTokenAsync(user,
   tokenProvider, token))
  {
    var identity =
      new ClaimsIdentity(
        CookieAuthenticationDefaults.AuthenticationScheme);
    identity.AddClaim(new Claim(ClaimTypes.Name,
     user.UserName));
    identity.AddClaim(new Claim(ClaimTypes.GivenName,
     user.FirstName));
    identity.AddClaim(new Claim(ClaimTypes.Surname,
     user.LastName));
    identity.AddClaim(new Claim("displayName",
     $"{user.FirstName} {user.LastName}"));

    if (!string.IsNullOrEmpty(user.PhoneNumber))
    {
      identity.AddClaim(new Claim(ClaimTypes.HomePhone,
        user.PhoneNumber));
    }

    identity.AddClaim(new Claim("Score",
     user.Score.ToString()));
    await httpContext.SignInAsync(
     CookieAuthenticationDefaults.AuthenticationScheme,
     new ClaimsPrincipal(identity),
     new AuthenticationProperties { IsPersistent = false });

    return true;
```

```
    }
    return false;
}
```

17. Update the `AccountController`, and add two new methods for two-factor authentication validation:

```
public async Task<IActionResult> ValidateTwoFactor(
 string email, string code)
{
  return await Task.Run(() =>
  {
    return View(new ValidateTwoFactorModel { Code = code,
     UserName = email });
  });
}

[HttpPost]
public async Task<IActionResult> ValidateTwoFactor(
 ValidateTwoFactorModel validateTwoFactorModel)
{
  if (ModelState.IsValid)
  {
    await _userService.ValidateTwoFactor(
     validateTwoFactorModel.UserName, "Email",
     validateTwoFactorModel.Code, HttpContext);
    return RedirectToAction("Index", "Home");
  }

  return View();
}
```

18. Start the application, sign in as an existing user, and go to the **Account Details** page. Enable two-factor authentication (you might need to recreate the database and register a new user before this step):

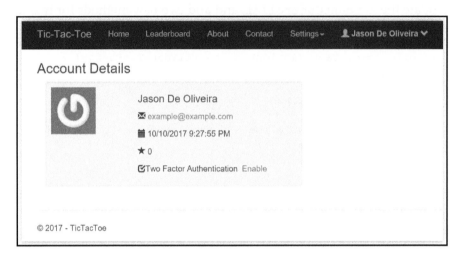

19. Sign out as the user, go to the **Login Page**, and sign in again. This time you will be asked to enter a **Two Factor Authentication Code**:

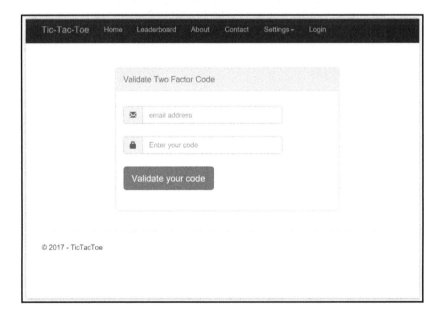

20. You will receive an email with the **Two Factor Authentication Code**:

21. Click on the link in the email and everything should be filled in for you automatically. Sign in and verify that everything is working as expected:

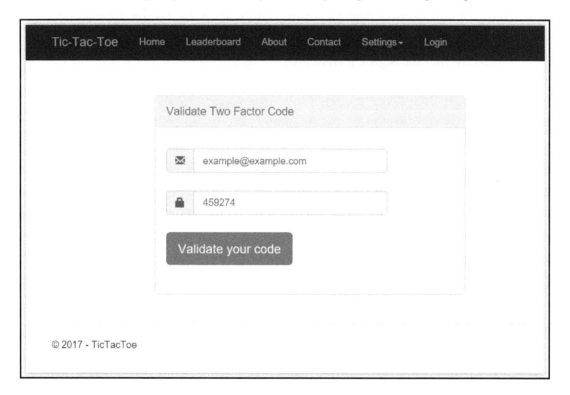

Adding forgotten password and password reset mechanisms

Now that you have seen how to add authentication to your applications, you have to think about how you want to help users to reset their forgotten passwords. Users will forget their passwords, it will happen, so you need to have some mechanisms in place.

The standard way of handling this type of request is to send an email reset link to the user. The user can then update their password, without the risk of sending the password in clear text through email. Sending a user password directly to a user email is not secure and should be avoided at all costs.

You will now see how to add a reset password feature to the *Tic-Tac-Toe* application:

1. Update the **Login Form**, and add a new link called `Reset Password Here` directly after the **Sign Up Here** link:

```
<div class="col-md-12 control">
  <div style="border-top: 1px solid#888; padding-top:15px;
  font-size:85%">
  Don't have an account?
  <a asp-action="Index"
   asp-controller="UserRegistration">Sign Up Here</a>
</div>
<div style="font-size: 85%;">
  Forgot your password?
  <a asp-action="ForgotPassword">Reset Password Here</a></div>
</div>
```

2. Add a new Model called `ResetPasswordEmailModel` to the `Models` folder:

```
public class ResetPasswordEmailModel
{
  public string DisplayName { get; set; }
  public string Email { get; set; }
  public string ActionUrl { get; set; }
}
```

3. Update the `AccountController`, and add a new method called `ForgotPassword`:

```
[HttpGet]
public async Task<IActionResult> ForgotPassword()
{
  return await Task.Run(() =>
  {
    return View();
  });
}
```

4. Add a new Model called `ResetPasswordModel` to the `Models` folder:

```
public class ResetPasswordModel
{
  public string Token { get; set; }
  public string UserName { get; set; }
  public string Password { get; set; }
  public string ConfirmPassword { get; set; }
}
```

5. Add a new View called `ForgotPassword` to the `Views/Account` folder:

```
@model TicTacToe.Models.ResetPasswordModel
@{
  ViewData["Title"] = "GameInvitationConfirmation";
  Layout = "~/Views/Shared/_Layout.cshtml";
}
<div class="form-gap"></div>
<div class="container">
  <div class="row">
    <div class="col-md-4 col-md-offset-4">
      <div class="panel panel-default">
        <div class="panel-body">
          <div class="text-center">
            <h3><i class="fa fa-lock fa-4x"></i></h3>
            <h2 class="text-center">Forgot Password?</h2>
            <p>You can reset your password here.</p>
            <div class="panel-body">
              <form id="register-form" role="form"
              autocomplete="off" class="form"
              method="post" asp-controller="Account"
              asp-action="SendResetPassword">
                <div class="form-group">
                  <div class="input-group">
                    <span class="input-group-addon"><i
```

```
                                   class="glyphicon glyphicon-envelope
                                   color-blue"></i></span>
                                 <input id="email" name="UserName"
                                 placeholder="email address"
                                 class="form-control" type="email">
                              </div>
                           </div>
                           <div class="form-group">
                             <input name="recover-submit"
                              class="btn btn-lg btn-primary btn-block"
                              value="Reset Password" type="submit">
                           </div>
                           <input type="hidden" class="hide"
                            name="token" id="token" value="">
                         </form>

                     </div>
                   </div>
                 </div>
               </div>
             </div>
           </div>
         </div>
```

6. Update the `UserService` and **User Service Interface**, and add a new method called `GetResetPasswordCode`:

```
public async Task<string> GetResetPasswordCode(UserModel user)
{
   return await _userManager.GeneratePasswordResetTokenAsync(user);
}
```

7. Add a new View to the `View/EmailTemplates` folder called `ResetPasswordEmail`:

```
@model TicTacToe.Models.ResetPasswordEmailModel
@{
   ViewData["Title"] = "View";
   Layout = "_LayoutEmail";
}
<h1>Welcome @Model.DisplayName</h1>
You have requested a password reset, please click <a
 href="@Model.ActionUrl">here</a> to continue.
```

8. Update the `AccountController`, and add a new method called `SendResetPassword`:

```
[HttpPost]
public async Task<IActionResult> SendResetPassword(
 string UserName)
{
  var user = await _userService.GetUserByEmail(UserName);
  var urlAction = new UrlActionContext
  {
    Action = "ResetPassword",
    Controller = "Account",
    Values = new { email = UserName,
     code = await _userService.GetResetPasswordCode(user) },
    Protocol = Request.Scheme,
    Host = Request.Host.ToString()
  };

  var resetPasswordEmailModel = new ResetPasswordEmailModel
  {
    DisplayName = $"{user.FirstName} {user.LastName}",
    Email = UserName,
    ActionUrl = Url.Action(urlAction)
  };

  var emailRenderService =
    HttpContext.RequestServices.GetService
      <IEmailTemplateRenderService>();
  var emailService =
    HttpContext.RequestServices.GetService<IEmailService>();
  var message =
    await emailRenderService.RenderTemplate(
      "EmailTemplates/ResetPasswordEmail",
       resetPasswordEmailModel,
    Request.Host.ToString());

  try
  {
    emailService.SendEmail(UserName,
      "Tic-Tac-Toe Reset Password", message).Wait();
  }
  catch
  {
  }

  return View("ConfirmResetPasswordRequest",
   resetPasswordEmailModel);
}
```

9. Add a new View called `ConfirmResetPasswordRequest` to the `Views/Account` folder:

```
@model TicTacToe.Models.ResetPasswordEmailModel
@{
  ViewData["Title"] = "ConfirmResetPasswordRequest";
  Layout = "~/Views/Shared/_Layout.cshtml";
}
@section Desktop{<h2>@Localizer["DesktopTitle"]</h2>}
@section Mobile {<h2>@Localizer["MobileTitle"]</h2>}
<h1>@Localizer["You have requested to reset your password,
 an email has been sent to {0}, please click on the provided
 link to continue.", Model.Email]</h1>
```

10. Update the `AccountController`, and add a new method called `ResetPassword`:

```
public async Task<IActionResult> ResetPassword(string email,
  string code)
{
  var user = await _userService.GetUserByEmail(email);
  ViewBag.Code = code;
  return View(new ResetPasswordModel { Token = code,
   UserName = email });
}
```

11. Add a new View to the `Views/Account` folder called `SendResetPassword`:

```
@model TicTacToe.Models.ResetPasswordEmailModel
@{
  ViewData["Title"] = "SendResetPassword";
  Layout = "~/Views/Shared/_Layout.cshtml";
}
@section Desktop{<h2>@Localizer["DesktopTitle"]</h2>}
@section Mobile {<h2>@Localizer["MobileTitle"]</h2>}
<h1>@Localizer["You have requested a password reset, an email
 has been sent to {0}, please click on the link to continue.",
 Model.Email]</h1>
```

12. Add a new View called `ResetPassword` to the `Views/Account` folder:

```
@model TicTacToe.Models.ResetPasswordModel
@{
  ViewData["Title"] = "ResetPassword";
  Layout = "~/Views/Shared/_Layout.cshtml";
}
```

```
<div class="container">
  <div id="loginbox" style="margin-top:50px;" class="mainbox
  col-md-6 col-md-offset-3 col-sm-8 col-sm-offset-2">
    <div class="panel panel-info">
      <div class="panel-heading">
        <div class="panel-title">Reset your Password</div>
      </div>
      <div style="padding-top:30px" class="panel-body">
        <div class="text-center">
          <form asp-controller="Account"
            asp-action="ResetPassword" method="post">
            <input type="hidden" asp-for="Token" />
            <div asp-validation-summary="All"></div>
            <div style="margin-bottom: 25px" class="input-group">
              <span class="input-group-addon"><i
                class="glyphicon glyphicon-envelope
                color-blue"></i></span>
                <input id="email" asp-for="UserName"
                placeholder="email address"
                class="form-control" type="email">
            </div>
            <div style="margin-bottom: 25px" class="input-group">
              <span class="input-group-addon"><i
                class="glyphicon glyphicon-lock
                color-blue"></i></span>
                <input id="password" asp-for="Password"
                placeholder="Password"
                class="form-control" type="password">
            </div>
            <div style="margin-bottom: 25px" class="input-group">
              <span class="input-group-addon"><i
                class="glyphicon glyphicon-lock
                color-blue"></i></span>
                <input id="confirmpassword"
                asp-for="ConfirmPassword"
                placeholder="Confirm your Password"
                class="form-control" type="password">
            </div>
            <div style="margin-bottom: 25px" class="input-group">
              <input name="submit"
                class="btn btn-lg btn-primary btn-block"
                value="Reset Password" type="submit">
            </div>
          </form>
        </div>
      </div>
    </div>
  </div>
</div>
```

```
</div>
```

13. Update the `UserService` and the **User Service Interface**, and add a new method called `ResetPassword`:

```
public async Task<IdentityResult> ResetPassword(
 string userName, string password, string token)
{
  var start = DateTime.Now;
  _logger.LogTrace($"Reset user password {userName}");

  var stopwatch = new Stopwatch();
  stopwatch.Start();

  try
  {
    var user = await _userManager.FindByNameAsync(userName);
    var result = await _userManager.ResetPasswordAsync(user,
     token, password);
    return result;
  }
  catch (Exception ex)
  {
    _logger.LogError($"Cannot reset user password
     {userName} - {ex}");
    throw ex;
  }
  finally
  {
    stopwatch.Stop();
    _logger.LogTrace($"Reset user password {userName}
     finished in {stopwatch.Elapsed}");
  }
}
```

14. Update the `AccountController`, and add a new method called `ResetPassword`:

```
[HttpPost]
public async Task<IActionResult> ResetPassword(
 ResetPasswordModel reset)
{
  if (ModelState.IsValid)
  {
    var result =
      await _userService.ResetPassword(reset.UserName,
       reset.Password, reset.Token);
```

```
        if (result.Succeeded)
          return RedirectToAction("Login");
        else
          ModelState.AddModelError("", "Cannot reset your password");
    }
    return View();
}
```

15. Start the application and go to the **Login** page, click on the **Reset Password Here** link:

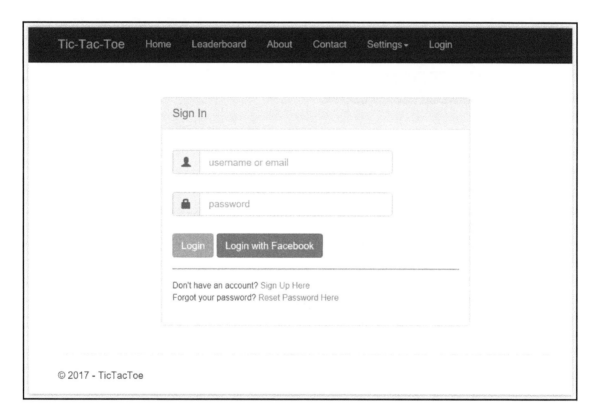

16. Enter an existing user email on the **Forgot Password?** page; this will send an email to the user:

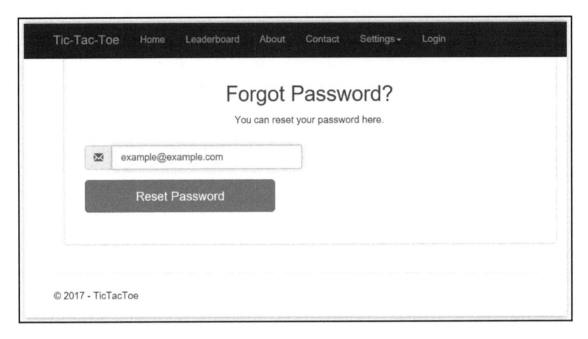

17. Open the **Password Reset Email** and click on the provided link:

18. On the **Password Reset** page, enter a new password for the user and click on **Reset Password**. You should be automatically redirected to the **Login** page, so sign in with the new password:

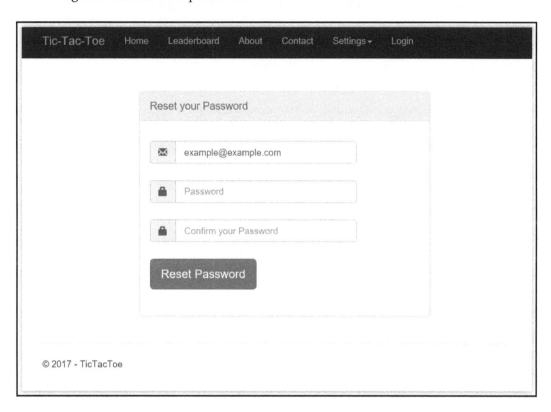

Implementing authorization

In the first part of the chapter, you saw how to handle user authentication and how to work with user logins. In the next part, you will see how to manage user access, which will allow you to fine-tune who has access to what.

The simplest authorization method is to use the [Authorize] meta decorator, which disables anonymous access completely. Users need to be signed in to be able to access restricted resources in this case.

Let's go and see how to implement it within the *Tic-Tac-Toe* application:

1. Add a new method called `SecuredPage` to the `HomeController`, and remove anonymous access to it by adding the `[Authorize]` decorator:

```
[Authorize]
public async Task<IActionResult> SecuredPage()
{
  return await Task.Run(() =>
  {
    ViewBag.SecureWord = "Secured Page";
    return View("SecuredPage");
  });
}
```

2. Add a new View called `SecuredPage` to the `Views/Home` folder:

```
@{
  ViewData["Title"] = "Secured Page";
}
@section Desktop {<h2>@Localizer["DesktopTitle"]</h2>}
@section Mobile {<h2>@Localizer["MobileTitle"]</h2>}
<div class="row">
  <div class="col-lg-12">
    <h2>Tic-Tac-Toe @ViewBag.SecureWord</h2>
  </div>
</div>
```

3. Try accessing the **Secured Page** by entering its URL `http://<host>/Home/SecuredPage` manually, while not signed in; you will be automatically redirected to the **Login** page:

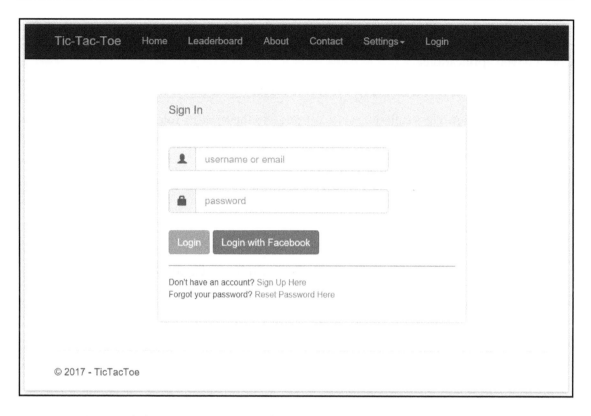

4. Enter valid user credentials and sign in; you should be automatically redirected to the **Secured Page** and be able to see it now:

Another relatively popular approach is to use role-based security, which provides some more advanced features. It is one of the recommended methods for securing your ASP.NET Core 2.0 web applications.

The following example explains how to work with it:

1. Add a new class called `UserRoleModel` to the `Models` folder, and make it inherit from `IdentityUserRole<long>`; it will be used by the built-in ASP.NET Core 2.0 Identity authentication features:

```
public class UserRoleModel : IdentityUserRole<Guid>
{
  [Key]
  public long Id { get; set; }
}
```

2. Update the `OnModelCreating` method within the **Game Db Context**:

```
protected override void OnModelCreating(ModelBuilder modelBuilder)
{
  ...
  modelBuilder.Entity<IdentityUserRole<Guid>>()
    .ToTable("UserRoleModel")
    .HasKey(x => new { x.UserId, x.RoleId });
}
```

3. Open the **NuGet Package Manager Console** and execute the `Add-Migration` `IdentityDb2` command, then execute the `Update-Database` command.

4. Update the `UserService`, and modify the constructor to create two roles called `Player` and `Administrator`, if they do not yet exist:

```
public UserService(RoleManager<RoleModel> roleManager,
 ApplicationUserManager userManager, ILogger<UserService>
 logger, SignInManager<UserModel> signInManager)
{
  ...
  if (!roleManager.RoleExistsAsync("Player").Result)
    roleManager.CreateAsync(new RoleModel {
    Name = "Player" }).Wait();

  if (!roleManager.RoleExistsAsync("Administrator").Result)
    roleManager.CreateAsync(new RoleModel {
    Name = "Administrator" }).Wait();
}
```

5. Update the `RegisterUser` method within the `UserService`, and add the user to the `Player` role or to the `Administrator` role during user registration:

```
...
try
{
  userModel.UserName = userModel.Email;
  var result = await _userManager.CreateAsync(userModel,
   userModel.Password);
  if (result == IdentityResult.Success)
  {
    if(userModel.FirstName == "Jason")
      await _userManager.AddToRoleAsync(userModel,
        "Administrator");
    else
      await _userManager.AddToRoleAsync(userModel, "Player");
  }

  return result == IdentityResult.Success;
}
...
```

Note that in the example, the code to identify whether a user has the administrator role is intentionally very basic. You should implement something more sophisticated in your applications.

6. Start the application and register a new user, open the `RoleModel` table within the **SQL Server Object Explorer**, and analyze its content:

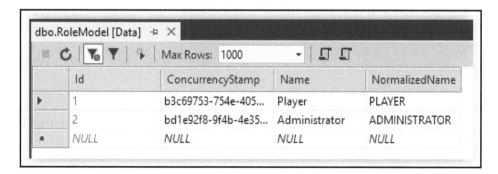

Id	ConcurrencyStamp	Name	NormalizedName
1	b3c69753-754e-405...	Player	PLAYER
2	bd1e92f8-9f4b-4e35...	Administrator	ADMINISTRATOR
NULL	NULL	NULL	NULL

7. Open the `UserRoleModel` table within the **SQL Server Object Explorer** and analyze its content:

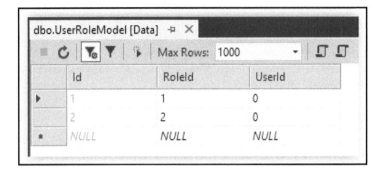

8. Update the `SignInUser` method within the `UserService` to map roles with claims:

```
...
identity.AddClaim(new Claim("Score", user.Score.ToString()));
var roles = await _userManager.GetRolesAsync(user);
identity.AddClaims(roles?.Select(r => new
 Claim(ClaimTypes.Role, r)));

await httpContext.SignInAsync(
 CookieAuthenticationDefaults.AuthenticationScheme,
  new ClaimsPrincipal(identity),
  new AuthenticationProperties { IsPersistent = false });
...
```

9. Update the `SecuredPage` method within the `HomeController`, and use the administrator role to secure access, and replace the `Authorize` decorator:

```
[Authorize(Roles = "Administrator")]
```

10. Start the application. If you try to access `http://<host>/Home/SecuredPage` without being logged in, you will be redirected to the **Login Page**. Sign in as a user who has the player role, you will be redirected to an **Access Denied Page** (which does not exist, hence the `404` error), since the user does not have the administrator role:

11. Log out and then sign in as a user who has the administrator role; you should now see the secured page, since the user has the necessary role:

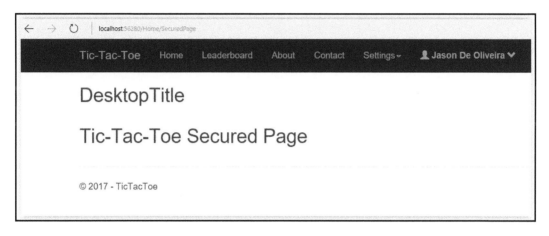

In the following example you will see how to sign in automatically as a registered user and how to activate claims-based and policy-based authentication:

1. Update the `SignInUser` method, and add a new method called `SignIn` in the UserService:

```
public async Task<SignInResult> SignInUser(LoginModel
  loginModel, HttpContext httpContext)
{
  var start = DateTime.Now;
  _logger.LogTrace($"Signin user {loginModel.UserName}");
  var stopwatch = new Stopwatch();
  stopwatch.Start();

  try
  {
    var user =
      await _userManager.FindByNameAsync(loginModel.UserName);
```

```
      var isValid =
        await _signInManager.CheckPasswordSignInAsync(user,
         loginModel.Password, true);

      if (!isValid.Succeeded)
      {
        return SignInResult.Failed;
      }

      if (!await _userManager.IsEmailConfirmedAsync(user))
      {
        return SignInResult.NotAllowed;
      }

      if (await _userManager.GetTwoFactorEnabledAsync(user))
      {
        return SignInResult.TwoFactorRequired;
      }

      await SignIn(httpContext, user);

      return isValid;
    }
    catch (Exception ex)
    {
      _logger.LogError($"Ca not sigin user
       {loginModel.UserName} - {ex}");
      throw ex;
    }
    finally
    {
      stopwatch.Stop();
      _logger.LogTrace($"Sigin user {loginModel.UserName}
       finished in {stopwatch.Elapsed}");
    }
}

private async Task SignIn(HttpContext httpContext, UserModel user)
{
  var identity = new ClaimsIdentity(
    CookieAuthenticationDefaults.AuthenticationScheme);
  identity.AddClaim(new Claim(ClaimTypes.Name, user.UserName));
  identity.AddClaim(new Claim(ClaimTypes.GivenName,
    user.FirstName));
  identity.AddClaim(new Claim(ClaimTypes.Surname,
    user.LastName));
  identity.AddClaim(new Claim("displayName",
    $"{user.FirstName} {user.LastName}"));
```

```
if (!string.IsNullOrEmpty(user.PhoneNumber))
{
  identity.AddClaim(new Claim(ClaimTypes.HomePhone,
   user.PhoneNumber));
}
identity.AddClaim(new Claim("Score", user.Score.ToString()));

var roles = await _userManager.GetRolesAsync(user);
identity.AddClaims(roles?.Select(r =>
 new Claim(ClaimTypes.Role, r)));

if (user.FirstName == "Jason")
identity.AddClaim(new Claim("AccessLevel", "Administrator"));

await httpContext.SignInAsync(
 CookieAuthenticationDefaults.AuthenticationScheme,
 new ClaimsPrincipal(identity),
 new AuthenticationProperties { IsPersistent = false });
}
```

Note that, in the example, the code to identify whether a user has administrator privileges is intentionally very basic. You should implement something more sophisticated in your applications.

2. Update the `RegisterUser` method in the `UserService`, add a new parameter to automatically sign in a user after registration, and re-extract the **User Service Interface**:

```
public async Task<bool> RegisterUser(UserModel userModel,
 bool isOnline = false)
{
  ...
  if (result == IdentityResult.Success)
  {
    ...
    if (isOnline)
    {
      HttpContext httpContext =
        new HttpContextAccessor().HttpContext;
      await Signin(httpContext, userModel);
    }
  }
  ...
}
```

3. Update the `Index` method in the `UserRegistrationController` to automatically sign in a newly registered user:

```
...
await _userService.RegisterUser(userModel, true);
...
```

4. Update the `ConfirmGameInvitation` method in the `GameInvitationController` to sign an invited user in automatically:

```
...
await _userService.RegisterUser(new UserModel
{
  Email = gameInvitation.EmailTo,
  EmailConfirmationDate = DateTime.Now,
  EmailConfirmed = true,
  FirstName = "",
  LastName = "",
  Password = "Azerty123!",
  UserName = gameInvitation.EmailTo
}, true);
...
```

5. Add a new policy called `AdministratorAccessLevelPolicy` to the `Startup` class, just after the **MVC Middleware** configuration:

```
services.AddAuthorization(options =>
{
  options.AddPolicy("AdministratorAccessLevelPolicy",
    policy => policy.RequireClaim("AccessLevel",
    "Administrator"));
});
```

6. Update the `SecuredPage` method within the `HomeController`, using a `Policy` instead of a `Role` to secure access, and replace the `Authorize` decorator:

```
[Authorize(Policy = "AdministratorAccessLevelPolicy")]
```

Note that it can be required to limit access to only one specific middleware, since several kinds of Authentication Middleware can be used with ASP.NET Core 2.0 (Cookie, Bearer, and more) at the same time.

For this case, the `Authorize` decorator you have seen before allows you to define which middleware can authenticate a user.

Here is an example to allow Cookie and Bearer:

```
[Authorize(AuthenticationSchemes = "Cookie,Bearer",
    Policy = "AdministratorAccessLevelPolicy")]
```

7. Start the application, register a new user with an `Administrator` access level, sign in, and access `http://<host>/Home/SecuredPage`. Everything should be working as before.

Note that you might need to clear your cookies and log in again to create a new authentication token with the required claims.

8. Try accessing the **Secured Page** as a user who does not have the required access level; as before, you should be redirected to `http://<host>/Account/AccessDenied?ReturnUrl=%2FHome%2FSecuredP age`:

9. Log out and then sign in as a user who has the `Administrator` role; you should now see the secured page, since the user has the necessary role.

Summary

In this chapter, you have learned how to secure ASP.NET Core 2.0 applications, including managing authentication and authorization for your application users.

You have added basic forms authentication, and more advanced external provider authentication via Facebook, to the example application. This should give you some good ideas on how to approach these important topics in your own applications.

Furthermore, you have learned how to add standard reset password mechanisms, because users forget their passwords all the time and you need to respond to this type of request as securely as possible.

We have even talked about two-factor authentication, which can provide an even higher security level for critical applications.

In the end, you have seen how to handle authorizations in multiple ways (basic, roles, policies), so that you can decide which approach is best suited to your specific use case.

In the next chapter, we will talk about the different options you will have when hosting and deploying your ASP.NET Core 2.0 web applications.

10
Hosting and Deploying ASP.NET Core 2.0 Applications

That's it, we are almost at the end of the book, which means that we have nearly finished the entire application development life cycle, and, thus, customers will be able to use your applications soon! Don't be sad; instead, be proud, because after reading and understanding this penultimate chapter of the book, you will have acquired strong skills to create and deploy your own mind-blowing applications with strong technical foundations!

Let's recap, from the beginning of the book until now: you have seen how to set up a development environment, how to use the various features of ASP.NET Core 2.0 to develop modern web applications, how to connect them to a database via Entity Framework Core, and, finally, in the last chapter, how to secure them against any malicious cyber criminals.

Now, we need to talk about the last step in the cycle, which consists of hosting and deploying your applications once they are production ready.

The goal of this chapter will be to explain the different options you have, how to choose the right ones, and how to deploy your ASP.NET Core 2.0 web applications using the most current technologies and cloud providers.

In this chapter, we will cover the following topics:

- Hosting applications
- Deploying applications in Amazon Web Services
- Deploying applications in Microsoft Azure
- Deploying applications into Docker containers

Hosting applications

You can build the best and most useful applications in the world, but if your customers cannot access them easily and from any device, you may not get the success expected. As you can see in the following diagram, applications need to be more and more omnichannel, which means customers need to be able to start on one device and then continue on another:

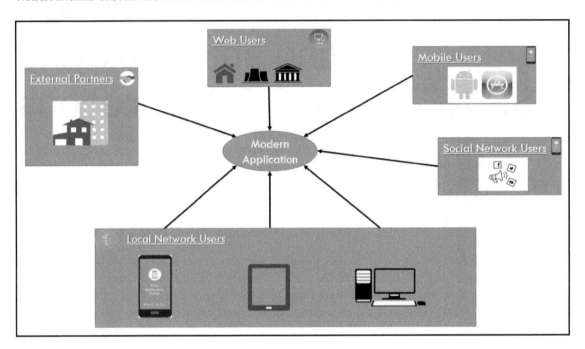

Your applications need to be deployable to multiple targets and, in some cases, multiple operation systems, to allow a high degree of flexibility and device availability. This is where hosting comes into play.

A host is responsible for application startup and lifetime management, which includes providing and configuring a server and request processing. Depending on how you are hosting your ASP.NET Core 2.0 applications, you can support different devices for your applications. The chosen technology has a significant impact on the possible device and operations system choices.

ASP.NET Core 2.0 fully supports all current hosting mechanisms on multiple platforms and operation systems. It all depends on your specific application context.

Some examples to host your ASP.Net Core 2.0 applications are as follows:

- Host on Windows via IIS
- Host in a Windows service
- Host on Linux using Nginx
- Host on Linux using Apache

During development time, or if you don't need to share your applications with others, it may be interesting to use self-hosting mechanisms or IIS Express, which provide a quick and easy solution for disconnected, proof-of-concept, or test projects.

However, if you start sharing your applications with others, you need some more sophisticated hosting solutions and the corresponding server technologies.

For example, to expose your ASP.NET Core 2.0 applications over the internet, you will need a web server, which is accessible outside of your local network. There are several possible solutions to achieve this goal.

One is using an internet host provider to host your web server. However, you will need to do the sizing and manage the server by yourself, which may be expensive and time-consuming. Another option is using public cloud providers, which offer much more flexibility and scalability, while allowing cost reduction and paying for what you need. The most famous ones are Amazon Web Services and Microsoft Azure which have data centers all around the world.

Furthermore, when using public cloud PaaS offers, you don't even have to manage the OS or the platform anymore. The cloud platform is doing everything for you. Instead, you can access cloud services, which provide web server or database server functionalities with high SLAs. Some examples are AWS Elastic Beanstalk and Microsoft Azure App Services.

After having seen the various hosting options at your disposal, you will be able to decide on your deployment targets. For publicly available web applications, you will want to deploy to a public cloud provider. The next sections will show you how to deploy to the most common and famous public cloud providers, and how to use the most recent technologies to do so.

Deploying applications in Amazon Web Services

Amazon Web Services, a subsidiary of *Amazon.com*, provides a public cloud computing platform for building, testing, deploying, and managing applications and services within globally available AWS data centers all around the world. It supports many different programming languages, tools, frameworks, and systems.

We will explore Amazon Web Services in the following sections and see how to create an account and deploy your ASP.NET Core 2.0 applications to AWS Elastic Beanstalk.

First, you have to sign up for an account on Amazon Web Services; it only takes five minutes, but you will need a credit card for that.

Let's go through the account registration steps:

1. Open a browser, go to `https://aws.amazon.com`, and click on the **Create a Free Account** button:

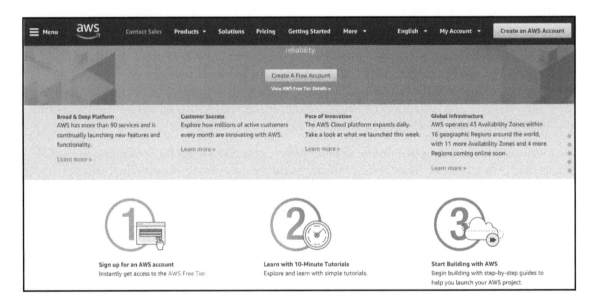

2. Fill the **Create a new AWS Account** form and click on **Continue**:

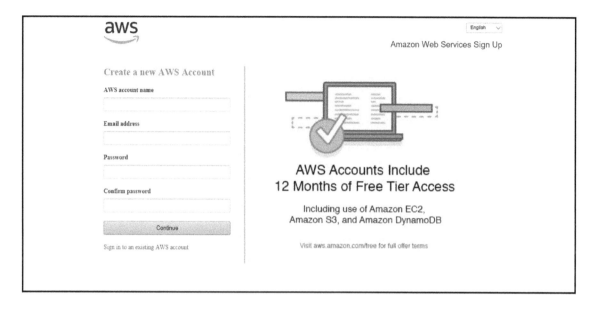

3. Fill the **Contact Information** form and click on **Create Account and Continue**:

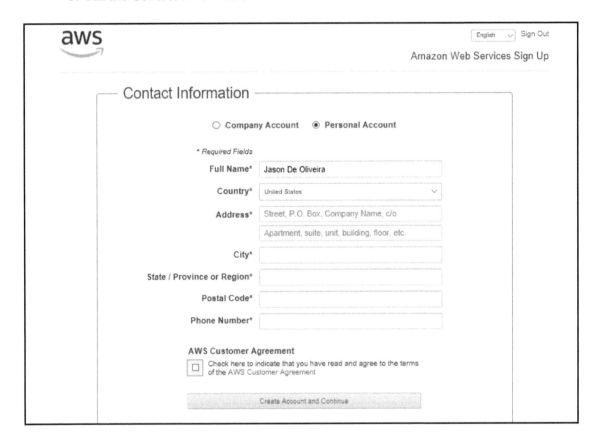

4. Fill the **Payment Information** form and click on **Continue**:

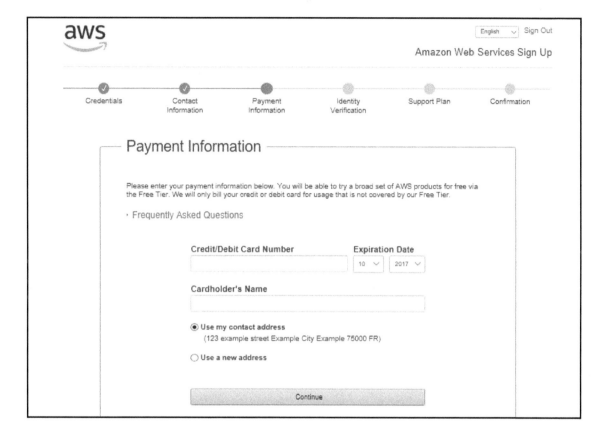

5. Fill the **Identity Information Verification** form and click on **Continue,** then select a support plan and click on **Continue**:

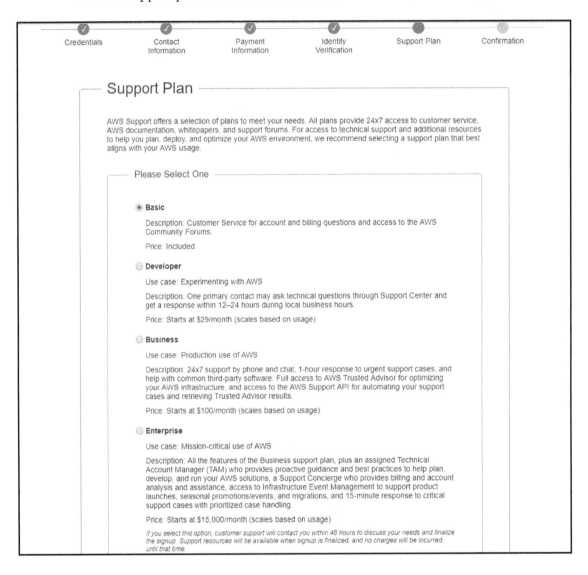

6. After the registration has been done, you are automatically redirected to the welcome page where you should click on the **Launch Management Console** button:

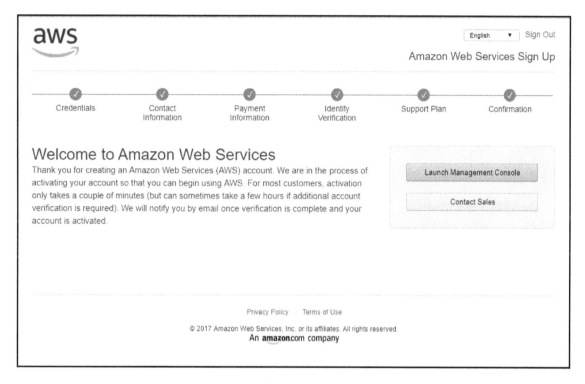

After having created your new Amazon Web Services user account, you are now ready to deploy your first ASP.NET Core 2.0 application in Amazon Web Services.

When working with Amazon Web Services, you basically have two choices to deploy your Asp.Net Core 2.0 web applications:

- Amazon Web Services Elastic Beanstalk
- Amazon Web Services EC2 Container Service

The next section will shed some light on how to deploy your applications in Amazon Web Services Elastic Beanstalk. So, stay tuned, engage your seat belt, and enjoy your ride!

Deploying applications in AWS Elastic Beanstalk

- AWS Elastic Beanstalk is a PaaS offering for web-based applications in Amazon Web Services, which includes auto-scaling. In this regard, it is comparable to Microsoft Azure App Services, which you will see in a later section of this chapter.
- It removes the need to manage infrastructure; instead, you only need to be concerned about building and hosting your applications. For a full DevOps approach, it is advised using this PaaS service if you want to work with Amazon Web Services.

> For more information on AWS Elastic Beanstalk, check out `https://aws.amazon.com/fr/elasticbeanstalk/`.

The following examples illustrate step by step how to deploy the *Tic-Tac-Toe* application in Amazon Web Services Beanstalk.

Let's start with the creation of the AWS Beanstalk application:

1. Sign in to AWS and go to the **AWS Management Console**, enter `Beanstalk` in the **AWS services** textbox, and click on the displayed link; you will be redirected to the **Beanstalk Welcome Page**:

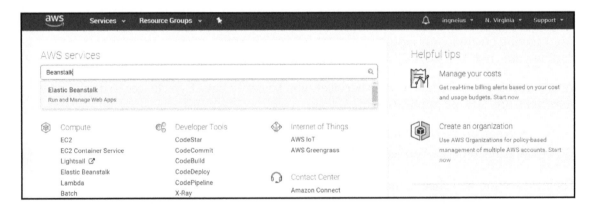

2. On the Beanstalk welcome page, select **.NET (Windows/IIS)** and click on the **Launch Now** button:

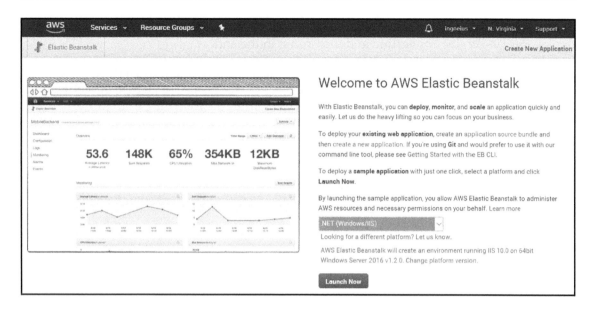

Note that you can change the IIS version and network settings (Network Load Balancer or Single instance) by clicking on the **Change platform version** link.

3. Wait until the Beanstalk application has been created; depending on your internet connection and AWS, this may take a while:

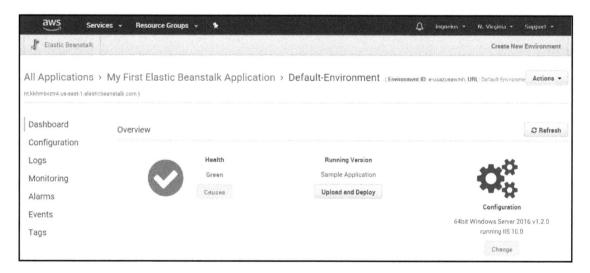

The technical environment needs to be prepared in the next steps, before being able to deploy the *Tic-Tac-Toe* application and then run it in the end.

As you may have seen in the preceding chapters, the application requires a database to persist user and application data. For this purpose, we will provision an SQL Server PaaS Service called RDS Service in Amazon Web Services, as in the following example:

1. Return to the **AWS Management Console** and click on **Elastic Beanstalk** within the **Recent visited services** section:

2. On the Beanstalk **All Applications** page, select the desired environment and then click on **Default-Environment**:

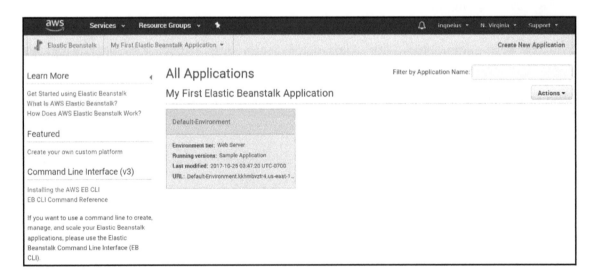

3. On the specific Beanstalk application page, click on **Configuration** in the left-hand menu:

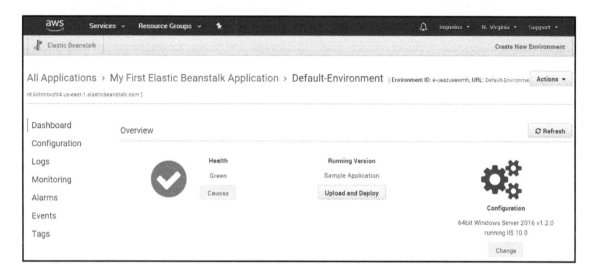

4. Scroll down and click on the **create a new RDS database** link:

5. Select as **DB Engine** SQL Server Express (**sqlserver-ex**) and enter a master username and password; leave the rest of the fields at their default values, click on the **Apply** button at the bottom of the page, and wait for the database creation to be finished:

 Note that, depending on your application's needs, the SQL Server Express Edition may not be enough, since it is limited in size, meaning that the Enterprise or Web Editions may be necessary, which will result in higher cloud provider costs. For the *Tic-Tac-Toe* sample application, it is, however, largely sufficient.

6. Go to the **AWS Management Console**, enter RDS in the **AWS services** textbox, and click on the displayed link; you will be redirected to the **Amazon RDS** page, click on **Instances** in the left menu:

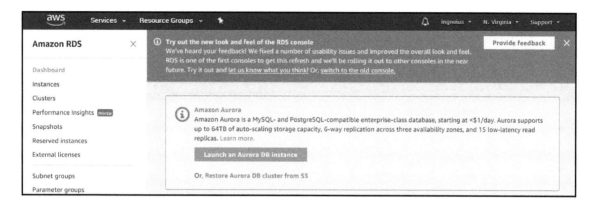

7. Click on your instance; the instance dashboard will be displayed. Scroll down to retrieve the endpoint address, which will be used to update the application connection string before deployment:

8. Scroll further down on the **Amazon RDS Instance Page** and click on the **Security groups**:

9. On the **Security Group** page, click on **Inbound** in the menu at the bottom of the page, then click on **Edit** for being able to update the inbound rules for the security group of the database you have just created:

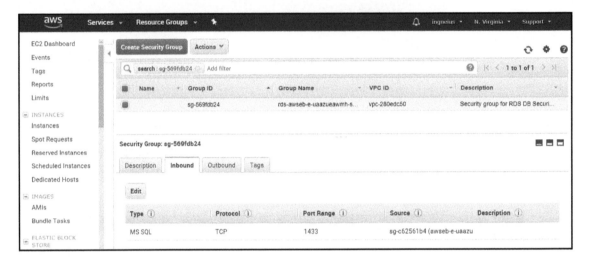

10. Click on the **Add Rule** button, choose **All TCP** as the type, **Anywhere** as the source, and enter a meaningful description, then click on the **Save** button:

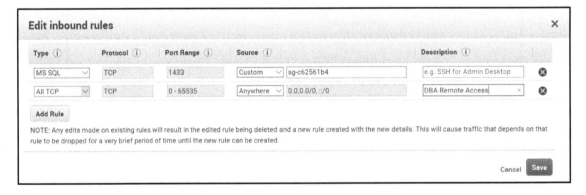

Note that you should configure the security group inbound rules stricter in a real production environment and set real IP restrictions. The source **Anywhere** should not be used for production environments.

11. Open **SQL Server Object Explorer** in Visual Studio 2017; sign in using the endpoint address, username, and password from before, then create a new database called `TicTacToe`:

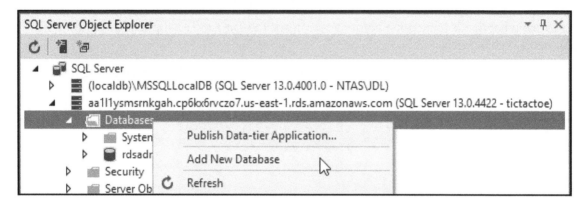

12. Update the `DatabaseConnectionString` in the `appsettings.json` file, and replace the parameters with the corresponding values:

```
"Server=<YourEndPoint>;Database=TicTacToe;
    MultipleActiveResultSets=true;
    User id=<YourUser>;pwd=<YourPassword>"
```

You have successfully configured the technical environment, which means that you are now able to publish the database schema as well as deploy the web application.

Are you eagerly awaiting to run the application in the cloud? Just stay concentrated and continue a little bit further and you will see your application running in Amazon Web Services very soon.

You have three choices when it comes to publishing the database schema:

1. Generate an SQL script to create the database from within Visual Studio 2017 via Entity Framework Migrations.
2. Change the default connection string in `Data\GameDbContextFactory.cs` and execute the `Update-Database` instruction within the **Package Manager Console**.
3. Run the application to create the database.

The most appropriate solution depends on the type and the size of your application and its database. As a rule of thumb, it is better to generate a script and then create the database for larger applications, while it is acceptable to create the database automatically when the application is running for the first time for smaller applications.

Let's see what needs to be done before you can see the *Tic-Tac-Toe* application running in Amazon Web Services:

1. Open the **Package Manager Console** in Visual Studio 2017 and execute the `Script-Migration` instruction as shown here:

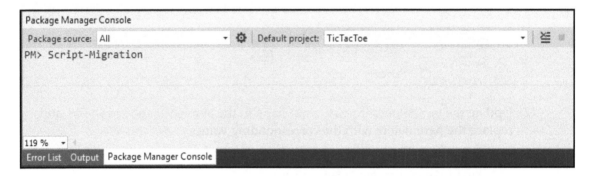

2. Take the generated script and copy it into a query window for the Amazon RDS database, then execute the script to create the database and the various database objects.
3. Download and install the **AWS Toolkit for Visual Studio 2017** from `https:// marketplace.visualstudio.com/items?itemName=AmazonWebServices. AWSToolkitforVisualStudio2017`:

4. Go to **AWS Management Console**, enter IAM in the **AWS services** textbox, and click on the displayed link; you will be redirected to the Amazon **Identity and Access Management** page:

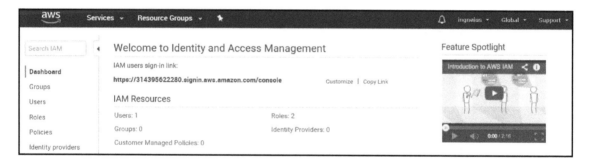

5. On the Amazon **Identity and Access Management** page, click on **Users** and then on the **Add User** button:

6. On the **Add User** page, give the new user a meaningful username and grant him **Programmatic access**, then click on the **Next:Permissions** button at the bottom of the page:

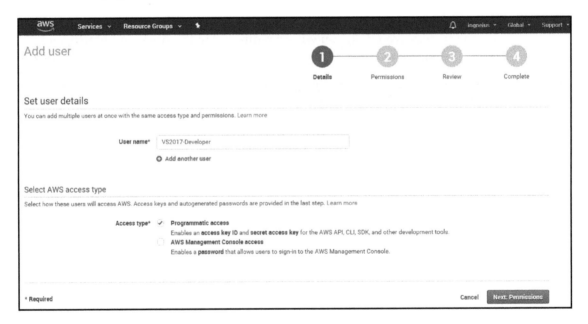

7. You now have to set the permissions for the new user; for that, click on the **Attach existing policies directly** button:

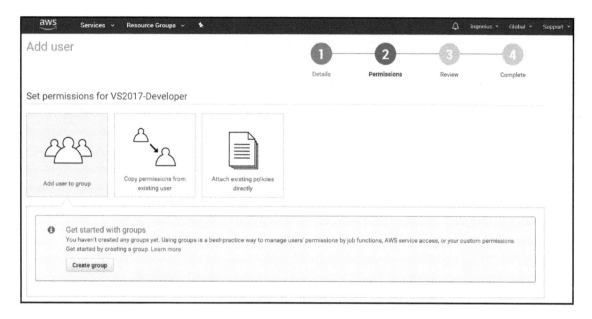

8. Select **AdministratorAccess** from the existing policies and click on the **Next:Review** button at the bottom of the page:

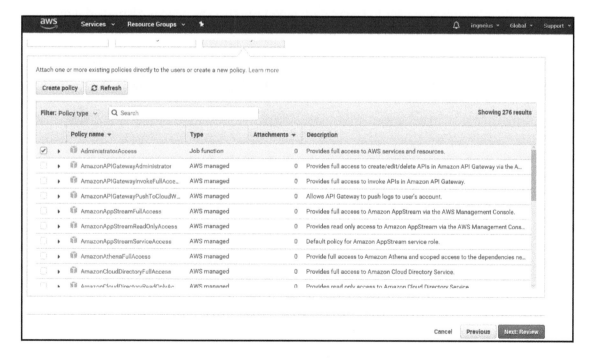

9. Verify that the **User name** and **AWS access type** as well as the selected policies are correct, then click on the **Create user** button:

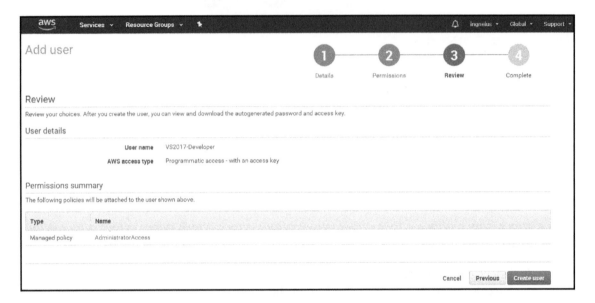

10. Wait for the new user to be created; when the success page is displayed, you can then download the `.csv` file, which we will use to configure Visual Studio 2017 with AWS:

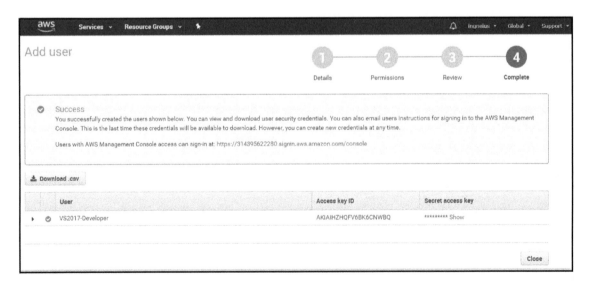

11. Open Visual Studio 2017 and display **AWS Explorer** by going to **View** | **AWS Explorer**:

12. Click on the **New account profile** button (the only active button):

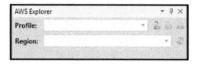

13. A wizard will be displayed; leave the **Profile Name** as default and fill the **Access Key ID** and **Secret Access key** with the values coming from the .csv file you have downloaded before during the new user creation process on AWS:

14. Since AWS is based on IIS as host for .NET Core applications, you now have to add a `web.config` file to the `TicTacToe` project:

```
<?xml version="1.0" encoding="utf-8"?>
<configuration>
  <system.webServer>
    <handlers>
      <add name="aspNetCore" path="*" verb="*"
        modules="AspNetCoreModule" resourceType="Unspecified" />
    </handlers>
    <aspNetCore processPath="dotnet"
      arguments=".\TicTacToe.dll"
      stdoutLogEnabled="true"
      stdoutLogFile=".\logs\stdout"
      forwardWindowsAuthToken="true" />
  </system.webServer>
</configuration>
```

15. You, furthermore, have to enable IIS integration; for that, open the `Program.cs` file and change the WebHost builder configuration to enable IIS integration, as follows:

```
public static IWebHost BuildWebHost(string[] args) =>
  WebHost.CreateDefaultBuilder(args)
    .UseStartup("TicTacToe")
    .CaptureStartupErrors(true)
    .UseApplicationInsights()
    .UseIISIntegration()
    .Build();
```

16. Right-click on the `TicTacToe` project and click on **Publish to AWS Elastic Beanstalk...** in the context menu:

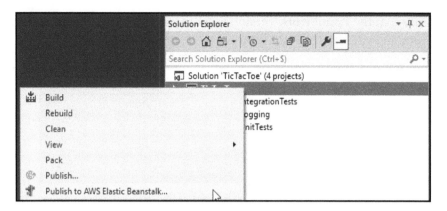

17. A wizard will be displayed; click on **Redeploy to an existing environment** and select the default environment you have created before, then click on the **Next** button:

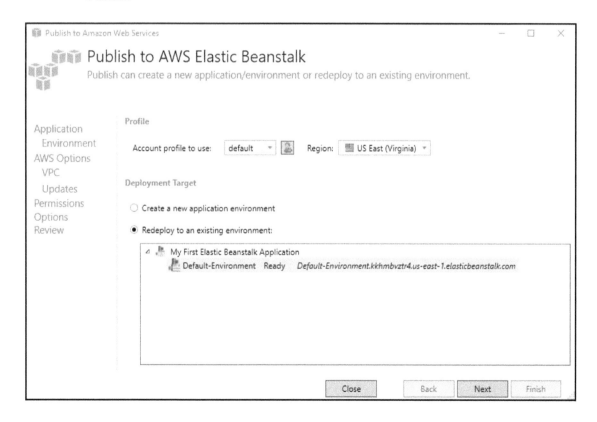

18. Verify that the **Framework** version is set to `netcoreapp2.0`; leave all default values and click on the **Next** button:

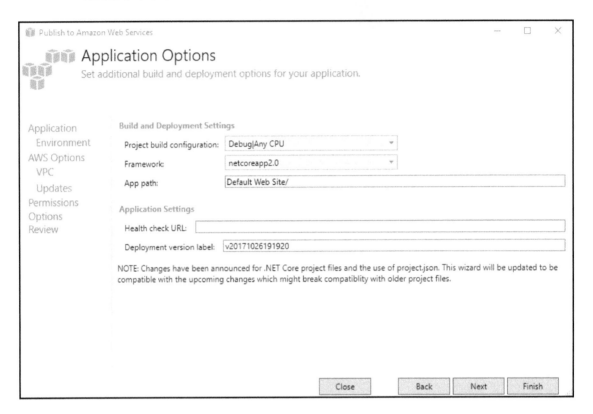

19. Select **Generate AWSDeploy configuration**, which will allow you to redeploy a copy of your application with AWS, then click on the **Deploy** button:

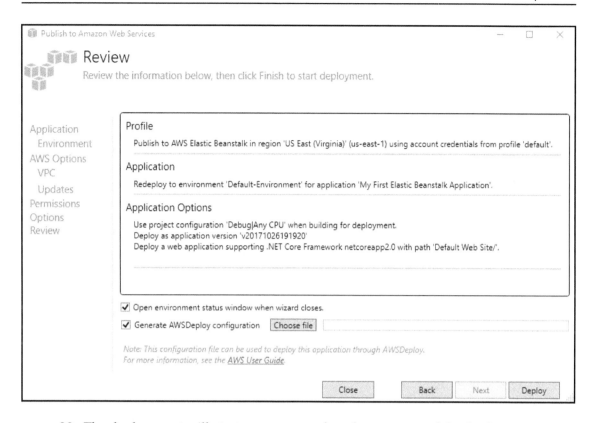

20. The deployment will start; you can see the advancement of the deployment process by going to **Output** | **Amazon Web Services**:

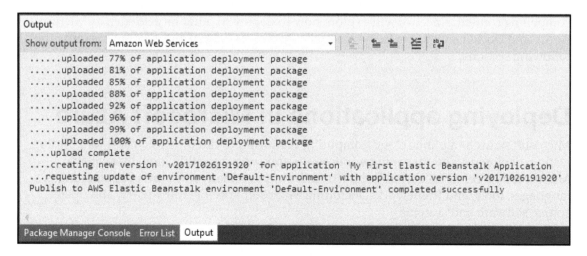

21. When the application is deployed, you can use the **AWS Explorer** to get the URL of the application, as follows:

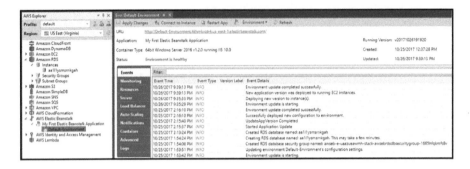

22. Open a browser and go to the application URL in Amazon Web Services, start the application and try to register a new user.

> Note that the application is not working as expected, you will get a 404 Not Found HTTP response. Everything is working locally and the deployment in Amazon Web Services was successful, but something is wrong. You will see in the next chapter, which is about logging and monitoring, how to analyze, diagnose, understand and fix this problem.

Congratulations, you have successfully deployed your first application in the public cloud. It is now available to the outside world and users can connect to it and start working with it.

This concludes the examples for Amazon Web Services. However, we still have some compelling content, since we will explore how to deploy to other targets such as Microsoft Azure and Docker containers in the next sections; so, stay sharp and continue reading the following sections.

Deploying applications in Microsoft Azure

Microsoft Azure is a public cloud computing platform provided by Microsoft for building, testing, deploying, and managing applications and services within globally available Microsoft data centers all around the world. It supports many different programming languages, tools, and frameworks, including Microsoft-specific, third-party, and open source software and systems.

When deploying web applications in Microsoft Azure, you basically have four choices:

- Azure App Services
- Azure Service Fabric
- Azure Container Services
- Azure Virtual Machines

However, before you can start deploying your applications in Microsoft Azure, you need to sign up for a subscription; so, let's do that right now:

1. You need a Microsoft account to be able to sign up for a Microsoft Azure subscription. You can use the same you have used for your **Visual Studio Team Services** (**VSTS**) subscription, but if you do not have one yet, create it by going to `http://www.live.com` and clicking on the **Create one!** link:

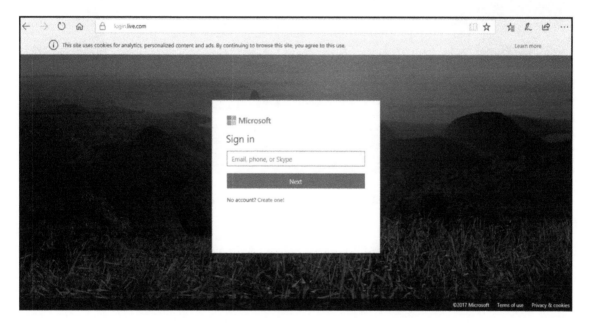

2. Go to `https://portal.azure.com` and log in with your Microsoft account; you will be asked if you want to take a tour. Select **Maybe later** (you should really take the tour later, though!) and you will be redirected to the **Microsoft Azure Management Portal**:

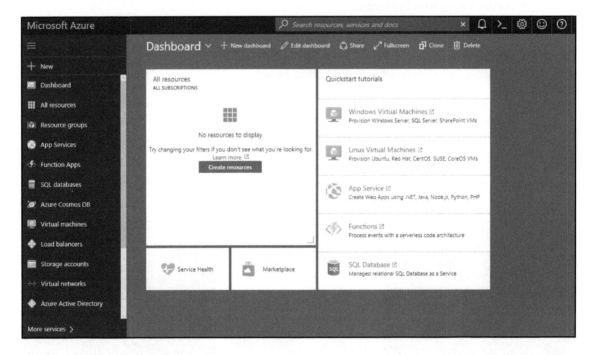

3. Click on **More Services** at the bottom of the left-hand menu, then click on the **Subscriptions** button:

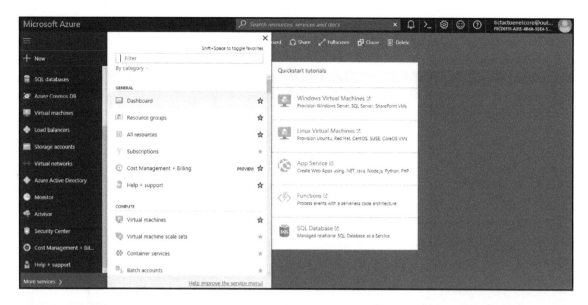

4. Click on the **Add** button:

5. Click on the **Free Trial** button and fill in the different forms until you have created your Microsoft Azure subscription:

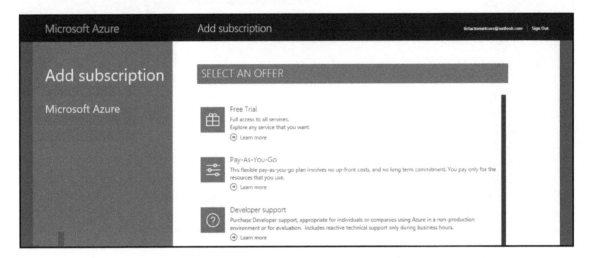

Exciting! You are now ready to provision the technical environment and, then, deploy your ASP.NET Core 2.0 web applications to the Microsoft Azure data center all around the world!

Deploying applications in Microsoft Azure App Services

Azure App Services is a PaaS offering for web-based applications in Microsoft Azure, which includes auto-scaling. In this regard, it is comparable to AWS Beanstalk, which you may have already seen in the section on AWS before.

It removes the need for managing infrastructure; instead, you only need to be concerned about building and hosting your applications. For a full DevOps approach, it is advisable to use this PaaS service if you want to work with Microsoft Azure.

 For more information on Microsoft Azure App Services, check out `https://docs.microsoft.com/en-us/azure/app-service/app-service-web-overview`.

The following examples illustrate how to deploy the *Tic-Tac-Toe* application to Azure App Services step by step:

1. Go to the **Microsoft Azure Management Portal**, click on **App Services** in the left-hand menu, and then click on the **Add** button:

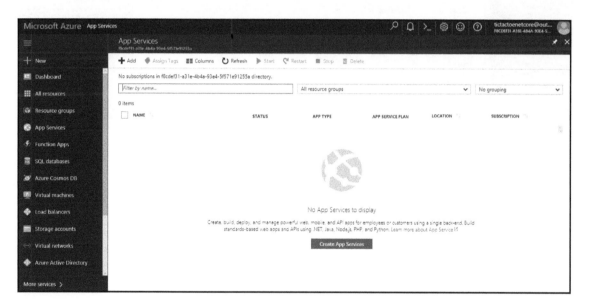

2. Click on the **Web App + SQL** button in the **Web Apps** section:

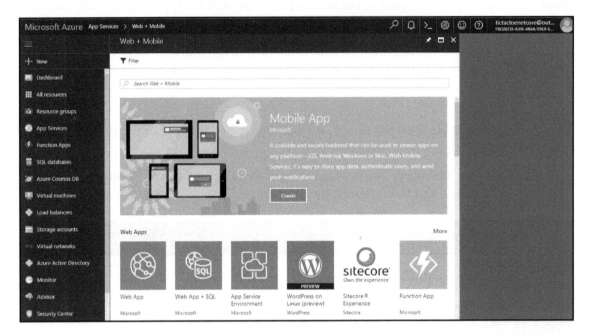

3. Read the service details and click on the **Create** button:

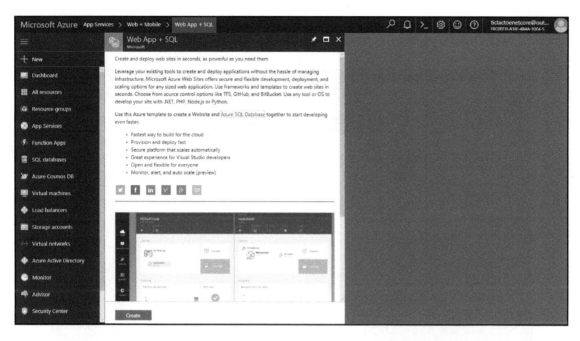

4. If you did not sign up for your Microsoft Azure subscription before, you can do that now by clicking on the **Sign up for a new subscription** link; you will be redirected to the same forms as you have seen at the beginning of the section:

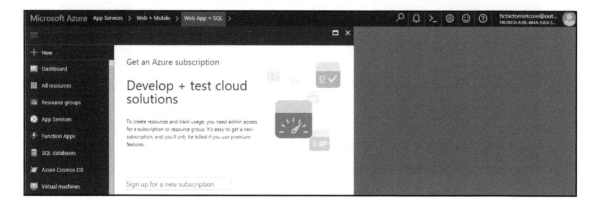

5. Choose a name for the application and a **Resource Group**, and click on the **SQL Database** button to configure the database options:

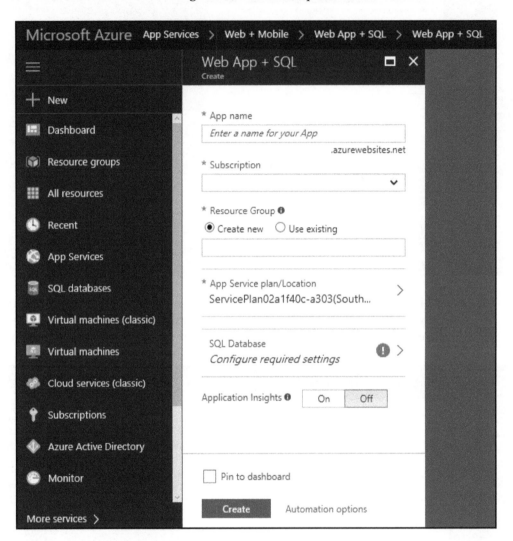

6. Click on **Create Database** and choose a database name. Leave the other options with their default values and click on **Target server**:

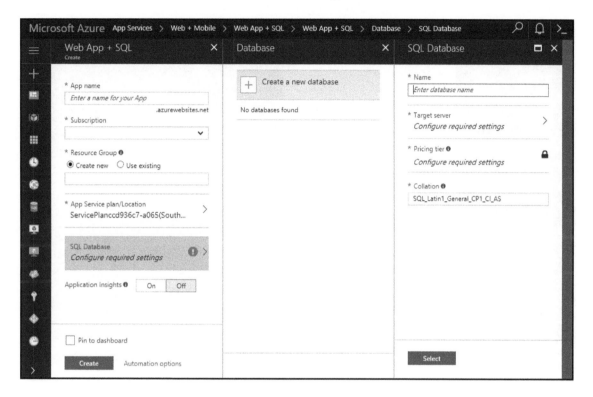

7. Enter some values for **Server name**, **Server admin login**, and **Password**, then click on the **Select** button, as shown here:

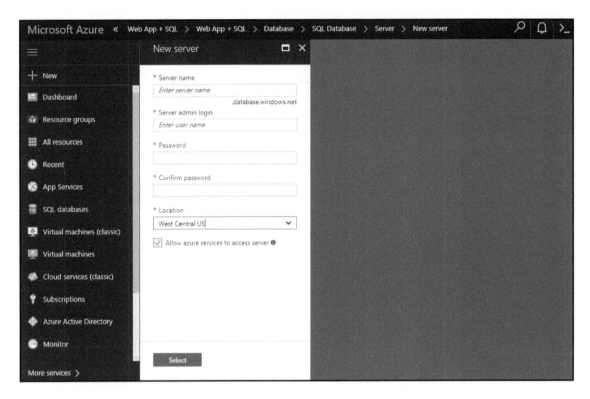

8. Click on the **Select** buttons for the new database server, the new database, and then finally on the **Create** button for the App Service; wait until it has been provisioned:

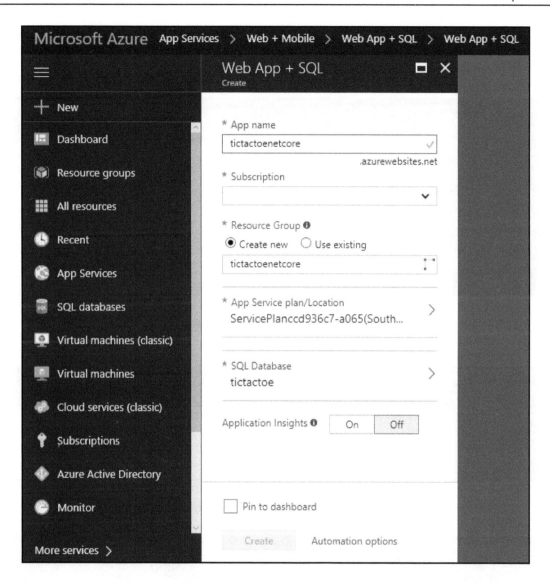

9. You need to allow access to the SQL Database to execute the database generation scripts for the `TicTacToe` application; in the left-hand menu, click on **SQL databases** and select the `TicTacToe` database:

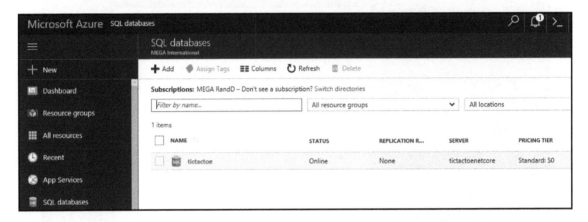

10. Click on **Set server firewall** to be able to add a new rule to allow access to the SQL Database from your IP:

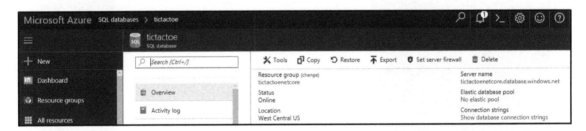

11. Click on **Add client IP**, verify your IP, and click on **Save** to add the new rule:

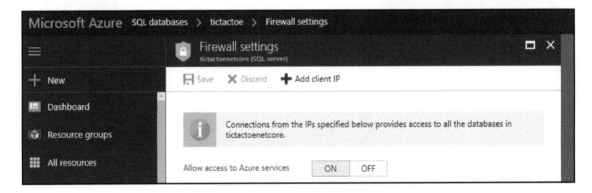

12. Click on **Connection strings** to retrieve the connection string for the `TicTacToe` Azure database you have created before:

13. Open Visual Studio 2017, go to the **SQL Server Object Explorer** and add a new SQL Server using the connection information from the `TicTacToe` Azure database connection string.

14. Add a new database to the Azure SQL Server, as you would have done in the Amazon Web Services example; it will be used to execute the `TicTacToe` database generation scripts:

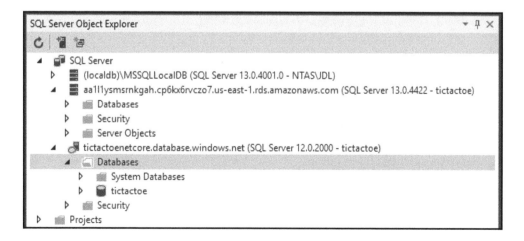

15. If you have not done it in the Amazon Web Services example before, open the **Package Manager Console** in Visual Studio 2017 and execute the `Script-Migration` instruction; otherwise, you can reuse the same scripts.

16. Take the generated script and copy it into a query window for the Azure `TicTacToe` database, then execute the script to create the database and the various database objects.

Now that the technical foundations have been provisioned and initialized in Microsoft Azure, everything is ready for the next step, which consists of deploying the sample application.

So, let's do exactly that—prepare the application and deploy it via Visual Studio 2017 into the Microsoft App Service you have created before:

1. Since App Services are based on IIS as the host for .NET Core applications, you now have to add a `web.config` file to the `TicTacToe` project; you should, however, already have done that if you have followed the Amazon Web Services example from before:

```
<?xml version="1.0" encoding="utf-8"?>
<configuration>
  <system.webServer>
    <handlers>
      <add name="aspNetCore" path="*"
        verb="*" modules="AspNetCoreModule"
        resourceType="Unspecified" />
    </handlers>
    <aspNetCore processPath="dotnet"
      arguments=".\TicTacToe.dll"
      stdoutLogEnabled="true"
      stdoutLogFile=".\logs\stdout"
      forwardWindowsAuthToken="true" />
  </system.webServer>
</configuration>
```

2. Furthermore, you have to enable IIS integration; for that, open the `Program.cs` file and change the WebHost builder configuration to enable IIS integration. You should, however, already have done that if you have followed the Amazon Web Services example from before:

```
public static IWebHost BuildWebHost(string[] args) =>
  WebHost.CreateDefaultBuilder(args)
    .UseStartup("TicTacToe")
    .CaptureStartupErrors(true)
```

```
.UseApplicationInsights()
.UseIISIntegration()
.Build();
```

3. Go to the **Microsoft Azure Management Portal** and click on **App Services** in the left-hand menu, select the TicTacToe application you have created before, click on **Get publish profile**, and download the Azure App Service **Publish** profile:

4. Right-click on the TicTacToe project, click on **Publish** in the context menu, then click on the **Import Profile** button, as shown here:

5. Select the downloaded Azure App Service **Publish** profile and the publish process should start automatically:

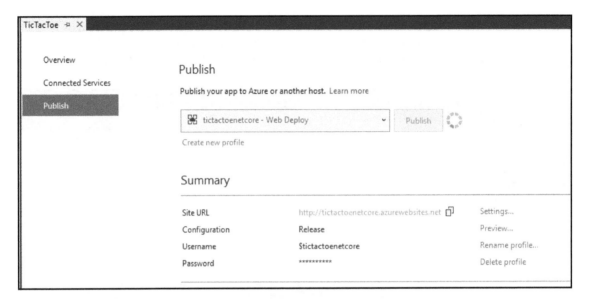

6. You can see the publish process in the **Web Publish Activity** view:

7. Open a browser and go to the application URL in Microsoft Azure, start the application and try to register a new user.

Note that the application is not working as expected, you will get a 404 Not Found HTTP response. Everything is working locally and the deployment in Microsoft Azure was successful, but something is wrong. You will see in the next chapter, which is about logging and monitoring, how to analyze, diagnose, understand and fix this problem.

This concludes the examples for Microsoft Azure. The next sections will explain how to deploy your application into Docker containers.

Deploying applications into Docker containers

Docker simplifies building, deploying, and running applications by using containers. Containers allow for the packaging of libraries, as well as any other dependencies, into a single application package (container image), which can then be shipped as a single coherent resource. This technology assures that the packaged application will run correctly anywhere where the container can be used, regardless of any environmental specific settings or configurations.

Here is a high-level schema of how Docker works:

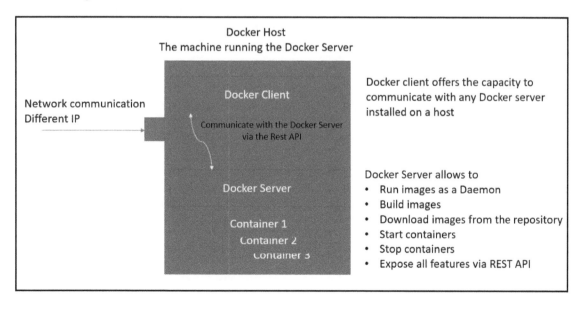

You basically have three choices when working with Docker containers:

- Use a VM locally or in the cloud with Docker for Windows or Docker Enterprise Edition for Windows 2016, depending on the operating system
- Use the Docker Hub (`https://hub.docker.com`) and the Docker Store (`https://store.docker.com`)
- Use either Microsoft Azure Container Services or Amazon Web Services EC2 Container Service

For more information on Docker, visit the following links:

`https://www.docker.com`

`https://docs.microsoft.com/en-us/dotnet/core/docker/docker-basic s-dotnet-core`

Deploying applications into Docker containers using Docker for Windows and Docker Enterprise Edition

Docker for Windows provides everything necessary to start using Docker containers in a Windows environment, whereas Docker Enterprise Edition for Windows 2016 is meant for companies that need to provide production environments based on the Docker technologies with the necessary support.

Let's see how to use Docker in Windows and how to deploy your application in this case:

1. If you do not have Docker for Windows installed yet, go to `https://docs.docker.com/docker-for-windows/install/`, click on the **Get Docker for Windows (Stable)** button, and install it:

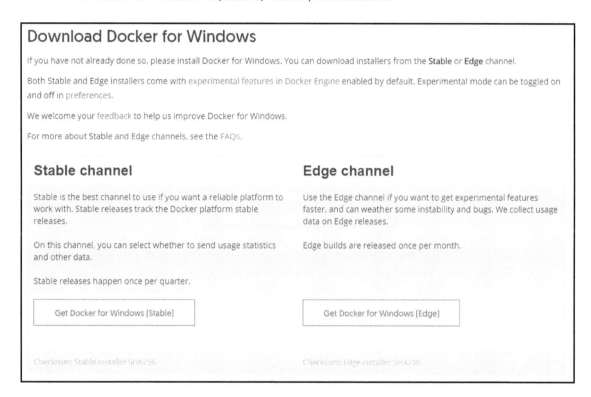

 To install the Docker Enterprise Edition for Windows 2016, go to `https://docs.docker.com/engine/installation/windows/docker-ee/` and follow the installation instructions. After the installation, you should skip the following steps and continue directly with the fourth step.

2. Right-click on the Docker tray icon and click on **Switch to Windows containers...** in the context menu:

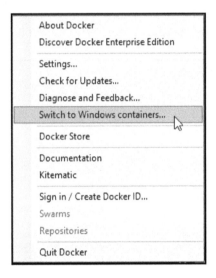

3. If the Container features have not yet been enabled in your Windows installation, Docker will ask to do it for you; click on the **Ok** button:

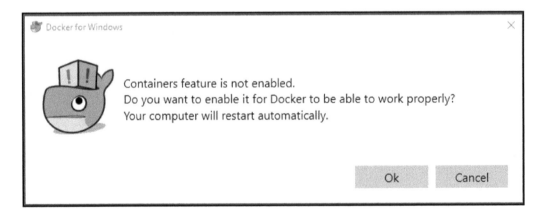

4. Open a new elevated Command Prompt, download the official Docker Microsoft SQL Server image, and execute the `docker pull microsoft/mssql-server-windows-express` instruction as follows:

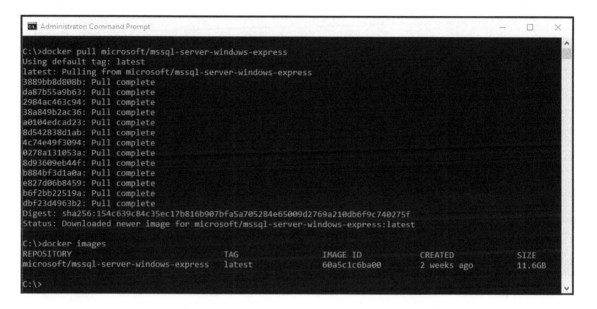

```
C:\>docker pull microsoft/mssql-server-windows-express
Using default tag: latest
latest: Pulling from microsoft/mssql-server-windows-express
3889bb8d808b: Pull complete
da87b55a9b63: Pull complete
2984ac463c94: Pull complete
38a849b2ac36: Pull complete
a0104edcad23: Pull complete
8d542838d1ab: Pull complete
4c74e49f3094: Pull complete
0278a131053a: Pull complete
8d93609eb44f: Pull complete
b884bf3d1a0a: Pull complete
e827d06b8459: Pull complete
b6f2bb22519a: Pull complete
dbf23d4963b2: Pull complete
Digest: sha256:154c639c84c35ec17b816b907bfa5a705284e65009d2769a210db6f9c740275f
Status: Downloaded newer image for microsoft/mssql-server-windows-express:latest

C:\>docker images
REPOSITORY                                    TAG        IMAGE ID        CREATED         SIZE
microsoft/mssql-server-windows-express        latest     60a5c1c6ba00    2 weeks ago     11.6GB

C:\>
```

5. Download the official Docker Microsoft ASP.NET Core image and execute the `docker pull microsoft/aspnetcore` instruction like this:

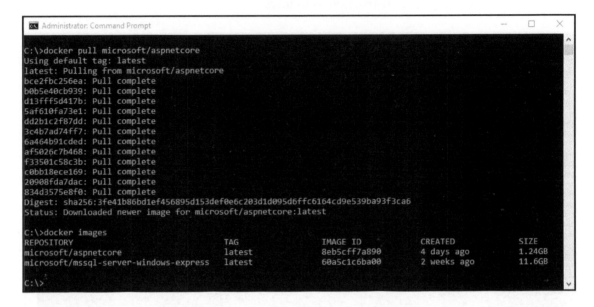

6. To be able to compile and publish applications from Visual Studio 2017 directly into Docker, you will also need to download the specific build image and execute the `docker pull microsoft/aspnetcore-build` instruction:

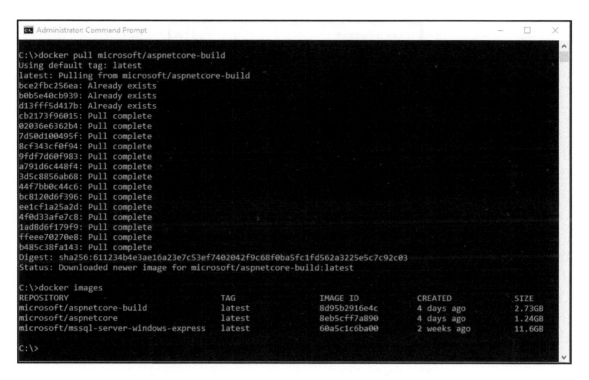

7. Open Visual Studio 2017, then open the `TicTacToe` project; in the menu, click on **Project | Docker Support** and select the **Windows** operation system:

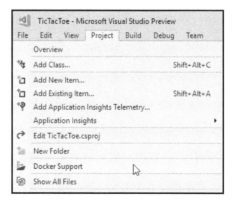

8. A new project called `docker-compose` will be autogenerated and added to the solution; it should contain a `.dockerignore` file (files to be ignored during deployment) and a `docker-compose.yml` file (deployment instructions):

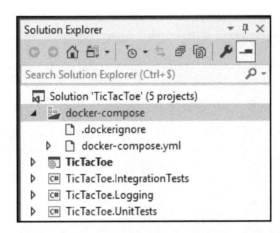

9. Update the `docker-compose.yml` file in the **Docker Compose Project** like this:

```
version: '3'
services:
  sql:
    image: "microsoft/mssql-server-windows-express"
    environment:
      sa_password: "123TicTacToe!"
      ACCEPT_EULA: "Y"
  tictactoe:
    image: tictactoe
    build:
      context: .
      dockerfile: TicTacToe\Dockerfile
    ports:
      - "8081:5000"
    depends_on:
      - sql
```

10. Update the `DefaultConnection` in the `appsettings.json` file in the `TicTacToe` project as follows:

```
"DefaultConnection":
 "Server=sql;Database=Master;MultipleActiveResultSets=true;
  User id=sa;pwd=123TicTacToe!"
```

11. Update the `Program.cs` file in the `TicTacToe` project; remove the Application Insights and IIS Integration because the Docker ASP.NET Core image is based on Kestrel instead of IIS:

```
public static IWebHost BuildWebHost(string[] args) =>
  WebHost.CreateDefaultBuilder(args)
    .UseStartup("TicTacToe")
    .CaptureStartupErrors(true)
    .Build();
}
```

12. Start the application by pressing *F5* (the `docker-compose` project should be set as a startup), the application should automatically be deployed into a Docker container now; verify that everything is still working as expected:

13. Open a Command Prompt and execute the `docker ps` instruction; to see all running Docker processes, there should be multiple running container instances:

Publishing images to the Docker Hub

You can upload your application images to the central cloud-based Docker repository called Docker Hub, and then use them in Microsoft Azure, Amazon Web Services, or any other Docker supported environments.

Note that there are also other Docker registries you could use, such as Azure Container Registry and others. Since Docker provides its own registry via Docker Hub, it is advised to use that though.

For more information on Docker Hub, check out `https://docs.docker.com/docker-hub`.

The following example showcases how to publish and upload the sample `TicTacToe` application to the Docker Hub:

1. Right-click on the `TicTacToe` project and select **Publish** in the context menu; since you have already created a publish profile in the examples before, you have to add a new one. Click on **Create new profile**:

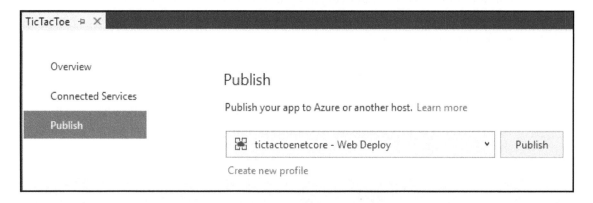

2. Click on the **Container Registry** button, select **Docker Hub**, and click on the
Publish button:

3. Enter your Docker Hub **User Name** and **Password** and click on **Save**:

4. Your container image will be published to Docker Hub; when it has been finished, go to Docker Hub and verify that the image has been uploaded:

Summary

In this chapter, we talked about the various options you have when it comes to hosting and deploying your ASP.NET Core 2.0 web applications.

You learned what hosting is and how to choose the appropriate solutions for a given use case. This will allow you to make better decisions for your own applications.

You have seen how to sign up for an Amazon Web Services account, how to provision the technical environment, and how to deploy ASP.NET Core 2.0 web applications.

Furthermore, you have seen how to sign up for a Microsoft Azure account, how to provision the technical environment, and how to deploy ASP.NET Core 2.0 web applications using this powerful public cloud computing platform.

We then talked about Docker and the various deployment choices you have when using this modern, increasingly adopted, and impactful technology. You are well prepared for the future since Docker may well completely change our way of thinking concerning deploying and managing applications.

In the next chapter, we will explain how to manage and supervise deployed web applications efficiently, which is very important for a DevOps approach.

11
Managing and Supervising ASP.NET Core 2.0 Applications

After having finished the development life cycle, we could have stopped there. However, this last chapter has been added to underline the importance of a thorough DevOps approach.

For now, we have only talked about the **Development (Dev)** side, but you should also embrace the **Operations (Ops)** side in **DevOps**, which consists of managing and supervising your applications during runtime.

This very important subject is often underestimated and sometimes, even worse, completely left aside. Developers tend to think that it is not a part of their job. They often say things like, *But it works on my machine* and *This is your problem not mine*. This is also commonly called the *Wall of confusion*. Agile methodologies and DevOps aim to avoid this kind of thinking, and this chapter will give you some advice and examples on how to better address those issues within your ASP.NET Core 2.0 applications.

The success of your application will be depending on how you can help **IT Operations** understand what is happening during runtime. This means providing them with means to manage and supervise applications quickly and efficiently.

Only then will you be able to provide high-quality applications with a low **Mean Time To Repair (MTTR)** for bugs, which can make the whole difference to becoming a future market leader within your specific markets.

Furthermore, it is easy for you to address these subjects when using ASP.NET Core 2.0, since, most of the time, you can take advantage of integrated or provided features without any bigger code changes.

In this chapter, we will cover the following topics:

- Logging in ASP.NET Core 2.0 applications
- Monitoring ASP.NET Core 2.0 applications

Logging in ASP.NET Core 2.0 applications

In `Chapter 10`, *Hosting and Deploying ASP.NET Core 2.0 Applications*, we explained how to deploy your ASP.NET Core 2.0 applications to Microsoft Azure, Amazon Web Services, and Docker. Let's go further, and understand how to add logging and monitoring in these environments, which is important to diagnose unexpected behavior and errors.

First, some theoretical background, and then, some practical example. Are you ready to learn what it takes to help IT Operations? Come on, it's the last chapter. Let's go!

Logging within applications consists of creating data to help understand what is happening during runtime. Several types of messages can be logged, such as information, warnings, and errors.

This data should then be persisted to log files, databases, SaaS solutions, or other destinations. To improve application performance, it is recommended to allow IT Operations to change the level of verbosity of the collected logging data during application runtime. In production environments, only warnings and errors should be logged for instance, while it makes perfect sense to enable logging everything during development time to be more efficient and to better understand exactly what is happening behind the scenes.

It is advisable to use a standard framework like ETW to structure and format logging data, so that IT Operations can use their preferred monitoring tools to quickly and easily read and diagnose error reasons. Famous logging frameworks such as Serilog or Log4Net also support standard output formats, so you could also use them if you like.

So, let's look at some concrete examples on how to handle logging for your ASP.NET Core 2.0 applications in different environments such as on-premises, in the public cloud, and in Docker.

In on-premises environments, logging data is stored in a log file most of the time. In this case, the application needs to have write access to write to the log file, and it is recommended to store all log files in a central folder called `logs` under the application path.

In Microsoft Azure, you have basically three different solutions to handle logging within your applications:

- **Standard file logging**: This is the easiest method, without any code modifications, but it is also the least powerful; you need to download files to retrieve logging data for your application.
- **Azure Application Service diagnostic**: This is the recommended solution, if you have not more than a single instance for your Application Service, since there are no log centralization features provided.
- **Azure Application Insights**: This is the most integrated and most powerful solution, which works across all application layers.

Amazon Web Services provides CloudWatch for logging and monitoring. The provided logging mechanisms are very similar to Microsoft Azure. When you have understood how to do it for Microsoft Azure, you will be able to apply your knowledge to Amazon Web Services easily and quickly, as you will see in the given examples.

 For more information, you can visit the Amazon Web Services CloudWatch website at `https://aws.amazon.com/en/cloudwatch`.

Docker does not provide any integrated monitoring or logging services like they exist for Microsoft Azure or Amazon Web Services. This means that, for adding, logging, and monitoring functionalities to your ASP.NET Core 2.0 applications in Docker, you have to use a log file. Furthermore, you have to provide your own centralized log recovery and analysis mechanisms to get consistent logging and monitoring data.

However, since applications can be instantiated multiple times, this may not be the best approach. Instead, you could also directly log to a centralized console, which should be the most efficient and most appropriate solution in a Docker environment.

Logging in Microsoft Azure

Ok, now that you have seen several solutions for logging in different environments, we will focus on Microsoft Azure. What happens if you take on the role of IT Operations, who need to diagnose why an application is not working as expected in Microsoft Azure? What are your choices, and what would be the best solution? That is exactly what you will learn in this section.

If you remember, we have already talked about logging on an application level in Chapter 4, *Basic Concepts of ASP.NET Core 2.0 - Part 1*, of this book. There, we added logging application events into a log file in a subfolder called logs of the application folder. This folder needs to be synchronized and monitored for disk space usage because, when it gets too big, it may as well become a failure reason by itself.

Furthermore, there are multiple sources of logs, since application logs and environmental logs (IIS, Windows, SQL Server, and so on) are handled separately. You have to combine all the information to get a holistic view of what is happening behind the scenes. This is very complicated and very time-consuming.

As you can see, it requires a lot of manual work to read and analyze application logs in this case. This becomes even more of an issue if you need to monitor and supervise a high number of applications at the same time. Doing everything manually is not really an option. We need to find a better solution.

Moreover, there are better and more integrated solutions in Microsoft Azure! If you deploy your applications in Azure Application Services, for instance, you can use the Azure Diagnostic Application Service. This feature can be enabled directly from the portal. Additionally, application logs and environmental logs are automatically centralized in a single place, which helps to find problems in a much quicker and more straightforward way.

Enabling Microsoft Azure Application Service diagnostic is very easy, so let's see how to do that now:

1. Open the **Tic-Tac-Toe Web Project** in Visual Studio 2017 and add a new extension called AzureAppServiceDiagnosticExtension in the Extensions folder:

```
public class AzureAppServiceDiagnosticExtension
{
  public static void AddAzureWebAppDiagnostics(IConfiguration
   configuration, ILoggingBuilder loggingBuilder)
  {
    loggingBuilder.AddAzureWebAppDiagnostics();
  }
}
```

2. Update the AddLoggingConfiguration method in the **Configure Logging Extension**, and add a case for the newly added **Azure Application Service Diagnostic Extension** from before:

```
public static class ConfigureLoggingExtension
```

```
{
  public static ILoggingBuilder AddLoggingConfiguration(this
    ILoggingBuilder loggingBuilder, IConfiguration configuration)
  {
    var loggingOptions = new Options.LoggingOptions();
    configuration.GetSection("Logging").Bind(loggingOptions);

    foreach (var provider in loggingOptions.Providers)
    {
      switch (provider.Name.ToLower())
      {
        case "console":
        {
          loggingBuilder.AddConsole();
          break;
        }
        case "file":
        {
          string filePath = System.IO.Path.Combine(
            System.IO.Directory.GetCurrentDirectory(), "logs",
            $"TicTacToe_{System.DateTime.Now.ToString(
            "ddMMyyHHmm")}.log");
          loggingBuilder.AddFile(filePath,
            (LogLevel)provider.LogLevel);
          break;
        }
        case "azureappservices":
        {
          AzureAppServiceDiagnosticExtension
            .AddAzureWebAppDiagnostics(configuration,
            loggingBuilder);
          break;
        }
        default:
        {
          break;
        }
      }
    }

    return loggingBuilder;
  }
}
```

3. Update the `appsettings.json` configuration file and add a new provider for Azure App Services:

```
"Logging": {
  "Providers": [
    {
      "Name": "Console",
      "LogLevel": "1"
    },
    {
      "Name": "File",
      "LogLevel": "2"
    },
    {
      "Name": "azureappservices"
    }
  ],
  "MinimumLevel": 1
}
```

4. Update the `Program.cs` file, change the WebHost builder configuration to enable IIS integration, and add the logging configuration as follows:

```
public static IWebHost BuildWebHost(string[] args) =>
  WebHost.CreateDefaultBuilder(args)
      .CaptureStartupErrors(true)
      .UseStartup("TicTacToe")
      .PreferHostingUrls(true)
      .UseApplicationInsights()
      .UseIISIntegration()
      .ConfigureLogging((hostingcontext, logging) =>
      {
        logging.AddLoggingConfiguration(
          hostingcontext.Configuration);
      })
      .Build();
```

5. Publish the **Tic-Tac-Toe Web Application** to an Azure App Services; if you do not know how to do that, you can look it up in Chapter 10, *Hosting and Deploying ASP.NET Core 2.0 Applications*.

6. Go to the **Microsoft Azure Portal Website**, click on **App Services** in the menu, select the **Tic-Tac-Toe App Service** you have deployed, and scroll down until you see the **Monitoring** section:

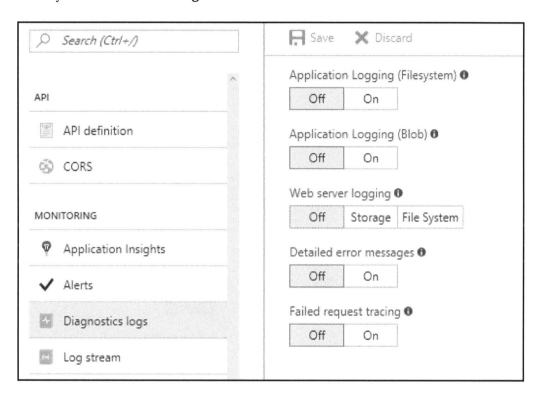

7. In the **Monitoring** section, click on the **Application Logging (Filesystem) On** button, select **Verbose Level**, enable **Detailed error messages** and **Failed request tracing**, and then click on the **Save** button:

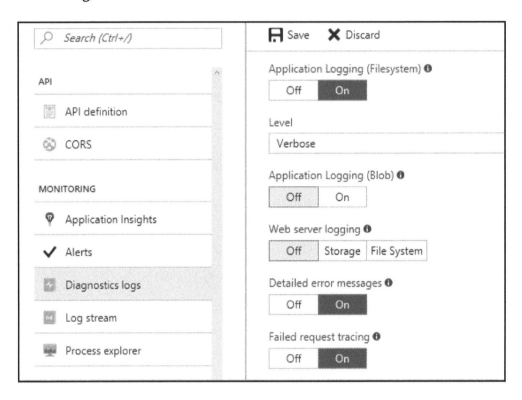

The *Tic-Tac-Toe* application will now start logging data into the Azure App Service filesystem. However, this is only the first step. You will need to retrieve the logs to be able to analyze them.

There are multiple ways of accessing the logs, depending on your specific needs. Some of them are specified here:

- Using FTP or FTPS to browse the `logs` folder
- Configuring Azure Blob storage and then downloading the blob content, which also has the benefit of centralizing logs for multiple services in a single place
- Using a dedicated application to retrieve logs automatically

Fortunately, the community has already worked on an open source solution on GitHub, called **Azure Web Site Logs Browser Extension**, which you can use. This solution consists of adding an extension to your Azure Portal.

You will now see how to add the **Azure Web Site Logs Browser Extension** to the Microsoft Azure Portal to analyze logs:

1. Go to the Microsoft Azure Portal Website, click on **App Services** in the menu, select the **Tic-Tac-Toe App Service** you have deployed in the preceding example, scroll down until you see the **Development Tools** section, click on **Extensions**, and then on the **Add** button:

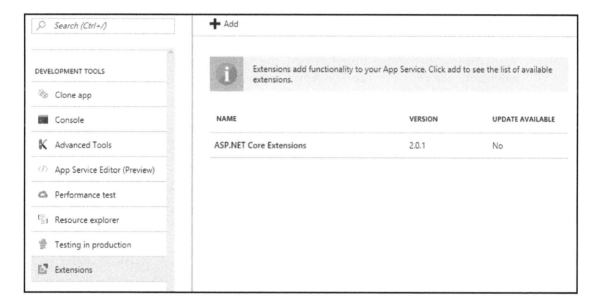

2. Select and install **Azure Web Site Logs Browser Extension** published by **Amit Apple**:

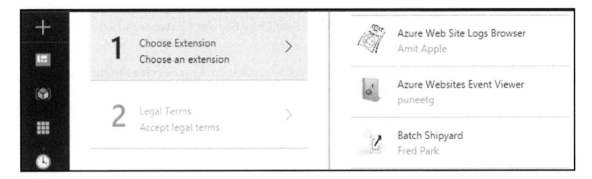

3. After the installation has been finished, the extension will be added to the active extensions for your **Tic-Tac-Toe App Service**:

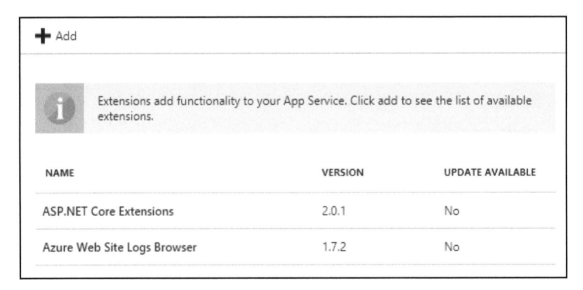

4. Click on **Azure Web Site Logs Browser Extension** and you will see an overview with the extension name, its author, and version number, as well as other additional information. Click on the **Browse** button:

5. A new browser window will be opened automatically, where you can see different log file sources; click on **File System - Application Logs**:

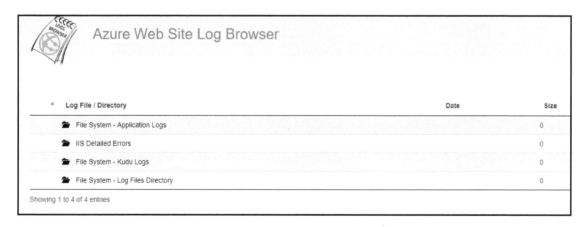

6. Select a log file with the diagnostic data you need to analyze:

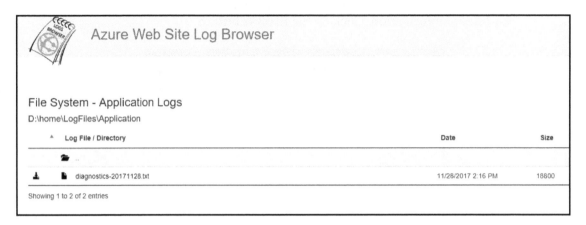

7. Read and scroll through the color-coded log file content. You will automatically see generated log entries, as well as log entries you have added by yourself in the preceding chapters:

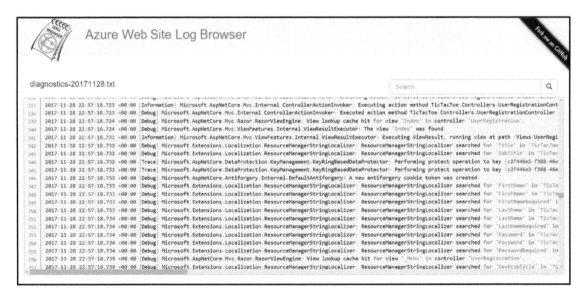

Logging in Amazon Web Services

If you are using Amazon Web Services, then adding logging to your ASP.NET Core 2.0 application will be very straightforward for you. You just have to write your application logs to the console, and the applications, which are deployed in Amazon Web Services Elastic Beanstalk, will automatically store their logs in Amazon Web Services CloudWatch. You will then be able to use the CloudWatch dashboard to analyze what is happening. This is comparable to Application Insights and its dashboard, which you have seen in the preceding example.

You will now learn how to access logs for applications you have deployed to the Amazon Web Services Elastic Beanstalk:

1. Publish **Tic-Tac-Toe Web Application** to Amazon Web Services Elastic Beanstalk; if you do not know how to do that, you can look it up in Chapter 10, *Hosting and Deploying ASP.NET Core 2.0 Applications*.

2. Start the application, go to **AWS Management Console**, enter Beanstalk in the **AWS Services** textbox, and click on the displayed link; you will be redirected to the Elastic Beanstalk welcome page:

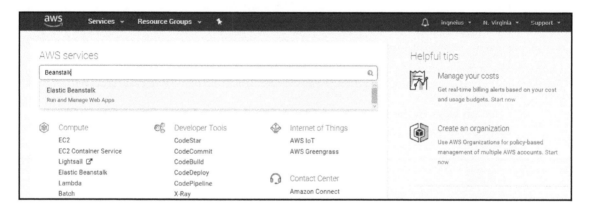

3. On the Elastic Beanstalk welcome page, select the *TicTacToe* application you deployed in the preceding step, as shown here:

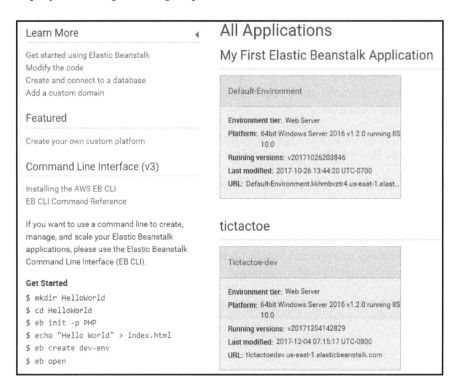

4. Click on **Logs** in the left menu and click on **Request Logs** | **Last 100 Lines**; you can now download the log files you need to analyze:

5. Download a log file and check its content:

```
AWSDeployment.log:

2017-12-04 12:47:04,603 INFO 1 AWSBeanstalkCfnDeployApp.DeployApp - Reading configuration from c:\Program Files\Amazon\ElasticBeanstalk\config\containerconfiguration
2017-12-04 12:47:05,587 INFO 1 AWSBeanstalkCfnDeploy.ContainerConfiguration - Setting SiteName to 'Default Web Site'
2017-12-04 12:47:05,587 INFO 1 AWSBeanstalkCfnDeploy.ContainerConfiguration - Setting AppName to '/'
2017-12-04 12:47:06,649 INFO 1 AWSBeanstalkCfnDeploy.Container - Could not find ElasticBeanstalk/environment section, creating in applicationHost.config
2017-12-04 12:47:08,259 INFO 1 AWSBeanstalkCfnDeploy.DeploymentUtils - Deleting directory (Default Web Site\aspnet_client\system_web\2_0_50727).
2017-12-04 12:47:08,259 INFO 1 DeploymentLog - Deleting directory (Default Web Site\aspnet_client\system_web\2_0_50727).
2017-12-04 12:47:08,259 INFO 1 AWSBeanstalkCfnDeploy.DeploymentUtils - Deleting directory (Default Web Site\aspnet_client\system_web\4_0_30319).
2017-12-04 12:47:08,259 INFO 1 DeploymentLog - Deleting directory (Default Web Site\aspnet_client\system_web\4_0_30319).
2017-12-04 12:47:08,259 INFO 1 AWSBeanstalkCfnDeploy.DeploymentUtils - Deleting directory (Default Web Site\aspnet_client\system_web).
2017-12-04 12:47:08,259 INFO 1 DeploymentLog - Deleting directory (Default Web Site\aspnet_client\system_web).
2017-12-04 12:47:08,259 INFO 1 AWSBeanstalkCfnDeploy.DeploymentUtils - Deleting directory (Default Web Site\aspnet_client).
2017-12-04 12:47:08,259 INFO 1 DeploymentLog - Deleting directory (Default Web Site\aspnet_client).
2017-12-04 12:47:08,274 INFO 1 AWSBeanstalkCfnDeploy.DeploymentUtils - Adding directory (Default Web Site\bin).
2017-12-04 12:47:08,274 INFO 1 DeploymentLog - Adding directory (Default Web Site\bin).
2017-12-04 12:47:08,290 INFO 1 AWSBeanstalkCfnDeploy.DeploymentUtils - Adding file (Default Web Site\bin\AWSBeanstalkHelloWorldWebApp.dll).
2017-12-04 12:47:08,290 INFO 1 DeploymentLog - Adding file (Default Web Site\bin\AWSBeanstalkHelloWorldWebApp.dll).
2017-12-04 12:47:08,306 INFO 1 AWSBeanstalkCfnDeploy.DeploymentUtils - Adding file (Default Web Site\bin\AWSSDK.Core.dll).
2017-12-04 12:47:08,306 INFO 1 DeploymentLog - Adding file (Default Web Site\bin\AWSSDK.Core.dll).
2017-12-04 12:47:08,321 INFO 1 AWSBeanstalkCfnDeploy.DeploymentUtils - Adding file (Default Web Site\bin\AWSXRayRecorder.dll).
2017-12-04 12:47:08,321 INFO 1 DeploymentLog - Adding file (Default Web Site\bin\AWSXRayRecorder.dll).
2017-12-04 12:47:08,337 INFO 1 AWSBeanstalkCfnDeploy.DeploymentUtils - Adding file (Default Web Site\bin\log4net.dll).
2017-12-04 12:47:08,337 INFO 1 DeploymentLog - Adding file (Default Web Site\bin\log4net.dll).
2017-12-04 12:47:08,337 INFO 1 AWSBeanstalkCfnDeploy.DeploymentUtils - Adding file (Default Web Site\bin\Newtonsoft.Json.dll).
2017-12-04 12:47:08,337 INFO 1 DeploymentLog - Adding file (Default Web Site\bin\Newtonsoft.Json.dll).
2017-12-04 12:47:08,352 INFO 1 AWSBeanstalkCfnDeploy.DeploymentUtils - Adding file (Default Web Site\bin\System.Net.Http.Formatting.dll).
2017-12-04 12:47:08,352 INFO 1 DeploymentLog - Adding file (Default Web Site\bin\System.Net.Http.Formatting.dll).
2017-12-04 12:47:08,368 INFO 1 AWSBeanstalkCfnDeploy.DeploymentUtils - Adding file (Default Web Site\bin\System.Web.Http.dll).
2017-12-04 12:47:08,368 INFO 1 DeploymentLog - Adding file (Default Web Site\bin\System.Web.Http.dll).
2017-12-04 12:47:08,399 INFO 1 AWSBeanstalkCfnDeploy.DeploymentUtils - Adding file (Default Web Site\bin\System.Web.Http.WebHost.dll).
2017-12-04 12:47:08,399 INFO 1 DeploymentLog - Adding file (Default Web Site\bin\System.Web.Http.WebHost.dll).
2017-12-04 12:47:08,415 INFO 1 AWSBeanstalkCfnDeploy.DeploymentUtils - Adding file (Default Web Site\Default.aspx).
2017-12-04 12:47:08,415 INFO 1 DeploymentLog - Adding file (Default Web Site\Default.aspx).
2017-12-04 12:47:08,415 INFO 1 AWSBeanstalkCfnDeploy.DeploymentUtils - Adding file (Default Web Site\Global.asax).
2017-12-04 12:47:08,415 INFO 1 DeploymentLog - Adding file (Default Web Site\Global.asax).
2017-12-04 12:47:08,415 INFO 1 AWSBeanstalkCfnDeploy.DeploymentUtils - Deleting file (Default Web Site\iisstart.htm).
2017-12-04 12:47:08,415 INFO 1 DeploymentLog - Deleting file (Default Web Site\iisstart.htm).
2017-12-04 12:47:08,415 INFO 1 AWSBeanstalkCfnDeploy.DeploymentUtils - Deleting file (Default Web Site\iisstart.png).
```

You have seen how to handle logging in various environments, on-premises and in the cloud; the next section will introduce you to monitoring, and how it can aid you to analyze problems in real time.

Monitoring ASP.NET Core 2.0 applications

In the previous section, you saw how to generate and analyze application logs for your ASP.NET Core 2.0 web applications, which will help you better understand unexpected behavior and application bugs. This will help IT Operations after an event has occurred to trace the different steps until the root cause of a problem has been found.

However, it will not help them to constantly monitor and supervise applications, since using logging mechanisms for this case will result in bad performances and negative overall application impacts. Logging is not the right solution for continuous monitoring!

The goal of monitoring is to analyze and supervise a large number of application metrics in real time, and to automatically detect application anomalies. The metrics need to have a very low message footprint for this to work efficiently.

The most commonly known monitoring frameworks for ASP.NET Core 2.0 are listed here:

- EventSource with ETW, which is very fast, and strongly typed, was introduced with .NET 4 and works only on Windows
- DiagnosticSource, which is very similar to EventSource, works cross-platform, like EventSource with ETW for Windows and like LTTNG for Linux

> For more information on ETW, go to the following website:
> `https://msdn.microsoft.com/en-us/library/windows/desktop/`
> `aa363668(v=vs.85).aspx`
>
> For more information on LTTNG, go to the following website:
> `http://lttng.org`

On top of these frameworks, most public cloud providers supply their own monitoring solutions. For Microsoft Azure, it is recommended to use Azure Application Insights for instance, while you should use CloudWatch for Amazon Web Services. These two monitoring solutions are fully SaaS and much more integrated with the respective public cloud provider portals.

Monitoring on-premises and in Docker

There are no standard monitoring solutions for on-premises and Docker environments as such, but there are some community-approved monitoring frameworks, such as EventSource or DiagnosticSource, which you can use to implement your own solutions.

Since these frameworks respect market standards such as ETW, IT Operations will be able to connect your ASP.NET Core 2.0 web applications using their standard monitoring tools, and they will like that very much!

An example would be Perfmon on Windows, which can receive ETW events and generate diagrams for monitoring purposes.

When using DiagnosticSource, you start by creating a listener. This listener receives application events and provides event names and parameters. The easiest way to create a listener is to create a POCO class, which contains methods that needs to be decorated with the `[DiagnosticName]` decorator, and is designed to accept parameters of the appropriate types.

The following example explains how to use DiagnosticSource to add monitoring to your ASP.NET Core 2.0 applications in on-premises and Docker environments:

1. Open **Tic-Tac-Toe Web Project** in Visual Studio 2017, and add a new folder called `Monitoring`; in this folder, add a new class called `ApplicationDiagnosticListener` as follows:

```
public class ApplicationDiagnosticListener
{
  [DiagnosticName("TicTacToe.MiddlewareStarting")]
  public virtual void OnMiddlewareStarting(
   HttpContext httpContext)
  {
    Console.WriteLine($"TicTacToe Middleware Starting,
     path: {httpContext.Request.Path}");
  }

  [DiagnosticName("TicTacToe.NewUserRegistration")]
  public virtual void NewUserRegistration(string name)
  {
    Console.WriteLine($"New User Registration {name}");
  }
}
```

2. Update the `Configure` method in the `Startup` class, add a `DiagnosticListener`, and subscribe to the `ApplicationDiagnosticListener` as shown here:

```
public void Configure(IApplicationBuilder app,
 IHostingEnvironment env, DiagnosticListener diagnosticListener)
{
  var listener = new ApplicationDiagnosticListener();
  diagnosticListener.SubscribeWithAdapter(listener);
  ...
}
```

3. Update **Communication Middleware**, add a new private member called `_diagnosticSource`, and update the constructor as follows:

```
private readonly RequestDelegate _next;
private DiagnosticSource _diagnosticSource;
public CommunicationMiddleware(RequestDelegate next,
 DiagnosticSource diagnosticSource)
{
  _next = next;
  _diagnosticSource = diagnosticSource;
```

```
        }
```

4. Update the `Invoke` method in **Communication Middleware**, and write an event
   if the diagnostic source is enabled:

```
public async Task Invoke(HttpContext context)
{
  if (context.WebSockets.IsWebSocketRequest)
  {
    if (_diagnosticSource.IsEnabled(
      "TicTacToe.MiddlewareStarting"))
    {
      _diagnosticSource.Write("TicTacToe.MiddlewareStarting",
      new
      {
        httpContext = context
      });
    }
    ...
```

5. Change the debugging settings in Visual Studio 2017 and set the project and
   emulator to `TicTacToe`:

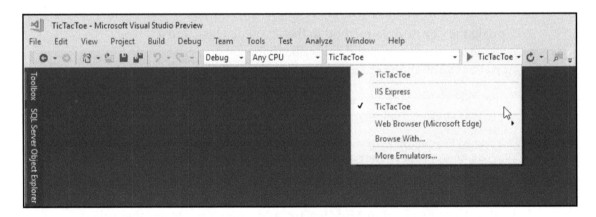

6. Start the application in Debug mode by pressing *F5*. A console will be opened automatically; register a new user and check the console output; you will see the **TicTacToe Middleware Starting** message, as shown here:

```
TicTacToe                                                                    —  □  ×
      Executed action TicTacToe.Controllers.UserRegistrationController.EmailConfirmation (TicTacToe) in 2657.7493ms
info: Microsoft.AspNetCore.Mvc.Internal.ControllerActionInvoker[2]
      Executed action TicTacToe.Controllers.UserRegistrationController.EmailConfirmation (TicTacToe) in 2657.7493ms
info: Microsoft.AspNetCore.Hosting.Internal.WebHost[2]
      Request finished in 2744.5098ms 200 text/html; charset=utf-8
info: Microsoft.AspNetCore.Hosting.Internal.WebHost[2]
      Request finished in 2744.5098ms 200 text/html; charset=utf-8
infoinfo: Microsoft.AspNetCore.Hosting.Internal.WebHost[1]
      Request starting HTTP/1.1 GET http://localhost:59929/CheckEmailConfirmationStatus
: Microsoft.AspNetCore.Hosting.Internal.WebHost[1]
      Request starting HTTP/1.1 GET http://localhost:59929/CheckEmailConfirmationStatus
infoinfo: Microsoft.AspNetCore.Authentication.Cookies.CookieAuthenticationHandler[8]
      AuthenticationScheme: Cookies was successfully authenticated.
: Microsoft.AspNetCore.Authentication.Cookies.CookieAuthenticationHandler[8]
      AuthenticationScheme: Cookies was successfully authenticated.
TicTacToe Middleware Starting, path: /CheckEmailConfirmationStatus
```

As already mentioned, sending logging and monitoring data to the console is a possible solution for on-premises environments, and a recommended solution for Docker environments.

Monitoring in Microsoft Azure

Microsoft Azure provides an integrated solution called Azure Application Insights, which allows IT Operations to monitor applications, resources, and services in real time. It works for the whole Azure subscription, and includes dashboards and diagrams for quick access to analytic data.

The following diagram illustrates some of the Azure Application Insights features:

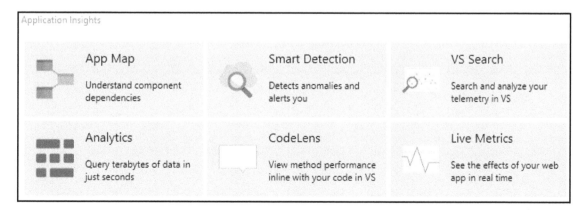

Let's use Application Insights in an easy-to-understand example; for that, you will start by creating a new Azure Application Insights resource in Microsoft Azure with its corresponding API key:

1. Go to **Microsoft Azure Portal Website**, click on **App Services** in the menu, select the **Tic-Tac-Toe App Service** you have deployed and configured in the preceding example, scroll down until you see the **Monitoring** section, click on **Application Insights**, fill out all the fields, and click on the **Ok** button. A new **Application Insights Resource** will be created for you:

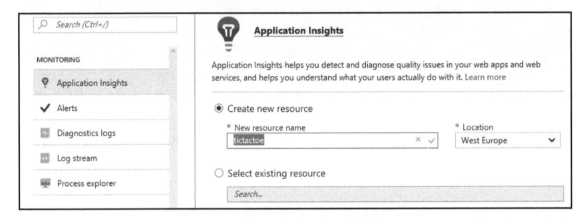

2. Click on **Monitor** in the menu. A new tab will be displayed. Go to the **Solution** section and choose **Application Insights**, then select the created **Application Insights Resource**:

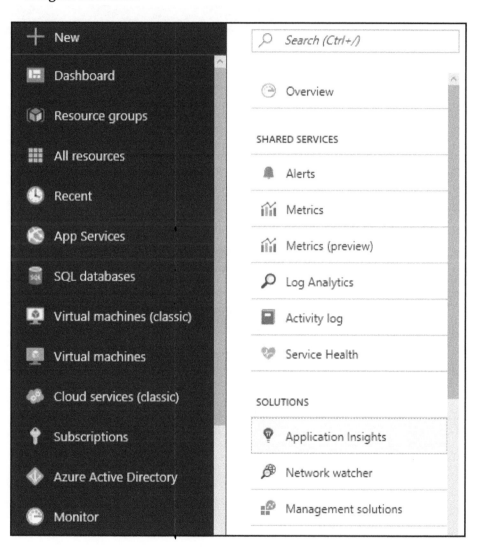

3. The **Application Insights Resource** tab will be displayed; scroll down until you see the **Configure** section, and then click on **API Access**:

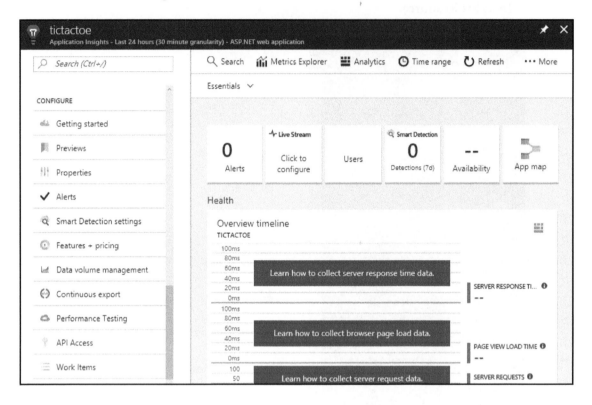

4. Click on **Create API key** to be able to generate a key, which will be used for the *Tic-Tac-Toe* sample application:

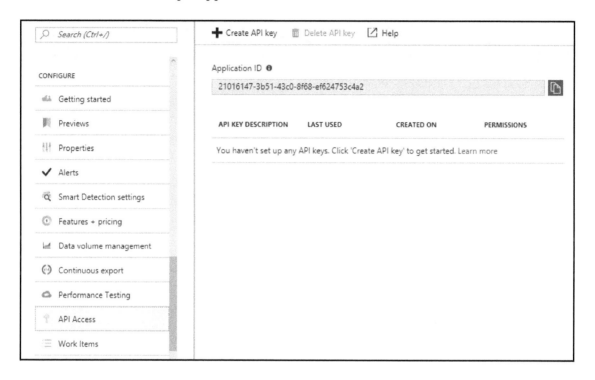

5. Configure the API key access rights (**Read telemetry**, **Write annotations**, **Authenticate SDK control channel**) and give it a meaningful name:

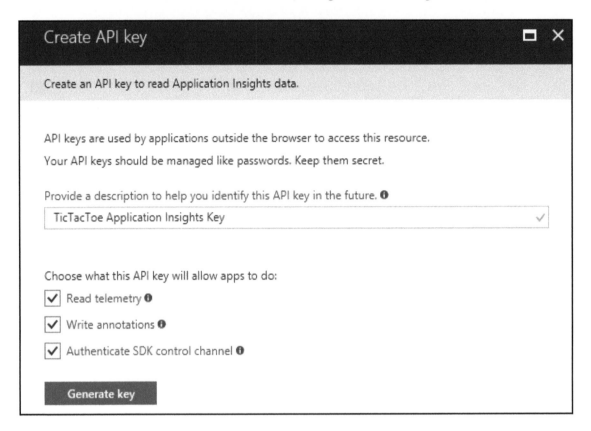

You have now finished the creation and configuration of the Application Insights resource in Microsoft Azure. Visual Studio 2017 contains some advanced built-in features that will allow you to connect your ASP.NET Core 2.0 application directly from within the IDE.

In the next steps, you will configure the ASP.NET Core 2.0 web application for Azure Application Insights:

1. Open **Tic-Tac-Toe Web Project**, click on **Project** in the top menu, and select **Add Application Insights Telemetry...**:

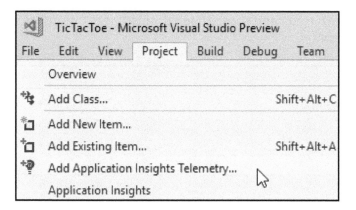

2. The **Application Insights Configuration** page will be displayed; click on the **Start Free** button:

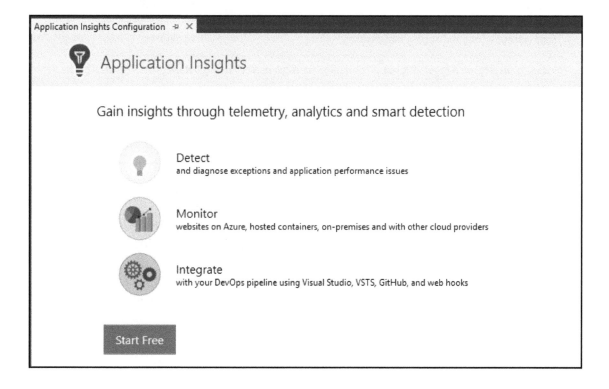

3. Enter your account and subscription details, select a resource, and click on the **Register** button:

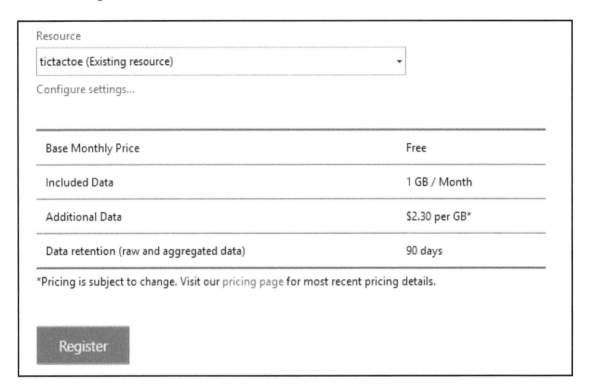

4. Republish the **Tic-Tac-Toe Web Application** to the Microsoft Azure AppService so that the Application Insights configurations are applied.
5. Go to **Microsoft Azure Portal Website**, click on **Monitor** in the menu, scroll down to the **Solutions** section and click on **Application Insights**, and then select the newly created **Application Insights Resource**.
6. The **Application Insights Dashboard** will be displayed; it serves to get a global overview, as well as to dive deep into the different monitoring areas:

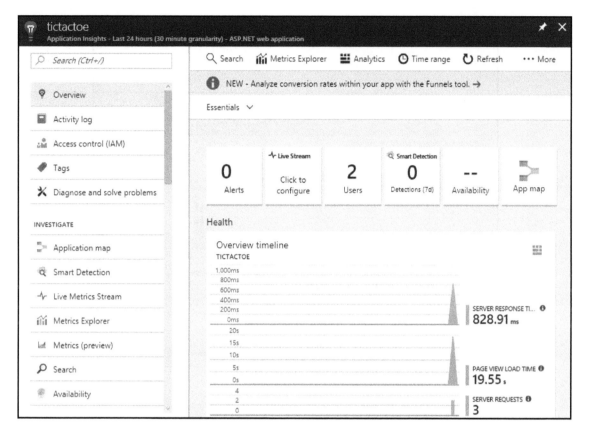

7. Click on **Search** to see the application flow; here, you can see that the error has occurred during the user registration process:

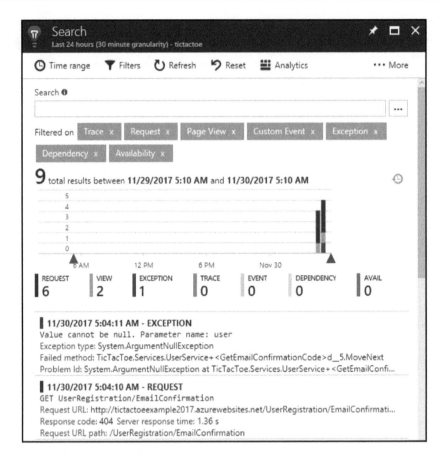

You may have already seen these errors in Chapter 10, *Hosting and Deploying ASP.NET Core 2.0 Applications*, after having deployed the *Tic-Tac-Toe* application to either Microsoft Azure or Amazon Web Services, as well as in the preceding logging section in this chapter. Everything is working locally and in Docker, but when you deploy it to the public cloud, it is not working anymore. Very strange! We cannot wait any longer; it really needs to be fixed!

We will now analyze the problem in more detail, and try to understand what needs to be done to solve it:

1. In Azure Application Insights, you can clearly see that there is a problem with the user registration, more specifically, a `404 Not Found` HTTP response.

2. When looking into the log file, as explained in the preceding section, you can see that the `UserRegistrationEmail` View in the `EmailTemplates` folder cannot be found, which then leads to additional errors:

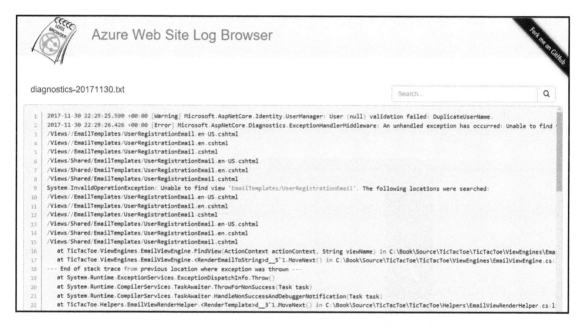

3. Go to the **Microsoft Azure Portal Website**, click on **App Services** in the menu, select the **Tic-Tac-Toe App Service** you have deployed and configured in the preceding example, scroll down until you see the **Development Tools** section, click on **App Service Editor (Preview)**, and then click on the **Go** link:

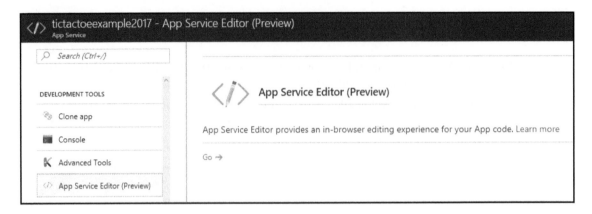

4. A new window with the **App Service Editor** page will automatically be opened; click on the **Search** button and search for the `EmailTemplates` folder, it cannot be found because all views are precompiled into a single DLL called `TicTacToe.PrecompiledViews.dll` during the publishing process:

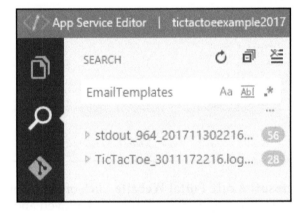

5. Apply a temporary fix for this problem by deactivating the pre-compilation during the publish process, open the `.csproj` file of the **Tic-Tac-Toe Web Project**, and add the following configuration elements in the `PropertyGroup` section:

```
<PropertyGroup>
  ...
  <PreserveCompilationContext>true</PreserveCompilationContext>
  <MvcRazorCompileOnPublish>false</MvcRazorCompileOnPublish>
</PropertyGroup>
```

Note that this is only a temporary fix for example purposes. You should reactivate pre-compilation and target the precompiled views in your code for a more industrialized and production-ready solution.

6. Republish the **Tic-Tac-Toe Web Application** to the Microsoft Azure AppService. Everything should now be working, including the user registration.

Note that you have to register a completely new user with a strong password such as `Azerty1234!`, for example, otherwise you might get additional errors if you don't. The application is missing some more advanced error handling due to lack of space within the book. Keep in mind that it was only given to better understand all the ASP.NET Core 2.0 concepts. You can, however, use the sample application as a base and then refine it as you like, and add the missing error handling.

You have seen how to configure your ASP.NET Core 2.0 web applications and are able to monitor them by using Azure Application Insights. You have even identified a problem during the user registration of the application. You have analyzed the logging and monitoring data, and you were able to solve the problem.

This works exceptionally well with .NET Core code, but, for now, you cannot see if any errors occur in the JavaScript parts of your applications. Since modern applications include a large number of JavaScript code, it would be great if you were able to monitor these parts also, right? Well, you can do that, you just have to adapt the code a little bit.

Let's see how to adapt the code and be able to monitor JavaScript application flows:

1. Start Visual Studio 2017 and open the **Tic-Tac-Toe Web Project**, update the `_ViewImports.cshtml` file in the `Views` folder, and add the Application Insights JavaScript snippet at the bottom of the file as follows:

```
@inject Microsoft.ApplicationInsights.AspNetCore
.JavaScriptSnippet JavaScriptSnippet
```

2. Update the **Layout Page** and **Mobile Layout Page**, and add the following line in the head section of the two pages:

```
@Html.Raw(JavaScriptSnippet.FullScript)
```

3. Update the `Startup` class and register the Application Insights service as follows:

```
services.AddApplicationInsightsTelemetry(_configuration);
```

4. Republish the **Tic-Tac-Toe Web Application** to the Microsoft Azure AppService so that the new Application Insights configuration is applied.

5. Start the application and open the **Application Insights Dashboard** in the **Microsoft Azure Portal Website**, click on **Search**, and then click on **Filters** and select **Request** only, deselecting all the other event types:

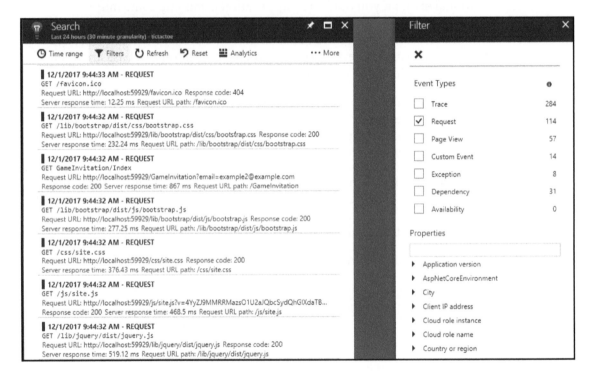

Great, you are able to constantly monitor your entire application, whether it be on the JavaScript side or on the .NET Core side, which will turn out to be quite useful in case of incorrect behavior.

In the last step, you will learn how to add and monitor custom metrics, which will allow you to trace business metrics in your applications:

1. Open the **Tic-Tac-Toe Web Project** and add a new service named `AzureApplicationInsightsMonitoringService` in the `Services` folder:

```
public class AzureApplicationInsightMonitoringService
{
  readonly TelemetryClient _telemetryClient =
    new TelemetryClient();

  public void TrackEvent(string eventName, TimeSpan elapsed,
   IDictionary<string, string> properties = null)
  {
    var telemetry = new EventTelemetry(eventName);

    telemetry.Metrics.Add("Elapsed", elapsed.TotalMilliseconds);

    if (properties != null)
    {
      foreach (var property in properties)
      {
        telemetry.Properties.Add(property.Key, property.Value);
      }
    }

    _telemetryClient.TrackEvent(telemetry);
  }
}
```

2. Extract the interface from the **Azure Application Insights Monitoring Service** and call it `IMonitoringService`.

3. Add a new option called `MonitoringOptions` in the `Options` folder:

```
public class MonitoringOptions
{
  public string MonitoringType { get; set; }
  public string MonitoringSetting { get; set; }
}
```

4. Update the `Configure` method in the `Startup` class, and register the **Azure Application Insights Monitoring Service** if it has been configured in the `appsettings.json` configuration file:

```
...
services.AddApplicationInsightsTelemetry(_configuration);
var section = _configuration.GetSection("Monitoring");
var monitoringOptions = new MonitoringOptions();
section.Bind(monitoringOptions);
services.AddSingleton(monitoringOptions);

if (monitoringOptions.MonitoringType ==
 "azureapplicationinsights")
{
  services.AddSingleton<IMonitoringService,
   AzureApplicationInsightsMonitoringService>();
}
```

5. Update `UserService` and add a new private member called `_telemetryClient`, and then update the constructor to initialize the private member as follows:

```
...
private readonly IMonitoringService _telemetryClient;
public UserService(RoleManager<RoleModel> roleManager,
 ApplicationUserManager userManager, ILogger<UserService>
 logger, SignInManager<UserModel> signInManager,
 IMonitoringService telemetryClient)
{
  ...
  _telemetryClient = telemetryClient;
  ...
}
```

6. Update the `RegisterUser` method in the `UserService` to use the `TrackEvent` method, and then add a custom metric called `RegisterUser` as follows:

```
...
finally
{
  stopwatch.Stop();
  _telemetryClient.TrackEvent("RegisterUser", stopwatch.Elapsed);
  _logger.LogTrace($"Start register user {userModel.Email}
   finished at {DateTime.Now} - elapsed
   {stopwatch.Elapsed.TotalSeconds} second(s)");
}
```

. . .

7. Update the `appsettings.json` configuration file, add a new `Monitoring` section, and configure it for Azure Application Insights:

```
"Monitoring": {
  "MonitoringType": "azureapplicationinsights",
  "MonitoringSettings": ""
}
```

8. Republish the **Tic-Tac-Toe Web Application** to the Microsoft Azure AppService so that the new Application Insights configurations are applied.

9. Start the application and open the **Application Insights Dashboard** on the **Microsoft Azure Portal Website**, click on **Search** and enter `RegisterUser` as a search term; you will only see the custom `RegisterUser` business metric now:

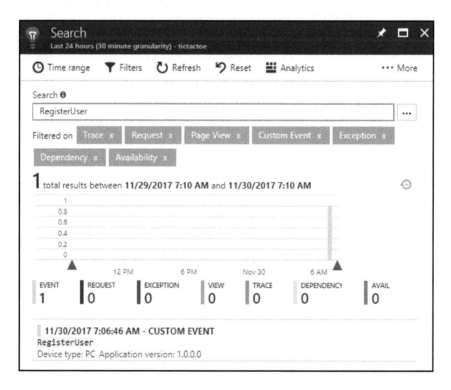

Monitoring in Amazon Web Services

Just like Microsoft Azure, Amazon Web Services provides an integrated solution, which allows IT Operations to monitor applications, resources, and services in real time. In Amazon Web Services, it is called CloudWatch. It provides nearly the same features as Applications Insights, meaning, it works for the entire AWS subscription and includes dashboards and diagrams for quick access to analytic data.

The following example illustrates how to use Amazon Web Services CloudWatch to monitor generic metrics and custom metrics so that you can learn how to do it for your own needs:

1. Open the **Tic-Tac-Toe Web Project** and download and install the **Amazon Web Services SDK for .NET - Core Runtime** NuGet package called `AWSSDK.Core`, as well as the **Amazon Web ServicesCloudWatch** NuGet package called `AWSSDK.CloudWatch`.

2. Add a new service called `AmazonWebServicesMonitoringService` in the `Services` folder, make it inherit the `IMonitoringService` interface, and implement the `Track` method with the AWS specific code, as shown in the following piece of code:

```
public class AmazonWebServicesMonitoringService :
 IMonitoringService
{
  readonly AmazonCloudWatchClient _telemetryClient =
  new AmazonCloudWatchClient();

  public void TrackEvent(string eventName, TimeSpan elapsed,
  IDictionary<string, string> properties = null)
  {
    var dimension = new Dimension
    {
      Name = eventName,
      Value = eventName
    };

    var metric1 = new MetricDatum
    {
      Dimensions = new List<Dimension> { dimension },
      MetricName = eventName,
      StatisticValues = new StatisticSet(),
      Timestamp = DateTime.Today,
      Unit = StandardUnit.Count
    };
```

```
    if (properties?.ContainsKey("value") == true)
      metric1.Value = long.Parse(properties["value"]);
    else
      metric1.Value = 1;

    var request = new PutMetricDataRequest
    {
      MetricData = new List<MetricDatum>() { metric1 },
      Namespace = eventName
    };

    _telemetryClient.PutMetricDataAsync(request).Wait();
  }
}
```

3. Update the `Configure` method in the `Startup` class, and register the **Amazon Web Services Cloud Watch Monitoring Service** if it has been configured in the `appsettings.json` configuration file:

```
...
if (monitoringOptions.MonitoringType ==
 "azureapplicationinsights")
{
  services.AddSingleton<IMonitoringService,
    AzureApplicationInsightsMonitoringService>();
}
else if (monitoringOptions.MonitoringType ==
 "amazonwebservicescloudwatch")
{
  services.AddSingleton<IMonitoringService,
    AmazonWebServicesMonitoringService>();
}
```

4. Update the `Monitoring` section in the `appsettings.json` configuration file, and configure it for Amazon Web Services CloudWatch:

```
"Monitoring": {
  "MonitoringType": "amazonwebservicescloudwatch",
  "MonitoringSettings": ""
}
```

5. Publish the **Tic-Tac-Toe Web Application** to Amazon Web Services Beanstalk, so that the new Amazon Web Services CloudWatch configurations are applied; if you do not know how to do that, you can look it up in `Chapter 10`, *Hosting and Deploying ASP.NET Core 2.0 Applications*.

6. Start the application. Go to the **AWS Management Console**, enter `CloudWatch`

in the **AWS services** textbox, and click on the displayed link; you will be redirected to the **AWS CloudWatch Welcome Page**:

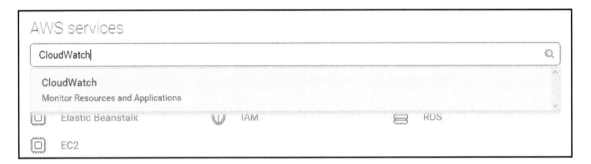

7. On the **CloudWatch** welcome page, click on the `TicTacToe` application:

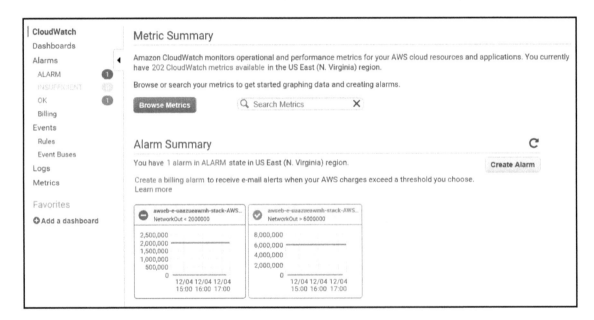

8. Click on an alarm to get more specific details about it:

9. Return to the **CloudWatch** welcome page, and enter `RegisterUser` as a search term in the textbox, then click on **Browse Metrics**:

10. You will see a diagram, as shown here, with the custom `RegisterUser` business metric:

Summary

In this chapter, we discussed how to manage and supervise your ASP.NET Core 2.0 web applications to help IT Operations to better understand what is happening during runtime before and after errors occur.

We talked about the concepts of logging, and how it can help reduce the time to understand and fix bugs. We illustrated different logging solutions on-premises, in Microsoft Azure, in Amazon Web Services, and in Docker.

You experienced how to configure logging in a Microsoft Azure environment using Azure AppServices and Azure Application Service Diagnostic, as well as the **Azure Web Site Log Browser Extension** for log file analysis in a detailed example.

You then saw how to do the same in Amazon Web Services by accessing and downloading application logs using Amazon Web Services CloudWatch.

We then introduced the concepts of monitoring and explained how to add monitoring in on-premises and Docker environments.

You configured Azure Application insights to monitor your ASP.NET Core 2.0 web applications in real time. You were even able to understand and solve the mystery behind the 404 Not Found problem.

In the last step, we showed you how to work with monitoring in an Amazon Web Services environment using Amazon Web Services CloudWatch.

In the next chapter, we will…well, there is no next chapter. You have seen everything this book has to offer. We hope that you liked it and that you found some value in understanding and assimilating the numerous examples we have given.

It is now up to you to make your own experiences and to further improve your ASP.NET Core 2.0 skills.

You can now start your journey as a veteran, as Nicolas Clerc (Cloud Architect, Microsoft France) has stated in his *Foreword* at the beginning of this book.

Good luck with that, and thank you for having taken the time to read the different chapters, and for having stayed with us for so long!

Index

Lightning Source UK Ltd.
Milton Keynes UK
UKHW05f0653011018
329811UK00006B/630/P